Conceiving Citizens

Conceiving Citizens

*Women and the Politics
of Motherhood in Iran*

Firoozeh Kashani-Sabet

OXFORD
UNIVERSITY PRESS

OXFORD
UNIVERSITY PRESS

Oxford University Press, Inc., publishes works that further
Oxford University's objective of excellence
in research, scholarship, and education.

Oxford   New York
Auckland   Cape Town   Dar es Salaam   Hong Kong   Karachi
Kuala Lumpur   Madrid   Melbourne   Mexico City   Nairobi
New Delhi   Shanghai   Taipei   Toronto

With offices in
Argentina   Austria   Brazil   Chile   Czech Republic   France   Greece
Guatemala   Hungary   Italy   Japan   Poland   Portugal   Singapore
South Korea   Switzerland   Thailand   Turkey   Ukraine   Vietnam

Published by Oxford University Press, Inc.
198 Madison Avenue, New York, NY 10016

www.oup.com

Oxford is a registered trademark of Oxford University Press

Library of Congress Cataloging-in-Publication Data
Kashani-Sabet, Firoozeh, 1967–
Conceiving citizens : women and the politics of motherhood in Iran /
Firoozeh Kashani-Sabet.
p.   cm.
Includes bibliographical references and index.
ISBN 978-0-19-530886-0—ISBN 978-0-19-530887-7 (pbk.)
1. Women—Social conditions—Iran. 2. Motherhood—Political aspects—Iran.
3. Women—Sexual behavior—Iran. 4. Women—Health and hygiene—Iran. I. Title.
HQ1735.2.K377   2011
305.48'89155—dc22   2010042522

1 3 5 7 9 8 6 4 2

Printed in the United States of America
on acid-free paper

For my children
and in the memory of
my beloved grandmother,
Maryam Rahmat Sami'i

CONTENTS

ACKNOWLEDGMENTS

Birthing this book has taken much longer than nine months. Quite literally, I lived the experience of pregnancy, loss, and birth as I researched and wrote about the history of reproduction. Although my speed of scholarly production slowed to a snail's pace, my capacity to understand children and to appreciate motherhood grew enormously. This newfound insight has informed my research into the historical scope of mothering and women's health in Iran. I began to reconsider my perspectives on feminism and the often bifurcated identities of women as professional or domestic. In this soul-searching process I recognized that women did not (and could not) realistically separate their lives so neatly into distinct categories. My analysis of maternalism and of the history of Iranian women reflects this important reality.

I began this project more than a decade ago as a study on hygiene. This approach made sense to me for two reasons. First, hygienic literature was prevalent in the form of popular advice to families in the expanding Persian press. Second, it addressed women's reproductive health in a colloquial and accessible way, providing a unique perspective on the social lives of Iranian women and men. Although other facets of women's health care did not receive nearly the same level of attention in the available literature (manuscripts, press articles, lithographed books), modernist discussions of mothering and reproduction revealed the ways in which gender impinged upon the management of health care in Iran. I learned in the process that popular perceptions of health, healing, and personal hygiene revealed a great deal about the social history of Iran and the Middle East.

I have centered my study on women's health and reproductive politics over a century-long period and chronicled issues that concerned maternalists (that is, proponents of reproduction, maternal health, and child care). I have also analyzed the ways in which activists confronted other social and political issues such as women's propriety, sexuality, suffrage, employment, and education. The debates concerning women's health did not occur in a vacuum. Many of the hygienists who disseminated popular notions about the benefits of vaccinations also sounded off on healthful mothering, child care, and the status of modern Iranian women (including comportment, attire, and schooling)—hence earning the label "maternalist." They also participated in the broad intellectual climate that pitted the traditionalist thinker against the secular modernist reformer—both of which had distinct opinions about women, mothering, and family life.

This work does not detail Islam's historical treatment of women's sexuality in Iran and the Middle East. However, since the topic of reproduction necessarily encompasses sexuality, it is important to understand the ways in which Islamic ideas of reproduction affected the maternalist discourse. The place of Islam in Iranian society exerts a profound impact on women's rights and reproductive politics. Although Islam legislated norms of behavior regarding sexual relations, marriage, and divorce, it left room for interpretation in concepts related to reproduction, education, and mothering. Any analysis of the women's movement in Iran must therefore grapple with this intellectual framework as it affected women's lives.

In the course of writing of this book, I came to terms with my views on modern medicine, especially in the areas of maternal care and pediatrics. I descend from a family of Rashti physicians. My two talented maternal uncles, Drs. Akbar and Ali Mehraban Samii, trained as surgeons in the United States, and the former returned to Iran to practice medicine for approximately fifteen years. My paternal uncle, Dr. Mohammad Mehdi Kashani-Sabet, was a much-loved family physician in Rasht who had trained locally and often combined both traditional and modern medical techniques in his practice.[1] My brother, Mohammed, and my cousins Soraya and Jason Samii have followed in their footsteps and practice medicine in the United States.

My decision to pursue history instead of medicine perplexed many of my family members. My uncle Ali, a brilliant thoracic surgeon, once famously (and lovingly) declared me the "mutant gene" of the family since I had rebuffed his entreaties to become a physician. I never realized how apt that epithet would be until the birth of my first child, when I would quickly learn to question certain medical norms and "standard" practices in modern pediatrics.

I have many people and institutions to thank for inspiration and support. The Presbyterian Historical Society and the Rockefeller Archive Center have generously given me access to troves of documents on the development of modern health care in Iran. The staff at various libraries and archives in Iran provided photocopies of manuscripts and relevant correspondence. Scholars in the fields of Iranian and Middle Eastern history have motivated me through their writings, sharp criticism, and, at times, friendship. In particular, I remain indebted to Afsaneh Najmabadi for her innovative and groundbreaking analyses of the women's movement in Iran. More than just an intellectual role model, Dr. Najmabadi has been a friend. Professor Hamid Dabashi has showered me with his generosity and included me in key conversations about the evolution of modern Iranian society. Over the years, Professor Reza Sheikholeslami has been a pillar of support, and it was a privilege for me to collaborate with him on a conference marking the centenary of Iranian constitutionalism in 2006.

My colleagues at the University of Pennsylvania have mentored me in many ways. Kathy Brown, Lee Cassanelli, Tom Childers, Lynn Hollen Lees, Ann Matter, Kathy Peiss, and Jonathan Steinberg have all provided much-needed professional support and personal advice when I most needed it. Without them, I would not have survived the nerve-racking tenure process. I gratefully add to my cohort of caring colleagues at Penn historian Eve Troutt Powell, whose decency is surpassed only by her intelligence. Scholars in other departments have also been most generous with their time. A friend from Yale, Professor Jamal Elias, is now a wonderful colleague in Penn's Department of Religious Studies. I thank my colleagues Rita Barnard and Demie Kurz from the Women's Studies Program at Penn for inviting me to present my research and for collaborating with me on many interesting events. Similarly, Dean Afaf Meleis of the Penn Nursing School and Professor Julie Fairman supported a symposium on disability history in the Middle East.

Scholars at other institutions have also provided valuable intellectual input. I thank Beth Baron, Matthew Connelly, Şükrü Hanioglu, and Judith Tucker for including me in pointed conversations as this project evolved. My editor at Oxford University Press, Susan Ferber, has an extraordinary eye for precision and clarity. I am fortunate that her insights have informed every page of this work. I thank the production team at OUP, especially Jo-ellyn Ausanka, for preparing this manuscript for publication. In addition, I extend my gratitude to my creative and efficient colleagues at the Penn Middle East Center (MEC), which I have had the privilege of directing since 2006. MEC staff members Jinhee Song and Jim Ryan have both contributed enormously to making the center a visible and active organization. Their support made it possible for me to take on this important administrative responsibility without totally sacrificing my research in the process. A gifted Penn graduate student, Chip Rossetti, helped me to compile the bibliography and index for this book, and I am most fortunate to have had his assistance and extraordinary professionalism.

I would like to add a few words about the images selected for reproduction in this work. The cover image and many of the pictures are copies from microfilms of old Persian newspapers, often of poor quality. Nonetheless, because of their relevance to the text, I have decided to include them despite their lack of clarity in some instances. Finally, despite attempts to contact relevant authorities, I was unable to obtain copyright information for these old newspapers, many of which are no longer in circulation and whose ownership in some cases changed hands after 1979.

Invitations to present my research at the Biennial Conference of Iranian Studies in 2000 and 2002, Princeton University in 2003, Barnard College in 2004, and the University of Pennsylvania in 2005 helped me to sharpen my arguments. I am grateful to Professor Eric Hooglund for encouraging me to publish my paper "Giving Birth: Women, Nursing, and Sexual Hygiene" in the journal *Critique: Critical Middle Eastern Studies* in 2002, after my presentation at the Conference of Iranian Studies. Although I eventually published this article elsewhere, I appreciate his early support of this project.

This study would have been impossible to complete without the backing and love of my extended family. The curiosity and passion of my nieces, Leila and Sara Kashani-Sabet, serve as constant reminders that writing has long been a Kashani-Sabet pastime. Keep writing, girls! My cousin Guive Sami'i is an absolute delight. I thank Guive and his devoted mother, Negar, for their good cheer and generosity. My "uncle" Iraj Sami'i, a gentle and caring man, often shared with me fascinating stories about our family that gave me a better appreciation of Iranian history. My cousin Roxanne Sami'i Brown, her husband, Justin, and their beautiful children, Emma and Noah, have brightened up many family holidays. I have also had the rare honor of being showered with the wisdom and kindness of Roxanne's grandmother, Nayyereh Ebtehai Sami'i. Our family matriarch, Nayyereh Khanum, is better known to the outside world as one of the first group of Iranian women elected to parliament in 1963. The activism and leadership of her genera-tion of women made it possible for me and my cohorts to pursue our careers more than thirty years later.

Finally, I must recognize the sacrifices of my immediate family. My mother, Fereshteh Sami'i, remains the rock of our lives. Thanks for all your love and help—always. My husband, Alireza Javaheri, never once com-plained about the fact that I would periodically convert our compact apart-ment into a tiny library, strewn with photocopies of documents and newspaper articles spanning nearly two centuries. A scholar by tempera-ment and training, Alireza has quietly sustained my intellectual pursuits for more than a decade. I can recognize this support only in the most humble way—*kheyli mamnun*. Without realizing it, my children have provided much fodder for this project. Reluctantly, they have shared their mommy with an unfamiliar public audience. Above all, they have enabled me to do more than just research the subject of motherhood. They have made me understand what it means to be a mother. To my children: God bless you!

Each of you has taught me so much. Thanks for reminding me every day of the things that really matter in life.

I dedicate this book to my precious children and to the memory of my beloved grandmother, Maryam Rahmat Sami'i. Better known as Nanejan, my grandmother used to take me to a maternity clinic near her home in Rasht when we would visit her for the Persian New Year. It was a ritual to pay homage to the children of that clinic, some of whom were born with disabilities. These casual visits left an indelible imprint on the mind of a sheltered and impressionable little girl. Now, more than thirty years later, I recall with fondness and gratitude Nanejan's subtle emphasis on the ideals that have guided me through adulthood.

Conceiving Citizens

Introduction

Childbirth brings life but also controversy. From the choice of delivering at home to opting for pain relief, women hear a cacophony of contradictory advice intended to guide them through these difficult decisions. Their preferences reflect different ideas about parenting, tradition, and control. Women and men of previous eras did not have access to the range of current technologies that tell them far more about birthing babies than they could have imagined possible. This dearth of information may have had its benefits, but it also meant that reproduction remained shrouded in mystery.[1]

Fact and fiction blended seamlessly in public perceptions of reproduction in Iran. As late as 1944, misinformation surrounded childbirth. One women's journal, *Banu*, even devoted its inaugural issue to this topic. "What do you know about the birth of babies?" it asked the reading public. Listing a series of true-or-false questions, the journal went through a set of common beliefs about reproduction to set apart science from superstition. Some questions dealt with identifying a baby's gender. Others offered information about correctly determining pregnancy weeks after conception.[2] Although the intent of this short piece was informational, its publication signaled a desire to propagate a new understanding of reproduction—or in other words, the origins of parenthood—even if some of the information presented remained unsubstantiated and contested.

A deceptively simple concept frames the narrative of this book: the mother. Why did mothers matter? How did maternity become tied to patriotic womanhood? What burdens did the idealization of motherhood place on ordinary women? How did maternalist policies impose new strictures on women's lives? This study unravels the historical experiences of motherhood in Iran to answer these questions. Embedded in this analysis is a general consideration about the political and professional visibility of women and the rise of ideologies that appropriated motherhood for political purposes.

The emphasis on motherhood in Iran spawned a social ideology known as maternalism. There is not, however, a perfect equivalent encapsulating the full range of the term in Persian. Unlike the word *feminist*, the term *maternalist* does not occur in the periodical press, not even as a Persian neologism. Yet the absence of such terminology does not negate the experience of maternalism in Iran. A range of words in Persian encompassed the subtle meanings of maternalism, including *madari*, or "mothering," or *mama'i*, meaning "midwifery," which concerned itself with reproduction as well as maternal and infant care. Maternalism became framed principally around these two concepts in Iran. The emergence of maternalism as a political discourse coincided with efforts to improve public sanitation and to define new social priorities for women.

By maternalism, I mean an ideology that promoted motherhood, child care, and maternal well-being not only within the strictures of family but also in consideration of nationalist concerns. Maternalists differed in their backgrounds and included physicians, hygienists, educators, journalists, feminists, and policy makers. Scholars who have studied maternalism in the Western context have shown its connection to domesticity and its impact on relationships outside the home.[3] In Iran, too, maternalism lauded domesticity and forged new associations between women and the state through the establishment of schools and the pursuit of unconventional professions. Maternalist objectives led to the creation of charitable, educational, and hygienic institutions that improved the general welfare of the citizen. Women benefited from the maternalist discourse by gaining new opportunities in the workforce and by becoming indispensable to the nation. Many entered new professions such as medicine and became symbols of Iranian industriousness.[4] Maternalism, however, did not necessarily project a feminist outlook. Nowhere does this distinction stand out as clearly as in the debate over reproduction and sexuality.

What distinguished the feminist from the maternalist? Simply put, feminists cared about women's rights; maternalists did not make that a priority. While maternalists strove to improve the health of women, especially pregnant women, and to prolong the lives of women and children, they did not all wish to establish gender equality or to combat patriarchy. The reproductive responsibility of women to the nation was simply too critical a matter to entrust to ordinary citizens, and overturning the status quo could inadvertently jeopardize national interests. Many maternalists also took on the subject of women's health because of national or religious priorities. In other words, maternalist priorities for Iranian policy makers mattered because they advanced the state's political ideology.

Feminism concerned itself with questions of equality before the law and addressed gender disparities at home, in the workplace, or in other public venues. Many feminists pursued charitable works and social projects intended to better women's status in society.[5] Above all, feminists strove to give women independence of choice in most relevant matters, including politics, reproduction, marriage, divorce, and attire. They captured women's voices and, along with maternalists, combated maternal and infant mortality through their participation in health care.

Maternalism became closely associated with the hygiene movement in Iran, often sharing and endorsing similar nationalist objectives. Iran's support for hygienic reforms emerged at a critical juncture when the country embraced a humanistic philosophy that not only aimed at curbing infectious diseases for human betterment but also tried to forge a nation of healthy patriots—both women and men.

The Iranian case stands out as an interesting historical phenomenon because, unlike in Romania, Japan, or Germany, no formal laws regarding childbirth, eugenics, or pro-natalism were mandated by the state in the late Qajar and early Pahlavi eras, when worries over depopulation were most strident.[6] Although maternalists promoted arguments that sought to increase birthrates, they were not solely repeating or recasting Western concepts of pro-natalism. The pro-natalist discourse appealed to some Iranians because such themes could be adapted to the more familiar Islamic injunctions regarding parenting and maternity. The debate on women's health and infant mortality in Iran can be situated within the hygiene movement that began in the nineteenth century. The interest in hygiene intersected with a maternalist discourse that inculcated the values of domesticity and celebrated the virtues of motherhood.

The history of hygiene and reproductive politics offers fresh insights into the social history of Iran and the Middle East. The scientific debate that at once improved public sanitation through vaccination programs and served as the philosophic pivot of nationalist policies would also transform concepts of mothering, reproduction, and citizenship. While elements of this narrative have been documented in recent works, other themes have remained insufficiently studied—namely, the conjunction between maternity, hygiene, and religious politics.

Women embraced or rejected state policies in family planning, health care, education, and politics. By pursuing individual choices that at times dissented from official and expected public norms, women learned to empower themselves. These choices included the sometimes unpopular decisions not to mother children and to abort fetuses. Some participated openly in popular politics despite its potentially life-threatening dangers. While I am unable to cover in equal depth each and every episode of control and resistance, I make a conscious effort to acknowledge dissent, deviance, and difference. I do so in part because certain studies of women and health care at times embed themselves in the very hegemonic structures they are trying to break down.

Beginning in the nineteenth century, some in the ruling elite pondered the reasons for Iran's political vulnerability and the reasons behind the country's territorial losses to Russia and Great Britain. Iranian thinkers expressed in prose and poetry their patriotic yearnings for independence, cultural dominance, and territorial expansion. Iranian women and men pursued their elusive quest for freedom and equality and experimented with constitutional rule at the turn of the twentieth century. For the first time, Iranian women gave voice to their specific concerns by pioneering schools, newspapers, and benevolent associations, forging new relationships with the state. In the process they attained a degree of social recognition as well as new political privileges.

The rise of scientific literacy, humanism, and hygiene brought to the fore new priorities for reformers and introduced new concepts about citizenship. Women gained visibility through the philosophical discourse of humanism and hygiene even as they embraced popular religion as a source of inspiration in their private lives. As Iranians acquired a new vocabulary to describe their homeland, they considered how best to forge a civic role for themselves. Women were not just conceiving citizens; they began to conceive of citizenship.

Many writers and state officials speculated about the nature of political empowerment and women's rights. The groundbreaking activism of Iranians, both women and men, during the constitutional revolution created a legacy of political participation that would empower them to challenge authority and patriarchy. Iran's ideology of "renewal" (*tajaddud*) defined many of the nationalist policies of the early Pahlavi era (roughly 1925–41) and informed state policies in matters of health, education, and family dynamics. The curricula of schools reinforced domesticity even as they trained women eventually to assume professions outside of the home. Maternalists inculcated the virtues of hygiene, family life, female industriousness, and sport through education and newly fashionable activities such as Scouting.

Iran experienced a dizzying array of social networks intended to control citizens and meet state directives. As the parameters of the Iranian state expanded, so too did the desire to control and supervise loose-knit communities and family life. Iran gradually developed a more sophisticated regulatory mechanism to impose its recommended norms of comportment, hygiene, and gender relations, partly out of concern over prostitution and the moral degeneracy of women and men. The hygiene movement informed but one facet of this social platform that attempted to control maternity and reproduction. Traditional care and modern medical practice did not always see eye to eye on pregnancy, miscarriage, childbirth, and child rearing. These differences tell us about more than just the culture of reproduction; they reflect the broad changes in Iranian society over the course of a century.

Iranian women defied the rigid parameters intended to circumscribe their identities. They did so by building their communities as teachers, nurses, writers, journalists, doctors, political spouses, and eventually politicians. Many women reinforced the trope of dutiful mother and wife even as they explored new professional opportunities. Yet this idealized mother was simply an unattainable archetype for the ordinary Iranian woman who struggled to fulfill the changing expectations of womanhood in response to the social and political vicissitudes of the nation. As literacy expanded and journalism matured in Iran, women narrated some of their feelings of dislocation and disappointment in their writings. What became of those who did not fulfill idealized images of womanhood? Some scripted an alternative narrative for themselves, while others shed a more realistic light on the travails of motherhood, sexuality, and marital relations in Iran.

Although the bulk of this book concerns women's health and sexuality, it is impossible to tell the history of women's health and the politics of reproduction as one of isolated social phenomena. As epidemics of plague, diphtheria, measles, cholera, and much more devastated struggling families, Iranians strove to educate themselves about the management of public sanitation and the workings of the human body. Grappling with the social realities of disease, Iranians questioned who was principally responsible for creating the conditions of health and hygiene: the individual or the state? The appeal of hygiene also lay in its ability to address multiple social causes. For this reason, it is unsurprising to see that the leading female activists who called for improvements in child care and women's education also appeared at the forefront of women's suffrage, unveiling, and reproductive rights.

This book consists of three parts. The introductory chapters set the social and intellectual framework that made it possible to explore the topics of hygiene and maternalism in the nineteenth century. Interest in science arose as part of the climate of reform in Iran during the Qajar and early Pahlavi eras. They explain some of the reasons why the creation of a healthy, clean, and productive community remained at the heart of modernist ambitions. The second part of the book focuses on the ways in which institutional change instilled maternalist objectives in the public arena. Schools, clinics, and welfare policies endorsed family life and encouraged healthful reproduction. As women became more independent at home and in the workplace, they no longer restricted their participation to traditionally female spheres such as education and nursing, but gingerly treaded onto less familiar terrain such as medical and political leadership. The third part of the book focuses on the political maturation of women in the late Pahlavi era. It documents the expansion of health care and education for women, the suffrage movement, and women's responses to family planning. Women's political activism caused a breach with certain religious thinkers who espoused maternalist ideology to reinforce women's familiar role as mothers and to limit women's activism in the political process. The final chapters consider the role of religion in the Iranian women's movement and its impact on social policies.

Maternalist concerns about reproduction and nationalism reverberated well beyond the boundaries of Iran and the Middle East. As Iran's participation in the international sanitary conferences of the nineteenth century demonstrated, the hygiene movement had gained momentum throughout Europe and America. Iranians engaged in health debates that concerned not just local physicians but doctors affiliated with the Russian, Austro-Hungarian, and British legations. The connection between population growth and national wealth emerged as talking points in Europe and elsewhere. In France, Great Britain, and Germany the woman question centered at times on discussions of depopulation and nationalism as well.[7]

The local experiences of Persian hygienists, mothers, and maternalists, however, distinguished their history from those of their counterparts elsewhere. While in France and America the registry of patients and eventually their sexual practices become surveyed and documented with increased efficiency and scrutiny, in Iran such policing techniques and surveillance of hygienic or sexual habits took longer to achieve. By the 1940s, the number of clinics and hospitals had mushroomed in Iran, but garnering statistics on the culture of mothering and the enforcement of health recommendations remained difficult. Visits to hospitals and clinics were not commonplace throughout the country, and such institutions did not maintain health records with regularity. More important, when family planners collided with maternalists over population politics, new measures and debates about reproduction did not become enforced by fiat despite the authoritarian nature of Iranian domestic politics and the emergence of a secret police force in 1957. These are interesting and revealing differences in Iran's experiences with reproductive politics as compared with those of Romania, China, Japan, and India.[8] At a time when the Iranian state decreed dress codes, why were reproductive policies left outside the legal framework of the country? Quite likely it is because Islamic injunctions encouraged childbirth and sexual morality, two social objectives that maternalists pursued as well. Many Iranian families embraced popular religion to explain their sexual practices and family relations. Others explored

new modes of conception made possible by innovative medical technologies that also raised ethical questions about reproduction.[9] Iranian women did not passively stand by and watch their men debate
politics and reproductive policy. By joining the medical ranks or
entering politics, they held their own as savvy partners and citizens.

A caveat regarding sources and historiography seems necessary
here. The theme of hygiene, and especially women's hygiene, has
received meager scholarly attention in Middle Eastern historical
studies, though social scientists have considered the significance of
reproductive politics in the contemporary period.[10] Iranian historiography succumbs to the same pattern; if anything, the subject is even
less thoroughly explored, although in addition to my research recent
studies have addressed different facets of health care in modern Iran.[11]
Still, historians know little about the origins of public health institutions and the background of local physicians and public health professionals administering medical aid. We lack accurate and reliable
statistics on prevalence of outbreaks, population counts, and accessi-
bility of hospitals and pharmacies. Where women's health is concerned, the gaps extend further. Archival and manuscript sources,
when available, remain scattered, making it difficult to establish general trends. Although archival documents and manuscript sources
from Iran and abroad were consulted for this study, many basic questions regarding the training and identity of Iranian midwives remain
only vaguely answerable.[12]

The literature on Middle Eastern women has been slow to explore
the salience of maternalism and hygiene despite the centrality of
these issues to the nationalist debate.[13] Scholars working contempo-
raneously have grappled with the theme of sexuality and women and
with that of health care in Iran over the last five years.[14] Important
differences will set my study apart from the historiography of the
field, however.[15] New historical data that include unpublished, hand-
written nineteenth-century Persian manuscripts and archival documents inform this study. By incorporating these untapped sources,
this book explores the age-old conflict between secularism and religion through the lens of hygiene, maternalism, and reproductive politics. This rich documentary evidence also enables us to consider the
ways in which the modern transmission of knowledge has privileged
science over traditional belief systems and even influenced sexuality,
fashion choices, veiling, and politics.

Recent scholarship on Iranian and Middle Eastern women's history, while concerned with issues of sexuality, focuses less on maternalism and reproductive politics.[16] Yet the practices and meanings of motherhood have hardly remained static. Changing attitudes about child rearing, reproductive biology, and maternalism reflect broad social and cultural shifts in Iranian society.[17] In addition, the history and relevance of women's hygiene in shaping the women's movement and the political and cultural evolution of modern Iranian society have been no less significant and revolutionary than the simultaneous discourses on veiling, education, and feminism itself. The controversies surrounding women's hygiene and reproductive politics, in fact, constitute a tertiary dimension of that debate.

Iran's experiences with maternalism and the social hygiene movement in the nineteenth century lacked the institutional backing present in America and Europe. Iran did not have an organization akin to the American Social Hygiene Association until later in the twentieth century.[18] Yet in Iran, as in America, various associations and individuals strove to set the moral debates that emerged from these new social orders.[19] Although much of modern Iranian history has pitted the religious classes and traditionalist thinkers against the secular modernist reformers, the hygiene movement in Iran and its maternalist preoccupations enabled men and women from both ends of the political spectrum to unite in an unpremeditated fashion in a social campaign intended to safeguard the virtue of Iranian society and to limit the perceived ills of sexual promiscuity. But they did not often do so, reflecting the divide between secularists and religious traditionalists. Women and men did not always see eye to eye on the issues of marriage, divorce, and employment outside the home, either. However, many agreed on the need to reduce the spread of sexually transmitted diseases and to prevent social behaviors that seemed to propagate such maladies.

These changing perceptions of sexuality and family relations had profound implications for modern Iranian society. Children—the desired fruit of marriage and sexual partnership—assumed a prominent role in defining family life and in shaping modern society. The child, as guarantor of human society, fulfilled the aspirations of the family and nation, and without healthy children Iran's future seemed threatened. The focus on childhood was even reflected in the publication of specialized texts on educating children.[20] A family was inconceivable without offspring, for children provided generational continuity and gave meaning to marriage beyond sexuality.[21] However, conventions of child rearing, often passed down through the generations, underwent significant change in the modern era. Demographic and nationalist pressures recast the culture of child rearing and mothering in nineteenth-century Iran, forging a maternalist ideology.

In the Islamic Middle East, where mothering remains a revered profession as well as a common marker of identity, an analysis of maternalism can shed light on the historical scope of motherhood and the contentious nature of reproductive politics. While the hygiene movement in Iran led to improvements in public sanitation and redefined conceptions of maternity and womanhood, it also generated another sweeping ideology: maternalism.

PART ONE

Hygiene and Citizenship

CHAPTER 1

ᖆᐧᖇ

Healing Iran

Hygiene and Social Change in the Qajar Era

In 1831, a serious plague epidemic swept through the capital, Tehran, as Iran was attempting to recover from its devastating loss to Russia in the Russo-Persian War (1826–28).[1] The plague of 1831 was neither the first outbreak of the disease in Iran nor the last. On May 24, 1877, the British consul in Rasht reported an outbreak of the plague in that city. Recalling the deadly trail of the plague's previous onslaughts, Alfred Churchill mused, "Very few persons in Resht are old enough to recollect the days when this town was attacked by the real plague. It was towards the year 1832 that this deadly malady manifested itself. In a few weeks half the population of a very flourishing town mustering upwards of 40,000 inhabitants had been lain low and the remainder had fled in all directions. Resht for a while became a charnel house—a city of the dead."[2] Churchill's account, though predisposed to sensationalism, dramatized the indignities wreaked upon innocent human lives by this uncompromising contagion.[3]

Nearly forty years later, another plague epidemic threatened the residents of Rasht. Hasan Khan, a Persian physician assigned the task of studying this illness, spent approximately fifty days in the city observing several patients afflicted with the plague. In a dispassionate account, Khan described the painful physical symptoms that accompanied the disease. As he remarked, "At first, the sick experienced fatigue, lethargy, fear, loss of appetite . . . and vomiting. The tongue was covered by a whitish or yellowish line."[4] These depictions exaggerated the sense of alarm surrounding the plague epidemic. Yet such detailed descriptions of the human physique also conveyed a deep scientific interest in understanding the mechanisms of the human body in conquering, or succumbing to, disease.

The infliction of such a deadly blight seemed a just sentence for an ignorant, soiled populace. The British consul unabashedly expressed his bleak impression of the "fanatical" Muslim natives ignorant about modern cures for disease in his account of the pandemic in Rasht. As Churchill remarked: "The least ignorant will prefer swallowing a piece of paper on which are inscribed the charm-imparting names of Ali and the Twelve Imams to the most efficacious medicines administered by a European Doctor."[5] In 1877, although the Persian minister of public instruction, I'tizad al-Saltanah, subscribed partly to Churchill's view and "admitted the apathy of the natives to all hygienic measures," by the last decades of the nineteenth century journalists and intellectuals stressed the virtues of cleanliness and sanitation.[6]

Diseases, it seemed, had become a commonplace of Qajar life—a reality that concerned not just Iranians but also European countries engaged in regular contact with Iran and other Middle Eastern societies because of trade and advances in communications. It was therefore unsurprising that a series of international sanitary conferences would be held to address epidemics and sanitation in the second half of the nineteenth century, indicating that the promotion of health and hygiene was not unique to nineteenth-century Iran but rather a subject of broad international appeal. In 1851, when the first international sanitary conference was convened in Paris, France, the themes of hygiene and humanism undergirded discussions of medicine and disease management. The conference was organized in an effort "to regulate in a systematic manner the quarantines and lazarettos" along the coast of Mediterranean countries. But the gathering also had a broader goal: to advance humanity through international cooperation and a "civilized" dialogue about hygiene and disease control. As one participant declared, "Hygiene is civilization. Without hygiene, civilization would only be a true social perversion." In 1866, when the subsequent international sanitary conference opened in Constantinople, 'Ali Pasha, the Ottoman minister of foreign affairs, reiterated similar sentiments. "This reunion," he declared, "is an incontestable proof of the immense step that civilization has taken in our century. Human fraternity, this fundamental law of all progress, gains more and more by the mutual guarantees that the civilized nations do not cease to give themselves. And what greater guarantee could we have offered entire humanity than the one we have before our eyes, in other words, to see governments that work toward civilization converge . . . to research and adopt measures that preserve against a disaster that desolates the human genre." Although Iran was absent from the 1851 sanitary conference in Paris, it sent representatives to the sanitary conferences of 1866 and 1874, thus participating in the larger humanitarian drive to bring hygiene to an international public.

The frequent outbreak of disease, which posed an ostensible threat to human life, spurred local discussion of and innovation in modes of public sanitation. The Qajar court even commissioned treatises on plague and other contagious diseases.[7] The pursuit of hygiene emerged in a social milieu in which policy makers, intellectuals, and even ordinary citizens became acutely conscious of the threat of deadly epidemics. Hygiene (*hifz al-sihhat*, literally "protection of health") emerged as a field of knowledge that incorporated rudimentary principles of science and medicine, particularly the elements of health. Hygiene, although inclusive of health matters, also embraced the themes of cleanliness and individual well-being, or humanism. In political terms the idea of hygiene was used to promote the creation of a clean, orderly, and sanitary society. Although hygiene interested Iranian administrators for demographic and humanitarian purposes, it also had a patriotic dimension that centered on the need to shield the homeland from pestilence and on the desire to forge a vigorous and physically fit citizenry—a public that could better serve the state.

Iran responded to crises in public health by making hygiene a salient social concern as well as a patriotic and humanitarian mission. Important institutions of hygiene emerged to combat infectious diseases. By 1874 the Sanitary Council (often referred to in British sources as the "Board of Health") formed in Tehran met on a somewhat regular schedule to discuss health matters. I'tizad al-Saltanah, the minister of public instruction, headed the Sanitary Council.[8] In addition, at "Ispahan and Kermanshah a sort of 'Assemblée Medicale' has been established" to improve the public response to epidemics.[9]

These attempts at enhancing public health met with limited success, however, prompting maternalists to consider the reasons for the persistence of high mortality rates in Iran.

As new institutions developed to improve public sanitation, court literature and newspapers drummed the theme of hygiene both as a social necessity and as a symbol of humanism and civilization. *Ruznamah-i 'Ilmi*, a nineteenth-century Qajar newspaper dedicated to promoting science, reported on the activities of the technical college Dar al-Funun, founded in 1851, and the Sanitary Council. In one issue, the journal discussed the Sanitary Council's desire to regulate the flow and use of drugs by having them tested first for safety by a college chemistry and physics teacher named Mirza Kazim before making them publicly available.[10] Another essay addressed the successes of the state hospital in treating complex illnesses. In fact, I'tizad al-Saltanah and other members of the Sanitary Council had inspected the hospital, highlighting a desire to scrutinize and observe public medical facilities and to promote empiricism, objectivity, and scientific rigor in these disciplines.[11] Medical discussions such as these tended to reflect optimism and a belief in the ability of modern science to conquer human illnesses, as new information and methodologies facilitated the transition from traditional to modern medicine in Iran. At the same time the emphasis on inspection and observation highlighted a desire to make the practice of medicine more scientific and accountable to public surveillance.[12]

The prevalence of epidemics correlated with the low level of public hygiene in Iran. These conditions impelled Qajar thinkers to expound on cleanliness, medicine, hygiene, and physical fitness in their works. In 1851 the first official Qajar gazette reported that in an effort to contain epidemics of plague and other diseases, state officials were patrolling the capital city and ordering residents to clean up their garbage to limit the spread of illness. Yet this source also confirmed little success and poor organization in the administration of these activities.[13] Pollution in major cities remained a source of concern for Qajar statesmen throughout much of the nineteenth century. As one observer summed up the situation, "Is it to be wondered that disease should not be generated in a country where wells and cess-pools are in close proximity, [and] where bodies of the dead are washed in the water the people drink?"[14] This impression was reinforced by the Russian consul in Astarabad, who similarly complained "of the uncleanly state of the town, the unwholesome condition of water, and the utter want of the necessary hygienic measures."[15] The Russian legation, in particular, expressed concern that the "house for washing the dead," or *murdahshur khanah*, was located in proximity to the Russian premises and that the water used for washing the dead would flow "into a 'kanat' (under-ground stream), which provides the parish with potable water."[16] Although Qajar officials often took necessary steps to improve sanitary conditions, the efficacy of disease control procedures sometimes varied from region to region.

In 1880, *Farhang*, a Persian journal published in Isfahan, ran a regular feature entitled "Hygiene and the Cleaning of Cities." Mirza Taqi Khan discussed numerous issues, such as the spread of disease through water as well as the proliferation of illnesses because of faulty sewage systems.[17] Moreover, he pointed out that the failure to remove household garbage from the streets on a regular basis heightened unsanitary conditions, particularly if rainfall added to waste putrefaction.[18] Thus, the success in combating disease remained limited despite the creation of the Sanitary Council and other organs. Other Qajar sources reported on different aspects of public health and sanitation. *Ittila'*, another important nineteenth-century journal, defined hygiene as the collective effort among the inhabitants of every city to eliminate disease through an emphasis on cleanliness (*nizafat*). This source identified certain causes of the persistent unsanitary conditions in Iran, which facilitated the spread of epidemics such as smallpox. These included (1) sickness or too much work in a communal labor setting, (2) intemperance in the consumption of intoxicating drinks, (3) lack of adequate sewage systems for managing waste and disorganization in their maintenance, (4) inattention to sanitation in the cities, and (5) a dearth of water, especially potable water. The absence of effective municipal offices responsible for providing such services exacerbated social hardships, making living conditions even more trying for Qajar subjects.[19]

Management of public baths gained significance as the state struggled to combat the outbreak of epidemics. The public bath (*hammam*) has long been a feature of Islamic urban architecture, and Qajar authorities entrusted urban social organization, including the supervision of public baths, to the local head, or *kadkhuda*, and other public figures.[20] As germ theory became known not only among Persian medical doctors but also among hygienists (who

were not necessarily trained in the modern medical sciences), discussions of hygiene focused on modes of disease transmission as well
as on cleanliness as an antidote to infection.[21] Concerns about cleanliness and contamination informed public health policies and influenced the regulations that would be drawn up for the maintenance of
public baths. For example, 'Ayn al Saltanah wrote that Larijan had
two public baths, an old one and a new one. Apparently the old one
was built during the reign of Shah Abbas (r. 1587–1629) and the new
one was constructed in 1891/1309 AH by Amin al-Mulk. He
observed that "the old bath is very dirty." Jewish men and women
visited the old public bath at night; Armenians, Jews, and foreigners
were not allowed in the new bath.[22]

Success in combating disease, however, remained inadequate
despite the construction of public baths, the creation of the Sanitary
Council, and the like. In the 1890s, Malik al-Muvarrikhin, a member
of the Qajar elite, observed that "the streets of the city [Tehran] are
very ruined and very dirty." Indeed, he claimed that the public roads
were "dustbins for the homes" of the capital—a situation heightening
unsanitary conditions and leading to the proliferation of illnesses
throughout the city. According to him, these filthy streets were "the
cause of air pollution and disease."[23] Despite the fact that Tehran had
been subjected to renovation and expansion under Nasir al-Din Shah
just decades earlier, the city's material setting required further attention and improvement.

In 1897, one journal contained a feature entitled "The Necessity of
Cleanness." Claiming that filth and squalor are "the cause of hatred
for the human soul," not to mention of "great detriment" to the
human body, the article proposed familiar measures for creating antiseptic conditions. Not only did the journal enjoin keeping one's
clothes and foods clean, it echoed the recommendations of the international sanitary conferences by stressing the importance of providing germ-free supplies of air and water.[24]

Because of its practical significance, other sources explored the
theme of hygiene as a way of expounding on social problems. A treatise from the early Muzaffari period (1896–1907) stressed the
state's responsibility in upholding antiseptic conditions. As its
writer, Khan-i Khanan, contended, "The necessities of life include
hygiene . . . [and] just as the state must make efforts to protect [the
country's] security [*hifz-i amniyat*], it is also obligatory to pursue

hygiene."[25] The attention to hygiene reflected an interest in improving social services from within the political structure.

If the circle of justice—a political concept of Persian governance that envisioned the ruler and society working in cooperation to ensure that a fair and righteous administration prevailed—had entailed the preservation of religion, it now also included support for community sanitation projects. This author emphasized the Islamic injunctions to keep clean in an effort to promote public morality and social policing. For instance, Khan-i Khanan argued that the police needed to regulate the amount of time and money that people spent in coffeehouses, which threatened to cause moral depravity. He also considered gambling and the offering of alcoholic beverages to students to be illicit activities that were forbidden in the Qur'an but existed in Qajar society.[26] Hygiene thus evolved as an expression not just of Qajar support for cleanliness but also of morality and eventually patriotism.

Hygiene was a subject at once personal and private but also social and public. The social perspective of hygiene took account of the country's unsanitary conditions, while its personal dimension concerned the human anatomy.[27] It thus became a way to conquer the human body—and by extension human society—through its emphasis on health, cleanliness, and the elimination of disease. Human empowerment might be attained if only people could comprehend their bodies and promote health through an understanding of nature and biology.

That understanding subsequently could be applied to political institutions in order to promote social weal. As one journalist commented, "Hygiene has illustrated the conditions of health and the provisions . . . that provide the endurance and continuation of life."[28] This celebration of life offered another optimistic assurance of Iranian humanism and modernity. Rigorous attention to hygiene not only promised a long and fulfilling existence but also professed an ideal life—whether personal or political—in which the need for healers and drugs might eventually be obviated.[29] By suggesting the possibility of creating an ideal man, it also gave a modernist interpretation to the concept of the perfect human being (*insan-i kamil*), an Islamic notion presuming the dominant position held by man in creation.[30]

The idea of hygiene and cleanliness had strong precedents in Islamic literature. The injunctions of *wudu* and *ghusl* equate the act of washing and cleanliness with religious purity.[31] As the Qur'an notes: "Truly Allah loveth those who turn unto Him, and loveth those who have a care for cleanness."[32] Modern Persian hygienists often emphasized that Islam itself was synonymous with cleanliness through the saying "*Islam pakizah ast*," literally, "Islam is pure"—often as a way of making hygiene compatible with the age-old traditions of Muslim belief.[33] Observance of personal cleanliness was obligatory and divine, since "all worldly and otherworldly duties are dependent upon hygiene," and each person maintained an individual responsibility to uphold his bodily health and cleanliness. For practical and religious purposes, then, "the reasonable, cautious human being must work as much as possible to protect his body."[34]

By linking hygiene to people's otherworldly duties, intellectuals also maneuvered around another thorny issue: the purported incompatibility of Islam with modern science. In a famous exchange with the French writer Ernest Renan, for instance, the controversial figure Jamal al-Din Afghani remarked that "the Muslim religion has tried to stifle science and stop its progress," but Afghani was also quick to point out that the Arabs had "rekindled the extinguished sciences, developed them and gave them a brilliance they had never had." This evidence, it was hoped, would again "prove" the Muslims' "taste for science."[35] Hygiene—a branch of science and humanistic learning—could forge a link between Islam, politics, and modern scientific thought with its stress on cleanliness, life, and the human anatomy.

In 1898 a prominent intellectual, Mirza Husayn Khan, Zuka' al-Mulk, maintained that "science and literature . . . are the pillars of humanism and the bases of civilization."[36] For him, the realization of human evolution and betterment rested in knowledge. He stressed the acquisition of knowledge in fields such as hygiene, medicine, and geography, since proficiency in the arts and sciences (*adab*)—or, in other words, humanistic endeavors—would allow Iran to strengthen its pillars of society and governance, and even restore its historical grandeur. Such scientific knowledge might bring about the eventual reduction of illness and the spread of hygiene, not to mention the realization of the ideal man. To demonstrate Iranians' proclivity for the salutary virtues of hygiene and scientific learning—as well as Iran's ability to become modern and "civilized"—Zuka' al-Mulk's newspaper, *Tarbiyat*, stressed the "scientific talent of Iranians," claiming that they "were and are the fountain" of scholarship in these disciplines.[37]

In addition to such grandstanding, *Tarbiyat* promoted the sciences by instituting a feature in the form of a discussion with Nayyir al-Mulk, Iran's minister of sciences. The column served to raise public literacy in the sciences and included information on subjects as diverse as electricity, ozone, and the temperature of the sun. To popularize the study of scientific fields, this publication even advertised the sale of relevant works in French at a local home in Qazvin.[38] The store of scientific knowledge, it was hoped, would help Iran understand its pathology of misrule in its attempt to regain stature among modern, "civilized" nations.[39]

Along with explanations of fields such as geography and astronomy, this journal regularly published articles on diseases and medicine—a scientific discipline concerned with human anatomy and the natural world. Medicine gained prominence not just because of its historical relevance but also because of its ability to offer treatments for prolonging and improving the quality of human life. The appeal of medicine and physiology reinforced the Qajar fascination with humanistic learning and with seeking medical answers to natural aberrations in reproduction and other scientific fields. As Zuka' al-Mulk explained, "For human beings the proper and healthy mode of living depends upon knowledge, from stone-cutting to woodwork . . . to medicine . . . [which is] the axis of well-being" and thus a science indispensable for every individual.[40]

To raise the public medical literacy level, Zuka' al-Mulk printed numerous essays on disease. Two such discussions concerned diphtheria and cancer. Contending that diphtheria was a contagion that had existed for a long time under different names, the paper proposed various hypotheses about its dissemination. The journal even published a biography of Louis Pasteur to foster interest in disease control.[41] As new schools developed during the reign of Muzaffar al-Din Shah (1896–1907), there would be a more marked intellectual distinction between the fields of medicine and hygiene, which, though nuanced and different in many respects, were sometimes lumped together. In 1900, the newly founded Luqmaniyah School, for instance, had two separate classes for hygiene and medicine.[42]

In 1898, a newspaper called *Ma'arif* ("learning" or "education") was founded as the organ of a society bearing the same name. Aside from regularly labeling the promoters of education and progress as "supporters of the world of humanism [*hava khahan-i 'alam-i insaniyat*]," *Ma'arif* argued for the education of women. Referring to an article published in another Persian journal, *Ittila'*, concerning the establishment of schools for women in the neighboring Ottoman lands, it supported education for Iranian women within the domestic sphere. Stressing that mothers needed to be educated in order to maintain hygiene at home and to improve the nursing of children, it contended: "If our daughters, like those in other civilized countries, learn about the necessary principles of livelihood and housekeeping, which consists of the refinement of manners and of household management, it will bring comfort to their marriages and children."[43] The writer therefore hoped that the Society of Education would take steps to create schools for the "nation's girls," who were after all the "future mothers and tutors of the country's sons."[44] Woman—like man—could better herself, especially as mother and patriot, through education.[45]

The infiltration of scientific thought encouraged the pursuit of hygiene as a way to keep the body fit. The human body became a subject of analysis as well as a metaphor for society. The conjunction of hygiene and patriotism allowed for human betterment, women's empowerment, and national advancement. Modern medicine and science, often described as "rational," was pitted against superstition, sorcery, and traditional modes of healing. Explanations of the human anatomy often centered on the male physique. There were, however, exceptions. One essay focused attention on the female anatomy by discussing morning sickness in pregnant women. This source even offered a purported cure, consisting of cocoa and distilled water, for nausea related to pregnancy.[46] Another writer, addressing primarily mothers and children's nurses, cautioned the children's caretakers against playing doctor and prescribing their own herbal cures for common childhood discomforts or illnesses. Lactating mothers were also encouraged to breast-feed their newborns, as "the best and healthiest milk is the mother's milk." In fact, women who decided against breast-feeding were regarded as negligent, not to mention more susceptible to uterine and breast cancers.[47] It is not surprising that these essays focused on women's reproductive (i.e., mothering) function—the one physiological difference that emphasized the importance of the female anatomy.[48] Still, in physiological discussions the prototypical human body remained the male form.

To encourage the proper maintenance and knowledge of the human body, Persian periodicals carried regular features on hygiene or related fields such as physiology.[49] In 1890, one source argued that hygiene needed to be attended to even before the founding of schools. What purpose did education serve if one suffered from physical weakness and debilitating diseases? The writer used the example of pastoralists to assert that country folk lived a more physically active and healthful lifestyle than those "civilized" urban dwellers who had accustomed themselves to comfort and leisure.[50] Regarding women's health in particular, this same piece went on to say that one could witness the well-being and physical stamina of pastoral women in their ruddy complexions, even as they carried their children in their arms and a load of firewood on their backs. The writer claimed that due to their physical condition pastoral women bore "twenty to thirty children"—no doubt an exaggeration of the women's actual reproductive capacity and activity—but apparently suffered few ill effects from their multiple pregnancies. Despite the physical hardships that pregnancy imposed upon them, their bodies remained strong and in the "utmost health."

The vigor of pastoral women was juxtaposed against the lives of pampered "civilized" women, who had "weak bodies," and who because of their infected blood "complain of one ailment or another." Such women lacked the strength even "to walk from their doorstep to the carriage." These weak women frequently suffered from infertility, the writer claimed. Even if they were fortunate enough to bear children, their bodies could not endure birthing more than two or three children, who in turn were feeble-bodied. The assumption that women coming from the leisured classes suffered from weakness and were prone to infertility gave the perception that urban (usually meaning privileged, upper-class) women lived an idle existence. They more than their "active" rural counterparts needed to change their lifestyles in order to prevent bodily decay. To maximize their reproductive capacity, and by extension to birth vigorous children, urban women needed to improve their physical stamina and alter their lifestyles and daily habits. Maternalists would take up vigorously the ideas embedded in this essay about women's fertility and their level of physical activity. Women's hygiene mattered insofar as it affected women's reproductive capacity, and hygienists addressed this theme from sundry perspectives.[51]

For men, too, social exigencies made hygiene and physical fitness attractive. In stressing the need to keep the human physique healthy, *Nawruz*, a journal devoted to culture and science, printed a column on the necessity of exercise for "nurturing and improving the [human] spirit and body." By keeping the body robust, exercise enabled people to take full advantage of their lives.[52] Hygiene appealed to reformers seeking to train a forceful and fit military. The military academy thus embraced physical exercise. In 1879, one newspaper noted that at the academy, gymnastics (translated simply as *varzish*, "sport") was being taught by Austrian instructors: "It is necessary for every soldier to tighten the muscles in his arms, legs, hips, and other body parts."[53] One writer argued that although the founding of schools had the benefit of nurturing children's minds, in Iran the "civilizing mission" of schools also had the unfortunate effect of making the youth physically inactive. It recommended incorporating gymnastics into the school curriculum and promoted "fast walking" to counter the ill effects of the sedentary lifestyle of many urban dwellers.[54] As with other facets of social reform, the pursuit of bodily health and exercise became a leitmotif of military indoctrination. The physically fit soldier would embody national vigor as well as male virility.

Defense of the state, not to mention human reproduction itself, depended not just on nubile women but also on fit, active men able to sire the next generation of healthy, dynamic citizens. The institutionalization of exercise as a palliative to physical decline would become a resounding theme of Pahlavi Iran, when exercise would become a regular activity of youth organizations. As fully productive members of the national community, healthy citizens would better promote the weal of the nation-state. Thus, physiology and hygiene—two distinct branches of scientific knowledge and two subjects intimately connected to human anatomy—became popular topics of research.

The fields of medicine, physiology, and hygiene required the acquisition of a specialized vocabulary.[55] The new language of science and hygiene slowly found its way into the humanistic discourse of Qajar political life, which was evolving simultaneously in the same intellectual milieu. In rethinking Qajar society, many nineteenth-century Iranian literati looked to science in their search to find solutions for the country's social and political ailments. Many intellectuals adopted the Enlightenment ethos of Europe and became enthralled with the idea of "natural laws" in discussions of the environment or society.[56] It was widely believed that progress would ensue because of the identification and application of natural laws to human societies. Just as geography located the natural laws of the environment, medicine identified the natural laws of the human anatomy. In their veneration of modern science, Qajar intellectuals sought to uncover the inherent natural mechanisms of human beings and their environment in order to attain (and ensure) societal progress and cultural advancement—a touchstone measured increasingly in national terms. Many of the same thinkers who promoted hygiene also placed emphasis on patriotism as a hallmark of modernity.

The debate on hygiene, mingled with the political transformations occurring in Qajar society, brought changes in perceptions and definitions of the country. Increasingly, intellectuals referred to their country as "homeland" (*vatan*) and to their commonwealth as "nation" (*millat*).[57] A territorial entity, *vatan* was regarded as the progenitor of Iranian society and the mainstay of the emerging nation. One journalist defined the concept of homeland thus: "*Vatan* is the place where a person is born and lives. Now, Iran is our homeland and our home, and in protecting it, it is our duty that we do not withhold our life, money, inhabitants, or wife and family."[58] If this patriot did not have all the answers, he did at least identify the need to promote hygiene and the sciences through the establishment of schools and other humanistic endeavors as a way to restore Iranian civilization and eminence.[59]

Others pursued hygiene as an expression of patriotism and appropriated medical terminology in an attempt to cleanse and cure their homeland. As one patriotic journalist contended, "Many of our people will suffer throughout the years unless there is hygiene in the country and until we understand its methods. And, of course, as our population declines, so too will our advancements."[60] On a literal level, hygiene accentuated the need to promote public sanitation and bodily health; on a political level, hygiene underscored the need to keep the homeland flourishing. In seeking remedies, Iran found itself slowly shifting toward a new setting—a modern environment that relied on scientific methods and solutions as well as innovative political structures to relieve the country of its various ills, whether social or political.

Motivated in part by territorial anxieties, which played an important role in giving the country its geographic shape, the birth of the

Iranian nation also took place because of social and political exigencies. From 1804 until 1905, for instance, Iran lost several outlying provinces through wars, treaties, or boundary delimitation efforts, including territories in the Caucasus and along its eastern boundary.[61] Faced with military, fiscal, and social troubles, Iranians searched for creative ways to fight their crisis of modernity. Many intellectuals espoused humanism in their discussions of progress and civilization. If modern empires—many of which also considered themselves "civilized" nations—boasted of railroads, steamboats, schools, and public hygiene, then Iran, to be counted among them, needed to procure similar articles of modernity These acquisitions included the introduction of innovative institutions as well as the invention of supporting nationalist polemics.[62]

Iran's transition to nationhood occurred in the midst of these simultaneous transformations and, in part, *because* of these concomitant technological, social, and scientific developments. This is not to suggest that Iranian nationhood emerged through a process of blind imitation or exclusively in a reactionary guise. On the contrary, the discourse on homeland expressly stressed the significance of the indigenous environment in forging patriotism. Still, there existed a desire to adopt and adapt alternative, nonindigenous structures to propel Iran toward nationhood—a move seen in Iran's struggle to create a parliament and write a constitution.

Though plagued by various afflictions, Iran slowly appropriated the lineaments of modernity and nationhood in attempting to eliminate its figurative diseases. The revolution of 1906 became a watershed in Iranian history precisely because Iranians not only tried to obtain some of the tokens of political progress that they had been discussing for decades but also succeeded in doing so. Even if the parliament—Iran's political hospital—could not cure all the nation's maladies, it could at least serve as a starting point for launching Iran's revitalization.

The dissemination of anatomical knowledge enabled writers to adopt a biological gaze when discussing the social sciences and the body politic. This development was necessarily modern because it was only after the eighteenth century that body organs and tissues became subjected to rigorous clinical scrutiny.[63] In Iran, too, interest in the body and hygiene as categories of understanding gained currency in the modern era. Newspapers and other literature projected and popularized this biological gaze by drawing an analogy between bodily health and political prosperity.

By 1906 a journal devoted to hygiene—*Hifz al-Sihhat*—began publication, reflecting public attention to health and sanitary matters. The periodical covered a broad range of topics and featured articles on subjects as diverse as dental hygiene and smallpox.[64] The emphasis on hygiene and sanitation prompted debate and administrative measures, pointing to the public interest in promoting cleanliness and sanitation.[65] A book on hygiene, *Sihhat-i Muzaffari*, published in 1906, was recommended to Iranian families and made available to schools. The office of the newspaper *Adab*, headed by Adib al-Mamalik, decided to distribute copies of this book to dignitaries in various Iranian cities.[66]

In 1907 several Tehran doctors formed a Society of Physicians to address the nation's sanitation and hygienic needs. Apparently the society convened twice weekly at the home of Sihhat al-Dawlah to discuss medical issues. Although the journalist Majd al-Islam Kirmani reported dissent between modernist and traditional physicians, he noted that the sessions often tackled matters of urban sanitation.[67] In the same year a Society for Cleanliness (Anjuman-i Nizafat), headed by Mirza Abu Talib, was created in Tehran to oversee sanitation of public baths in the capital. Mirza Abu Talib was described as an educated person who supported constitutionalism and was well versed in the "praiseworthy qualities of humanism."[68] Public baths were necessary for instilling cleanliness and sanitation, but over time they had become a reservoir of germs, threatening public sanitation. The dearth of clean water remained a significant public health challenge, hindering efforts to improve sanitation. The consequence of poor public hygiene heightened awareness of the social impact of disease and mortality. Such fears impelled some hygienists to link patriotism with population preservation. As Majd al-Islam Kirmani remarked, "Preservation of the populace is the most important element of civilization, and preservation of the populace is dependent upon the presence of men knowledgeable about medicine."[69] Nationhood—the quintessential symbol of modernity—could not be wholly achieved without other accouterments of civilization such as hygiene. In embracing nationalism, Iranians tried to forge an ideal patriotic society and to create a healthy and enduring national community.

The Municipal Council (Shaura-yi Baladiyya) also came into existence at this time, and one of its main tasks was the maintenance of
public hygiene.[70] This responsibility began at the local level, and in
drawing up the municipal regulations (*qanun-i baladiyya*), Majlis delegates obligated themselves to maintain the nation's cities in material
terms as well as in medical ones. The sixth article of the urban regulations, for instance, specified a commitment to hygiene (*hifz-i sihhi*)
and "the establishment of pharmacies and the like."[71] The creation of
the Municipal Society (Anjuman-i Baladiyya) provided an opportunity for citizens to promote hygiene through institutional means.
During one of its sessions, the Municipal Society even composed a
hygiene charter (*nizamnamah-i hifz-i sihhi*) to stress the need to sustain sanitary conditions. Considerable discussion surrounded the
creation of a hygiene commission. Mu'adib al-Islam, nominated by
the members of the Municipal Society to assume leadership of the
commission, declined to do so, fearing the commission's inability to
execute its orders without the necessary judicial and surveillance
forces in place, not to mention that the commission lacked sufficient
funds to make it viable.[72]

During the period of the second Majlis, from 1909 to 1911, several
political parties even instituted public hygiene in their political plat-
forms. The Society of the Seekers of Advancement of Iran (Jam'iyat-i
Taraqqi Khahan-i Iran), for instance, included among its goals "the
preparation of the items necessary for hygiene and the establishment
of hospitals." Similarly, the party of Ijtima'iyun-i Ittihadiyun listed
improvement in public hygiene as one of its objectives.[73] One journalist even reported the creation of a medical commission on military
hygiene (*hifz al-sihhat-i nizami*), since infirm cavalrymen could not
effectively protect the homeland. A healthy army, like a robust citizenry, could better ensure the defense of a country faced with chronic
border skirmishes.[74]

Efforts to promote institutions of public health and hygiene
spread more rapidly to the provinces during these years, in part
because of the creation of provincial societies. In Gilan, a hygiene
assembly as well as a medical council, which included some of the
well-known doctors of the province, would convene twice a week.
There is a reference to the Hygiene Society, or Anjuman-i Sihhat, in
Qum as well, though little information exists about its activities.[75]
While details regarding the membership and function of these

hygiene assemblies are lacking, their existence points to the public interest in promoting sanitation to curb the occurrence of epidemics and to reduce mortality.

Even schoolbooks instilled hygiene as a requisite object of a nation's civilizing mission as well as a primary function of its municipalities. In 1911, Iranian journalist and politician Sayyid Zia' al-Din Tabataba'i noted in a textbook intended for elementary schools that the duties of the municipality included cleaning the streets and baths and providing the necessities of hygiene.[76] Two other textbooks published shortly after this one reiterated the municipality's responsibility in elevating public sanitation.[77]

Why did hygiene appear at the forefront of patriotic debate? If Iran strove to project an image of political vigor, particularly at a time of declining fortunes, then the country's material conditions needed to reflect the health of the homeland (*vatan*). The nation's control over its sanitation methods mirrored its authority over other areas, such as its finances, its social policies, and its women. Aside from the material need to eliminate disease, public health became a symbol of national weal and male authority.

The debate on hygiene grappled with a range of topics—venereal disease, cleanliness, health, sport, beauty, disability, and drug abuse— in an attempt to impose social order upon Iranians. Personal habits in matters of dress, drinking, and home life contributed to forging a sanitary society, along with the need to promote cleanliness in modern Iranian society. Although in this manner the hygiene movement that began in the nineteenth century placed social limits on Iranian citizens, it nonetheless brought improvements in public sanitation through its emphases on vaccination programs, nursing, and financial support for clinics and hospitals. Maternalists appropriated hygiene themes to discuss women's issues such as healthful reproduction, marriage, and venereal disease in Iran. They relied on familiar tropes, especially the image of the mother, to depict gender roles.

Motherhood offered female patriots a visible social role in the national drama.[78] In a telling cartoon dating back to the constitutional period, the daughters of Iran are called upon to restore the health of the nation. Depicted as an invalid, the "mother of the homeland" (*madar-i vatan*) is surrounded by attentive daughters ministering to her needs.[79] The caption reads: "Oh, oh, kind mother, why have you fallen into such affliction, resting on your sickbed?"[80] Distressed over

Woman Depicted as Motherland. *Shikufah.*

the hardships of the motherland, the daughters promise to nurse their ailing mother back to health, vowing, "Our dear mother, as long as your daughters are alive, we will not allow you to become so abject. We will not stop curing you."

The depiction of Iran as a feeble woman, although reinforcing stereotypes of female weakness and inferiority, made room for female political participation in the polity, a point illustrated in this cartoon by the determination and political will of Iran's young daughters to rescue the homeland. By contrast, the nation's son, shown in the opposite corner of the picture, sleeps indifferently even as his female compatriots beseech him to awaken from his slumber and tend to his motherland. In Iran, as elsewhere, the modern preoccupation with nationalism drew upon mothers to record a narrative that gave women and men new civic responsibilities.[81] By personalizing the motherland and its troubles, patriots interpreted civic duties in filial terms. The defilement of this ideal in the form of territorial and bodily invasion or rape negated the very impulses of modernity and civilization.[82] Though focused on man, the ideals of Iranian constitutionalism eventually embraced woman in the adoption of a female persona for the homeland and in urging education and health care for women.

The portrayal of women as sympathetic healers, or nurses, and as embodiments of the homeland gave women a vital political presence and paved the way for their participation in shaping policy. A venerated figure, the mother became not just a metaphor for the homeland but a crucial participant in the conception of the nation. Her image intruded into discussions of public health and politics. Patriarchy relied upon mothers to raise a generation of girls and women who could serve its interests. Architects of national policy looked to mothers to raise virtuous daughters who pursued honorable careers in teaching and nursing but did not necessarily challenge the patriarchy. While mothers, and indeed the theme of motherhood, were often treated with reverence in Persian prose, this concept did not always get translated into improved social policies for women.[83] Activists devoted the following decades to helping women attain material progress in their lives. In the process, they gave new meaning to motherhood and expanded the dimensions of women's participation in Iranian society.

CHAPTER 2

✑

Population Politics

Infant Mortality and the "Crisis" of Midwifery

Travelers to Iran in the nineteenth century often decried the startlingly high rate of infant mortality. In 1843, Reverend Justin Perkins, who opened the American Presbyterian mission in northwestern Iran, observed that a "much larger proportion of children, die in infancy, in a given population among all classes in Persia, than in America."[1] Perkins noted that while births "are far more numerous," few children survived to adulthood. While he acknowledged the difficulty in explaining "the cause of such mortality," Perkins speculated that poor hygiene and the early age of marriage were possible contributing factors.[2] Writing in 1856, Lady Mary Sheil, wife of British envoy to Persia Sir Justin Sheil, remarked that "the mortality among children is immense, owing to neglect, ignorance, and laziness." Citing the shah's French physician, Sheil continued: "Dr. Cloquet . . . expressed to me his conviction that not above three children in ten outlived their third year."[3] Sheil faulted the local culture of child rearing, including women as the traditional caretakers of children, for this deplorable condition. She described a society in which fairly affluent mothers apparently disliked nursing infants and one that purportedly allowed "nurses" to calm children with bits of opium.[4]

Nearly four decades later, British official George Nathaniel Curzon documented other scenarios to explain the high mortality of women and children. Upon visiting Iran in 1892, Curzon cited a report by the Austrian physician Jakob Polak that one of the "main causes of the decline of population" in Iran was related to the "unfavourable position of women, including the facility of divorce, early marriage, and premature age, the length of the suckling period, and the thereby impaired fertility of the sex." Other possible reasons for population decline included the "decay of sanitary police, and consequent greater ravages by typhus, dysentery, cholera, plague, and, more particularly, owing to the inadequacy of inoculation, by small-pox—the mortality of children in the second year of their age being very striking."[5] A year later, James Bassett, an American missionary serving in Iran for twenty years, wrote that the "mortality among Persian children is very great. The graveyards show that this statement is true."[6] Though pinpointing different reasons for the prevalence of infant mortality, these travelers recognized this issue as a consequential social problem facing nineteenth-century Iranian society.[7]

Nasir al-Din Shah, the longest-ruling Iranian monarch of the nineteenth century, enlisted the support of European doctors to improve sanitation in Iran. One French physician, Joseph Désiré Tholozan, served the king as his private physician and also composed treatises on the etiology of plague and cholera in Iran. His works, along with those of other European doctors, were translated into Persian in the nineteenth century in an effort to disseminate current information on hygiene. An unpublished Persian manuscript containing translations of Tholozan's writings on smallpox sheds light on the impact of that disease on children. The translator provides a brief history of Edward Jenner's theory of vaccination, pointing out that smallpox vaccinations had significantly reduced the death rate among children in England, where smallpox had reached "epidemic" proportions. In Iran, too, "where this practice [of inoculation] has appeared," it was hoped that widespread smallpox vaccinations would eventually diminish fatalities caused by the ailment.[8] Still, childhood illnesses that regularly felled Iranian babies included "measles, scarlet fever, whooping cough, mumps, chicken pox," typhoid fever, and diphtheria. Unsurprisingly, "the commonest illness of all is smallpox." Though adults also became victims of smallpox, "it is considered a children's illness, because people hardly ever grow up without having had it."[9]

Persian sources reported the mortality of children resulting from epidemics as well. In 1894, the Persian newspaper *Nasiri* confirmed

Curzon's conclusions about the fatality of smallpox by acknowledging that "every year many children die or become maimed because of the lack of smallpox vaccinations."[10] In 1898, another source condemned Iran for doing little to combat the threat of smallpox—a "negligence" that had caused numerous preventable deaths. Smallpox not only claimed many lives but disfigured its survivors, making them, in the words of the prolific scholar Mirza Husayn Khan, Zuka' al-Mulk, "hideous and ugly."[11] Every year smallpox wreaked devastation among children, killing or disabling them (*naqis mishavand*).[12] In addition to smallpox, a measles epidemic in Tehran had claimed the lives of many children back in 1896; the deaths had occurred largely from gangrene, believed to be a side effect of measles.[13] By the end of the century, Persian hygienists pondered the fatalities caused by epidemics even as they penned treatises about overhauling public sanitation.

As these indicators show, curbing infectious diseases and prolonging the lives of mothers and children, whose health was particularly compromised in the nineteenth century, made sense both medically and socially. This impetus would have little political significance, however, had it not been co-opted by Iranian modernists and policy makers in the first half of the twentieth century to control the sexuality of women and men in the interests of the nation. For the next fifty years Iranian officials, physicians, intellectuals, and women activists would investigate the high incidence of infant and maternal mortality, offering socially prescriptive measures to counter the possibility of depopulation.[14]

Such arguments were not unique to Iranian nationalism, of course. Countries such as Great Britain, the United States, and France combated similar issues.[15] Indeed, some Iranian medical professionals in the 1920s and 1930s, influenced and even trained by both American and French physicians, predictably echoed elements of the pro-natalist arguments used in the United States and France. In the Qajar period, lasting from 1796 to 1925, however, Iran's experience with such policies remained inchoate and was alternately circumscribed and supported by the teachings and practice of Islam. The Qur'an writes: "Wealth and children are the ornaments of this life."[16] In two other passages the concept of wealth is again directly linked to the notion of childbearing, illustrating Qur'anic views of childbirth as a manifestation of divine beneficence. Moreover, the state not only went through ideological and political transformations but struggled to remain viable even as it implemented new welfare policies in the domain of public health. With the exception of the constitutional years (1906–1911), the Iranian government remained largely authoritarian, but the absence of institutional precedents made it difficult for the state to police its social welfare policies. Finally, unlike certain Western nations, Iran was unique in its scapegoating of midwives and women as a leading cause of infant mortality in the country. These concerns generated impassioned debates about the reproductive role of women in the family and the polity. Child rearing and mothering adapted to nationalist and demographic pressures. While women did not always frame the debates on population, their vital contribution to human reproduction placed them at center stage when it came to hygiene and maternalist politics.

Iran experienced epidemics of plague, cholera, smallpox, measles, and diphtheria with regularity, like other regions of the nineteenth-century Middle East. In 1875, epidemic diphtheria had appeared in Shiraz and increased until 1876, when it began to diminish. Later that year, diphtheria broke out in "some of the villages, but not in the town of Kashan, affecting children from 3 to 10 years old." Similar outbreaks were reported at Qum and Tehran, where in the autumn of 1876, the diphtheria epidemic was described as virulent, "particularly amongst children."[17] A report of the Board of Health pointed out that a "sort of epidemic small-pox of the confluent form committed, two months ago, great ravages, attacking both old people and children; out of 750 cases of the latter, only 37 recovered."[18] Weeks later, a memorandum from the March 1877 meeting of the Board of Health in Tehran reported the spread of smallpox to Persian Kurdistan, as well as several deaths from diphtheria. There was also concern about the increase of diphtheria in Tabriz.[19] Although vaccinations were known to curb epidemics of smallpox, they had not yet become common practice among Iranians. C. J. Wills, a British medical officer in Iran, observed in 1879 that "vaccination is not in favour; inoculation, or the direct communication of the disorder by placing the patient in the same bed with one suffering from smallpox of the most virulent type, is the method pursued."[20]

In addition to medical reports, memoirs recorded personal experiences with infant mortality during these years. Yahya Dawlatabadi notes in his autobiography that his younger brother died at the age of six.[21] Similarly, 'Abd Allah Mustawfi recalls that his sister Roqiyeh "died in her youth." Mustawfi also points out that his nephew, the son of his brother Mirza Ja'far, "died in infancy," though he does not specify the cause of death.[22]

Personal accounts such as these confirm the prevalence of infant mortality and indicate that epidemics contributed significantly to this outcome, perhaps more so than the "ignorance" of midwives. Yet the discourse of hygiene singled out unskilled midwives as a major contributing factor to mortality in Iran, a controversial assertion. This scapegoating becomes particularly revealing, for Iranian physicians of the same era were at times no less (and possibly more) prone to superstition and unscientific approaches to medicine than were midwives.[23] Yet hygienists and other modern reformers made little effort to address the quackery that sometimes passed for objective science in the male domain. The unorthodox treatments, limited training, and questionable methodology of male physicians infrequently became scripted as primary contributors to infant mortality in Iran, even though efforts were made to standardize the training and certification of physicians as well.[24] Yet it is important simultaneously to deconstruct the dominant (and often triumphant) discourse on modern science and medicine that was so prevalent in Iran and the Middle East. An analysis of maternalism will help to explain this fundamental difference, for midwives assumed more than just a transitory function in the social life of Iranian women. Although they performed obstetrics, midwives also treated common ailments, accepting a measure of responsibility for the general health of women and children.

Mirza Najaf Quli Khan, a physician in Tabriz, reported in 1899 that the cause of population decline in Iran (*nuqsan-i nufus-i mardum-i Iran*) could be traced to unskilled midwives who dispensed care with filthy hands and in unsanitary conditions. As he caustically remarked, "These uneducated executioners are ready to destroy the population."[25] This physician's sharp scrutiny and sobering observations echoed the public outcry for improved hygiene and birthing conditions in Iran.

Since the medieval period midwifery had ranked high as a profession because of midwives' valuable role in facilitating the process of birth. As Ibn Khaldun wrote in the fourteenth century, "Crafts noble because of their object are midwifery, the art of writing, book production, singing, and medicine. Midwifery is something necessary in civilization and a matter of general concern, because it assures, as a rule, the life of the new-born child."[26] Despite its status as an intellectual endeavor, it was a profession that was "as a rule restricted to women, since they, as women, may see the pudenda of other women."[27] Midwives had a civic responsibility to help women through the travails of childbirth, but it was unclear exactly how female midwives gained access to this knowledge (other than through personal experience).

Even before the modern era, Iranian women considered hygiene and childbirth a component of their domestic existence. A seventeenth-century work, *Kulthum Nanah*, written by Jamal al-Din Muhammad ibn Husayn Khvansari (d. 1713), recounts the daily habits of Iranian women of the Safavid era and discusses the superstitions midwives tended to incorporate in their practice.[28] This work so impressed some Orientalists that it was translated into English and French in the nineteenth century. A narrative of the habits and beliefs of the common folk, *Kulthum Nanah* discusses the customs of bathing, marriage, and pregnancy. From reciting incantations to performing prayers, from suspending onions to waving a sword, midwives performed unconventional healing rituals to ensure the health of the newborn and the mother.[29] By relating some of the superstitions common to childbirth, this anecdotal account reinforced the "unscientific" approach that traditional midwives adopted when delivering babies. Even this informal treatise stressed hygiene in women's everyday lives. On bathing, for instance, it comments on mundane rituals such as women washing their "head three times with soap," while noting that women helped one another apply a depilatory to remove their underarm hair. Bath time, it seemed, was a social hour for women, as they were encouraged to chat and even to talk about their relations with their husband.

Western travelers reported other customs common in Iran. James Justinian Morier, the British diplomat and writer who first visited the country in 1808, observed that "when a woman feels the pains of labour, she not only calls the *mamaché*, or midwife (who is generally an old woman), but also all her friends and relations."[30] Once the child is born, the birth attendants "wash it, clothe it, and swathe it in a long bandage, called the *Kandak*, that entirely encircles the child from its neck downwards ... They then place it under the same bedclothes with the mother."[31] It is interesting to note that such practices have endured not only in Iran but also in the West, suggesting that

Persian midwives of the nineteenth century were not completely ill-informed or misguided in recommending procedures considered routine even today. Morier noted that the midwife then pronounced the profession of the Muslim faith in the child's ear and drew a sword to perform a special ceremony.[32]

Religious works imparted rituals that promised to maximize a couple's chances of siring healthy, attractive children and avoiding unwelcome outcomes such as miscarriage, difficult labor, and disability.[33] In Islam, as in other cultures, menstrual blood signified impurity.[34] Shi'i hadith considered intercourse between a husband and wife to be illicit (*haram*) during menstruation. It was further believed that pregnancy achieved during an eclipse would result in a miscarriage. Certain prayers promised to ward off the devil so that prior to intercourse a man's sperm, and by extension his offspring, would not be tainted by satanic spirits.[35] Another tradition held that pregnant women should eat quince in order to give birth to children with smooth skin. Other written incantations were used to protect a mother from experiencing a difficult labor and to ensure the safe delivery of the child.[36] Women who had newly delivered were urged to eat something moist so that their children might be blessed with forbearance.[37] As birth attendants, midwives were often entrusted with the responsibility of acting on such common practices and recommendations. Some midwives, however, also assisted women with abortions. A medical journal reported, for example, that in Iran abortions were common and that "it constituted a specialty" for midwives. Several herbs or drugs were used to induce an abortion.[38]

By the late nineteenth century, as Iran became engrossed by the potential healing powers of Western medicine, male physicians and hygienists disparaged the unempirical methods of local midwives. C. J. Wills, a British medical officer attached to the Telegraph Department in Iran, commented on the culture of midwifery, a description that reinforced the impression that midwives seemed to give pregnant women poor care. Writing in 1879, Wills painted a gruesome picture of the birthing process, during which mothers sometimes endured physical injury. Local traditions of childbirth and midwifery, which remained mainly "in the hands of Jewesses and old women," sustained the belief that labor proceeded more successfully if the expecting woman was not lying down. As Wills explains, "The patient is placed in a crouching position, sitting on her heels, with her feet raised from the ground by means of two bricks . . . the patient on no account is permitted to lie down. The successful termination of the labour is supposed to be the result of gravitation." If a complication presented itself, such as "the presentation of an extremity, or of the cord, the midwife simply drags at it till something gives way." Such a procedure could rupture the womb, which was "a common thing." New mothers generally visited the public bath on the sixth day after delivery and resumed their ordinary activities shortly thereafter.[39] Midwives in Iran were not alone in recommending a sitting position to induce labor, but their limitations in tackling complications related to childbirth did at times endanger the health of mothers and newborns. A French medical study of different birthing practices around the world confirmed the popularity of this birthing position in Iran and even included an illustration of it.[40] Another position favored in Iran depicted the midwife assisting the woman in labor from behind.[41] Emile Duhousset, a military officer who had served on a mission to Iran in 1858, offered an anthropological perspective on the culture of birthing there.[42] Duhousset remarked that labor was anything but a private affair; rather, numerous female attendants participated in the event. Some witnesses read passages from the Qur'an, while others brandished swords to ward off evil spirits.[43] Duhousset based some of his remarks on depictions of birth drawn by Persian artists.

In 1896, Samuel Graham Wilson, commenting on medical practices in Iran, concluded that "there is a great deal of superstition in the treatment of disease." He gave testimony about a difficult case of childbirth at which a Persian doctor attended—a description that evoked a virtual medical circus. As Wilson recalled: "He could only stay in the next room and send in directions through the midwife. He asked them to call the woman physician. There were half a dozen women about when she arrived. They were so fanatical that she could hardly get her hands washed, lest she defile the bowl. . . . Meanwhile a mollah led a sheep into the room and around the couch of the woman. It was then sacrificed for her life. The doctors left without doing anything."[44] Wilson's description fit into familiar accounts in which the disparagement of local medical customs often was justified by the outcome of events. Arguably, Wilson and other critics made valid assessments of Qajar medical practices. Yet it is telling that that Wilson's work, like many others in this genre, scarcely provided examples of medical successes in Iran. How is it, one wonders, that

anyone survived childbirth given the degree of ignorance and superstition that was apparently rampant in nineteenth-century Iran?

Reverend Isaac Adams, a physician and Christian missionary
born in Iran in 1872, reported on the condition of Iranian women.
In the village of Sangar, Adams observed the common habit of
"beating of their wives." According to Adams, "it is quite common
there to see a woman's head bruised and her clothing torn." Con-
cluding that he had been raised "among ignorant and ill-influenced
people," Adams made similarly alarming comments about the
dearth of medical services available to women.[45] He noted, for example,
that during epidemics men typically fled the cities to seek refuge in
the mountains but left their women and children behind to perish.
In addition, he noted that male doctors, "not daring to touch
them, even to feel their pulse or look at their tongue," left them
there "to stand the pain and suffering to the end without any relief."
During childbirth, they "often perish under the barbarous hands of
the ignorant midwives."[46] Adams' words echoed those of other
Western missionaries and medical professionals who had lived in
the country.

By the turn of the century, although midwives remained central to
the birthing process, their role was no longer appreciated. Iranian
midwives presided at births, but they did not receive formal schooling,
nor were they skilled in the modern techniques of obstetrics. As
Mirza Najaf Quli Khan, the physician from Tabriz, said deridingly in
1899, if newborns were lucky enough to survive the ignorance of
midwives, they would then have to endure the incompetence of nannies and wet nurses. These caregivers often bathed the infants in cold
water and bundled them tightly in blankets, needlessly exposing
them to pneumonia or restricting their natural movements. These
grievances, although anecdotal and devoid of statistics, exposed the
culture of child rearing in Qajar Iran. Yet as Mooshie G. Daniel, a
native of Urumiyah, observed in 1898, "The modern midwife is
greatly needed in Persia, as many women die for want of attention,
and it is against the law for male doctors to give them treatment."[47]

It is disconcerting that hygienists tended to single out midwives as
culprits in infant mortality; indeed, the maternalist discourse origi-
nated in the nineteenth century with male hygienists and physicians
who questioned the role of traditional female caretakers and then
reassessed the culture of mothering and childbirth in Iran. After the

publication of the first women's journals, many educated Iranian women also donned the mantle of maternalist and criticized midwives as well, but they had as their primary aim the betterment of women's status rather than an overarching desire simply to inflate population figures for nationalist purposes.

European medical doctors expanding Western medical knowledge in Iran influenced the field of midwifery as well. Jean-Etienne Schneider, a French physician who had served the Persian king Muzaffar al-Din Shah and who headed the Sanitary Council for a time, had hoped to charge a French midwife, Mlle. Marguenot, with the task of educating Persian midwives about childbirth. According to Schneider, Persian midwives "had no idea of sepsis, anti-sepsis, and . . . through their ignorance have caused many cases of puerperal fever, with many fatalities," but nonetheless they possessed authority and influence over the traditions of childbirth in Iran.[48] Schneider described Mlle. Marguenot as having struggled "almost daily" against superstitions and the prejudices of indigenous women in the domestic service of Persian ladies.[49]

Persian maternalists propagated this negative image of midwives as well. In 1904, Mirza Husayn Khan, Zuka' al-Mulk, founder of the newspaper *Tarbiyat*, advertised the publication of a textbook on midwifery composed by Mu'tamid al-Sultan, a respected Persian physician. Zuka' al-Mulk lamented that the book had not been published earlier so that it could have been read by "ignorant, uncaring midwives" and thus have averted the "innocent martyrdom" of a thousand people by "stubborn old women."[50]

Although little is known about the training of midwives in the nineteenth century, an extant manuscript entitled "A Treatise on Midwifery" offers medical advice on the process of facilitating childbirth. The text, apparently completed in Jumadi al-Thani 1294 AH/June 1877, discusses the physiology of a woman undergoing labor, as well as the various possible positions of the fetus, highlighting scenarios that might be dangerous to either the mother or the child.[51] This specialized medical treatise lacks the accusatory tone of popular hygienic discussions of midwifery in the late Qajar era that denounced midwives as enemies of public health. Instead, it focused on imparting obstetrical knowledge to the physician and the midwife about pregnancy, including determining the competence of the uterus through its shape—either a "pear" or a "clock"—and recognizing the movements of the fetus in an effort to identify the position and condition of the fetus in utero.[52]

Another manuscript attached to this work and completed roughly around the same time, in May 1877, offered insights into women's ailments.[53] It is unlikely that midwives ministering care to women throughout Iran referred to these specialized, unpublished texts, given that by most existing accounts midwives were generally regarded as illiterate. Despite their limited use and circulation, the production of these rare manuscripts suggests that some Qajar physicians or hygienists were expressing a desire to approach reproduction in a systemic, empirical fashion. The medical documentation of childbirth was a first step in this process of control, which would give men some authority over the management of childbirth in Iran, a field that at least in the nineteenth century typically eschewed male involvement and government control.

The attacks upon the practices of traditional midwives mimicked the intellectual controversies that had been brewing among Iran's medical elite throughout the nineteenth century. The introduction of Western medicine in Iran began with the arrival of European and American physicians affiliated with sundry religious or diplomatic missions. In 1851, the opening of the Dar al-Funun, Iran's first modern educational facility, brought additional European instructors in the sciences to Iran. European doctors also served as private physicians to Qajar kings in the nineteenth century and instructed a generation of Persian students in the Western sciences. However, some traditional physicians and members of the 'ulama opposed the growing appeal of Western medicine. Eventually it was agreed that students at the Dar al-Funun would be taught both modern Western medicine and traditional Persian medicine.

Epidemics and unskilled midwives, however, were not the only causes of infant mortality. Famine and poverty compounded the social hardships confronting Iranian families of the nineteenth century. One journalist discerned that "in Iran, the poor do not have enough food, and for this reason the health of poor children is generally worse than that of adults. In particular, toward the end of summer and the beginning of autumn, food sources are mainly limited to fruits," most of which were consumed by adults. Children, it claimed, subsisted mostly on rice.[54] When epidemics visited the country, children became easy targets because they were often malnourished and more susceptible to contracting contagious diseases.[55] The Tabrizi physician cited above, Mirza Najaf Quli Khan, noted that married couples on average suffered the loss of six or seven children. Aside from dealing with the emotional hardship of death, the anguished couples then had to cope with the possibility of infertility, since some women experienced difficulties in procreating after multiple births. Mirza Najaf Quli Khan's observations support Lady Sheil's statistics on infant mortality and in fact suggest a possible increase in mortality figures by the turn of the century.[56] These accounts, however anecdotal, confirmed the prevalence of child mortality as well as the common occurrence of sterility and infertility in married life.

With all this emphasis on reproduction, what became of infertile couples? The British physician C. J. Wills, who had visited Iran in the nineteenth century, labeled sterility "that terror of the Oriental woman."[57] Another traveler to Iran considered it a truism that "every Oriental woman wishes to have a child—for the sterile woman is covered with opprobrium, and sterility spells divorce."[58] In Hamadan, a legend held that infertile women who visited and touched the famous stone statue of a lion would be able to bear children. In July 1906, Ali Khan Qajar, Zahir al-Dawlah, the governor of Hamadan, confirmed the popularity of this site among barren women on his visit there.[59] A. V. Williams Jackson, a renowned professor of Persian antiquity at Columbia University, also mentioned the fame of this lion monument, acknowledging that "barren women touch its brow to remove the curse of sterility."[60]

One women's journal explored the conditions of infertility and impotence for those already afflicted. Some believed that special herbs could relieve infertility and impotence resulting from external causes. However, other women resorted to superstition in their desperation to find a cure for their infertility. To combat this, *Jahan-i Zanan* reprinted the contents of a manuscript found in a Mashhad library recommending that women wear a charm around their necks with a specific incantation intended to induce pregnancy. Such superstitions, the journal concluded, impeded women from getting educated and seeking proper medical help.[61]

Reliable figures on Iran's nineteenth-century population are not readily available, but in 1898, Mirza Husayn Khan, Zuka' al-Mulk, reported that based on travelers' accounts (left unspecified), Iran's population at the time totaled over 8 million.[62] By 1920 Julian Bharier lists the population as 11.37 million. A decade later the population had increased once more, to 12.59 million.[63] As these statistics show, Iran, unlike France, actually experienced a slight growth in population, despite high mortality rates, during the interval when concerns about depopulation consumed maternalists. Perhaps the low level of public hygiene, including the dearth of clean running water, the frequency of pandemics, and the scarcity of clinics and other institutions of modern health care, heightened fears of depopulation, particularly since Iranians, already uneasy about the viability of their country as an independent nation, remained under military threat along its boundaries. Finally, because the government had not conducted reliable censuses, maternalists may not have been aware of the gradual increase in population. Nonetheless, as shall be seen, maternalists manipulated the debate on population to impose social control over sexuality and women's reproductive rights.

Despite the general but slow trend toward population growth, in 1907 another journalist sounded the alert that "many of our people will suffer throughout the years unless there is hygiene in the country and until we understand its methods. And, of course, as our population declines, so too will our advancements."[64] This frightening scenario launched a hygiene movement in Iran that conspicuously co-opted social programs for political aims as it assumed control of women's bodies. Attention to women's health emerged in this context and was not always restricted to reproduction. Rather, this interest spurred innovation in treating common female problems such as cramping related to menstruation and pregnancy.[65] The debate on hygiene significantly affected the role of women as advocates of public health and as midwives of the nation. Although threats of epidemics did not disappear with the spread of modernist conventions, they whetted the patriotic drive to advance public hygiene.

The study of hygiene, as opposed to medicine, opened up vistas for women's involvement and cultural enlightenment precisely because it was perceived as a less elite, more plebeian discipline—one better suited for the subaltern, including women. A physician needed to labor for years to gain his expertise, whereas, according to one observer, "one can spread the science of hygiene without any effort . . . to the minds of the general public."[66] Medical students in Iran did eventually include women in their ranks, but that momentous step would take place decades later. Until then, hygienic education would attempt to prevent the escalation of dangerous epidemics through simple measures. In the process, mothers and midwives served as the primary conduit of hygienic education and practice, particularly concerning newborns.

Maternalists concentrated on women's reproductive health and recorded in print their trepidation about depopulation, midwives, and inadequate sanitation. In the process, male figures (hygienists, physicians, and religious leaders) who may have had little actual experience in obstetrics gradually chipped away at the authority of often seasoned female midwives in the birthing process. Even as the hygiene movement created possibilities for volunteerism and investment in maternal health, it reinforced patriarchy through modern schools and clinics. These transformations in the culture of maternal health care altered the dynamics of gender relations in Iran. While new institutions of health and education often upheld male authority, they eventually armed women with some of the tools they needed to assert their independence in the volatile politics of reproduction and motherhood.

As modern physicians certified their new learning in specialized educational settings, they justified their criticism of traditional medicine, obstetrics, and child care, knowledge of which, unlike modern medical knowledge, was often passed down informally and unscientifically. The secular state, working superficially within the confines of an Islamic framework, initiated public programs that popularized the rudiments of maternal and child hygiene through schools, newspapers, and even film. It also scripted a narrative that accepted as its premise the superiority of modern Western medical knowledge and practice.

PART TWO

Marriage, Maternity, and Sexuality

CHAPTER 3

cᐱɔ

From Celibacy to Companionship

The Evolution of Persian Marriages

I n 1877, a discussion on the celibacy of priests spurred debate in the Persian journal *Akhtar* about marriage as a fundamental social institution. The rejection of celibacy was not a novel concept in Islamic literature. Popular Shiʿi traditions rejected celibacy as well. For example, the renowned Safavid-era theologian Muhammad Baqir Majlisi (d. 1698 or 1699), credited with propagating commonly practiced Shiʿi rituals, repudiated celibacy and instead wrote about the wisdom of marriage and procreation.[1] Building on these historical precedents, the writer of this article argued that endorsement of a monastic way of life (*rahbaniyyah*) ran contrary to Islam, as well as to the laws of nature and basic common sense. Restricting marriage was akin to denying the existence of God. Just as there was no difference between "aborting a fetus" (*isqat-i jinin*) and "killing a person" (*kushtan-i adam*), so there was no distinction between "forbidding marriage" (*man'-i izdivaj*) and abortion, for marriage "causes the production and creation of human beings." By denying the natural desire within them, priests were flouting the wisdom of God and a fundamental human impulse. This writer considered such precepts to be a perversion not only of nature but also of religiosity.[2]

Iranian marriages had fallen under scrutiny and reassessment in response to shifting public needs and political expectations. The dearth of extant marriage records from the nineteenth century makes it difficult to assess whether Qajar society was experiencing an actual rise in celibacy and a decline in marriage. However, modernity imposed changes on the role of women and men in society, changes that became reflected in family life. The evolution of Persian family life, especially in urban centers, required a new look at the meaning and social significance of marriage. Muslim marriages in Iran still required witnesses, documentation, and parental acquiescence, but over time they became more than just a legal contract. For decades Iranians grappled with these ideas, and eventually they put forth new legislation intended to regulate personal relations between women and men.

A woman's chastity or promiscuity was bound to her family's honor. Many believed that Persian society had an obligation to help women remain virtuous. To do so, the state needed to create opportunities for women's industriousness, education, and domesticity. The absence of such "respectable" opportunities could bring about temptation and vice, leading errant women toward promiscuity and prostitution. Morality was not solely bound to religion, however. The question of women's morality influenced the secular debates about women's health, marriage, and education. Women, as well as men, preoccupied themselves with the meanings of feminine virtue in an increasingly secular and interconnected society.

Matrimony had an important communal dimension. Marriage laws not only delineated the economic relationship between husbands and wives but also prescribed a social hierarchy that laid out the civic duties of women and men. In addition, marriage provided the state with a means of managing its population. After all, it was the government's sanction and enactment of religious and civic law that enabled women and men to marry, to serve as witnesses, or to officiate at a wedding ceremony. By outlining a code of conduct, marriage could preserve the virtue of citizens and further the moral objectives of the state. Marriage, as the starting point of family life, emphasized ideals such as unity, loyalty, virtue, and industriousness, which could also strengthen the bonds between citizens and the state. As Iran experimented with new forms of political governance at the turn of the twentieth century, the family became an appealing metaphor for describing the evolving relationship between citizens and the state.[3]

In the late Qajar era the purported erosion of marriage as an institution appeared connected to the moral laxity of Iranian society. The
spread of venereal disease, accompanied by a perception of increased
sexual promiscuity, reinforced the sense that Iranian society was
becoming socially decadent. To counter celibacy and to curb sexual
promiscuity, several writers addressed the virtues of marriage. In the
late nineteenth century, a Persian translation of an Ottoman, and later
Indian, rendition of a French manual on marital hygiene was published, endorsing marriage and discussing the physiological processes
of human reproduction. Like French hygienists of the nineteenth
century, the manual's author, Sayyid Muhammad Shirazi, "paid more
attention to pregnancy and birth than to menstruation or sexual
intercourse."[4] The purpose of marriage, Shirazi wrote, was to increase
population, for marriage served not just the individual but humanism
(*adamiyat*) and civilization (*tamaddun*) as well. He believed that
human beings found it "impossible to live in seclusion and alone."
Alluding to various religious and cultural traditions, Shirazi maintained that moral and practical exigencies necessitated marriage. The
ancient Greek philosophers, he wrote, viewed marriage as a "great
service to the homeland" that ensured "the duration of the nation."
Islam, too, opposed a monastic lifestyle (*rahbaniyat*). According to
hadith, or Islamic traditions, "He who is able to marry should marry,
for it keeps the eye cast down and keeps a man chaste; he who cannot,
should take to fasting, for it will have a castrating effect upon him."[5]
Even the Prophet Muhammad, Shirazi claimed, had stated that the
"best women are those who bear many children," thus illustrating the
extent to which women had been encouraged to produce offspring.
In short, there was no higher purpose to marriage than human reproduction and continuation of the human race.[6]

Single men and women, Shirazi went on, might suppose that they
were free from the burdens of family life and child rearing, and that
they enjoyed longer life spans than married couples. However, he
assured them, a review of available death records would surely prove
the contrary. Because bachelors lived unregulated lives—their meal-
times, for instance, were unspecified—not to mention that their
solitary lifestyles invited fornication and adultery (*zina'*), they faced
health risks that threatened to reduce their longevity. Married men,
on the hand, lived orderly lives and enjoyed a happy existence because
of their families' kindness and attention. The same held true for

married women. Although they confronted "veritable" fears due to pregnancy and childbirth, they experienced the joys and pleasures of spending time with their husband and children—experiences that extended their life span. Marriage, he concluded, was a virtuous and "natural act."[7] Such truisms left little room for doubt or dissent—the intent, no doubt, of the author and the government censors who supported such translating endeavors, for the texts were regarded as social correctives, not as open cultural fora.[8]

Shirazi took editorial liberties with his translation, as his numerous references to the sharia' make clear. One can nonetheless assume that a significant portion of his work derives from the French original. Yet Shirazi's musings are interspersed throughout his translation, and the text therefore represents one of the earliest Persian texts on marital hygiene in the modern era. In this work Shirazi articulates some of the basic tenets of reproductive health and sexuality with which Iranian maternalists would grapple in the first half of the twentieth century. By adopting a biological gaze and a scientific posture, he discussed the biology of human reproduction with uncanny openness and candor. Why was such direct discussion of sexuality possible? Hygienic literature such as Shirazi's work made it possible to discuss socially sensitive topics such as sexuality and reproduction because sexuality was couched in a pseudoscientific language intended to bring about a higher societal good: improved public sanitation and personal hygiene, as well as the birthing of healthy children. From an ethical standpoint, discussions of marriage and marital hygiene also addressed the desire to promote morality and virtue among Iranian women and men by endorsing legal and sensible marriages. At the same time, Shirazi and other maternalists were creating norms of behavior that, though not legally enforced, identified personal choices in matters of health, marriage, and even dress as "appropriate" or "inappropriate."

Shirazi's discussion of marriage reinforced such simplistic truisms, and the didactic tone of the text emphasized his writings as a corrective for Iranian families who veered from his suggested norms of marital hygiene and conduct. Legal marriage, Shirazi remarked, was one of the laws of metaphysics. Eschewing marriage and acting contrary to this natural order resulted in "lunacy" and "illness," whereas engaging in marriage and obeying the laws of nature brought about health and vigor. Ancient physicians, he noted, often attributed the illnesses of young women to love, and marriage seemed to cure the woes of young women.[9] The proper age of marriage was difficult to determine, however, given the variability in the physical and psychological development and readiness of women and men. He admonished those who insisted on a child's marriage before the child displayed physical maturity, calling it "harmful" and "in error." Girls in particular who were married too young not only suffered from weakness but also had immature uteruses and thus could not nurture strong children in the womb.[10] Older couples, too, were at risk for siring weak and chronically ill offspring. Similarly, marriage between couples with a wide age difference between them often did not bring about happiness and health. Children of such marriages, Shirazi postulated, inherited the physical condition of their aged parent and appeared "weak, ill, hunchedbacked," and "unsightly" (*bad shikl*).[11]

Mention of venereal disease stirred controversy by suggesting sexual impropriety in an Islamic society. These discussions also pointed to the need to provide rudimentary sexual education and awareness within marriage. An early Iranian maternalist, Shirazi focused on the ways in which healthful reproduction might be achieved. While Iran did not legislate eugenics, maternalists who pioneered texts on reproductive hygiene articulated and propagated such concepts. For example, Shirazi urged potential marriage partners (and their parents, who often engaged in negotiating marriage proposals) to educate themselves about their physical health. He encouraged families to expose any medical concerns prior to marriage in order to deter the couple from bearing children who might also inherit similar difficulties. In fact, he believed that such flawed individuals, including women whose physical characteristics impeded them from birthing healthy children, should be barred from marriage and reproduction in order to avoid spreading these inadequacies to the next generation. Shirazi even suggested that a law be instituted preventing individuals with "impaired physical features" (*ma'yub al-'aza*) and "inherited illnesses" (*mawrusi al-amraz*) from marrying.[12] A marriage based on fitness and vigor was considered the starting point of healthful reproduction and might even be an antidote to illicit sexual relations. Yet Shirazi gave tacit recognition to the reality of extramarital affairs, and his text even provided a putative cure for gonorrhea, a sexually transmitted disease known at the time.

Shi'i traditions placed a premium on marrying virgin brides. One tradition implored men to marry virgins so that they would bear the men numerous children. Another tradition claimed that virgin brides had a pleasing smell in their mouths. In addition, they had dry uteruses and their bodies were apparently better equipped to carry children. The same tradition maintained that the breasts of virgin brides produced more milk than those of nonvirgins.[13] Even Shirazi had confirmed that among certain families it was customary to display a bloody sheet after a husband and wife first engaged in sexual relations, and that failure to provide such evidence of virginity often led to the disgraced bride being sent back to her father's home.[14] In short, the "best women" (*bihtarin zanan*) were those who gave birth copiously, and nature rewarded virgins by enabling them to carry numerous children in their wombs. By contrast, the "worst women" (*badtarin zanan*) were those who controlled their husbands, bore no children, and flirted with other men.[15]

While it was possible to identify some of the desirable elements in a potential marriage partner, Qajar families were not always able to attain marital bliss. Some writers investigated the causes of unhappy marital unions among Iranians. In her memoirs, the Qajar princess Taj al-Saltanah, betrothed at eight years of age, lamented her marriage to Hasan Khan Shoja' al-Saltanah and the Persian tradition that had placed her in this predicament. Taj al-Saltanah, a daughter of the nineteenth-century Persian king Nasir al-Din Shah, defied stereotypes of harem life.[16] A restless soul, Taj despised conventions such as marriage, opting instead for refined pastimes such as reading and mastering the art of epistolary prose. Born in 1883, Taj grew up within the cloistered walls of the harem. Her mother, Turan al-Saltanah, was the shah's cousin, and her parents had wed through an institution known as *mut'a* (temporary marriage).[17] As she rued, "Of mankind's great misfortunes one is this, that one must take a wife or husband according to the wishes of one's parents."[18] Even on her wedding day, Taj al-Saltanah could not conquer her misgivings about her forced fate. As she recalled, "Never will I forget that moment, when freedom and dignity were snatched away from me. . . . In all fairness, however, I should not be the only one cursing that day; that poor wretched youth ought to have felt the same as I did."[19] An honest and heartfelt description of her woes, Taj's reflections gave voice to some of the common frustrations experienced by women and men of her generation.

Other observers found some merit to Persian unions, even as they condemned the custom of polygamy. In 1891, the Ottoman writer Ahmed Bey noted that polygamy in Iran is "hardly practiced" except among "the royal family and some rich old mullahs," although he may have understated its popularity among ordinary folk. Those engaged in polygamy, Ahmed Bey asserted, were "generally despised."[20] Another source found in 1911 that in Iran only 2 percent of the population engaged in polygamy.[21] Still, an American missionary report from 1914 stated that "polygamy and concubinage must be driven out" of the country, suggesting that polygamy, albeit rare, was actively practiced among certain Iranian communities and was likely underreported.[22] Few accounts exist of the relationship among the multiple wives of men, yet it is safe to assume that interactions among competing wives were not always harmonious. In 1921, an American missionary gave testimony of a bitter dispute involving two village wives. Apparently a quarrel had ensued between the two wives over a petty matter of heating the oven. In a fit of anger the second wife had thrown the baby of the first wife "from the roof to the ground," but the child had fortunately "escaped harm." The second wife had also bitten off a piece of the lip of the first wife. Finally the landlady intervened and had the second wife beaten. The landlady also removed a pair of gold earrings belonging to the second wife and gave it to the first wife to help pay for the medical expenses associated with having her lip sewn up by a mission doctor.[23]

In addition to polygamy, some Western travelers to Iran spoke out against the travesty of marrying off child brides. Because family honor hinged on the chastity of girls, some Iranian parents encouraged their daughters to wed at a young age to avert the temptations of sexual experimentation before marriage and the shame associated with it. Early marriage seemed preferable to promiscuity or, worse, prostitution.[24] In 1911, the British missionary Napier Malcolm remarked that "the usual age for a Muhammadan girl to marry is thirteen or fourteen, but in many places they marry as early as eight or nine."[25] Girls generally had little say in this matter, perhaps due to their youth, as Malcolm speculated. Arranging marriages before couples had reached the age of puberty made little sense and often obligated them to endure miserable marriages.

In Iran, as elsewhere, marriage gave women and men certain privileges such as citizenship, access to welfare services, and the right to inheritance.[26] Marriage also reinforced a division of labor that ordered society along recognizable gender lines. Although a number of accepted norms of marital conduct changed in Iran over the course of a century, the view that men served as protectors of their women remained relatively static. Scholars have convincingly argued that Iranian men were taught to assume responsibility for the welfare and security of their women. This "male guardianship" of women saddled men with paternalist obligations as fathers and husbands. Just as women needed to embrace domesticity to forge a harmonious family life, men had to assume their manly duties. In 1907, as the journalist Mu'ayyid al-Islam averred, material progress in Iranian society necessitated "manliness" (*mardanigi*) and "brave action" (*harkat-i dalira-nah*). Bravery became one of the requisite virtues of male patriotism, as without brave men and soldiers the nation's survival remained at risk and women's purity might become compromised. But bravery meant more than just success on the battlefield. Brave men used their male authority both at home and in the public sphere to support their women. "Congregating and talking," Mu'ayyid al-Islam said deridingly, did not effect change or help to eliminate social ills.[27]

In a subsequent essay, Mu'ayyid al-Islam contended that the least passionate individuals are those who "do not pay attention to their wife and daughter, who abandon them without expenses or livelihood." Instead, such persons wasted their savings on "meaningless expenses" (*kharjhayah bihudah*) in gambling houses (*qumar-khanah'ha*), brothels (*fahishah-khanah'ha*), and the like.[28] Still, he observed that the predicament of women with irresponsible husbands paled in comparison with the distress widows faced, especially if they were left alone to care for their children. In fact, he concluded that widows were the most helpless and "abandoned" (*dar mandah*) women, and because they represented the nation's honor (*namus*), widows required men's protection.

Widows were quite common in Iran because of the prevalence of child marriages. As John Wishard, chief of the American Presbyterian Hospital in Tehran, noted, "Many of these children are married, often at the age of twelve, to men old enough to be their grandfathers, and this means a large number of widows."[29] Wishard pointed out that because many widows "are left without means of support, there is only one road open for them, and that road leadeth to destruction."[30] Some widows chose to become "plural wives" or temporary ones, as polygamous or temporary marriage offered them rights that might not otherwise be available to them.

The plight of widows had worsened in the months after the granting of constitutional government. Mu'ayyid al-Islam reported that several widows had congregated outside the Tupkhanah, near the parliament itself, in protest and seeking government financial assistance for their withheld pensions. That the widows had gathered in such a public place emphasized the failures of the country's men in defending their vulnerable female citizens. They had not only let down the widows but also dishonored the nation.[31] The public display of such negligence embarrassed the male leaders of the country, including the delegates of the newly founded parliament, since it showed their inability to achieve a basic aspect of manliness: protection of the nation's female citizens. Mu'ayyid al-Islam regretted that these profligate leaders squandered money on lavish feasts but did not consider contributing funds to relieve the widows' misery. To ease the embarrassment of having to explain the public's inaction toward suffering widows, he volunteered to have the office of his newspaper function as a depot for the collection of charitable contributions. These contributions were to come from the nation's leaders and others to help lessen the impact of poverty on widows and their families.[32] Another newspaper, *Rahnima*, also objected to the hardships that these widows had endured, a situation forcing them to put up tents outside Artillery Plaza in Tehran during the hot summer months. As this anonymous writer decried, the widows lived for months, "hunchbacked," in these tents with little air circulation. Some became sick from living under unsanitary conditions, while others perished. Yet few, if any, passers-by offered to assist these disadvantaged, abandoned women.[33]

Among the most important social changes brought during the constitutional years was the termination of the harem as an institution. Under Nasir al-Din Shah, the harem had grown into a considerable royal and social institution. To control costs, Muzaffar al-Din Shah shut down his father's harem after Nasir al-Din Shah's assassination in 1896.[34] The dissolution of the harem, a symbolic institution confined to the rich, meant that even Iran's privileged classes were shifting their views on marriage. Like many ordinary Iranians, Persian royalty would grapple with the purpose of modern marriage in order to adapt to the exigencies of contemporary society. The harem had at once signified male authority and female complicity in upholding polygamy as a necessary condition of married life. With the passing of this quintessential institution of polygamy, Iranians of all classes could begin to imagine monogamy as the preferred expression of modern marriage.

Family life had to adapt itself to the political changes transforming Iran. In 1907 the popular Persian newspaper *Habl al-Matin* declared patriotism a "necessary duty," surpassing even one's commitment to life, property, and family. It argued: "Your wife and children are only enjoyable when the homeland and Islam are not trampled upon."[35] This was a bold and revealing statement. National exigencies, it seemed, had superseded familial obligations even in a society that considered the family a fundamental social unit. Middle Eastern households had traditionally forged kinship networks intended to support women and children. But as Kandiyoti explains, "The 'protective net' which households were supposed to extend over their more vulnerable members—women, children and the elderly—grew increasingly threadbare. . . . The material basis of traditional authority relations within the family between the young and the old and between genders was subjected to persistent assault."[36] Too, in Iran the economic demands of urban life and the expansion of state bureaucracy necessitated a different set of skills and preparedness from both women and men in the domestic sphere and the professional world. The modern family served as a conduit for the propagation of nationalist mores and a vehicle for the enforcement of gender roles conducive to new maternalist ideals. Nationalism had created a different political language for Iranian men and women.[37]

Marriage provided an ethical framework for social and family relations. An essay written in 1911, likely by the journalist Sayyid Hasan Mu'minzadah, supports this point. Mu'minzadah declared that four essential factors gave life meaning and purpose. These fundamentals included the mind (*'aql*), property (*mal*), and a wife (*'ayal*) and child (*farzand*). He described the wife as the "mistress of the house" (*kadbanu*), a modest and upright woman who managed the man's home according to the man's wishes, and who cared for his property. The ideal wife birthed, nursed, and nurtured her children. She served as a partner in the home alongside the man in her life. The emphasis on seeking out this "ideal" wife placed pressure on the Iranian woman to subsume her needs to her husband's by making his comfort and well-being her priority, instead of allowing the woman to focus on herself as an equal partner in the marital relationship. In return, the ideal wife gained her husband's constant approval. The goal of married life was the protection of honor (*hifz-i namus*), often used to mean the honor and welfare of the family.[38]

In 1911, the editor of *Amuzgar*, a weekly newspaper published in Rasht, addressed marital relations in a short essay. Although this journal focused on topics of political and intellectual import, it is noteworthy that a brief discussion on marriage ensued: "Marital relations are one of the main issues of life, and its significance is such that all religions and nations of the world have established laws governing marital relations. Anyone who behaves contrary to these laws cannot be considered a person of decency and character." The wedding night was ideally a blessed event. Even prophets and leaders celebrated their weddings with feasting. In Iran, however, although marriage was regarded as one of life's milestones, it marked the beginning of "misfortune"—a misery brought about as a result of women's ignorance.[39] This misogynistic trope targeted women as the cause of men's suffering in the family, as well as a source of domestic discord.[40] Without education, women would not grasp the real intent of marriage and partnership, whereas women's schooling might actually improve marital relations between Iranian men and women.[41]

Because marriage was considered a predictable event in the lives of many Iranians, early Persian women's journals often discussed marital relations between couples, even suggesting ways for creating happy unions, though not openly addressing sexuality. In 1910, *Danish*, the first newspaper edited by a woman in Iran, pointed out that disagreements over money often led to marital conflict and cautioned that women should avoid asking their husbands for money on a daily basis. Instead, women were encouraged to maintain a monthly household budget.[42] Men were also reminded that they ought to speak to their wives about their experiences outside the home, particularly since few urban women spent much of their day out of the house. For this reason, men needed to anticipate that their wives might at times express frustration about their overwhelming child care responsibilities.[43] To prevent other causes of dissent between husbands and wives, men were urged to respect their wives' family members and to refrain from making derogatory comments about their in-laws even in jest.[44]

Another women's journal, *Shikufah*, also published several pieces on marriage.[45] One essay stressed the friendship and unity between husbands and wives, arguing that they resembled "two individuals in one skin."[46] Instead of viewing marriage as an institution that reinforced hierarchy between women and men, such writers advocated marriage as a reciprocal partnership between women and men. Still, marriage retained its necessary public function in Iranian society. In 1915, one passage echoed the words of Sayyid Muhammad Shirazi's nineteenth-century manual on marital hygiene in its emphasis on marriage as a way to encourage human reproduction. Population growth (*takathur-i afrad*) depended on marriage, and human beings, by nature, shunned solitude to seek this natural union.[47] Unlike Shirazi, however, the writers of *Shikufah* acknowledged that marriage in Iran remained risky, somewhat akin to fishing for oysters in deep waters: if one was fortunate, the shell would contain pearls, and if not, it would brim with something far less desirable. For this reason, marriages built on blind luck and ignorance were discouraged because of their potential for disastrous unhappiness.[48] By making happiness and compatibility a focus of modern Iranian marriages, such writers were advocating a novel approach to marital relations.

In the aftermath of the First World War, discussions of marriage once again assumed social significance. Although the two earliest Persian women's journals, *Danish* and *Shikufah*, had ceased publication by then, other women's magazines appeared on the horizon and reignited the debate. In 1921, Fakhr Afaq Parsa launched a new journal called *Jahan-i Zanan* (Women's World). Born into a religious family, Parsa apparently had married her husband at the age of nine but nonetheless was encouraged to get an education.[49] In the second issue of her bimonthly journal, Parsa reiterated the claim that men and women sought companionship to lead meaningful lives and to fulfill their needs. She contended that men who did not have a woman's "shadow" cast over them languished in solitude. In the absence of Persian statistics on demographic indicators, Parsa cited instead European figures to show that the mortality rate among unmarried men in Germany, France, and Britain was higher than the mortality rate among their married counterparts in those countries. In short, Parsa concluded that marriage brought longevity.[50]

In a subsequent issue, Parsa printed a translation of an essay written by Feride Ezzat Selim from Istanbul that explored the "painful

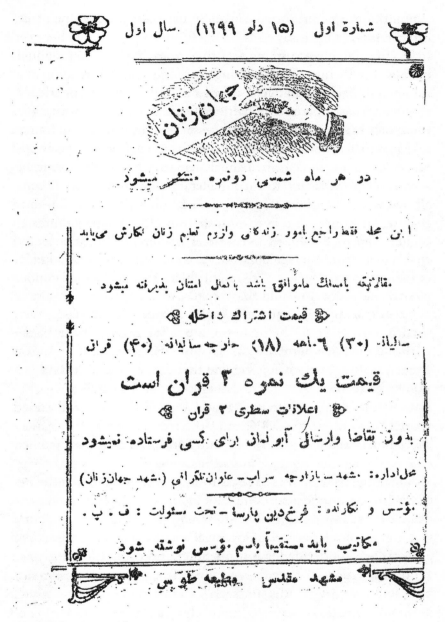

شمارهٔ اول (۱۵ دلو ۱۲۹۹) سال اول

جهان زنان

در هر ماه شمسی دونمره منتشر میشود

این مجله فقط راجع بامور زندگانی ولازم تعلیم زنان نگارش می‌یابد

مقالاتیکه بامسلك ماموافق باشد باکمال امتنان پذیرفته میشود

❧ قیمت اشتراک داخله ❧

سالیانه (۳۰) ۶ ماهه (۱۸) خارجه سالیانه (۴۰) قران

قیمت یك نمره ۳ قران است

❧ اعلانات سطری ۲ قران ❧

بدون تقاضا وارسال آبونمان برای کسی فرستاده نمیشود

علل اداره: مشهد ـ بازارچه ـ سراب ـ عاون‌التجار اقای (مشهد جهان زنان)

مؤسس و نگارنده: فرخ‌دین پارسا ـ تحت مسئولیت: ف ـ پ ـ

مکاتیب باید مستقیماً باسم مؤسس نوشته شود

مشهد مقدس مطبعه طوس

Cover of Jahan-i Zanan. *Jahan-i Zanan.*

predicament" of Muslim women, especially after marriage. Although women assumed much of the burden for creating a happy marriage and household, husbands also had emotional obligations to their wives, which did not vanish after they satisfied their own sexual needs. However, many husbands virtually ignored their wives. While

young brides grieved over their miserable domestic life, their husbands visited prostitutes.[51]

In 1922, Muhtaram Iskandari, along with several other women,
founded the Patriotic Women's League of Iran, and prominent activists such as Fakhr Afaq Parsa served on its executive committee. A
year later, Iskandari, the daughter of a Qajar prince, began editing an
eponymous newspaper published under the auspices of the league.
Like previous journals edited by Iranian women, *Majallah-i Nisvan-i
Vatankhvah* addressed women's hygiene, marriage, and child rearing;
it even included segments on the literary achievements of accomplished women worldwide. Above all, Iskandari stressed the need to
give Iranian women access to education in order to enable them to
become informed mothers and desirable spouses.[52] Education would
enable women to manage their homes better, and this improvement
in the quality of domestic life might then bring about harmonious
marital relations between husbands and wives.

Instead of making marriages family affairs, some consideration
needed to be given to the wishes of the actual people in the union:
the bride and the groom. In 1921, *Jahan-i Zanan* carried an article on
women's suffrage worldwide, highlighting the political successes that
women had achieved. It reported, for instance, on the political participation of women in Australia, Norway, and Finland, who had gained
the right to vote in 1902, 1906, and 1913, respectively. Yet Parsa, who
likely authored this article, noted with derision that in Iran "women
still do not have the right to choose husbands."[53]

A lengthy essay on marriage customs in Iran condemned the be-
trothal of mere children to one another. It was a deep-rooted societal flaw, not just a parental shortcoming, the article claimed, one
that perpetuated Iran's dysfunctional culture of matrimony. The
go-betweens—extended family members and community elders—
kept these unfortunate traditions alive. Unhappy marriages, moreover, encouraged youths to seek extramarital relations, which
invariably brought disgrace to the family and exposed them to venereal disease. In other words, marriage alone was no guarantee of
population growth or morality. Marriages needed to be based on
companionship to give meaning and bring longevity to a relationship.[54] The unsuitability of marrying off child brides to old men
recurred as a cautionary tale in discussions of Persian matrimony. In
1924, after the closure of her journal *Jahan-i Zanan*, Fakhr Afaq
Parsa published in another magazine the heartrending story of an

شمارهٔ ۱

مجله

﷽ جمعیت نسوان وطنخواه ایران ﷽

۱۳۰۲

علمی   ادبی   واجتماعی

﴾ صاحب امتیاز ومدیر مسئول — شاهزاده ملوك اسكندري ﴿

(در هر برج یك مرتبه طبع ونشر میشود)

محل ادار

خیابان ارامنه پل امیر بهادر جنب كارخانه چراغ برق
كوچه اسدالله خان سرهنك نمره ۱۹

وجه اشتراك

در داخله : سالیانه ۱۵ قران   شش ماهه ۸ قران
در خارجه : سالیانه ۲ تومان   شش ماهه ۱۱ قران

تك شماره سی شاهی

﴾ قیمت اعلانات سطری یك قران ﴿

﴾ بدوشیزگان مدارس در قیمت بطور كلی تخفیف داده میشود ﴿
كهن جامه خویش پیراستن   به از جامه عاریت خواستن

—﴾ در (مطبعهٔ قناعت) بطبع رسید ﴿—

Cover of Nisvan-i Vatankhvah. *Majallah-i Nisvan-i Vatankhvah.*

anonymous woman who had been forced by her father to marry a
fifty-year-old man when she was only eleven years old. After years of
suffering from the insults of her in-laws, this woman ran away with
her children and eventually managed to get a divorce, but not before
having contracted numerous incurable diseases. Her message to

other women was simple: mothers needed to protect their daughters from abusive marriages.[55]

In 1926, a preliminary report made the following pessimistic observation about the living conditions of Iranian women: "Women have no civic rights. They live in ill ventilated houses, and take no exercise. This, combined with early and repeated pregnancies, tends to lower their physical resistance to sickness."[56] The low levels of hygiene not only affected domestic life but also spilled into the sphere of public responsibility. Journalists functioning as social critics endorsed marriage and marital hygiene in the popular press during Reza Shah's reign both to circumscribe the spread of venereal disease and to endorse population growth and preservation.[57]

One female activist, 'Iffat al-Muluk Khvajahnuri, proposed the opening of sports clubs that were geared toward women and taught sports better suited to women's bodies, such as tennis.[58] Khvajahnuri also encouraged physical fitness for other women in the context of healthful reproduction. She described Iranian girls as "the people who will become the future mothers of the nation." Iran, Khvajahnuri wrote, had pinned its hopes on these young women "who in order to renew the greatness of this dear nation would produce brave and strong youth."[59] Both women and men needed to keep healthy in order not to succumb to weakness, opium addiction, and idleness. In a subsequent article on sports, Khvajahnuri cited the absence of sports in Iran as a major contributing factor in the loose morals of Iranians and in their physical and psychological decline.[60] This physical discipline among Iranian families of the ancient era, who would teach their children riding and archery, apparently had enabled Iran to attain imperial grandeur.[61]

Sport and fitness even became positive attributes for a potential marriage partner. As one writer remarked, "The most important trait of a suitor is complete health . . . and participation in endeavors such as regular exercise." Many youngsters, upon getting married, completely stopped exercising, thus committing a grave error, for "exercise facilitates blood circulation and purifies the blood . . . which is important [for the quality of] semen" and therefore for the health of future progeny.[62] In other words, marriage need not eliminate exercise from a couple's daily life. Young married couples were exhorted to continue exercising after marriage to maintain their physical vigor and the vitality of their offspring.[63]

In addition to promoting fitness, the discourse on marriage abounded with advice to young brides about how "to hold on to husbands" (*shawhar-dari*).[64] One article questioned why divorce was on the rise in Iran, while marriage was on the decline. Women and their expensive tastes—that is, their penchant for luxury products and fancy attire, often unaffordable for most men—were faulted for being one cause of divorce among modern Iranians.[65] Related pieces warned Iranian women not to view marriage as a material or "commercial" union, but rather to define it as "an old duty based on the need to continue the generation and to procreate."[66]

The fear that polygamy might increase the spread of venereal disease among women of childbearing age became a powerful reason to deliberate the salutary virtues of monogamy. One man, for instance, was singled out for having infected three of his wives with syphilis, all of whom had died while giving birth, presumably from complications related to infection from venereal disease.[67] In 1926, a report prepared for the Rockefeller Foundation noted that "the number of wives which a man may take is limited to four, but there is no limit to the number of concubines he may have. Polygamy is not the rule among the peasant class, except in the Caspian provinces, where the women work in the rice-fields." The same study found that "the age of marriage of girls is from nine years upwards."[68]

In 1928, several articles in the Persian daily newspaper *Ittila'at* explored the decline of marriage in Iran. One writer unequivocally declared that marriage should be based on the "heartfelt desire" of a man and a woman, though this "desire" meant more than just a lustful infatuation if there was to be a lasting union. In marriage, men and women had distinct responsibilities and needed to regard themselves as partners in raising their children. Husbands had an obligation to respect and protect their wives, as well as to provide for their education and enlightenment. Wives needed to provide for their husbands' comfort and to manage the household frugally. While some of these duties were delineated along familiar gender lines, others emphasized marriage as a partnership between equals.[69]

This bevy of commentary on the unenviable condition of Iranian women in miserable marriages may not have effected immediate political change, but it gradually paved the way for introducing legislation aimed at securing women's personal rights and health through this time-honored institution. In 1931, a marriage law was passed that placed some regulations on child marriage. Two years later, the Tehran Marriage Court of First Instance enacted an important judgment enforcing the recently passed legislation. Evidently an illiterate cobbler had married a twelve-year-old girl. After deliberating, the court sentenced the cobbler, "his sister and another 'wooing agent,' [and] the officiating mullahs . . . to varying degrees of correctional imprisonment."[70] The American legation may have rushed to conclusions when it cited this judgment to claim that the Marriage Law of 1931 had "practically stopped child marriage in Iran."[71] In remote Iranian villages the new law had barely made inroads. As one writer cautioned: "Are we aware that many widows, divorcees, and underage girls are without jobs. . . . Do we realize that men can throw their wives out of the house whenever they want. . . . Are we aware that in villages, away from the capital, they marry off a ten-year-old girl to a sixty-year-old man in contradiction to the provisions of the law of marriage?"[72] Recent legislation could not wholly supersede local traditions of family life, and Iranian women continued struggling to secure basic social and economic rights.

The marriage law of 1931, debated simultaneously in the press along with discussions of venereal disease and marital hygiene, made only vague references to the health of couples eager to engage in matrimony. Article 3 of the law required a health permit from a licensed physician for couples under the required minimum age of eighteen for men and fifteen for women. The permit needed to certify that the couple was physically ready for the union and that marriage would not be physically harmful to them. In addition, the civil code required men to report any other marriages to legal officers performing the ceremony.[73] Other sections dealt with women's dowries, and Article 1040 enabled engaged couples to request certificates of health from each other, although they were not legally bound to do so.[74] Some religious leaders voiced opposition to these reforms. Reportedly, "mullahs who preached against the new marriage laws have been warned not to do it again, or have been exiled to another city."[75] Despite concerns about the proliferation of venereal disease, the law ironically permitted men to "take an unlimited number of temporary wives, each for a period of one hour to ninety-nine years."[76] Revisions to the marriage law in 1937 did not tackle health matters concerning engaged or married couples with any rigor, either.

The Persian criminal code, published by the Ministry of Justice in 1933, attempted to rectify shortcomings in the provisions that dealt with "offenses against decency and morality (rape, sodomy, abduction, adultery, prostitution, et cetera)." The American chargé d'affaires described the new law as "modified and partially modernized Islamic personal status jurisprudence." This legislation departed from sharia' law in important respects. First, the penalty for sodomy, rape, adultery, and incest was no longer death, but was set at "imprisonment of from six months to life."[77] Second, as a consequence of this law, a "woman is now theoretically competent to bring suit against her husband on charges of adultery or non-support." However, the husband "still enjoys full right of divorce."[78]

The debate on marital hygiene did not deal with the religious politics of *mut'a*, or temporary marriage, focusing instead on the secular rationalizations of the state about procreation and population control. These debates made few inroads among the religious classes who upheld the practice of *mut'a* in Iran. Shi'i jurists have argued that temporary marriage could, in theory, prevent the spread of prostitution since men could achieve sexual fulfillment. As Shahla Haeri explains, "Temporary marriage, the 'ulama believe, not only keeps men sexually satisfied, it prevents them from visiting prostitutes; hence, public health is guaranteed and morality is upheld. The 'ulama reject any association between temporary marriage and a possibility of health hazards like venereal disease."[79] Both venereal disease and prostitution existed in Iran despite, and perhaps because of, the practice of *mut'a*. Although religious thinkers and secular reformers did not always agree on marriage laws and veiling, the maternalist focus on sexual modesty and family life provided these seemingly oppositional groups with a common cause. Public conversations about propriety in Iran's dominant Islamic culture drew not just on religious texts and sayings but also upon modern hygienic knowledge, which condemned the spread of adultery and prostitution. Public discussions of celibacy, sexuality, and marriage did not openly address homosexuality (*liwat* or *hamjins bazi*) as another kind of social deviance, which, like adultery, remained strictly prohibited in Islam but was practiced in contemporary society.[80] The incidence of homosexual and adulterous relationships may partly explain why the institution of marriage was viewed as being in "decline" even after two decades of maternalist emphasis. Ease of divorce was considered another reason.[81] In 1945, a cartoon printed in a women's magazine illustrates the public cynicism about marriage and rising concerns about the prevalence of divorce in Iranian society. The image on the left depicts a bride and groom who gaze with consternation at the Office of Divorce and contemplate the possibility that their marriage, too, might end in divorce. In front of the Office of Divorce is a line of unhappy women and men parting ways.[82]

Public scrutiny of Iranian marriage had an impact on the fate of child brides. Some evidence suggests that the age of marriage did in fact rise over the long term. In 1924, one writer explained that although statistics on marriage were wanting from nineteenth-century Iran, it appeared from "looking at the fathers of today who were the youth of twenty years ago" that marriage was in decline. The author of this essay then asserted that while Iranian youth in the nineteenth century typically married between the ages of twenty and twenty-five, after the constitutional period Iranians from twenty-five to forty years old were no longer forming families and even "despise marriage."[83]

Nearly three decades later, a report completed by the Rockefeller Foundation in cooperation with Iranian health authorities found that "although in the past 'child brides' were said to be common, there is now in existence a law prohibiting females from marrying before the age of 16."[84] Their survey found that "only nine of the married females were less than 15 years of age." The report also noted a decline in polygamy: "Of the married male population only 66 out of a total of 1,876 were found to have two wives at the time of the survey and only two had three wives."[85] The authors speculated that "economic factors" likely made it "difficult" to sustain polygamous relationships.

Monogamy emerged as the common form of union because it flouted Islamic institutions such as *mut'a* and was in line with the evolution of marriage elsewhere in the world, especially the West. The

Divorce Office. *Banu.*

ascendancy of monogamous marriage was epitomized by the wedding of the shah's young heir, Muhammad Reza Pahlavi, to Princess Fawzia of Egypt in 1939. The Persian popular press covered the news of the shah's engagement with fascination.[86] The symbolic significance of the marriage was not lost on British diplomat Nevile Butler, either, who conceded that the event was "of some historical interest." Previously, Iranian kings drew "upon their own countrywomen, not necessarily of illustrious birth, to fill their harems." Polygamous marriage, however, created "internecine struggles for succession," as the king's wives vied for his attention in part to secure for their sons the coveted throne.[87] Muhammad Reza Pahlavi's marriage gave the appearance of "bridging, or perhaps ignoring," the Shi'i-Sunni divide and was not "expected to be popular among the Iranian ulema."[88] In preparation for the wedding, "beggars are being rounded up by the police authorities and conveyed to other towns."[89] There were constitutional obstacles to the marriage since Princess Fawzia was not of Iranian origin, though she was eventually granted Iranian nationality.[90] In Egypt, despite the lavish expenditures on this wedding, there was "little enthusiasm . . . for this alliance," given "acute world tension and anxiety."[91] The marriage contract was concluded at Abdin Palace in Cairo on 15 March 1939 at a "simple" ceremony and "in accordance with Islamic Law," and a celebration of the couple's marriage followed in Iran.[92] Although the wedding had symbolic value, the marriage lasted less than a decade. Ironically, the shah's divorce became emblematic of the challenges that accompanied modern marriage.

Infidelity. *Banu.*

In 1945, the women's magazine *Banu* published an essay about men's infidelity. It found that men scarcely expressed the same love and attachment to their wives after a few years of marriage. Instead, the article claimed that men had a "protean and covetous" nature that predisposed them to seek the companionship of others. Some women, fortunate enough to discern their husbands' true emotions, might be able to avert infidelity by providing them the proper attention and affection. But as the writer noted in jest, "Each day, it is necessary to discover a new secret in the art of husband-keeping [*shawhar dari*]."[93] In short, it seemed that many women had reluctantly acknowledged the likelihood that their husbands might be unfaithful to them or seek another wife. The scrutiny of marriage in Iran had not necessarily lessened marital discord.

Iranian attitudes toward marriage changed over time, but not always for patriotic purposes. Like other institutions, marriage had to adapt itself to the needs of contemporary society. These transformations culminated in the termination of the harem as a royal prerogative and the embrace of monogamy as the preferred expression of modern marriages. Monogamy did not always bring Iranians happy and enduring unions, nor did it eliminate the risk or reality of extramarital relations. Even though the crown prince embraced monogamy, the country's other social classes did not always follow suit. Nonetheless, the public debate on marriage transformed the culture of matrimony in Iran with its emphasis on health certificates, age limits, and companionship. Some women assumed a degree of control over the selection of husbands, and if nothing else, they were advised to receive a certificate of good health from a future spouse.

CHAPTER 4

෴

Sexual Mores, Social Lives

The Impact of Venereal Disease

I n 1894 Abu al-Hasan Khan Tafrishi, an Iranian physician who
headed Tehran's main hospital, translated into Persian excerpts
of a French hygiene manual at the behest of the Iranian minister of
science, Mukhbir al-Dawlah.[1] Aside from explaining basic human
biological processes, he touched on the characteristics of various
contagious diseases, including smallpox, cholera, plague, and syphilis. He viewed syphilis as a disease consigned to prostitutes, whom
he held directly responsible for its transmission. Prostitution not only
caused emotional distress for couples but also endangered their
health through the spread of sexually transmitted diseases. As he
explained, "The prostitute carries the poison of this dangerous disease
[syphilis], and death is considered the best end to it." Once dead, the
prostitute would no longer be able to infect other people and cause
unnecessary ailments, including deafness and blindness, in others.[2]
At times a sacred site, a woman's body could by turns be construed as
a repository of evil, especially in its pursuit of sexual fulfillment. The
prostitute best exemplified this double-edged reality. Arguing that
"the prostitute is a public menace," Tafrishi railed against prostitutes
for not bemoaning their reputation or caring about people, since they
constantly infected more people, who then spread the disease to
others. It was an ailment that "destroyed homes" (*khanahman suz*)

and "spoiled generations," for men could unintentionally infect their wives and children.[3] In other words, syphilis threatened the future capital of the nation: its population. In Iran, where outbreaks of famine, plague, and cholera already claimed many lives, syphilis mainly endangered the populace through the possibility of disability, and so prostitution and the proliferation of venereal disease were considered menaces.

Popular manuals such as Tafrishi's were authored predominantly by men and were also largely composed *for* men in order to impart information about sex and women's bodies. Men, like women, did not always feel comfortable talking about sex, and the popular print media made it possible to create a space for the discussion of subjects normally considered taboo.[4]

The dearth of medical records makes it difficult to estimate the impact of syphilis in the Qajar era. Jean-Etienne Schneider, a European physician who practiced medicine in Iran, confirmed its prevalence there in the nineteenth century. He also noted that the country lacked a sanitary police force that could manage cases of venereal disease. As Schneider explained, "Among these Muslim people, there is no question that a woman cannot be examined, even if she is a courtesan."[5] Not only was it "inconvenient" to discuss women, but little attempt had been made to determine an accurate count of them. He admitted that these obstacles rendered it difficult even to measure the progress of syphilis in the country. Nonetheless, Schneider considered the disease widespread.[6]

While some specialized medical texts discussed reproduction, their readership was likely limited to medical practitioners. It is nonetheless significant to document what Qajar physicians understood about venereal disease. In 1877, a Persian medical treatise on women's illnesses addressed syphilis, for example, and recommended treatment with mercury for women of childbearing age.[7] The Austrian physician Jakob Polak also reported on the use of mercury in Iran as a treatment for syphilis.[8] Western works dealing with syphilis and marital hygiene were also translated, and hygienists of the nineteenth century candidly addressed these subjects in their manuals.

Travelers and memoirists wrote about the prevalence of prostitution, which, many believed, contributed to the spread of syphilis. In 1858, author and physician William Sanger noted that "numerous open and avowed" prostitutes lived in Iran, "among whom the dancing girls were conspicuous for the beauty of their persons and the melody of their voices." Apparently the dancing girls held "considerable sway until the time of Futteh Ali Khan [r. 1797–1834], who crowded his palace with concubines, and from among them issued edicts to suppress immorality, prohibiting the dancing girls from approaching the court, and exiling them to the distant provinces."[9] In fact, during the Safavid era, "public brothels were very numerous, and largely contributed to the national revenue, no less than thirty thousand prostitutes paying an annual tax in Ispahan alone."[10] Although during the Qajar era "no licenses were given," prostitution thrived and "public brothels" operated in several Iranian cities.[11] As Rudi Matthee has observed, "In the absence of surviving court records, ego-documents, and sources narrating the period's social history, and with only a few visual images and the occasional negative textual reference available, Safavid prostitution would virtually remain a closed chapter were it not for the accounts by Westerners visiting the country."[12] Similar observations can be made for the early Qajar era as well. Although one wonders what access, if any, Sanger may have had to dancing girls in Iran, the endurance of this image is telling.

Some Western observers decried the institution of temporary marriage as a form of "legalized prostitution." Shi'i Islam allowed women and men to arrange a marriage contract for a set period of time through the institution known as *mut'a*. Some Shi'i scholars believe that this form of partnership had existed during the time of the Prophet Muhammad.[13] As James Bassett explained, "Of all the social and religious customs, no one is more baneful in its influence over women than the custom of Sekah marriage. . . . It is legalized prostitution sanctified by a brief religious rite."[14] Robert Speer described the custom in this way: "Short period *sighehs* in the big cities are quasi-prostitutes. . . . In other words, a gigantic system of prostitution, under the sanction of the Church, prevails in Meshed."[15] However, both Bassett and Speer were Christian missionaries with a vested interest in denouncing a curiously Muslim social convention such as *mut'a*. As Homa Hoodfar has observed, while Western writers expressed dismay about the prevalence of polygamy in Islamic societies, they rarely acknowledged the incidence of "mistresses" and the large number of children born out of wedlock in their own societies.[16]

In 1902, an American serving with the Presbyterian mission reported on widespread "prostitution" in the holy city of Mashhad: "Prostitution has not been abolished. It flourishes in Meshed under ecclesiastical sanction, and in the cities." Speer referred to the practice of temporary marriage common among the Shi'i, which allowed men and women to contract a marriage of short or long duration. Iranians, however, made a distinction between fornication not sanctified by temporary marriage, including prostitution, and what certain Western travelers commonly labeled "legalized prostitution," or *sigheh* marriage. These Western sources provide a necessary window into prostitution in Iran, especially since there is a paucity of documentary evidence. However, writers such as Speer also wished to disprove the notion that Islamic injunctions "have abolished the vice of prostitution, and made Moslem lands in this vital respect cleaner than Christian lands."[17] In other words, some travelers may have exaggerated the prevalence of prostitution or may have deliberately conflated prostitution with what Persian locals considered licit sexual relations. That said, indigenous writers also acknowledged the existence of prostitution, and some even grappled with its moral and physical implications. In his memoirs, 'Ayn al-Saltanah recorded that the physician of Larijan, Mirza Muhammad Khan, had put together "good entertainment" and that he had "10 to 20" female prostitutes.[18] One Qajar reformer, Khan-i Khanan, acknowledged that urban security (*nazmiyah*) did not have a handle on prostitution. Recognizing both the reality of prostitution and its potential harms, he recommended that prostitutes be examined, if possible, and treated to check the spread of venereal disease.[19]

By 1900, the Iranian press candidly acknowledged syphilis as a common malady believed to spread in part because of prostitution.[20] In 1904, another source stated that "in northern Persia syphilis reigns in a frightful manner."[21] One journal even advertised medications sold by a local pharmacy (ironically called the Islamic Pharmacy) with the potential to cure syphilis and gonorrhea.[22] Several years later, another newspaper announced the availability of a "new drug for treating syphilis" that had been tested and recently been imported from Paris.[23]

Sources outside the urban centers of Tehran and Tabriz began to address the dangers of syphilis. In 1903, the newspaper *Muzaffari*, published in the southwestern coastal city of Bushehr, began a

regular column on hygiene. Aside from offering rudimentary explanations of germ theory, it edified readers about the transmission of
syphilis. In addition to sexual intercourse, it was argued that syphilis
could be spread orally by sharing drinks or opium pipes with infected
individuals as well as through public baths.[24] Mirza Najaf Quli Khan,
a physician writing for *Adab* in 1902, cautioned his readers against
using opium pipes, as well as tea and coffee cups in coffeehouses,
because of the possibility of contamination. He surmised that on
average one hundred people daily shared opium pipes at coffeehouses,
many of whom could be infected with syphilis or other contagious
diseases such as influenza.[25] It is telling that even periodicals with a
less gender-specific focus strove to educate the Iranian public about
the consequences of promiscuity and, by extension, the dangers of
venereal disease. In 1905, another writer reported that "ignorant
people" who had not paid attention to their personal hygiene and
thus contracted syphilis or gonorrhea could seek the assistance of a
local physician, Mu'ayin al-Hukama, to cure their disease. Apparently
this physician had successfully treated several patients with such ailments who went on to have numerous children.[26]

Hygienists also targeted public baths in their efforts to curb infection. Najaf Quli Khan complained about the loincloths and bath
towels that people contaminated with venereal diseases such as syphilis and gonorrhea wore while bathing, thus infecting the healthy
bathers.[27] Given Islamic beliefs about adultery, it was more socially
acceptable to regard syphilis as a contagious disease whose prevalence owed less to sexual indiscretion or moral impurity than to low
levels of personal hygiene. By 1925, Joseph Gilmour, who had investigated the sanitary conditions of Iran for the League of Nations,
remarked that "when enquiring into the possibility of the transmission of syphilis by the public baths, no medical men could tell me of
any actual case of chancre they had seen where the infection could be
traced to the bath." As late as 1940, when Dr. Rosalie Morton visited
Iran, she remarked that "poor people seldom bathe their entire bodies"
and that many "do not go to the public baths for months," but that "it
is quite a usual thing to go after acquiring an infectious disease."[28]
Despite what Persian hygienists, or "medical popularizers," and
physicians believed, syphilis could rarely, if ever, be spread through
public baths.[29] The infection is typically passed sexually, although the
syphilis bacterium, *Treponema pallidum*, discovered in 1905 by Berlin

scientist Fritz Schaudinn and his associates, can be transmitted through breaks in skin and mucous membranes, as well as from mother to child during pregnancy. It is currently believed that the disease can go through four stages, and infection usually occurs during the two initial stages.[30]

The medical discourse of syphilis in Iran extended back to the medieval period; indeed, one of the earliest Islamic works on the subject is a Persian manuscript completed in 1569 CE by 'Imad al-Din Mas'ud Shirazi.[31] Modernist understanding of the disease, however, particularly discussions of hereditary syphilis, echoed French views on the subject. For example, Alfred Fournier (d. 1914), first chair of syphilology at the Hôpital Saint-Louis, determined that an infected patient would suffer from insanity in later stages of the disease.[32] According to Jill Harsin, "Fournier himself was partly responsible for the growing list of health problems attributable to syphilis."[33]

On its prevalence in Iran, 'Ali Aqa, the editor of *Muzaffari*, estimated that out of every twenty people in Iran, at least two had contracted syphilis.[34] This figure seems somewhat exaggerated; European travelers to the country, including physicians, often wrote about epidemics there, and while smallpox, plague, and cholera attracted international attention, syphilis did not. Still, it is safe to assume that venereal disease had become commonplace in Qajar society. One observer attributed the spread of syphilis, gonorrhea, and other diseases to the filthy water that bathers used to wash themselves.[35] Another writer spoke out against the apparent lack of public hygiene in Tehran, commenting that "syphilis has overtaken the city."[36] Although Islam required cleanliness before prayer, it was believed that water supplies in Iran were often polluted because people who had contracted syphilis or gonorrhea bathed themselves in those settings, making it difficult to fulfill religious obligations using clean water.[37]

The prevalence of syphilis touched on another public concern that became audible during the constitutional revolution: the morality of Iranian society and the honor of the nation's men as defenders of women's virtue. The failure to draw up and enforce prostitution laws meant that brothels existed and sometimes were subject to public attacks. In 1907, for example, Yusuf Mughis al-Saltanah reported that several sayyids had raided brothels in Tehran.[38] The inadequacy of policing mechanisms and the dearth of municipal services reflected this lawlessness.

At core was the issue of sexuality and public morality, a topic that sometimes caused divisions among different sectors of Iranian society. Even within the confines of an Islamic state, the topics of sexuality and promiscuity were cautiously being broached in popular journals. In 1907, an anonymous essay for the popular newspaper *Nida-yi Vatan* acknowledged the prevalence of prostitution in the capital city, Tehran. The writer contended that many turned to the false lure of prostitution because of "hunger" and "lack of direction" in their lives, and advocated that such women first express remorse and renounce prostitution completely, then find husbands to marry, presumably in order to help the reformed prostitutes lead a life of virtue.[39] It is interesting that this writer, likely a man, did not engage in moralizing, but instead argued for the moral redemption of prostitutes and their reintegration into society as reformed women and potential marriage partners.

Given the political instability of Iran and the frequency of food shortages, prostitution persisted as a public dilemma. During the First World War, one newspaper reported that fornication was so prevalent that it would lead to moral corruption if the government did not take immediate measures to curb it. As this writer lamented, "In this city the number of profligate and unaccounted-for women has increased so much that one must cry at its condition."[40] The presence of prostitutes and the surge in "unaccounted-for women" reflected the weakening of political (and therefore male) authority in the country. In times of political uncertainty, Iran's moral dilemmas exacerbated men's concerns about the absence of guardianship over Persian women, most glaringly witnessed in the prevalence of prostitution. The spread of venereal disease compounded these gender-related anxieties. One cartoon gave expression to these public concerns about the moral degeneration of Iranian society. An invalid representing Iranian society lies on the ground suffering from various ailments such as poverty, ignorance, syphilis, and prostitution, which have caused bodily harm.[41]

In 1921, the Pasteur Institute, jointly operated by French physicians and Iranian health authorities, opened its doors in Iran. Its main branch offered medications and serums intended to cure or alleviate symptoms of plague, gonorrhea, and syphilis. For the destitute, the institute provided these services free of charge.[42] The following year, a French medical publication reported that syphilis "has expanded in

Image of Invalid Personifying the Nation and Afflicted by Various Social Ills, Including Prostitution. *Nahid.*

a frightening way in Iran, whether by contamination or heredity," speculating that polygamy "facilitates the propagation of this disease."[43] A missionary medical report confirmed the existence of the disease even in small communities such as Turbat, a city south of Mashhad that was estimated to have fifteen thousand inhabitants in 1922. The missionary medical staff stated that "the prevalence of syphilis appalled us. . . . The patients' own statement of having had the disease seemed to be of considerable value, for it is so common that they have learned to recognize many of its ordinary symptoms."[44] By 1925 medical professionals affiliated with the Presbyterian mission in Mashhad estimated that of the patients receiving services there, "the definitely syphilitic [constituted] over 10%."[45]

Some physicians stressed that Iranian youth needed to seek out healthy marriage partners to order to ensure healthful reproduction. In 1921, Dr. Shaykha Khayyiri published a short piece in the women's journal *Jahan-i Zanan* on the legal restrictions on marriage in the United States against those ill with contagious diseases, particularly venereal disease.[46] Dr. Khayyiri supported this idea, contending that healthy parents typically bore healthy children, whereas infected parents produced sick offspring who tended to die in childhood. While Dr. Khayyiri absolved such children of blame for their fate, she was less generous toward their parents, who she believed had married and procreated despite knowing that they carried a debilitating disease.[47]

In 1922, a journal devoted to scientific and literary issues voiced concern that syphilis often went undiagnosed by local Persian physicians. It therefore advocated further research and training for doctors working in this area. In particular, the writer, Fath Ali Masih al-Saltanah, noted that Iranian physicians rarely used blood tests to diagnose syphilis; in the absence of such tests, Iranian doctors sometimes found it difficult to diagnose the disease because patients refused to divulge all their symptoms. Consequently, patients sometimes received treatment only after the disease had progressed to a more serious stage.[48] Masih al-Saltanah urged doctors who had studied bacteriology to teach their skills to other physicians.[49] In the meantime, another writer advertised the latest drugs against syphilis and gonorrhea, regarding the diseases as a legacy of Qajar misrule.[50]

Three years later, the most celebrated Persian women's journal, *'Alam-i Nisvan*, brazenly took up this subject in an essay titled "The Outbreak of the Illness of Syphilis in Our Country." The article claimed that nature had presented this disease to those who had "stepped outside of the circle of humanity and entered the wadi of perversion"—in other words, adulterers. The piece also recognized that those who had not committed any sexual sins were equally at risk for the disease. Syphilis might be just punishment for the "truly guilty" (*gunahkaran-i haqiqi*), but this writer regretted the pain it had caused its innocent victims, that is, young women and children. The essay emphasized that the disease was transmitted through sexual intercourse with an infected person as well as through the use of public baths.[51] Presumably as a deterrent, the article also discussed the effects of syphilis on pregnancy and the physical ailments of children born to women who had contracted it.

The Rockefeller Foundation, a private American philanthropic organization established in 1913, expressed an interest in understanding and addressing Iran's sanitary conditions during the Pahlavi era. In 1926, the Rockefeller Foundation reported that "the sanitary conditions of Persia are appalling. This refers especially to Tehran and the towns. The most important fatal or debilitating diseases are malaria, tuberculosis and syphilis." Tuberculosis was found to be "a town disease" that affected women more than men, possibly because of "the secluded lives they live, combined with early marriage, frequent pregnancies and want of fresh air." In addition, syphilis, though prevalent, appeared "to be of a benign type. Signs of congenital syphilis are not noticeable among the people."[52] The report stressed that "prostitution is forbidden by the Moslim [*sic*] religion," but the report did not mention efforts to deal with prostitution, particularly in connection with the spread of syphilis.[53]

In the same year, a six-month report on the sanitary conditions of Iran, completed by Persian health officials and presented to the Interior Ministry, made similar findings and offered suggestions for fighting venereal disease (*mubarizah ba amraz-i zuhravi*). The report found that prostitution was on the rise, and along with it went venereal disease. It stressed further that compulsory military service, mandated in 1925, would contribute to the spread of venereal disease to rural and tribal communities, which in the past had apparently shown a lower incidence of such illnesses. Some young men, who might typically serve a minimum of two years in urban centers to fulfill their military service, would engage in illicit sexual relations and likely contract such diseases. Upon returning to their villages, they would then spread the disease to their communities. To ward off this scenario, the report recommended the creation of health services throughout the country for the inspection of prostitutes. Licensed doctors would take charge of treating infected patients and presenting them with certificates of health. Municipal authorities would also be required to register prostitutes in an effort to regulate them.[54] In 1928, the *Pars Yearbook* noted that a clinic existed for treating patients suffering from syphilis and gonorrhea; this treatment center, apparently geared primarily to women, was in Shahr-i Naw, a locale in Tehran known to be frequented by prostitutes.[55] One traveler to Iran reported that some efforts had been made to keep "a register of women" there.[56]

Journalist Rawshanak Naw'dust overtly dealt with the reality of prostitution in the magazine she edited for women, observing that women turned to prostitution if they lacked solid, supportive family relationships and financial means. For this reason, she pointed out, "aside from the minority of skilled and wealthy women, prostitutes were generally poor and hard-working women."[57] A proponent of independent employment for women, Naw'dust argued that prostitution would remain a social dilemma in Iran until women achieved a measure of financial independence and were no longer beholden to their spouses for support. She explicitly tied prostitution to the dearth of employment opportunities for women in urban centers, and the limited financial remuneration of women in rural areas. Expanding women's access to respectable professions that offered decent wages and financial remuneration became a focus of women's activism, in part, because working women would no longer need to resort to prostitution to support themselves. However, such changes did not occur overnight, and it was still essential to monitor prostitution. Curiously, despite concerns over promiscuity and the spread of venereal disease, the shah refused to sign a bill that had passed in 1933 "making it illegal to keep a brothel."[58]

Tehran clinics mentioned cases of venereal disease without targeting prostitution or polygamy as a possible cause of its proliferation. The Municipal Council, founded during the constitutional years, listed seven clinics in Tehran that administered health care gratis to the poor. These clinics offered treatment for a range of illnesses including syphilis and gonorrhea. Services provided by the Municipal Council allowed ordinary citizens to seek medical assistance even for sexually transmitted diseases without subjecting them to moral discipline. In the month of October/November 1927, approximately 596 individuals were treated at the Municipal hospital for various diseases. Of this number 250 had been treated for gonorrhea, while 220 had been seen for syphilis, although we do not know the gender of the patients.[59]

Aside from causing physical discomfort, syphilis was an embarrassing social disease. In particular, women and girls who were unfortunate enough to contract it were susceptible to gossip and disparagement. For instance, this author claimed to have knowledge of a four-year-old girl who had contracted syphilis from a public bath. "Thank God the girl was four years old," Qa'im Maqami wrote, "or else on top of this pain, her parents would also have to tolerate the disparaging remarks of people about their daughter" and her sexual misconduct.[60] While syphilis was a recognizable public health concern, it was not an acceptable social malady, for it confirmed publicly the existence of sexual promiscuity. Moral degeneracy might in turn derive from sexual promiscuity, social pitfalls with which male and female modernists grappled. Qa'im Maqami's observation pointed to the informal social networks such as the "gossip" circuit of neighbors and friends that monitored sexual behavior among Iranian families.

Institutions of state and religion were not the sole arbiters of maternalism, family life, and sexual behavior.

Female journalists such as Rawshanak Naw'dust urged women to take their health seriously and to beware of new drugs advertised in newspapers. Rather, Naw'dust encouraged her readers to consult physicians or to seek free medical assistance at public clinics as soon as they detected sores or any other discomfort suggesting an infection with either syphilis or gonorrhea. Women did not necessarily need to fear venereal disease; instead, they had to inform themselves and tackle it head-on.[61]

If public health considerations alone would not impel the Iranian state to deal with venereal disease, then patriotic priorities would. According to one writer, "This fatal disease threatens the Iranian nationality by encouraging moral decay [*inhitat-i akhlaq*], laziness, weakness, and cowardice."[62] Recommended methods of prevention included prohibiting infected individuals from getting married and the creation of hygiene centers in the provinces. It was further suggested that public baths be placed under the supervision of the Sanitary Council. Public health centers even invested money for the purchase of films, to be shown free to the general public, advising them about the dangers of syphilis and gonorrhea and the most effective prophylactic measures to take.[63] In a particularly empowering move, young women were encouraged to take responsibility for their health by ensuring that their fiancés had received a clean bill of health from a physician prior to marriage.[64]

Apart from creating unwelcome health risks, venereal disease infection forced women to seek out male doctors—a prospect that apparently made many Iranian women (and men) uncomfortable. As one journalist pointed out, "The majority of women are shy about going to male physicians." Thus, many turned to less qualified "foreign midwives who gradually give themselves the label of 'doctor' to appear more competent and experienced than they really are."[65] Women who consulted foreign health professionals often perished because of malpractice, another unintended consequence of syphilis. Women were not the only ones whose lives and fertility were adversely affected. Venereal disease undermined male virility through its physical emasculation of men. As a disincentive, men were reminded of their role as "head of the family" and advised not to put their wives and children at risk.[66]

The government gradually recognized venereal disease as a public health issue. The civil code listed tuberculosis, syphilis, and gonorrhea as infections from which future brides needed protection.[67] Syphilis and gonorrhea also created commercial opportunities for those hoping to make money off the infected by enticing them with easy but possibly ineffective cures. Numerous advertisements promised spurious syphilitic cures and "anti-gonorrheal injections" (*ampul-i zid-i suzak*). One ad, which appeared with some regularity in the newspaper *Ittila'at*, claimed to make available "the best and latest remedy for syphilis," which would take effect quickly after consumption of the first dose of medicine.[68] For men, these remedies proved all the more attractive, as male virility was celebrated in this machismo culture that glorified the king, the army, and the athlete as embodiments of male vigor. Indeed, the same newspaper that printed public announcements for anti-gonorrheal injections also advertised a male aphrodisiac pill called Hadaco for men with possible fertility problems who hoped to sire offspring. In addition to treating male infertility, the pill also promised to relieve psychological weakness and pallor, conditions to which modern male citizens needed immunity.[69] A subsequent advertisement focused on the ills of gonorrhea, including the fact that it caused blindness in infants, and urged those infected with the disease to take Hadaco capsules.[70]

Such quick fixes did not amount to much, as syphilis and gonorrhea spread throughout the population during the early Pahlavi

Hadaco. *Ittila'at.*

period. In 1933, a hygiene journal dedicated to propagating health and to forging a "fit and vigorous" Iranian populace asserted in its first issue that Iranian society was not sufficiently informed about this "frightening disease [i.e., syphilis] that has troubled and alarmed all of humanity."[71] Dr. Tutiya, a physician and the editor of this hygiene periodical, reported that cases of syphilis had increased at a disturbing rate and seriously threatened future generations of Iranians. Unlike other contagious diseases, it could "transform future generations" and "transmute the race."[72] Syphilis remained of special concern in pregnant women, as the infection could pass through the placenta to the fetus, causing severe disabilities in a newborn.

Gonorrhea, singled out in various publications as another debilitating venereal disease, also endangered married couples by potentially causing sterility and reducing Iran's healthy population of patriotic citizens. The physical side effects of gonorrhea were manifested in eye ailments, so infected pregnant women were advised to have their condition treated to avoid passing the disease on to their newborn. Midwives were instructed to wash the eyes of newborns with boiled water immediately after birth to forestall infection, indicating that Iranian health practitioners were at least aware of the role of gonorrhea in loss of sight and in potential sterility.[73] In order to prevent blindness related to gonorrhea, Iranian health officials had adopted the practice of using silver nitrate on newborns by the 1920s, a procedure introduced by French physicians in 1884.[74]

A Persian pediatrician, Dr. Fereydun Kishavarz, explored the effects of syphilis on newborns. Kishavarz contended that its treatment with mercury, a therapy adopted "centuries ago," remained "definitely effective" in helping children suffering from congenital syphilis, though arsenic and potassium iodide were possibly more effective in treating congenital syphilis. Since congenital syphilis was deemed an "extreme" infection, it necessitated the "most potent" therapy, though the side effects of heavy metal poisoning were not addressed.[75]

Accurate statistics on the prevalence of syphilis, gonorrhea, and other contagious diseases in Iran are not readily available. However, the medical report of the American mission in Mashhad in 1935–36 found that "syphilis is very prevalent, and is not being adequately treated, largely because of the high cost of the necessary medicines."[76] Patients often did not pursue treatments regularly despite efforts by the missionary medical staff. As the mission report explained, "We hand out printed folders on the disease, emphasizing the necessity for continued treatment."[77]

Monthly Iranian governmental records gathered from 1935 do not offer enough data for comparative purposes. Nonetheless, it is worth noting that syphilis and gonorrhea had spread well beyond Tehran to other cities such as Isfahan and rural communities. In July 1936 three men and eight women had contracted syphilis. In the Bakhtiyari region in August, there were four reported cases of syphilis in men and six in women; two cases of gonorrhea were reported in men and one in a woman. This suggests that at least in this small monthly sample, women outnumbered men as victims of sexually transmitted maladies, even taking into account the likelihood of underreporting.[78] An internal government memorandum from April 1938 reported that on average 70 percent of the population of Azerbaijan province was infected with the disease. Syphilis, the report claimed, also accounted for the rise of insane individuals, whose condition "is a result of this disease."[79] This figure seems unusually high, especially when compared with statistics from other regions of Iran, and the report does not discuss the methodology employed to calculate this percentage. Still, these statistics imply that the provinces of Iran experienced different rates of infection. Studied collectively, they suggest that venereal disease, while undoubtedly commonplace, may not have proliferated as widely in certain areas as nationalists had led the public to believe. Even if the frenzy over syphilis and gonorrhea was exaggerated, the seriousness of the threat ultimately led to the expansion of clinics.

Some physicians advocated awarding certificates of health to uninfected individuals. For example, Dr. Alavi emphasized that sterility could be the most serious consequence of gonorrhea, as it undermined the "social value of men and women," whose public responsibility it was to procreate. Infected individuals, Dr. Alavi believed, should be barred from "entering society" until their health had been restored and they no longer posed a reproductive threat to sexual partners.[80] In 1939, Dr. Ali Mustashfi, a contributor to the hygiene journal *Sihhat Nima-yi Iran* and an advocate of health certificates for engaged couples, delivered a speech on the dangers of gonorrhea. At a meeting of the Society for the Cultivation of Thought (Sazman-i Parvaresh-i Afkar), Mustashfi stated that if left untreated, gonorrhea often caused swelling in male reproductive organs and possibly tubal defects in women. Given political anxieties over national demography, Mustashfi's disquisition on gonorrhea exacerbated fears of physical disability while anticipating potential problems associated with infertility. To curb the incidence of gonorrhea, Mustashfi recommended avoiding intercourse with people infected with the disease. In a particularly forward-thinking move, he even suggested the use of a "protective covering" (*ghulaf-i hafizah*), in other words, condoms—although, he noted, "one cannot completely trust" this method of prevention.[81] To protect partners further, Mustashfi recommended that people infected with syphilis marry only after being treated for eighteen months and if symptoms were not found during a clinical examination.[82] Similarly, prostitutes, whether healthy or infected, were advised to report to a commission on sexually transmitted diseases for checkups and to receive health certificates.[83] Marital health permits, while offering some protection to partners against venereal disease, could needlessly impede others from engaging in matrimony. To some extent, they lent legal authority and legitimacy to the belief that the purpose of Iranian marriages was primarily procreation, not self-satisfaction.

Despite the successes of modern medicine, women and their physicians could not always control the biological soundness of their fetuses. Few, if any, known personal narratives exist of women from the Qajar or early Pahlavi eras who mothered children with disabilities. Yet many families lived with disability, and many women nursed disabled children. The deviant and the disabled lived alongside the "normal" despite public reticence about them. This absence is particularly revealing because popular Iranian journals of the same era frequently discussed the culture of child rearing in Iran but omitted issues related to disabled children. Though maternalists cluttered Persian journals and newspapers with advice to mothers, they ignored the care of disabled infants, who they sometimes argued suffered because of the sexual indiscretions of their parents. Some Iranian maternalists equated promiscuity and the prevalence of syphilis with the spread of birth defects.[84]

Disabilities in newborns were often, rightly or wrongly, ascribed to syphilis. To underscore this point, *Sihhat Nimayah-i Iran* published pictures of several infants with deformities purportedly caused by syphilis.[85] The visual images were presumably meant to shock readers and discourage sexual indiscretion and experimentation. Yet these pictures, and the debates surrounding special-needs children, showed the limitations of the Iranian state and the public in dealing with the social reality of disability. While the state acknowledged disability among children, it offered little support for their physical and educational remediation.

Physical deformities resulting from the complications purportedly related to syphilis evinced the inadequacies of the Iranian medical establishment and public in grappling with the consequences of disability. The attention to venereal disease grew out of the desire to limit the spread of prostitution and related illnesses such as syphilis and gonorrhea, conditions viewed as soiling the populace and harming future generations of Iranians. In fact, the hygiene journal cited above, *Sihhat-nimayi Iran*, frequently published pictures of children with physical deformities believed to be caused by syphilis. It claimed that children born to syphilitic parents often died at birth; if they managed to survive, their quality of life was severely impaired because syphilis attacked the nervous system, possibly causing blindness, deafness, or insanity. These very real and dangerous consequences of syphilis necessitated a public campaign aimed at educating Iranians about the ramifications of venereal disease. However, the pictures of

Child Disabled from Syphilis. *Sihhat-nimayi Iran.*

physically deformed children and adults, whose condition may or may not have been a consequence of syphilis, provoked fear and sensationalism. Such medical authorities shunned syphilitics and other physically disabled people and barred them from full participation in Iranian society.[86]

While educating Iranians about the transmission of sexual diseases gave them some agency in protecting their reproductive health, it did not eliminate illicit sexual activity in Iran. In 1934, the League of Nations Committee of Inquiry into traffic in women and children found that measures put into place to limit foreign travel by Iranians, as well as provisions in the marriage law restricting the union of Iranian women to foreigners without prior sanction, helped to curtail the unlawful movement of Persian women. According to the league's report, "These two measures have been mainly instrumental in the stoppage of the traffic in Persian women to other countries which had formerly existed, especially during the war, and which was facilitated in some cases by the migration of such women as the wives of Persian pilgrims to the holy places of Iraq, where they had been abandoned, or as wives of visiting Arabs who returned to that country and divorced them."[87] The league pointed out that "there were only a few prostitutes of Persian nationality found outside Persia—namely in Iraq and British India."[88] Iraqi authorities, however, claimed that "almost half of all the prostitutes in Iraq were of Persian origin. The considerable number of prostitutes of Persian race found in Iraq who were nationals of Iraq was composed partly of women who were Iraqi by birth and partly of those who have acquired that nationality by marriage."[89] The Committee of Inquiry noted that during the war "there was a steady influx of Persian prostitutes to Mesopotamia," most likely because a foreign army was stationed there.[90] A former Persian official serving in Baghdad and Basra reported that "during his term very shortly after the war, he had had occasion to repatriate 300 Persian prostitutes to Persia."[91] This traffic of Persian women gave further proof of the prevalence of prostitution in Iran and the concomitant social quandaries that it engendered.

Addressing prostitution in an official capacity ran the risk of acknowledging the moral laxity of Iranian society, a reality that maternalists had addressed in general terms. Still, some state and medical officials supported measures to protect the sexual health of the country's young people. In 1938, Ahmad Matin Daftari, the minister of justice, presented a bill to the parliament compelling engaged couples to receive state-approved health permits prior to marriage, a measure supported by avid maternalists, including Persian physicians.[92] Ahmad Sayyid Imami, a professor at the college of medicine, was in favor of health certificates as early as 1931, when the marriage law was being revised. Imami cited concerns not only about venereal disease but also about ailments such as kidney and heart disease, which often caused hardships for pregnant women during labor and delivery. Imami posed ethical questions about whether women with such physical limitations should be denied marriage or childbirth, outcomes that could exacerbate population worries in Iran. He believed that women with certain health problems should be allowed to marry after undergoing simple medical procedures.[93] Although infertility remained a touchy subject, it was a corollary to reproduction. Some Iranian couples did not readily divulge such personal matters, even to their family physician.[94] As medical researchers investigated the causes of infertility and explored possible new reproductive technologies, the Persian popular press tried to keep up with these changes.

Despite worries about promiscuity and sexual morality, images of the Iranian woman in the popular press were lustful and physically revealing. These depictions contradicted the moral message implicit in discussions of venereal disease and marriage, which skirted around the socially explosive issues of adultery and polygamy. Women appeared as attractive and sexually desirable partners. The use of cosmetic products by Iranian women manifested a desire to enhance physical beauty. Customs records from 1935 indicate that 100,000 rials' worth of cosmetic products—including facial powders, soaps, perfumes, creams, and nail polish—had been imported to Iran, revealing widespread consumer investment in these goods.[95] By 1938, women were cautioned not to use cosmetics products wastefully and obsessively but rather to apply makeup sparingly, both to protect their skin from overapplication and to safeguard their virtue (*matanat*).[96] Still, beauty continued to be marketed in urban centers and the popular press.[97] One article took this trend to new heights by endorsing rhinoplasty for women, whose unseemly noses had apparently diminished their outward attractiveness.[98] Women were exhorted to become beauty-conscious, as outer beauty not only reflected well on the modern citizen and state but also reinforced individual self-esteem and confidence.

The dolling up of Iranian women produced a boom in the Iranian fashion industry as Western modes of dress, whether locally tailored or designed by foreigners, increasingly became the vogue for Iranian citizens. Fashion houses (*khayyatkhanah*) and related technologies such as the sewing machine glutted the Iranian market.[99] Women were not the only targets of this beauty culture, however.[100] Men, too, became a focus of this consumerism within the expanding cosmetics and fashion industries. In 1928, when a decree was issued that Iranian men were to wear Pahlavi hats, one advertisement urged its fashion-conscious male readers to take full advantage of this opportunity and enhance their wardrobe by purchasing flannel outfits and raincoats to complete the new look.[101]

Like the cosmetics industry, pharmaceutical companies received an economic windfall from the hygienic movement in Iran. Local drugstores increased in number and advertised their services with regularity in print media.[102] New drugs, or "elixirs" of life, promised to cure numerous ailments, from backaches to hemorrhoids, while others pledged to strengthen weak nerves. Hygiene thus became an antidote to infirmity, delaying physical decay and death through its focus on health and beauty, marriage and reproduction. Human betterment might be achieved if women and men could conquer their bodies and promote healthful reproduction through an under-standing of hygiene and human physiology.

The maternalist discourse—and, I would argue, the hygiene move-ment in general—liberated the modern Iranian woman by opening up discussion of previously taboo subjects such as sexuality and encouraging a public reassessment of family life and women's rights in the domestic partnership. As Foucault has written, "The central issue, then ... is not to determine whether one says yes or no to sex ... but to account for the fact that it is spoken about [and] to discover who does the speaking."[103] This observation is pertinent to Iran given that in 1943, syphilis, prostitution, and opium addiction were identi-fied as persistent social challenges for the country.[104] The campaign to control prostitution and venereal disease may not have sufficiently curbed these ills in Iranian society, but it created a public space in which the discussion of such topics became permissible.

While prostitution had long existed in Iran, it assumed a different social and national significance with the modern impetus to overhaul

public health. The spread of prostitution was responsible for the proliferation of diseases such as syphilis and gonorrhea that not only
caused personal harm but also weakened the national workforce and
undermined the constitution of the patriot. As writers and policy
makers explored the reasons for the existence of prostitution, health
officials launched a public campaign that controlled sexuality and
childbirth as it popularized the rudiments of maternal and children's
health. Because venereal disease afflicted women and children with
sterility, blindness, and other unwelcome side effects, it necessitated
prompt medical attention. The reproductive capacity of Iranians
remained threatened so long as venereal disease targeted the nation's
most vulnerable citizens. For this reason, state health officials and
medical practitioners went beyond moralizing about the ills of prostitution and supported the registry of prostitutes. They strove to provide medical treatment to prostitutes without penalty of imprisonment
(or, worse, death) in order to check the proliferation of venereal
disease. Some argued that the virtue of ordinary citizens paralleled
the morality of the Iranian state. Discussions of venereal disease and
prostitution, however, became about more than just public morality.
This debate had enormous implications for women's rights in Iran, as
it recognized that women were often put at physical risk through their
marriages. Women had little choice but to take action to protect
themselves and the health of their offspring.

CHAPTER 5

Giving Birth

Modern Nursing and Reproductive Politics

B irthing babies seems a mundane event. Yet even a cursory review of the history of maternity in Iran reveals the controversial culture of birthing. What women and men understood about reproduction shaped their choices about the type of care to seek during childbirth. Although specific rituals related to childbirth differed in form and spirit, and often changed with the times, their existence showed a desire to protect women in labor from some of the unknown dangers of childbirth and to assume control over a mystifying and momentous event in people's lives. The accumulation of knowledge about procreation in Iran altered men's relationships to female bodies. Male figures (hygienists, physicians, and religious leaders) who may have had little actual experience in obstetrics gradually chipped away at the authority of often seasoned female midwives in the birthing process.[1]

Transformations in Iran's culture of childbirth significantly affected gender relations, and the development of modern nursing manifested the authority of modern (male) physicians, as well as the indispensable participation of women in public health management. Women's experiences with conception, pregnancy, and childbirth—whether as mothers, health care professionals, or both—mirrored the broad cultural changes occurring in Iran. In the twentieth century, Iranian physicians slowly made the transition from traditional to modern medicine, although this shift was not devoid of dissent. Despite the infiltration of Western medical thought, entrenched beliefs and superstitions sometimes made it difficult to disseminate new scientific knowledge about reproduction. Even physicians who may not have resorted to talismans to ward off the evil eye had limited access to new approaches to childbirth and maternal care.

Many Persian physicians of the modern era typically drew upon both Islamic and Western medical literature to treat patients.[2] Historically, Islamic notions of conception differed from Western ones, although Greek views of reproduction influenced both schools of thought. Medieval Muslim scholars did not privilege a man's contribution to conception over a woman's role, but patriarchy remained ingrained. In fact, relying on the Qur'an, some medieval Islamic jurists argued that neither the male matter nor the female matter was more significant than the other. Islamic medical philosophers such as Ibn Sina and Ibn Rushd, however, asserted the dominance of the male sperm in reproduction.[3] These discrepancies suggest that the medieval Islamic world did not have a uniform view of reproduction and female sexuality.[4]

The dearth of medical information about women's internal anatomy meant that female sexuality—and hence human reproduction—remained poorly understood. Information about pregnancy appeared in folkloric literature and was scattered in medical works. In early modern Iran, Safavid physicians built on medieval Islamic medical knowledge to learn about female ailments and reproduction. Although some medical specialization had emerged, male doctors did not typically treat gynecological matters. Rather, midwives treated female conditions, but since most were illiterate, they left no account of their empirical experiences. Few anatomical works focused on the pelvis and other internal parts of the female anatomy, and as a result, male physicians knew little about women's internal reproductive organs.[5] Medical manuscripts from the Qajar era typically focused on the etiology and treatment of epidemic diseases such as cholera or smallpox, or they provided general discussions on anatomy and hygiene. One treatise, however, addressed women's diseases specifically, providing explanations and treatment of diseases related to the uterus, including uterine cancer and ovarian irregularities.[6]

In the modern era, as Western medicine rapidly made headway among the elite, Western physicians often spoke of traditional Persian physicians and midwives in derogatory terms. Yet this clash represented more than just a conflict between the East and the West. Similar phenomena had already taken place in other cultures, such as in early modern England, a society that was not influenced by Western colonialism or Islamic belief. Illiterate Muslim women were thus not alone in attaching new meaning to religious concepts related to conception and reproduction. Nor did their unscientific beliefs make them more benighted or ignorant than their Western counterparts, as some modern hygienists contended.[7] What matters here is that both Protestant and Shi'i women, for example, became subjected to similar structures of power intended to circumscribe their individual authority and their independent decision making in matters of reproduction and sexuality.

Because of limitations on state power, many Western-educated physicians in Iran strove to control mothering, childbirth, and sexuality less through legislation and more through a public campaign aimed at altering the traditional lifestyle and hygienic culture of the ordinary citizen. These were not dominant, however. In July 1934 the number of medical professionals educated in Iran slightly exceeded the number of foreign-trained health practitioners.[8] Nonetheless, Western-style medicine made headway in Iran, reflected in such proposed changes as reducing the influence of local midwives.

The interest in reproduction was tied to a discourse on cleanliness and bodily health. Healthful procreation became appropriated by statist interests and attempts to populate communities with fertile, chaste, and family-oriented subjects. In times of political crisis the need to uphold patriarchy intensified, and control over women and their sexuality reinforced male authority. As Iranians came to understand the process of reproduction better, they strove to regulate maternal care through the expansion of nursing and the regulation of midwifery. These changes became possible as the political climate in Iran emphasized state centralization and the top-down supervision of health care. Iranian medical officials hoped to curtail infant mortality through improvements in municipal services and the expansion of clinics.[9] Although male physicians gradually assumed control over the fields of obstetrics and gynecology, they had to acknowledge the salience of involving women in the politics of reproduction.

Women's health remained a key to understanding demographic trends, and it became the state's prerogative to question and supervise women on the tenets of mothering and child rearing. Essential to this project was the need to form a modernist culture that lauded matrimony, domesticity, and motherhood. Popular newspapers as well as school curricula reinforced women's familial responsibilities, even as they invited women to complement their household duties with work outside the home.[10]

In 1908, *Tamaddun*, one of the "best newspapers" of the constitutional era, serialized a satirical column on the state of sanitation in Iran.[11] The discussion took the form of a fictitious exchange between a father named Haydar Khan and his son. As the column continued week after week, Haydar Khan disparaged the 'ulama, or religious scholars, whose duty, he believed, was to inculcate the meaning of cleanliness (*nizafat*). He also targeted Iranian midwives, blaming their ineptitude for having created a virtual public health crisis in the country.

In a telling passage Haydar Khan recalled the gruesome birth of his son, whose complicated delivery almost led to the death of both mother and baby. The presiding midwife, who apparently had tried all possible positions for inducing labor, eventually concluded erroneously that 'Afifah Khanum's distended stomach was not a result of pregnancy but rather the consequence of a malignant condition that was sure to bring her untimely death. Losing hope, the midwife simply rubbed oil on her patient's back and stomach to assuage her suffering, and, instead of sending for a physician, burned wild rue to ward off evil spirits. 'Afifah Khanum's death was averted only when her husband, Haydar Khan, quickly called for a doctor to rescue his wife and child from the grip of the caring yet uninformed midwife.[12]

This episode illustrated the hazards women and children faced during labor and delivery, even as it derided midwives and their common superstitions. Haydar Khan and 'Afifah Khanum represented an ordinary Iranian couple at the turn of the century—that is, citizens who had not benefited from travel abroad, who did not have access to Western physicians like members of the Qajar aristocracy, and who relied on local *hakims* and midwives for basic medical services. Recounted in part to condemn the dearth of qualified midwives, this story called attention to the prevalence of maternal and infant mortality resulting from what should have been a predictable consequence of matrimony: childbirth. The lack of sanitary facilities, the article showed, posed serious health risks to women and children.

Writers and health officials considered the hazards of depopulation as they advocated policy shifts in childbirth practices. Women's sanitation seemed especially salient as hygienists, physicians, and public officials, alarmed by the high rate of infant mortality, strove to nurture a growing generation of healthy, able-bodied patriots. Although victims themselves, women curiously were singled out as the enemies of public sanitation. They were regarded simultaneously as potential founts of hygienic knowledge and perpetrators of medical ignorance. Women could help to promote hygiene as easily as they could hinder it. In Iran and elsewhere, modern physicians gradually assumed authority over childbirth and, in the process, sullied the image of the traditional midwife, who may have succumbed to magic or talismans and was often faulted for the tragedy of infant mortality in Iran. Traditional midwives in Iran could scarcely compete with the legitimacy of a new generation of licensed physicians who came to embody scientific authority and rationality.[13]

Little information is available on indigenous medical institutions that came into existence at the turn of the century to serve women. In 1908, the newly founded Himmat Hospital in Tehran provided midwifery services, but it likely had limited capacity and popularity. Female patients, moreover, had to be accompanied by a family member who would be willing to care for them.[14] Because the majority of births in Iran still occurred at home with the help of other women, it was imperative to teach all women the basic principles of hygiene.

Writers from varying backgrounds advocated instructing women about matters of personal and public health to reduce illness and death among women and children. Yet they also touted hygiene as a necessary component of maintaining a clean and orderly household and society. Journals published at the turn of the century for and by women focused on hygiene and child care to impart essential information to women.[15] Several essays dealt with hygiene and pregnancy, once again highlighting the valuable role of women as progenitors of Iranian society. Pregnant women were cautioned to protect themselves against catching colds, encouraged to eat well, and discouraged from wearing tight clothing.[16] The journal *Danish* even thanked a female American doctor for administering care to Iranian women, since the paucity of female physicians meant that people previously had turned to "women without knowledge" for assistance, particularly in the delivery of children, even though such women dispensed care with "impure hands filled with microbes."[17] Hygiene and cleanliness thus became touchstones of patriotic womanhood.

In addition to addressing the dilemmas of midwifery, maternalists dwelled on other facets of child rearing and women's health. Because poor mothering and inadequate midwifery surfaced as the main culprits of high infant mortality, hygienists urged mothers to stop playing doctor. In one article mothers and nannies were cautioned not to treat every ailment experienced by children in the same way. "My sisters, my mothers," the writer implored, "where did you train to become a doctor? Where did you learn about the properties of herbs? You are right to know about the beneficial properties of chamomile tea in healing children's stomachaches . . . but not all stomachaches are the same."[18] Instead, mothers and nurses were instructed to consult physicians before administering healing herbs to their sick children, an example of the transition between traditional and modern medicine in Iran.

Breast-feeding, deemed the starting point of good health for children, was stridently endorsed by maternalists in hygienic literature. There were, of course, religious and historical precedents for this emphasis. The Qur'an, for example, states that "mothers shall suckle their children for two whole years."[19] Moreover, women who viewed breast-feeding as a social inconvenience and opted for wet nurses were admonished and shamed. As one journalist goaded, mothers who "out of ignorance" decided against breast-feeding in order to "keep their clothes clean, to sleep well at night, to entertain guests . . . or go to weddings" demonstrated their callousness and probably would not be much moved if their children died, either. In other words, non-breast-feeding mothers, whose ranks apparently were growing, hardly resembled mothers at all. "With deep regret," he wrote, "I confess that the mothers of today have forgotten their holy duty."[20] To lend further credence to his view, this writer cited the work of a British physician, Edward Ellis, who had written on children's diseases and had endorsed breast-feeding in his works.[21] This reference to a Western medical authority on breast-feeding seems ironic, since classical Islamic physicians also considered the breast milk of the child's own mother the most beneficial food for a newborn.[22] However, if for medical reasons a mother could not breast-feed, then an appropriate wet nurse was the next best alternative. The qualities of a good wet nurse, according to Muslim doctor Ibn Sina, included the right "form and physique," relatively young age, and personal character.[23]

Persian women writers, drawing on Islamic and local traditions, advocated breast-feeding to reduce illness and death among women and children. Some even claimed that children breast-fed by their own mothers were more capable than children nourished by the milk of a wet nurse or manufactured milk (*arza'-i san'ati*). In the early twentieth century, as today, controversy existed over the use of manufactured milk and its connection to infant mortality. Some believed that children "frequently" fed artificial milk products died at eight or ten years of age.[24] Another writer maintained that women should not consider themselves too weak to breast-feed after birth. If they were strong enough to endure labor, they could certainly manage breast-feeding. In addition, the writer pointed out that breast-feeding did not cause physical harm by inducing anger or backaches in women, but rather could alleviate certain diseases and restore a woman's uterus to its normal condition.[25]

Pregnant women, often singled out in hygienic literature because of their vital role in abating population worries, were urged to take responsibility for creating "antiseptic" conditions for childbirth. They were instructed to provide their designated midwives with a clean change of clothes prior to delivery, soap and boiled water, and clean sheets for the procedure.[26] Pregnant women were particularly warned to avoid midwives who had contracted syphilis and thus could infect newborns.[27] In turn, midwives were cautioned not to rush the process of delivery and "yank out" the baby "like a rubber tissue," needlessly threatening the infant and mother.[28]

Caring for a newborn was no easy task. At a time when women routinely birthed at home with little knowledge of statistical norms for birthweight and other metrics of newborn health, one women's journal provided such basic guidelines for families. An average birthweight was considered to be just over three kilograms (or approximately six and a half pounds), with boys weighing slightly more than girls. Women were taught that although children typically dropped some weight after birth, breast-fed children would regain their birthweight after a week. Children breast-fed by their own mothers were considered to enjoy good health and to be more likely to develop superior cognitive abilities than babies fed by wet nurses or consuming artificial milk.[29]

Some writers encouraged women to abandon the advice of elderly women and instead to embrace modern hygiene to care for their children. In her journal *Jahan-i Zanan*, Fakhr Afaq Parsa provided translations of an article from Turkish that emphasized this point. The translated text warned mothers of newborns to be wary of the "sayings of old women, the doctors of the home." In fact, this anonymous writer maintained that infections appearing in children were often caused by the actions of mothers who, for example, had failed to seek vaccinations and available treatments. Another impediment was the absence of short books on hygiene for families that could guide women and men to maintain a healthful lifestyle.[30] Other articles focused on cooking, considered another necessary component of hygiene and bodily health.[31]

Iranian women were not always eager to adopt new hygienic recommendations. One observer claimed that Persian mothers preferred adhering to the sayings of Khulthum Nana, the apocryphal matron who advised women on their social mores, instead of accepting modern hygienic knowledge. As a result, Iranian children routinely perished because of the lack of attention paid to the prevention and treatment of common childhood illnesses.[32] According to this source, while Iranian women typically gave birth to approximately ten to twelve children, the children rarely survived. By contrast, in "civilized nations," where women typically birthed fewer children, the population had remained constant or had increased because of the success in implementing hygienic measures that had curbed infant mortality.[33] One writer, Iffat al-Muluk Khvajahnuri, suggested convening public hygiene sessions to educate Iran's largely illiterate population about proper child care and personal hygiene. She contended that attention to hygiene was an urgent matter that could not be postponed until the majority of Iranians had attended school and become educated.[34] Muhtaram Iskandari argued further that hygiene took precedence over military concerns since Iran needed healthy mothers and children to populate its army.[35]

Without competent nurses and midwives, public officials feared, the population would fall. In 1925, the League of Patriotic Iranian Women submitted a proposal to the parliament urging Majlis delegates to address the matter of population decline related to contagious diseases and its impact on national priorities. The first article suggested requiring blood tests and other physical examinations for couples before marriage. The second item called for sending students of modest means to Beirut and Egypt in order to instruct them in midwifery. The third point stressed that locally made clothes ought to be used in schools to support indigenous industries.[36] That women took an active role in promoting potential legislation that might serve to improve their health, and to further national ambitions, showed modest political progress, even though none of these measures was immediately embraced by the parliament.

The crisis of midwifery unsettled public health officials who hoped to combat infant mortality in part by regulating midwifery. Although the reverence for midwifery as a profession had abated somewhat since the medieval era, many Persian women's journals supported academic nursing, which they viewed primarily as a "womanly" occupation and a suitable alternative to traditional midwifery.[37] In 1916 one woman described nursing (*parastari*) as a vocation "that is everywhere considered women's responsibility" and ill-suited to men, for nursing was a "talent that is natural in women."[38]

In 1916, modern training schools for nurses began operating in Iran under the auspices of Presbyterian missionaries.[39] The mission acknowledged that "the profession is new to this part of the country and our training school is distinctly in the experimental stage."[40] To initiate formal nursing education, the Presbyterian missionaries provided basic guidelines for the first class of nurses in northwestern Iran, to include no more than "six candidates at a time." Nursing applicants were required to "give evidence of good moral character, average good health, intelligence and earnestness of purpose."[41] The first six months of training were regarded as "probationary," after which time approved candidates would be admitted to full-time training. The courses of study included physiology, anatomy, practical nursing, and obstetrics.[42] The first class of nurses graduated in 1919–20, and graduation ceremonies, attended by "leading Persian physicians of the city," were held in the men's ward of the Tabriz hospital, which was "emptied and decorated with American and Persian flags for the occasion."[43] By 1919, the American Mission hospital in Tehran had classes for training native nurses,[44] and in 1922, the American Mission hospital in Tabriz reported that "we now have eight native girl nurses in training, four having recently come in after graduating from our Girl's school."[45]

The same medical report found that in an eleven-month period, out of fifty obstetrical cases only five were Muslim women. According to this source, the "Persian Moslem women only come occasionally and then in extremity. These five were such cases. . . . Four of these women had already been under the care of native mid-wives for hours or days. All four died within a few days after delivery at the hospital. The other case came in time, and received the benefit of a Cesarian."[46] These statistics, however unreliable, suggest that birthing conditions for Muslim Iranian women remained risky even within the setting of a Western-style hospital, and that maternal death was not an unusual occurrence. Why, then, were Muslim women in areas that offered Western-type medical services reluctant to take advantage of them? Perhaps one explanation may be that "time of sickness is always one of special opportunity for the Christian message so nurse and doctors have a great privilege in administering to the eternal souls as well as relieving bodies torn by sickness and pain." In other words, some Muslim Iranian women may not have wanted to subject themselves to proselytizing.[47] Another explanation may have been that "there is quite prevalent among the people a prejudice to hospitals, since they seem to regard them much as a case of 'Abandon all hope, ye who enter here.'" In other words, some may have refused hospital services out of fear for their life.[48] Finally, the social stigma of approaching a male physician discouraged many Iranian ladies from seeking medical assistance. It was observed that "women from the lower classes and some from the upper classes as well, will come to a male physician for such ailments as eye, ear and stomach trouble. . . . Our obstetrical work is limited almost entirely to the Armenian and foreign community."[49] By 1925, the missionary medical staff acknowledged that it "will be a long [time] before Persian women will come freely to the hospital for confinement but now and again we have a patient who realizes the advantages we have to offer."[50] In particular, one Persian woman who had apparently received excellent obstetrical care shared her experiences with an aristocratic woman, who "came to the hospital for her own confinement." Still, delivery in a hospital remained a rarity for Persian women at the twilight of Qajar rule.[51]

As a measure of political stability reigned in Iran during the early Pahlavi years, institutions of health emerged to improve sanitation.

The Iranian Red Lion and Sun Society met some of the needs of women, orphans, and the needy. Conceived in 1921, the society began operations in 1923 and gained international recognition from Geneva in 1924. Regional offices were established in several provinces, including Azerbaijan and Khorasan. In 1926 a branch was opened in Qum, where members of the 'ulama welcomed the inauguration of the regional branch. Other regional branches included Sari in 1929, Isfahan in 1932, and Rasht in 1936.[52]

In 1925, when the League of Nations commissioned a report on the sanitary conditions of Iran, it found that the municipality of Tehran managed a workhouse for the indigent as well as an orphanage that accommodated more than seven hundred children, many of whom were "found wandering in the streets and are homeless." A hospital, which handled infectious diseases and other serious illnesses, was attached to the orphanage. Overall, the report concluded that "the children appeared happy and well nourished."[53] In addition, the municipality of Tehran administered a "lunatic asylum," intended to serve only a hundred individuals, although in actuality the asylum cared for a slightly higher number of psychologically challenged people. Some orphanages, formed to meet the needs of abandoned children, were encouraged to treat healthy children well, as healthy orphans could grow up to become productive citizens of the state and alleviate worries over population decline.[54] The state invested little in assisting the disabled; rather, the emphasis remained on preventing disability and death among children.

Infant and maternal mortality prompted economic investment in midwifery and nursing. In 1926, a school of midwifery, apparently connected with the Pasteur Institute, opened in Tehran.[55] Applicants were required to provide evidence of being at least eighteen years of age and to have a certificate of good standing from their previous school, as well as records of exams and other related documents from the last years of high school. But these educational standards limited women's access to Persian nursing schools. In 1929, the American Hospital in Mashhad reported that nursing instruction "must, of course, be very elementary as our Persian nurses have had very little education, a few of them still being illiterate."[56] The expansion of nursing instruction thus played a role in improving basic literacy levels among women as well.

At the same time Persian nursing schools were emerging, advertisements for private clinics and the services of foreign-trained midwives were published in the leading Persian newspaper, *Ittila'at*, indicating not only a rise in private practice but also the commercialization of midwifery as a potentially lucrative medical service.[57] One certified midwife, Khanum-i Shahbaz, publicized her services in an advertisement claiming that she had received a permit in midwifery from the Ministry of Education, as well as a license from London to practice nursing and midwifery. Located in Tehran, her maternity clinic contained five beds and even offered prenatal care.[58] Because of the absence of regulation, women intellectuals faulted Iranian policy makers for not adequately confronting the "very important question" of instituting sufficient training centers for midwives—a question that was "immeasurably urgent for the next generation."[59] One female journalist argued that it was "the duty of educated women . . . to inform their sisters about hygiene by publishing magazines . . . and organizing conferences."[60]

In 1926, Dr. Amir 'Alam, who served as vice president of the Red Lion and Sun Society, acknowledged that untrained midwives posed a significant threat to mothers and infants.[61] He envisioned the establishment of birth centers (*dar al-waladah*) run by professionally trained midwives to assist with labor and delivery—an advancement that might eventually reduce women's mortality. Such centers could freely provide disadvantaged women with easy access to the latest techniques in obstetrics. Newborns would be turned over to parents once it had been determined that the children were in good health. Amir 'Alam's maternalist concerns, however, had a distinctly patriotic purpose, for state-run birth centers could directly oversee the process of childbirth. As he explained, "One of the main sources of the wealth, power, and greatness of nations is population size," and birthing centers, he argued, indirectly contributed to that cause by reducing dangers to the health of mothers and newborns. Moreover, state-operated birthing centers could decide whether parents were ready to assume responsibility for their child, intruding into what was once considered exclusively the parents' domain.[62]

Maternalists took for granted women's choice about whether to bear children. To make maternity appealing to young women, one female journalist celebrated pregnancy as a distinctive advantage of womanhood. As Rawshanak Naw'dust wrote in the inaugural issue of her magazine, "Whose countenance is more confident and proud than that of a pregnant woman's? If attention is paid, it will be understood that no sultan at the height of his power will glow with more pride."[63] The belief that a pregnant woman "glowed" and that pregnancy conferred upon her a privileged and coveted status was a familiar one. However, it was sometimes difficult to celebrate pregnancy when would-be mothers had to deal with the possibility of infant mortality.

In 1927, one observer asked, "Why, with the existence of a number of married couples, and the fact that boys and girls get married at a young age, is the population of Iran less than that of foreign countries? Is it not because of the ignorance of mothers, nurses, and even midwives? Why should Iranian midwives not be educated or be knowledgeable . . .?"[64] Inadequate birthing facilities and a dearth of certified caregivers remained a cause of infant mortality and maternal deaths during childbirth. Other recommendations intended to alleviate anxieties over population decline included the imprisonment of women for anywhere from one to three years for having an abortion. Those assisting women in this "murder" were similarly subject to prosecution.[65] Although these measures did not necessarily translate into law during the period under review, they expressed the opinions of a select cadre of Iranian physicians and health professionals. Their recommendations circumscribed the decision-making power of Iranian women in reproduction.

Population worries prompted the expansion of nursing education. If women's education in itself was not a desirable end, nonetheless it made sense to school women in order to address the problems of infant mortality, maternal death, and, by extension, population decline. In 1930 a graduate of the Midwifery School in Tabriz delivered a scathing attack on the members of her profession. As she rhetorically asked, "Is population not the real asset of the state? Is it not the duty of every government to protect the life of its citizenry?"[66] Why then had the state not disqualified uncertified midwives from delivering babies? Unlike other "civilized" nations, which had taken necessary steps to protect the welfare of mothers, Iran entrusted its future to those who had "no scientific knowledge." This "certified" midwife contended that the Iranian state should "universally ban" the practice of midwifery by uncertified caregivers. Yet the reality of finding a qualified midwife proved problematic, especially for the poor, since they did not have many choices in this matter and often were ministered to by any available childbirth practitioner. Some female maternalists, while endorsing social welfare programs, nonetheless echoed the official line by laying blame for women's mortality almost exclusively on the midwives themselves.[67]

In 1930 the government approved the charter for another school of midwifery, to be supervised by the Ministry of Health. The School of Midwifery (Amuzishgah-i 'Ali-yi Mamayi) offered a three-year course of study, after which students would receive a certificate of competence from the Ministry of Education. The subjects of academic instruction included the study of anatomy and hygiene in the first year. Clinical training gave midwives experience in the following areas: minor surgery, general nursing skills, the modes of drug dispensing, cleanliness, and precautionary measures to take in the event of epidemics. The second year of study concerned pregnancy and obstetrics, as well as child rearing and women's particular ailments. In the third year midwives became skilled at handling atypical births.[68]

Nursing education received a boost in 1935 when the Women's Hospital (Marizkhanah-i Nisvan) opened in Tehran and included a College of Midwifery. The drive to create a cadre of licensed midwives, again touted as a promising step toward health and prosperity for women, children, and the Iranian family, was headed by Dr. Bakhtiyar. The first class consisted of seventy female students, all of whom had completed their high school education, and the instructors were recruited from among high-ranking physicians. The three-year course of study prepared the students for midwifery and qualified them to manage a similar college of midwifery elsewhere in the country. The hospital itself served as a "big, educational classroom" for nursing students, who benefited from the experience and leadership of seasoned physicians in treating pregnant women. Iran's leading male physicians such as Dr. 'Abbas Adham, Dr. Amir 'Alam, and Dr. Bakhtiyar supervised obstetrics, gynecology, and nursing education in this way.[69] This trend continued in 1936 as Dr. Jahanshah Saleh assumed primary instructional responsibility at a newly founded nursing school jointly supervised by an American medical professional. Later that year, a specialized pediatric nursing school emerged to improve children's health care.[70]

The Ministry of Education approved the charter for the establishment of additional nursing schools in 1936. These regulations stipulated that students complete a two-year program and that the nursing schools themselves be free and connected to a hospital to facilitate clinical training. Nursing applicants needed to have graduated from a

Picture of Nurses. *Ittila'at.*

three-year secondary school before matriculating. Only unmarried women between eighteen and twenty-five years of age were allowed to enroll, although exceptions were made for experienced nurses who had been working in health care institutions before the founding of such modern nursing programs. The emphasis on youth education undermined the role of older and more traditional women, who in the past had often served as midwives. The nursing curriculum mandated instruction in child care and covered the rudimentary principles of pharmacology and anatomy. In addition, nurses received training in treating common childhood illnesses as well as diseases and conditions specific to women, especially pregnancy.[71] With the establishment of the Faculty of Medicine at the University of Tehran, medical students also received specialized training in the fundamentals of obstetrics and in the treatment of syphilis.[72]

Nursing schools, though crucial institutions of modern health care, did not completely eliminate maternal and infant deaths. Precise records regarding infant mortality rates for this period are difficult to obtain. The following observation by British officials in Iran sheds some light on why procuring these statistics proves tricky:

> The only figures available are those issued by the Municipality of Tehran. Death certificates are employed in the capital, but their use is not compulsory. They are collected by the washers of the dead, who are not supposed to perform their duties unless a certificate is produced. . . . It will be seen from the list given below that in the case of more than one-eighth of the total deaths in Tehran in twelve months, the cause

has been returned as unknown, and that in sixty-five a return of "sudden death" has been made.[73]

Despite these difficulties, British sources offered the following mortality figures in 1925, as reported by the municipality of Tehran. There were 809 reported deaths caused by smallpox, and the age distribution of these deaths indicated that the majority occurred among children four years of age or younger.[74] In the same period, 22 deaths occurred during childbirth, while the number of still-births was estimated as 173.[75] The report also pointed out that "the number of deaths from puerperal fever is certainly underestimated" at eight dead. Six years later, in 1931, the Iranian Ministry of Foreign Affairs distributed a statement on the death toll in Tehran during a one-month period. Eight reported deaths were attributed to syphilis. Several deaths occurred due to typical childhood diseases such as measles, smallpox, croup, and whooping cough, although age ranges were not listed for the deaths.[76] New regulations intended to improve the collection of birth and death information gradually changed the management of health care. The Department of Health mandated that "statement of the cause of death must be signed by a doctor before the body-washers are permitted to accept bodies."[77] Attending doctors and midwives also had to report births.

New regulations emerged to manage pharmacies, and "public baths, tea houses and eating places, butcher shops and candy stores are being inspected."[78] Despite these advances, high infant and child mortality rates distressed families and public health officials alike. One reason for the persistence of infant mortality may have been the dearth of prenatal care in Iran. In 1933, a "leaflet in Persian on pre-natal care, adapted to Persian customs," was being prepared. Pre-natal care would enable pregnant women to receive urgent medical care for serious complications such as eclampsia.[79] Another familiar reason for the high death rate among infants remained the incompetence of midwives.

A physician newly arrived in Mashhad, Dr. Adelaide Kibbe, discerned "several undeveloped projects" for future work. The first concerned the teaching of local midwives: "These 'mammas' . . . ready with dirty herbs, or sticks, or fingers, remain in the background, a sinister menace to every woman." The second matter concerned children. As Kibbe described, "What a field lies here! Babies are brought to the clinic unwashed, joggled all day long ... stuffed with tea or sweets or even cucumbers, or soothed with a 'bit' of opium."[80] Even after decades of education and activism, it appeared that some Iranian families found it difficult to abandon tradition.

Although new clinics appeared in Tehran, other cities and provinces lacked sufficient institutions of public hygiene. An internal governmental report on the sanitary condition of Kerman and its environs found that qualified physicians there remained scarce and that malaria was rampant, leading to high infant mortality. According to this report, although most married couples sired approximately six or seven children, only one or two survived. This report further pointed out that venereal disease was less visible here than in other parts of Iran, but that sexually transmitted diseases nonetheless were on the rise. The office of the Kerman inspection authority, which prepared the report, recommended that the government invest in building a hospital there and when possible to provide necessary drugs and medications free of charge to the inhabitants in order to reduce mortality rates.[81]

Outside of Tehran, some observers considered obstetrics "an untouched field." The staff of the American Hospital in Mashhad maintained that the "'mammas' (midwives) are illiterate women who have never had any opportunity to learn." In addition, the hospital staff pointed out that none "of the young women from the government's well-organized midwifery school in Teheran have come to Meshed, let alone to any of the lesser cities of Khorasan, and there is no government control of midwives."[82] Although the benefits of the government's midwifery school had not yet spread to the provinces, nonetheless it is significant that an independent party such as the mission staff had cited it as "well-organized." Dr. Adelaide Kibbe, who had written this portion of the report for the American Hospital in Mashhad, confirmed that Persian women "still prefer the home-like old 'mamma' ... and accept as kismet (fate) what too often follows, dead babies, puerperal infection, crippled lives."[83] During the interwar era many Iranian families preferred the convenience and familiarity of birthing at home to the foreign experience of delivering in hospitals or maternity clinics. For this reason, midwives who were willing to care for pregnant women in their homes remained central to the birthing process in Iran even though they were "illiterate."

Nursing schools finally appeared in other major Iranian cities, including Mashhad, Tabriz, Isfahan, and Shiraz.[84] Although women did not matriculate in the School of Medicine when the University of Tehran opened its doors in 1934, female enrollment accounted for 3 percent of the total student participation in the Faculty of Medicine by 1941.[85] In places such as Kermanshah, where the government had yet to launch a midwifery school, the American mission hospital worked in tandem with the state to provide obstetrical services. In fact, the government was "very willing to grant" the hospital "a permit to conduct our school of nursing in conformity with the government program."[86] In 1937, the hospital reported a rise in the number of visits by Persian women seeking obstetrical care. This increase was attributed in part to the high-quality care provided at the hospital: "The Iranian women are beginning to learn what it means to be properly cared for and they appreciate good nursing care and advertise it after they leave the hospital."[87]

Health authorities took other important steps to improve public sanitation and to curtail infant mortality. In 1932 the cabinet passed regulations to make vaccinations available without payment for children from birth to twenty-one years of age. Parents were instructed to take newborns up to six months to statewide centers to give their children the first of four injections necessary to prevent smallpox. These state-approved centers would then provide a certificate documenting the vaccination. The next installments of the vaccine were to be administered between six and seven years of age; between twelve and thirteen years of age; and between nineteen and twenty-one years of age. Parents or caretakers discovered to be negligent in this matter were at first reprimanded and then subjected to prosecution.[88] Hygiene remained an imperative for the Iranian government at the dawn of the Pahlavi dynasty. The need to increase public access to clean water as well as the desire to reduce the incidence of infectious diseases and mortality rates among infants informed public health policy throughout the twentieth century. There were significant demographic, humanitarian, and health care reasons for this emphasis: frequent epidemics, high infant mortality, maternal deaths and disability related to childbirth, and prostitution.

New schools played a vital role in inculcating the value of physical fitness through their curricula. Like her male counterpart, the modern Iranian woman was exhorted to engage in physical exercise to become a more productive member of the national polity. As Hajar Tarbiyat, head of the Society for Women, explained: "Women more than men require bodily and spiritual health. . . . Therefore, it is necessary to pay attention to the bodily health of girls and their engagement in physical exercise from childhood."[89] Presumably, women's bodies needed specialized and constant training to assist them with the difficult ordeal of pregnancy and the necessary task of nurturing "strong-minded men" for the nation.

In addition to encouraging physical fitness, the Pahlavi state made the cleanliness of cities, towns, and villages a priority for local municipalities. A government memorandum dated August 1936 urged village authorities to assist with sanitary measures, particularly among those who engaged in animal husbandry. The state stressed that, where possible, villagers should be encouraged to tend to animals away from settled urban areas and to keep their homes as hygienic as possible.[90] Popularization of hygiene and the stress on cleanliness were communicated through the newly founded Sazman-i Parvaresh-i Afkar as well.

The expansion of health facilities, particularly the establishment of state-run clinics and hospitals, as well as benevolent societies brought hygiene to more households and geographic areas during the Pahlavi regime. Women of the royal family served as benefactors of welfare organizations supporting women and children. Princess Fawzia, for example, oversaw the newly instituted Association for the Protection of Pregnant Women and Children (APPWC). One of the private palaces had even been converted into a bright room in which pregnant women and children received medical care provided by the APPWC.[91] Princess Shams Pahlavi initiated another organization called the Association of Benevolence (Bungah-i Niku Kari) that had a special pediatric hospital. Indigent mothers and children received medical services gratis at these centers, which were financed in part by private individuals.[92]

State policy showed curious contradictions despite the concern over women's health. In February 1936, for instance, just over a month after the promulgation of the revolutionary unveiling decree, a British diplomatic report from Tabriz noted the difficulties veiled women faced when approaching medical establishments. According to this source, "Doctors were forbidden to admit veiled women to hospitals."[93] Confronted with the "passive resistance" of many women and members of the 'ulama to the decree, the state even compelled medical professionals to turn away women in need. This policy seems in direct contradiction to the obstreperous rhetoric urging Iranian women to rely on modern hospitals and clinics for medical care. Faced with a potential public conflagration over the unveiling issue, however, the state ranked its priorities. Temporary measures, which excluded veiled women from "the baths, the cinema, [and] the use of public carriages," appeared justified in carrying out the women's renewal movement.[94]

In 1938, Dr. Sami Rad wrote a series of articles on children's health, reiterating that the principal hazards to children's well-being remained "ignorant old women, illiterate midwives, opium . . . and inadequate nutrition."[95] Although more than two decades had elapsed since the establishment of the first nursing schools in Iran, the medical attitude toward midwives had apparently changed little. Nonetheless, female health practitioners had gained enough visibility to promote women's welfare, capitalizing on the opportunity to instruct a new generation of midwives and nurses on the modern principles of maternal and child hygiene. In 1938, for instance, Malihah Adibzadeh, a graduate of the government's college of midwifery, published a column in the daily newspaper *Ittila'at*, discussing women's physiological changes during pregnancy and advising them on matters of hygiene.[96] Speaking before the Society for Women in 1940, Dr. Bakhtiyar, who headed the College of Midwifery, offered a historical assessment of midwifery's evolution in Iran. According to him, prior to the 1920s Iran had lacked sufficient hospitals specializing in obstetrics. One maternity clinic (*zayishgah*) contained only two beds, used principally for urgent cases, while the Women's Hospital had only six beds, which were frequently unused. By contrast, in 1939 the Women's Hospital accommodated sixty beds and enrolled eighty students in midwifery classes. Its maternity clinic, which also offered courses in nursing, increased its capacity to forty beds, which "are always full." The municipality of Tehran further planned to build a maternity clinic to include one hundred beds.[97] If somewhat exaggerated, Dr. Bakhtiyar's figures nonetheless broadcasted recent advances in women's health care while bringing women's medical concerns to the fore of hygiene efforts and national politics.

Obstetricians likely encountered birth abnormalities such as conjoined twins in their practice, but these aberrations were barely addressed in discussions of child care. The image of conjoined twins perhaps illustrated the most glaring example of birth defect, or "oddity," for the Iranian public. The very phrase used to describe such bodily deformities, *aja'ib al-makhluqat* (oddities of creation), became an expression of wonderment about human peculiarities. The reference to conjoined twins as "oddities" defined their physical difference as either monstrous or animal-like, thus embodying the antithesis of the human condition. That physicians and observers continued using this terminology well into the twentieth century suggests the acceptance of physically deformed individuals as existing somehow outside the pale of "normal" humanity, despite the fact that the lives of conjoined twins could be filled with typical human experiences such as travel, entertainment, and procreation.

Discussions of deformity, often couched in negative terms, departed from the positive and life-affirming language and message of Iran's health-related propaganda. Like other countries, early twentieth-century Iran became enthralled by the promises of hygiene and the curative potential of modern medicine, precisely because it was hoped that modern medicine might obviate disease, deformity, and even ugliness. The hygiene movement in Iran embraced health and fitness while simultaneously eschewing disease and disability. Although the popular press endorsed beauty and health, it rarely published pictures of disabled people, even in articles about the consequences of infectious diseases with the potential to disable and disfigure. At the same time that charitable organizations provided new services to the disabled, the state regarded disability as a social condition that needed to be circumscribed. This attitude partly explains the absence of photographs depicting the disabled community in the popular press and the dearth of social services for disabled people during the early Pahlavi era.[98] In short, ugliness and deformity were not modernist, patriotic virtues—or even "feel-good" topics intended to convince citizens of the benefits associated with the hygienic movement—and thus did not become common discussion points in Iran's heavily sanitized press.

In the 1930s, a scientific journal dedicated to the popularization of hygiene notably departed from this trend, however. Edited by a French-educated Iranian physician, Dr. Tutiya, the journal *Sihhat-nimayi Iran* (Iran's Hygienic Image) frequently published pictures of people with physical deformities. These depictions featured

Aja'ib-i Khilqat. *Adab.*

conjoined twins, identified as *aja'ib al-makhluqat*. The term used to connote "typically developing" in Persian, which is originally an Arabic phrase—*sahih al-khilqah*—makes explicit that "correct" and "incorrect" types of human being exist.[99] Deviations from the norm represented not just difference but oddity.

The journal's introductory issue discussed the birth in Tehran of a set of conjoined twins connected at the chest. Apparently the twins perished shortly after birth "because of neglect." Their parents, in an effort to hide the deaths, buried them in their yard, but the police discovered and later retrieved the bodies of the twins. The journal does not mention whether the parents suffered any criminal consequences for their neglect, pointing out only that the mother had a history of giving birth to twins.[100]

In her study of teratology, or "the study of monsters," in the British Empire, Carrie Yang Costello argues that obstetricians encountered birth abnormalities at the time of delivery and that such children were termed "monsters." Costello points out that discussions of teratology, which has commonly become known as the study of birth defects, did not consider the treatment of such infants, not because treatments did not exist but because medical discussions of deformities spoke to a "cultural fetish."[101] Iranian discussions of *aja'ib-i khilqat* displayed a similarly "freakish" curiosity about people with physical differences, rather than an enlightened or informative medical approach intended to assist and educate Iranian physicians.[102] In nature, Dr. Tutiya wrote, one frequently observed physically deformed infants, but his essay offered little in the way of treatment options or other medically relevant information about the care of conjoined twins.[103] The discourse on deformed children created norms of physical and mental fitness to which modern Iranian citizens needed to aspire. While hygienists redoubled efforts to limit the spread of infectious diseases and the disabilities resulting from them, they were slow to reach out and recognize the legal rights and educational needs of the disabled, including children. Despite these limitations, public health officials pioneered many organizations that targeted the elimination of illnesses such as malaria, smallpox, and venereal disease.

What impact did the hygiene movement have on women and children? Women's and children's health received a boost from this vigorous campaign. Although hygienic conditions for these two populations remained far from ideal—according to Byron Good, a study undertaken by a company called Overseas Consultants in 1949 found infant mortality in Iran to be over 50 percent[104]—still, some measure of vital progress had been achieved. In the context of public health care, women trained as professional nurses, not just midwives, serving to increase the longevity of infants, mothers, and the infirm.

Hospitals built separate women's wards to treat obstetrical cases. Women gained the opportunity to train in the latest techniques of nursing and midwifery and thus prepared the ground for the first class of female physicians. In addition, women paid attention to venereal disease, as well as to pregnancy and child rearing. To be sure, the mortality of women and children decreased somewhat in the early Pahlavi years, but the ever-expanding state also intruded further into the lives of citizens as a result of the maternalist discourse.

Caught in the crossfire, women informed this hygienic culture even as they vied for control of their sexuality and family life. In 1940, Dr. Morton concluded, "The health influence of women is a new movement. . . . Along with railways and factories will come wholesome baby foods, proper nursing bottles, plumbing, and bathing facilities, disinfectants, healthful clothing, and all the rest of the modern hygienic materials by which Iran may turn from the road of doom and keep going upward to new health and happiness."[105] Even if Morton's optimism seems somewhat misplaced, the attention paid to the female role in human reproduction brought new career possibilities for women.

In 1944, Dr. Iran A'lam, head of Tehran's maternity service, reflected on her career in an interview with a women's magazine. Daughter of the famed physician Dr. Amir A'lam, Dr. Iran A'lam had received her medical degree from France, specializing in women's health and gynecology. She returned to practice medicine and served women of varying social backgrounds. As she confessed, "The best pleasures for me are when I cure a patient and can alleviate her pains."[106] The professional achievements of Dr. Iran A'lam perhaps served as the best testimony to both the historic impact and the limitations of the politics of reproduction in Iran. Dr. A'lam did not shed her traditional identity as mother and wife despite having pursued a medical career. Instead, she maintained that "women's first responsibility is to managing her home and to taking care of her husband and children."[107] This statement may seem ironic given the groundbreaking accomplishments of Dr. A'lam. Her comment was an indication, however, that maternalist ideals remained deep-rooted even among the growing class of professional women. The entry of Iranian women into the professional workforce did not always impose upon them a choice, but rather offered them multiple identities as physicians and nurses, mothers and wives.

Picture of Iran A'lam. *'Alam-i Zanan.*

Originating amid somewhat justifiable fears about population decline, the hygiene movement that in its inception had provided liberating and humanistic ideals of extending human life and achieving human betterment became appropriated by statist and nationalist obsessions about population growth, fitness, and social control. As Iran grappled with its social welfare policies, maternalist ideology would alternately broaden or restrict women's choices in matters of marriage, maternity, and personal hygiene. Women emancipated themselves somewhat from the patriarchy of modern medicine and the hygiene movement by shaping the nation's social agenda. In Iran, as elsewhere, the impact of modern medicine remained revolutionary, and official discussions of health care reflected the newfound authority and legitimacy of contemporary physicians. Although women did not overturn medical patriarchy, they gave expression to their reproductive concerns, not just as breeders but at times as peers.

CHAPTER 6

cᴧɔ

Schooling Mothers

Patriotic Education and Women's "Renewal"

I n 1907, one writer labeled Iran's women "the most unfortunate
and the most miserable people of the world." Because many lacked
jobs, they became dependent on men for their economic livelihood.
Despite having to endure such hardships, "ignorant, unfair men"
refused to grant Iranian women any "rights of humanity" (*huquq-i
insaniyat*).[1] This provocative article, though fomenting little institutional change, was nonetheless a significant public recognition of the
inherent need to honor the rights of Iranian women in the evolving
political climate of early twentieth-century Iran. Prior to this, few
public utterances openly addressed the inferior position of Iranian
women or acknowledged their basic human rights, including their
right to an education.

Two years later, another Iranian journalist reiterated the sentiment, conceding that his countrywomen mattered less than "the
animals of other nations." Although granted various privileges
through Islamic law, or sharia', they lacked "human rights" (*huquq-i
bashari*).[2] For sure, Iranian women lacked many basic political and
social privileges. Much has been written about the failures of the
Iranian constitution of 1906 and its denial of suffrage to women.
Still, women pursued groundbreaking activities during those years.[3]
And to frame the story of Iranian women at the turn of the century

around this sour note would miss the historical progression of women's social activism, as well as the level of public engagement and debate that opened up some political venues, promoted public health, and presented enhanced educational opportunities for modern Iranian women.

Since the nineteenth century Iranian writers and policy makers had made education a priority, and in the coming decades Iran would invest significant capital to expand education and literacy.[4] In 1897, a Qajar courtier, Khan-i Khanan, composed a fascinating treatise that espoused institutional reform in various sectors of Iranian society, including its educational infrastructure. Khan-i Khanan argued for the education of women since mothers played a crucial role in the upbringing of children.[5] Endorsement of women's education became a talking point in the flourishing Persian press at the turn of the century.[6] In 1904, one writer submitted an editorial to the newspaper *Ittila'* in support of women's education. This anonymous essayist noted that some considered women "naturally deficient" (*naqis al-fitri*) and thus not in need of education. However, this writer asserted that women deserved to become literate in order to raise informed children. Educated women would pass on knowledge to their offspring, instead of corrupting them with superstitions.[7]

The constitutional revolution introduced a heightened phase of social activism as women founded clubs, societies, and schools. They raised funds for the "maintenance of one free school for orphans and one industrial school."[8] In 1910, volunteers who had organized a school for orphaned girls also made available clothes and supplies free of charge.[9] Notices appeared seeking female teachers qualified to teach the Qur'an, Farsi, and sewing.[10] In addition, the parliament made provisions for education and mandated that the government foot the bill for building schools.[11]

Women asserted their political will in other ways as well. When American financial advisors, led by W. Morgan Shuster, were expelled from the country as a result of Russian pressure, "bands of women went to tea houses and other shops and destroyed the Russian goods ... or to the mosques to deliver speeches, hoping to arouse the men to patriotic action."[12] Economic hardships and the lack of basic food items impelled Iranian women to go to the home "of Mr. Shuster demanding bread." Some Muslim women turned to Christian missionaries, who organized a "class in needlepoint, in which such poor women might be trained so they could at least earn their bread," although such classes were accompanied by "prayer and a gospel talk."[13]

What access did Muslim Iranian women have to educational facilities at the turn of the century? Missionary and other religious schools existed for various minority groups that also accepted Muslim girls.[14] During the constitutional period, numerous schools appeared around the country, but mostly in Tehran and often of limited duration, providing girls an elementary education in home economics and basic literacy.[15] However, the dearth of qualified teachers hampered efforts to bolster education. Even existing schools such as the Dar al-Funun and the Military Academy faced budgetary shortfalls and could not pay their teachers.[16] One bystander complained that, despite the talk about education, Iran lacked a teacher training college, illiteracy remained rampant, and many rural communities were deprived of educational opportunities.[17]

The impetus to educate Muslim women faced some controversy. A prominent Shi'i scholar, Shaykh Fazlallah Nuri, commented on the social changes spurred by the constitutional revolution and virtually equated the education of women with profligacy. The consumption of alcoholic beverages and "the propagation of brothels," he claimed, signaled the hazards of eroding Islam from public life. These perils included opening schools to educate women and girls.[18] Nuri was writing at a time when the country reeled from strife over differences about the role of Islam in Iran. Although the constitution declared Twelver Shi'ism the official religion of the country and eventually set quotas for the participation of non-Muslims in the parliament, conservative scholars such as Nuri wondered about the impact of secular legal innovations on the application of Islamic law.

Not all religious scholars shared Nuri's trepidation about female education. Mrs. Safiyah Yazdi, the wife of a leading mujtahid, Aqa Shaykh Muhammad Husayn Yazdi, in fact pioneered a school for girls called the 'Iffatiyah School. Interestingly, the Yazdis' daughter went on to study the modern sciences and their granddaughter earned a doctorate in medicine and practiced as a gynecologist. The 'Iffatiyah School eventually turned into a secondary school and included distinguished scholars among its faculty.[19] Another woman responded directly to Nuri's censure. In a long editorial, this unidentified author demanded from Nuri the exact passage in the Qur'an and hadith that prohibited women from acquiring knowledge.[20] Nuri, of course, could not pinpoint a Qur'anic passage that forbade women from reading and writing. But this was not the only issue. What mattered was the way in which women threatened the old order. A famous exchange between memoirist of the revolution Nazim al-Islam Kermani and Sayyid Muhammad Tabataba'i, a jurist at the forefront of the movement, reminded readers that some believed that women's seclusion needed to be secured before girls' schools could thrive in Iran.[21]

In 1909, Iran emerged from its civil war bruised but intact. Nuri was executed for his association with Muhammad Ali Shah, the monarch who had precipitated the civil war by refusing to acknowledge the authority of the newly constituted Majlis. Emboldened by their victory, patriots supporting constitutional rule wrote with heroism about the will of the Iranian nation. One essayist remarked that even women, "who are hiding behind their veils," would take their head and neck scarves and convert them to weapons to defend Iran.[22]

Over the next two years Majlis delegates passed reforms that promoted secular education for women. However, existing schools in Iran faced a shortage of funds and teachers. Public morality also remained a concern for some. Complaints from Najaf, Iraq, reached an editorial office in Iran that the civil war had not been fought in order to eradicate Islam from the country and to allow the sale of alcoholic beverages in the streets. Journalists and their newspapers, essayists warned, ought not to lose sight of their objectives by filling their pages with advertisements about the sale of pianos and alcoholic drinks.[23]

Formal female activity had its limits at the turn of the century, as women were denied voting privileges. In 1911, when Majlis delegates debated the women's suffrage bill before them, one deputy, Hajji Vakil al-Ru'aya, argued that women had the right to vote. Shaykh Asadollah, however, challenged Vakil al-Ru'aya by asserting that women had no such political prerogatives as the "weaker sex," since they lacked the capacity for judgment.[24] In 1911, women lost the suffrage battle, but this defeat did not stop them from voicing discontent about the social hardships in their lives. As the capital faced food shortages, five hundred women took to the streets of Tehran and demonstrated outside the home of the premier, Sipahdar. The police finally dispersed the women, "several being wounded, one possibly mortally."[25] This incident would not be the last time that an Iranian woman would give her life to stand steadfastly for her convictions. Many women activists pursued their political aspirations in other ways. This included another push for suffrage. In 1913, Iran was represented at the Congress of the International Woman Suffrage Alliance, although Iran remained unaffiliated with the alliance. Carrie Chapman Catt of New York, the international president, noted that Iran and some other countries lacked "an organized woman suffrage movement."[26] Although Iranian women failed to organize an effective suffrage movement until later in the century, they enhanced their educational and professional opportunities after World War I.

To avoid giving the impression that women would be led astray if educated, advocates of women's literacy centered female education on the notion of patriotic motherhood. As nationalism became state policy, particularly during the Pahlavi years, women's education endorsed patriotism as it inculcated the virtues of family life, marriage, and motherhood. The content of women's education reflected this emphasis.[27] Although the concept of patriotic motherhood politicized domesticity to fit state interests and priorities (and continues to do so under the Islamic Republic), it enabled Iranian women to regard themselves not just as participants in the domestic realm but also as contributors to the civic community.[28] Perhaps unintentionally, patriotic motherhood opened the door for women's education in fields outside of home economics and nurtured their political socialization.

In 1905, the newspaper *Hadid* articulated this new meaning of motherhood in its embrace of literacy for women. Women were the essential lifeline of humanity, it argued, and for this reason they needed to be educated. According to its editor, Aqa Sayyid Muhammad Shabistari, "Women are the basic elements of the social fabric of humanity. . . . Mothers, no matter how kind they may be, if they are ignorant, they are the enemies of humanity."[29] As Iranians grappled with disease control, they made hygienic education a mantra of patriotic motherhood. Infant life expectancy was reduced by smallpox, measles, scarlet fever, and other diseases, as well as the unsanitary medical practices of physicians and midwives, who were blamed for the crisis of infant mortality.[30] The high incidence of mortality threatened women and children and undermined the nation's ability to raise a community of dutiful compatriots.

Women were the true nurses and caretakers of a hygienic household, and thus a natural conduit for spreading the salutary and patriotic virtues of hygiene and humanism. It behooved them to become educated and learn the principles of hygiene: "Whenever the kind mothers know something about what a microbe is, the innocent children, who are the new generation of the homeland, will not fall prey to hard-to-cure illnesses or the arrow of death."[31] Practical considerations such as fear of the spread of disease in the household, as well as in the nation, made it necessary for women to receive a rudimentary education, especially hygienic education, even if they were discouraged from learning abstract subjects such as mathematics or philosophy in their formal training or social indoctrination. As Shabistari argued, "For women, logic and . . . jurisprudence are not necessary."[32] In practice, however, it became difficult to restrict women's education into narrow categories of learning.

If the struggles of the constitutional and Pahlavi years restricted women's ability to venture too far beyond the perimeters of home and family—and, when they did leave those confines, usually in ways sanctioned by the state—it also emboldened Iranian women to fight and seek respect for their position in society as educators, as participants in civil society, as standard-bearers of patriotism and modernity, and finally as mothers and wives. These enterprises helped extend the ideal of patriotic *motherhood* to that of patriotic *womanhood*. The modern Iranian woman would become not just a capable homemaker but also a laborer, an athlete, a teacher, a nurse, or a state employee.[33] This feminine ideal was a womanhood in tune with the nationalist discourse of the secular state, while alternative expressions of feminism, particularly those tied to Iran's rich religious culture, were somewhat muted. Still, the secular women's movement left a legacy of activism, institutional reform, and cultural ideology that has enriched the country's contemporary religious culture. Even if religious symbols disappeared from the official rhetoric of the women's movement, the emphasis on themes such as morality and chastity in the debate on physical and mental hygiene had religious undertones eventually picked up by traditionally minded activists.

In 1910, the first newspaper written by a woman for women began publication in Iran. Entitled *Danish*, meaning "knowledge," it primarily aimed to educate readers about their maternal role, focusing on child care and home management. That "knowledge" became this journal's mission spoke to the new status women had gained in the public sphere following the constitutional revolution. But it was a domestically focused knowledge imparted to Iranian women. A cursory look at the themes in *Danish* suggests that maternity, child care, and home management dominated discussion despite the political awareness that had resulted from the constitutional revolution. Though eschewing politics, *Danish* made literacy and formal schooling an objective for Iranian women, even calling them obligatory. To attract readership, the journal's editor, Dr. Kahhal, advised: "For women who cannot read, it is submitted that men read this journal to them every week, so they won't be deprived of its advantages; perhaps this will cause them to take up literacy."[34] The periodical endorsed female industriousness and the pursuit of work as a means to social betterment.[35]

Even newspapers that were not gender-specific contained features on women's schooling, although female education remained embedded in the domestic sphere or became linked to nationalist priorities. The weekly journal *Amuzgar* (Instructor) argued that educated women "became a source of comfort for boys." Citing a tradition attributed to the Prophet Muhammad, the writer averred that "stupid, ignorant women should not be in charge of nursing their children." While the acquisition of knowledge was in itself a noble aspiration, for women "what matters after receiving an elementary education is the learning of ethics and living [*'ilm-i akhlaq va zindigani*]."[36] Women's schooling needed to reflect these values and instill the requisite skills and virtues of matrimony and motherhood.

Women's education made sense since mothers bore the responsibility of educating sons. The writer, presumably a man, even argued that women's schooling promoted their modesty (*nijabat*) and moral decency.[37] Others promoted women's education as an end in itself, while keeping in mind the need to protect women against moral corruption. In 1911, the Society for the Advancement of Iran included in its charter a clause giving special attention "to educating women and to establishing special women's schools with teachers who have correct comportment [*mu'alimat-i sahih al-akhlaqi*]."[38] Although support for women's schooling became an ethos of Iranian feminism, some proponents circumscribed the nature of female learning. Yet the nature of the threat to men and to women's virtue sometimes remained vague and unspecified in male discourses on women's education. Education meant empowerment, but women needed to be empowered within the domestic sphere and with a larger goal in mind than mere self-indulgence.

In 1912, a second women's journal, *Shikufah* (Blossom), began publication in Tehran under the editorship of Maryam Muzayyin al-Saltanah, a woman committed to female education. Here, too, the domestic concerns of women in their roles as wives, mothers, and daughters were elaborated. She touched on topics such as pregnancy, marital relations, and especially patriotic motherhood—that is, mothers committed to the family who also identified with the ideals of the nation, whether in promoting national goods or in spreading the sentiment of love of homeland (*hubb-i vatan*).[39] *Shikufah* made patriotic motherhood both respectable and requisite for modern Iranian women. Maryam Muzayyin al-Saltanah encouraged women to pursue the virtues of education, hygiene, and cleanliness, making practical knowledge about the basics of "patriotic housewifery" the focus of her articles.[40] She also tried to set parameters on women's education to safeguard women's virtue. For instance, "a woman who in the street or the bazaar jokes with a foreign man and removes the veil between him and herself cannot be called a cultured and educated woman."[41]

The mere founding of these women's journals (notwithstanding their domestic emphasis) stood out as revolutionary.[42] While promoting education and literacy for women, these journals also forged a cult of domesticity, with the intent of lending a new import and gravitas to activities that had long been a part of women's lives. But who exactly was the patriotic mother? Both male and female journalists often cast patriotic mothers as attentive women who strove to understand and promote the essentials of hygiene and cleanliness within the domestic sphere, particularly where pregnancy and child rearing were concerned.[43]

Mothering was not just a simple inborn instinct. As the numerous references in *Shikufah* to children's hygiene, breast-feeding, and familial relations make clear, such duties required forethought, planning, and sometimes specialized knowledge. In addition, without patriotic motherhood societal progress would be limited. In a column entitled "The Services of Women to Society Are Not Less than Men's but Are Actually More," it was argued that children's first schooling took place on their mother's bosom, and that even the great philosophers and inventors were educated until the age of twelve by their mothers. Women thus provided the essential care and rudimentary training that enabled great thinkers to excel in mathematics, sciences, and other fields.[44] Finally, in discussing literacy, female industriousness, or equality, the journals helped to blur the boundaries of domesticity.

Male patriots, who also had family obligations, could "prove" their patriotism through self-sacrifice often in warfare and through official service to the state. In 1912, for instance, a textbook on civic studies, *Ta'limat-i Muduniyah*, to be used presumably in boys' schools, there was an interesting chapter on family and homeland (*khanahvadah va vatan*). It defined a person's duty to the homeland "as working toward its advancement" and not withholding life and property for its protection. A husband's responsibility to his wife consisted of treating her with kindness and providing for her comfort and happiness.[45] Men's civic obligations need not surpass their familial ones.

There is little information on existing schools for girls during World War I. In 1916, Samuel Jordan, credited with founding the Alborz Boys' College in Tehran, maintained that Tehran had approximately seventy schools for boys and about forty for girls. Jordan observed that despite the war, Iranians had not diminished their "deep enthusiasm . . . for education and their abiding faith in it as the only hope for the future."[46] Another report written during these years from the American Presbyterian mission in Urumiyah noted the "difficulties of organizing school work where girls are not expected to go to school."[47] Notwithstanding these obstacles, Sadiqah Dawlatabadi, daughter of the leading Shi'i jurist Shaykh Hadi Dawlatabadi, opened a school for girls in Isfahan called Umm al-Madaris (the Mother of Schools).[48] Iran also established its first state schools for girls in 1918.[49] In 1923, an announcement in a Persian newspaper advertised that the Franco-Persian School was accepting girls for the elementary and middle school years.[50]

Although Iranian women made education a focus of their activism after World War I, they continued pushing for suffrage. In 1919, the International Woman Suffrage Conference issued a resolution articulating its desire "that the franchise be granted to the women of all countries on the same basis as men; that married women shall not be deprived of their nationality without their consent, and that existing inequalities between men and women shall be removed."[51] The resolution sought equality in employment opportunities for women and men and parity in the "moral standard" of both sexes. Although this congress had no legal impact on the lives of women in Iran, its demands would later be echoed in resolutions adopted by the United Nations, an international organization that Iran would join and whose resolutions regarding women would be bitterly opposed by some religious groups in the country, including the Fedaiyan-i Islam.[52] In May 1926, an Iranian delegate attended the International Congress of the Woman Suffrage Alliance, held in Paris.[53]

Majlis delegates, however, dodged the issue of suffrage and instead took up the subject of women's education.[54] Some considered illiteracy an impediment to women's equality and social progress.[55] Others wondered whether the founding of schools would be sufficient to change attitudes and public ethics. As one writer speculated: "Will literacy teach patriotism . . . unfortunately one must emphatically answer 'No!' From reading a book no one can acquire wisdom and ethics."[56] Yet motherhood and motherly love could teach values that might prove impossible to inculcate through schooling and education alone: "Yes, in the word *mother*, in this meaningful word, the future of humanity is made. If the heart of a mother becomes devoid of this love, families will be ruined . . . and humanity will be sacrificed."[57] The content of women's education instilled maternalist themes such as child rearing and marriage, along with literacy.

These subjects predominated in the pages of the periodical press. In 1922, for instance, *Bahar* considered the position of women in the twentieth century. Reflecting on the advances of the "civilized" world, this piece bemoaned by contrast Iran's backwardness. Such discussions, of course, were not new among Iranian intellectuals, but at this time momentous political changes had taken place in Iran.[58] Just a year earlier, Reza Khan and Sayyid Zia al-Din Tabataba'i had orchestrated a coup that marked the eventual demise of the Qajar regime. Moreover, the country was recovering from the hardships of the First World War, which had hampered efforts to bolster public education for both women and men. This article maintained that Iran's troubles were rooted in the ignorance of its women, who in the past had been denied basic opportunities. However, the writer posited that "wherever women have shared in social responsibilities . . . order and stability have been evidenced in society."[59] Lauding the positive contributions of women historically, and in particular their success in overcoming prejudices encountered over their purportedly inferior abilities, this piece concluded optimistically with the statement that the twentieth century was the century of women (*qarn-i bistum qarn-i zan ast*).[60]

Women redoubled their literary output after the war, and new publications inculcated the virtues of patriotic motherhood. In 1921, Fakhr Afaq Parsa, editor of the newly founded journal *Jahan-i Zanan* (Women's World), argued for women's literacy since educated women could benefit from reading necessary literature on hygiene and household management (*khanah dari*). Without access to this written advice, girls had no choice but to gain knowledge of home economics from uneducated nannies, thus perpetuating a cycle of dysfunction in the home.[61] Afaq cited a saying attributed to the Prophet that the pursuit of knowledge was incumbent upon men and women. "Pursue knowledge," she quoted, "even if it takes you to China."[62] The schooling of women appeared less threatening to men and to the patriarchal status quo if situated in the familiar surrounding of the home. As Afaq contended, a man's duty was to work "outside the home," whereas a woman's role was "maintaining the home."[63] Yet during its short run her publication also carried features on housekeeping that went beyond teaching women about child care, including an essay on preventing fire hazards in the home.[64]

This journal provided a rough estimate of students attending schools in Tehran and Mashhad. Using statistics cited in another women's journal, *'Alam-i Nisvan*, Afaq reasoned that approximately twenty women out of a thousand in Tehran had access to an education in a population of approximately 500,000, while in Mashhad the number amounted to no more than three per thousand in a population of approximately 200,000.[65] Afaq went on to compare the dearth of educational facilities in the province of Khorasan with the neighboring country of Afghanistan, which had recently opened a school for girls in Kabul.[66]

The burgeoning women's movement, partly in conformity with the secular emphasis of the state, typically adopted non-religious symbols to convey its message of political activism and inclusion for women. In a schoolbook from the late Qajar era designed specifically for girls' schools Joan of Arc, by virtue of her patriotism, appeared a more appropriate paragon for modern Iranian girls than did Fatima.[67] Yet some women journalists such as Fakhr Afaq looked to Islamic history in search of exemplary women as they tried to promote modern virtues like education. The inaugural issue of her journal, *Jahan-i Zanan*, maintained that during the golden age of the *khilafat* women's social stature improved, and many learned women lived among the Arabs of the first Islamic century. She then went on to argue that during the Umayyid period "women's misfortune began."[68] Afaq Parsa was forced to shut down her paper after she published a scathing letter by a woman from Kerman who had criticized the slow pace of reform for women in Iran.[69] When this letter was printed, the 'ulama apparently objected to its contents, and Afaq's journal ceased publication.[70] Afaq did not end her career after this episode, however, and continued publishing her views in other women's magazines, including the one associated with the Patriotic Women's League.

Popular women's literature reinforced mothering as a modern profession for the expanding community of readers. In 1923, a magazine affiliated with the Patriotic Women's League of Iran began circulation under the editorship of Muhtaram Iskandari. Writing at a time when Iran faced political uncertainty, Iskandari, who headed the League, made the tutelage of women a focus of her patriotic activity by founding a school for the education of adult women.[71] The lead article in her magazine, *Majallah-i Nisvan-i Vatankhvah-i Iran*, dealt with women's education and stressed that "only the acquisition of knowledge brings progress for human beings and their children." Ethics or manners (*akhlaq*), Iskandari continued, came from the Arabic root *khalq*, meaning "creation," and so the study of ethics needed to focus on perfecting human beings and their nature.[72] In a subsequent essay, Iskandari contended that the only reason women in the East were regarded as "cognitively deficient" was because they had little access to education, a condition worsened by the inattention of Eastern men to this matter.[73] Women's education, however, had to embrace themes of moral and national import such as physical fitness, marriage, hygiene, and population growth in order to be relevant.

Modern educators stressed hygiene as a social necessity as well as a patriotic duty, and emphasized the need for women to maintain an active lifestyle.[74] Women took on the role of nurses, both literally and figuratively, in incorporating hygiene into the girls' curriculum. A schoolbook written for girls in 1923 reflects this point. Devoting approximately one-third of the text to the subject and to the practice of cleanliness (*nizafat*), the book included a section on caring for the sick (*mariz dari*), which it considered a "natural" function of women and a skill that necessitated women's familiarity with elementary medical principles.[75] In addition, the six-year course of study for girls in elementary school included a class each year on hygiene. In the fifth and sixth years, the class pursued a curriculum that included a detailed exploration of disease, cleanliness, and pollution.[76]

Writers for the league's magazine composed short pieces for women about hygiene and germ theory as well. Mothers, the journal argued, could celebrate medical advances such as the development of vaccinations that cured or lessened the side effects of childhood diseases such as diphtheria. In fact, mothers had an obligation to become informed about available drugs that physicians could administer to help sick children recover from potentially life-threatening illnesses.[77]

Muhtaram Iskandari's untimely death on 26 July 1924 (23 Dhul-hijja 1342 AH) at the age of twenty-nine was reported by a colleague, Nur al-Huda Manganah Nurani, as a tragedy for Iranian women. Despite suffering from chronic ailments, Iskandari had devoted herself to women's causes, including the establishment of an industrial school.[78] Another contemporary, Sadiqah Dawlatabadi, commemorated Iskandari by encouraging Iranian women to continue Iskandari's activism and to organize schools, conferences, and charitable associations for the needy and unemployed.[79] After Iskandari's death, Mastureh Afshar assumed editorship of the league's newspaper, and the league continued functioning until 1932.[80]

As Iran faced separatist impulses among its tribes, state-endorsed education stove to domesticate the homeland by scripting a homogenous ideology that instilled love of homeland (*hubb-i vatan*).[81] The authoritarian nature of patriotic education fit in well with maternalist objectives that emphasized social hierarchy through the family.[82] Some writers remained sanguine about women's advancement. Others perpetuated the cult of domesticity in arguing for women's secular education. In 1924, the Persian journal *Farangistan*, which was published in Berlin, printed a column on the education of women (*tarbiyat-i zan*). It stated that in Iran whenever women were mentioned, the image of a weak and mentally unsound creature appeared before one's eyes. In actuality, such a picture would elicit derision in Iran of the 1920s. While women were not necessarily incapacitated, they were, however, dissimilar from men. According to this writer, because men and women had different physical and emotional characteristics, they had to be educated in different ways. Women needed to concern themselves with the tasks of the home and seek professions that took into account their particular physical and emotional makeup. In Europe men became involved in "hard labor," such as working in mines, while women became writers, nurses, and the like.[83] Presumably, in Iran the division of labor needed to mimic these same lines.

In 1925, another journal, *Farhang*, reflected on the position of women in society, arguing that had school doors been open to women as they had been to men, the female population would have benefited equally from this access to education. It further stressed that the nation's progress and prosperity depended on the education of its women. However, the article pointed out that Iran's current schools, with their incomplete educational agendas and meager budgets, were inadequate for the critical task of intellectually nurturing youth. Instead, learned women had to participate vigorously in promoting female education through the establishment of associations.[84] Other steps that could be taken to improve women's status in society included the founding of journals geared to women, the publication and translation of books that highlighted women's past accomplishments, and the production of theatrical performances with instructive value.[85]

One of these women's magazines, *Payk-i Sa'adat-i Nisvan*, founded by Rawshanak Naw'dust in Gilan, made patriotic motherhood and education a frequent subject of discussion.[86] This journal, reflecting a socialist perspective, received assistance from the Iranian Cultural Society, which affiliated itself with Soviet politics.[87] Many of the themes and activities it took up, however, resembled those of women working outside a socialist framework. For instance, in its first issue it celebrated motherhood and the role of pregnant women as progenitors of society, as had earlier women's journals. As Naw'dust glowingly remarked, "What expression is prouder than that of a pregnant mother's?"[88] Pregnant women, she claimed, let it be known with their eyes that they were the ones who nurtured human populations. Unlike other contemporary writers, Naw'dust did not consider marriage a natural and preordained human act, but rather an artificial one.

Promoting some of her socialist beliefs, Naw'dust took up the cause of the working class and the rural women in the northern

Iranian province of Gilan who labored under difficult conditions in the rice fields. She urged "open-minded and active" women to pay attention to the needs of diligent rural women and to lead them to the path of education and enlightenment. Rural women "who live in darkness, away from education," earned so little from their labors that they might fall to prostitution if they were deprived of two days' worth of work, she warned.[89] Naw'dust contended that "the only steps taken for improving the situation of Iranian women have been pursued by enlightened women from the middle class," including teachers and students. By contrast, upper-class women concerned themselves with superficial and cosmetic improvements in the lives of Iranian women. She criticized women who were unaffiliated with various benevolent societies and who pursued "feminist" ideals individually. As Naw'dust explained, "Many individual women who are not connected with associations have 'feminist' beliefs and view the question of women's freedom . . . apart from national interests, while others . . . regard all men without exception as their enemies." This passage includes one of the earliest overt uses, if not the first, of the term *feminism* in a Persian newspaper. Feminism, Naw'dust believed, could not be practiced in social isolation or in exclusion from national interests. In her view, the Iranian women's movement was bound with the ideals of patriotic womanhood, despite her affinity for the working classes. As she wrote in the second issue of her journal: "Honorable women . . . if you raise patriotic children, know for certain that [you] have remedied all the hardships of Iran. If I were in your place, the first word that I would teach my child would be 'Iran.'"[90] Motherhood became entwined with patriotism.

In 1926, *Ittila'at* provided statistics for elementary schools throughout Iran. These figures showed the wide range of variation in the availability of schools to women. While Azerbaijan had several foreign schools for girls, Khuzistan was reported as having none.[91] That same year, a preliminary report prepared for the Rockefeller Foundation found that "the greater part of the population is illiterate. There are small schools in most of the villages where children are taught to read and write."[92] The same report maintained that the "latest available figures from the Ministry of Public Instruction show that in 1924 there were in the country 252 Government schools, 229 National schools, 108 Private schools, 87 Foreign schools, 240 Religious schools (Mosques), and 1,026 'Maktab' schools, or a total of 1,942 establishments. Of the above, 1,796 were for boys, and 146 for girls."[93] In other words, investment in education for boys was ten times greater than that for girls, at least based on the number of schools. In addition, the government schools "provide education to 73,534 boys, 17,485 girls and 4,979 students in religion."[94] Moreover, many buildings used as schools were ordinary houses that could not accommodate large numbers of students.[95] While there were eight secondary schools for boys, only one existed for girls. This disparity offers one explanation for the high rate of illiteracy among women. It also explains the ardent desire of activists to expand educational opportunities for women.

The culture of early education impeded the pursuit of knowledge beyond the elementary level since many Iranian children often quit school in order to join the workforce: "As a rule, the children do not remain long at school as they start to work at a very early age."[96] Adelaide Kibbe, a physician working in Mashhad, similarly noted the presence of children in the labor force: "Little children, and skillful workers they are, too, work all day long in a rug factory for not enough food, no school or sunshine or play."[97] Child labor existed not only in the carpet industry, but also in other urban and rural sectors. In addition, the architecture of schools was not designed expressly for educational purposes. Even in the capital itself, "schools are not buildings especially designed as schools. They are, for the most part, ordinary dwelling-houses which have been hired by the Ministry, as a rule, the rooms are not large enough for the number of pupils and there is over-crowding."[98]

What role, if any, did Islam have in women's education and the cultural feminism of the early twentieth century? Before the inauguration of the Pahlavi regime in 1926, two schoolbooks published for use in girls' schools made only oblique references to Islam, and schoolgirls conversing are depicted in chadors (full-body coverings).[99] Aside from these incidental references, the available schoolbooks for girls from the late Qajar and early Pahlavi eras did not discuss Islam in a meaningful way. However, the guidelines in 1924 for girls' elementary schools included courses on the Qur'an and on religion that taught the basics of prayer (*namaz*) and obedience to God and his Prophet.[100] Other regulations aimed to uphold the modesty of girls through proper attire by emphasizing that schoolgirls should wear dark colors (gray, black, brown, or navy) and long-sleeved shirts that did not open in the front.[101]

The Ministry of Culture reported that in 1918–19, 244 elementary and middle schools existed in Iran. More than 24,000 students were enrolled at these schools, with girls accounting for just over 1,800. Girls made up nearly 8 percent of all students enrolled in the country.[102] Although statistics on women's schooling are not uniformly available on an annual basis, in 1928, *Payk-i Sa'adat-i Nisvan* published an overview of the educational facilities for women in Iran's northern province of Gilan, noting that within five years, the number of women's schools had increased, as had the number of women attending those schools.[103] The formal—that is, state-endorsed—education of women in schools or other nationalist institutions would become critical to mobilizing a segment of the female population, quite often a privileged one. Educational indoctrination inculcated through the study of manners or ethics (*akhlaq*) as well as the pursuit of physical fitness would promote dynamism and vigor in the modern Iranian. Citizens healthy in mind and spirit could best serve the nation.

While the state could not entirely control people's habits at home, it could advocate certain values, including hygiene and sports, through its schools. In order for exercise to become more than just a passing fad, it had to be made a part of every Iranian's daily life. In other words, a culture of health, fitness, and athleticism had to be forged. One article created an antecedent for Iranians' purported penchant for sports by pointing out that sports historically had been a prominent feature of the great civilizations of the Greeks and the Romans, as well as the glorified society of pre-Islamic Iran. In those cultures, too, physical exercise was considered a "regular activity" in people's lives.[104] In 1925–26, the Iran Bethel School for girls, run by American Presbyterians, reported that physical education had become more common and comprehensive and that from "the sixth class up a hygiene text-book was used in connection with the gym classes."[105] The Bethel School's gradual appeal to upper-class Muslim Iranians families showed the ways in which the Western curriculum had infiltrated women's education.[106]

In 1927, a law passed making physical fitness a requirement in schools and introducing sports in the daily life of the Iranian youth. The law stipulated that physical exercise would become mandatory in all new schools and that except for holidays exercise would form a regular part of the school regimen.[107] A charter for the Pish Ahangi (Boy Scouts) of Iran was also established as a way of promoting "virtuous behavior" and to ingrain the culture of fitness and health throughout the country. It was followed by a Girl Scouts organization.[108] As Sa'id Nafisi, a well-known scholar and university professor, remarked in reflecting on the creation of the Boy Scouts and Girl Scouts and the establishment of athletic facilities in Iran: "The stronger, the more powerful, and the healthier the human body is, the more a person will advance in his work, and [thus] his mind will be healthier . . . and his aptitude greater for the acquisition of knowledge."[109] Nafisi regarded scouting as an effective way to promote physical and spiritual fitness in the interest of forging a more industrious and powerful citizenry.

Sport became intimately associated with Iran's youth culture of the 1930s, in which physical fitness was considered a by-product of a hygienic lifestyle. For women, too, exercise gained social significance, as can be seen in a program from the Society for Women (Kanun-i Banuvan) in 1935. The society operated an outdoor sports facility, where women could practice tennis, volleyball, and basketball.[110]

Schoolbooks mandated by the Education Department (Vizarat-i Ma'arif) played a part in defining the ideals of patriotic womanhood. Many of these texts circumscribed women's activity to the domestic sphere but then strove to make domesticity a patriotic commodity. The comportment of women, whether inside or outside the home, became a feature of modern education, and this behavioral emphasis in female education was carried out under the rubric of *akhlaq*, or manners. An analysis of the content of women's textbooks also reveals the trend toward secularism in women's education and the gradual effacement of Islam from women's textbooks.[111]

Descriptions of women's character often depicted ideal types—the "kind mother" or the "obedient daughter"—as recognizable paradigms. Women's nature predisposed them to "gentleness," "empathy," "honesty," and "sincerity," and a woman achieved happiness once she became "the queen of her husband's heart and the head of the household" (*malakah-i dil-i shawhar va ra'isah-i khanah*). Even manhood (*tukhm-i mardi*) depended on the influence of the woman within the family.[112] A harmonious family life depended on the proper comportment of both women and men. At times, men needed to be "brave, strong, warlike," while on other occasions they profited from being "humble, forgiving, and kind."[113] For men, too, gender roles and male ideals fluctuated and became rewritten as experiences of family life changed. Yet it was often difficult for both women and men to conform to these ideal types in their daily lives.

Badr al-Muluk Bamdad, a secular educator and social activist, composed two noteworthy textbooks used in girls' schools. In 1931, Bamdad published the second edition of a textbook on *akhlaq*, or manners, which conformed to the program of instruction of the Ministry of Education for the third year in women's middle schools. The topics discussed in 1931 complemented the teachings of the Qajar era.[114] It continued much of the emphasis placed on women's proper comportment in society, but reflections abounded on personal codes of conduct. In particular, rationality, bodily exercise, willpower, industriousness, and accountability for one's actions were lauded as salutary virtues. Bamdad also stressed cleanliness as the "best mode of avoiding illness."[115] As she explained, "Before all else we require bodily health. . . . What joy or fruits can a life that is lived in the cradle of misery and illness bring?" Mothers and housewives could make personal hygiene a part of their daily living skills, in addition to their children learning it at school.

Women who promoted disorderly behavior in the household (*bi nazmi*) were admonished, for "not until the little familial governments (*hukumat'ha-yi kuchak-i khanavadagi*) are in order will the state agencies become orderly."[116] In other words, orderliness and organization in administrative settings began in a well-regulated home and family. Women's domestic responsibilities still ranked high among their patriotic duties, particularly as women seemed predisposed by their "nature" to form a family. As Bamdad explained, "It is for this reason that the program of the girls' schools has been organized in such a way as to prepare them for managing the home. For reading and writing alone would produce people who would not be of use to the family or to the nation"[117] Still, Bamdad included a section called "Work" in her textbook, in which she stated that "choosing a profession is one of the most important matters of life," an indication that employment outside the home was gradually becoming more desirable for Iranian women.[118]

Sadiqah Dawlatabadi, a contemporary of Bamdad's, also endorsed women's work. Writing in 1932, she observed that Iranian women were benefiting from their newfound independence to work in stores and reap the rewards of their labors. She enjoined working women to pioneer other businesses and to expand the professional opportunities of women beyond the fields of education and government, where jobs remained limited. Women were suited not just to fields such as midwifery, teaching, medicine, and secretarial work, but could also launch stores and businesses. Sewing, too, offered self-sufficiency by giving women the skills to create useful and attractive outfits themselves, without having to rely on tailors. Economic self-sufficiency and financial independence became key messages of Iranian feminists.[119] Traditional female crafts such as weaving and knitting retained their appeal as skills fit for Iranian ladies. Such industriousness not only displayed the talents and self-sufficiency of the modern Iranian woman, but it also brought about economic profits through the increased sale of yarn.[120]

The field of journalism offered upper-class women additional opportunities to pursue social activism and to promote the cause of women. The government cited women's increased participation in journalism as a successful indicator of the women's movement.[121] In 1932, writer and activist Zandukht Shirazi founded a periodical entitled *Dukhtaran-i Iran* (The Daughters of Iran). In its pages, she expressed gratitude to those who were supporting her endeavor, connecting the life of the periodical not only with herself but with Iranian women and girls more generally.[122] But as one of the male writers of *Dukhtaran-i Iran* observed, female journalism appeared rather short-lived. While every now and then a few women would successfully launch a magazine, the periodical would instigate controversy and then be phased out. Isma'il Javid, the writer of this essay and an acquaintance of Kazemzadeh Iranshahr, who published an eponymous Persian journal in Germany, averred that the movement toward women's independence suffered from the absence of unity among women and the distance of women from one another.[123] By distance, he was presumably referring to their seclusion in the home. Women of the pen, on the other hand, could serve their cause by inviting other women to join in a "national unity of Iranian women" (*vahdat-i milli-yi zanan-i Iran*) through their prose and publications.

Although women had pioneered associations and even political groups prior to this time, the power of the word, as Javid observed, might broaden the scope of women's involvement and possibly lessen the pervasive presence of patriarchy. This subtle shift had already led to the expansion of cultural associations geared toward women across various Iranian cities and devolved the responsibility of empowerment to women themselves. But more could be done to involve women. The underlying theme of women's intellectual independence spoke to a somewhat understated element in the secular women's movement of the early Pahlavi era. Male intellectuals such as journalists, doctors, and policy makers had scripted much of the official discourse of the women's movement in the early Pahlavi era, whether it concerned reproductive politics, education, or unveiling. Ironically, as Javid himself noted, "the young girls of Iran must endeavor somewhat in their education and ethical growth to achieve a measure of independence of thought . . . and no longer need the approval of men."[124]

The Pahlavi state, however, often determined the aims of secular female education. Badr al-Muluk Bamdad, for instance, composed another textbook for use in women's schools, entitled *Home Management*, a text to be used primarily in high schools for women. In 1931, the book was already in its seventh printing. That an educated, patriotic woman—and not a man—had authored this work did little to change the philosophy of female education. In fact, the "science" of housekeeping and household management had only grown more refined. This continuity is not surprising given that state endorsement was necessary for the publication and dissemination of such schoolbooks.[125]

Citing the 'ulama, *Home Management* claimed that "it is only through creating orderly families that one can produce strong societies and ethnic groups." Housekeeping contributed positively to the creation of a vibrant national community and thus was considered "the prerequisite for the prosperity of the nation."[126] Because of its perceived role in forging an orderly, obedient family and society, home management was elevated to an academic discipline and "science," about which, like other sciences, "great scholars" had written voluminous tracts. Since the nineteenth century, Iranian intellectuals had heralded the virtues of science, and the elevation of housekeeping to a science increased the import and urgency of the subject in women's schools. By labeling housekeeping a science, Iranian schoolteachers and thinkers also seemed to suggest that the creation of an obedient, orderly society had a scientific formula intimately linked to the home and family. If such values could be enforced at the familial level, then the Iranian nation would finally become the orderly, harmonious society to which many patriots aspired. In an ideal household, women succeeded in curtailing strife and disobedience. Instead, they promoted the ideals of hierarchy and obedience, cleanliness and culture. These values could be uniformly inculcated through the educational system and its media of instruction: schoolbooks and mothers.

Anticipating criticism from certain quarters, *Home Management* acknowledged that in the past some women had managed to run their households effectively without school instruction. The text, however, justified the teaching of home management as an attempt to disseminate the experience of knowledgeable housewives to their unseasoned counterparts, since the mistakes of poor household management could not easily be undone.[127] *Home Management* covered subjects as diverse as child rearing and table manners, even including a picture that showed the proper arrangement of utensils on a dining room table.[128] Bamdad aimed to canonize housewifery and patriotic womanhood through such carefully scripted educational texts. Mothers' instruction would produce diligent, patriotic male citizens in the service of the homeland and deferential female companions in the service of patriotic men. Iranian women and society thus became domesticated through the educational system in an effort to secure patriarchy and patriotism.[129]

In 1936, Hajar Tarbiyat, a modernist educator, gave a speech before the Society for Women at which she unequivocally remarked: "The current conditions of today's world necessitate that women must be skillful, vigilant, learned and must know everything in addition to being able to succeed at administering their home and nurturing their child, which is one of their natural duties."[130] The expectations and demands of modern Iranian women had become more ambitious and comprehensive, in part because the aims and content of women's education had broadened considerably. Formal schooling and academic training, despite the rigid guidelines promulgated by the state, not only recast the culture of domesticity in modern Iran but also introduced additional venues of industry that complemented women's traditional responsibilities. While reinforcing the importance of their domestic roles, Iranian society allowed women eventually

to expand their roles through increased access to educational opportunities, changes in the curriculum, and professional involvement in
civic life. Women did not really break out of the cult of domesticity,
but they did venture beyond it. Women eventually founded a wide
array of associations and sociopolitical networks that would broaden
their involvement and decision making in civic matters.[131]

Patriarchy continued influencing the language and emphasis of the
women's movement, particularly among male writers and activists
who inspired and supported female literacy.[132] This trend persisted in
part because of the time-honored belief that women actually fared
well under patriarchy and that their material well-being depended
upon the men in their lives: their fathers, husbands, and sons. Early
Iranian feminists, however, broke the myth of benevolent patriarchy.
For this reason female activists such as Zandukht Shirazi, Rawshanak
Naw'dust, and Sadiqah Dawlatabadi lauded women's efforts to pursue careers outside the home, a concept reinforced in the curricula
of girls' schools.

By 1929 women at the high school level studied academic subjects
other than household management, such as mathematics, history,
geography, physics, and foreign languages, and prepared for becoming
instructors themselves. While the curriculum embraced domesticity,
it included instruction in many other fields, a process that gradually
prepared a growing number of women for assuming new occupa-
tions. In 1937, for instance, in girls' middle schools, the subjects of
household management (*tadbir-i manzil*), child care (*bachihdari*),
and sewing (*khayyati*) were only three among the seventeen classes
that women were required to take in a three-year course of study. In
total, more class time was allotted to the combined study of Persian,
history and geography, foreign language, mathematics, and science
than to stereotypically female courses such as sewing.[133] Here one
witnesses a gradual shift in the women's movement from the emphasis on patriotic *motherhood* to that of patriotic *womanhood*. Women
would no longer be judged exclusively through motherhood, but
rather through literacy, education, fitness, and professions outside
of homemaking.

By 1936, women also gained the possibility of pursuing higher
education at the University of Tehran, established in 1934, and twelve
female students became the first women to enroll there.[134] That same
year, the Ministry of Interior reported that 58,600 girls were enrolled

in elementary and traditional schools, and approximately 2,000 women were employed as teachers. Girls attending middle schools numbered over 3,400. Numerous women also attended industrial schools as well as institutes of fine arts and fashion.[135] Even if these figures are somewhat exaggerated, when analyzed along with other accounts, they suggest that educational opportunities for women had grown at an unprecedented pace during the interwar years. An analysis conducted by the daily newspaper *Ittila'at* showed that in 1922, only 180 girls attended a grade school, whereas by 1937, more than 3,000 girls had completed an elementary education.[136]

Not only had the number of schools for women increased, but the range of educational facilities had broadened as well. In January 1935, the British Legation in Iran acknowledged that "progress must be recorded" on the subject of education. As the counselor at the legation, V. A. L. Mallet, observed, "I was interested to see children from the black tent dwellers in the Lar Valley plodding several miles to school in another tent 'village' last summer. The standard is probably low enough, but the number of at least partial literates in the next generation will be several hundredfold that of the present adult literate population."[137] Rural communities would gain better access to education with the creation of the Literacy Corps (Sipah-i Danish) in 1963.[138]

In addition, charitable institutions emerged to nurture and school orphans. In 1938 the Arts School and Orphanage of Shahpur opened its doors. At the start the orphanage housed 130 girls and 70 boys. By 1959, the numbers had jumped to 200 girls and 120 boys. Funds for its operation came directly from a *waqf*, or Islamic charitable endowment, entrusted to the king. The children received training in the arts and had the opportunity to take a range of classes. Girls could enroll in classes for cooking, sewing, home economics, and music. They could also train to become a physician's assistant. Children received certificates for the completion of their training.[139] Charitable work not only fulfilled the social and religious obligations of royal patrons but also helped to win them public support and approbation.

The expansion of schools and the emphasis on public education extended to adults as well as children. In January 1939, based on a press report, the number of adults attending classes had increased to over 100,000, indicating that the courses "are steadily growing in popularity." Moreover, the adults came from diverse backgrounds and included "peasants, masons, labourers, bath attendants, butchers, chauffeurs, waiters," and the like.[140]

By 1942, Sadiqah Dawlatabadi, a tireless advocate of women's rights, had given the journal she first began editing in 1921 a specific mission—"to educate the mother" (*tarbiyat-i madar*).[141] While Dawlatabadi made motherhood a serious topic of discussion, she also carved a literary space within her journal for exploring differences of opinion about the women's movement. Dawlatabadi passionately defended the activities of the Society for Women against its detractors such as political activist Maryam Firuz, even as she recognized some of the limitations and cultural excesses of the Reza Shah era.[142] Patriotic motherhood perhaps unintentionally opened up other career vistas and political possibilities for Iranian women. Although the demands of domesticity persisted, many women succeeded in exploring a world outside of the home. If initially female education strove to mold efficient house managers and spouses, it eventually extended beyond those parameters to forge a literate and diversely skilled professional female citizenry.[143]

In 1944, Queen Fawzia, the shah's first wife, addressed Iranian women in a recently founded magazine, *Alam-i Zanan*. The queen maintained that women's most significant social responsibility was "raising upright children for the country."[144] Although echoing such clichés, the magazine went on to feature Iranian women who had moved far beyond their identities as mothers. The first issue included a biography of Dr. Shams al-Muluk Musahab, the first Iranian woman to earn her doctorate in Persian literature and a future senator. Musahab's academic career mirrored the shifts that had taken place in women's education. As a youngster, she had received her primary education at home from her mother. Eventually she attended various girls' schools and was invited to pursue her doctorate in Persian literature. An accomplished writer, Musahab served as principal of Parvin High School, supported by the state, and worked actively with the Women's Party (Hizb-i Zanan), established in 1943. Although committed to women's education, Dr. Musahab did not shirk her familial obligations in pursuit of her career. On the contrary, she considered her domestic life of primary concern, a virtue Musahab claimed to have inherited from her mother.[145] For Musahab, domesticity went hand in hand with literacy and education.

Picture of Dr. Shams al-Muluk Musahab. *'Alam-i Zanan.*

Women from different ends of the political spectrum worked to enhance educational opportunities for girls in Iran even as they embraced motherhood. While the subjects of female education and motherhood had widespread support, consensus could not easily be reached on the veil. Nowhere would women's unity and patriotism be tested more severely than in the state's decision to impose the unveiling of Iranian women. This controversy would cause a sharp divide among the different classes of Iranians.

CHAPTER 7

❦

Defrocking the Nation

Unveiling and the Politics of Dress

From travelogues to memoirs, historical literature teems with absorbing accounts of Islamic women and the veil. The harem and the practice of seclusion undoubtedly have something to do with this fascination. Veiling, dictated by law and tradition, consumes contemporary societies beyond the boundaries of Iran. This curiosity makes sense from a historian's vantage point since Iranian women have twice become subjected to contradictory legal injunctions on veiling, and no study of Iranian women would be considered complete without a mention of veiling.

In Iran, clothing became a barometer of politics. The controversy over dress—the decision to veil or not to veil, the choice to wear or eschew the tie—expressed more than just a personal preference. The choice of attire not only reflected consumer interests and popular tastes but also revealed political proclivities.[1] State intervention in fashion signaled an attempt to impose uniformity and control upon the individual. A citizen's outfit expressed either social conformity or political dissent.

Western visitors to Iran in the nineteenth century described Iranian society through descriptions of women's and men's attire. Tastes in attire exposed social mores and affected the public interactions of women and men. It is perhaps helpful to re-create—however imperfectly—the public appearance of Iranian women as gleaned from various travelogues and images. In 1807, a traveler to Iran, Edward Scott Waring, reported that Persian women typically did not "encumber themselves with many clothes. . . . A Peerahun and a pair of Zeer Jamus is the whole of the dress; the trowsers [*sic*] are made of thick velvet, and their shift either of muslin, silk, or gauze."[2] Waring reported that many Iranians he encountered were typically "too poor to be fashionable," though variations in the color of their robes denoted differences in class and employment. Merchants, for examples, did not wear "scarlet or crimson cloths." Although by some accounts silk clothing was prohibited, "they avoid this by mixing a very little cotton with them."[3] When Persian women left the home, they concealed their faces and covered their bodies with a "cloak, which descends from the head to their feet."[4] That Persian women concealed their faces and bodies fascinated male observers, some of whom dwelled on the inferior and benighted social codes mandated against women by Islam.[5] Persian society remained far from perfect in its treatment of women, but this inequity reflected not just local traditions but also a prevalent pattern of patriarchy in the nineteenth century.[6]

Clothing embodied local customs and represented social distinctions between rural and urban communities, as well as gender. Justin Perkins, an American missionary who spent eight years in northwestern Iran, commented on the meanings of headdress among the different classes of people in Azerbaijan. As Perkins explained, "The *Seyeds* are the reputed lineal descendants of the Prophet. . . . They are distinguished by a green or blue turban. Only the religious orders wear a turban. The other classes, from the king (except on state occasions) down to the beggar, wear the black conical cap."[7] Not only did clothing set the religious man apart from the layman, it also indicated social station. As another Western writer remarked in 1828, "The dress of women of lower class has a rather dismal effect: it is commonly of a very dark colour."[8] Even the foreign observer perceived differences in class and culture through dress.

Contacts with Europe influenced the sartorial taste of Iranians and reflected modern sensibilities, some of which were replicated in the shah's harem. In his memoirs, the courtier Abdollah Mostofi observed that women's "fashions were always set by the ladies of the court. It began with the princesses and on to the wives of the aristocracy and eventually everyone. That was how women began to shorten their dresses."[9] Mostowfi marked the year (1882–83) in which "the young fashionable ladies' dresses hiked from ankle-length to knee length," following the shah's return from his trip to Europe.[10] Another courtier, Dust Ali Khan, Muayyir al-Mamalik, noted that women of the harem set fashion norms for other Iranian ladies.[11] The shah's fascination with ballet costumes is also commented upon in a Western account by Eustache de Lorey, a member of the French Legation in Tehran. According to de Lorey, the shah "bought a quantity of ballet-girl costumes, and on his arrival in Teheran had all his harem dressed like operatic fairies."[12] The shah's fascination may appear frivolous, but it also revealed changing consumer tastes and a predilection for Western attire among certain classes of Iranian society.

Qajar reformers urged consumers to wear outfits made from locally produced fabrics. Although many Iranian domestic products could scarcely compete with Western goods on the international market in the nineteenth century, locally crafted shawls and carpets received the attention of Western consumers. Writing in 1840, Justin Perkins remarked: "It is surprising with what skill the Persians manufacture some articles, with the simplest utensils. I have seen shawls valued at a thousand dollars apiece, and carpets very far superior to those of Turkey."[13] Writers encouraged the use of locally produced clothing to promote Iranian industry and goods (*ravaj-i amti 'ah-i Iran*) and self-sufficiency particularly in an era when Iran began relying upon Europe in commerce and trade. One reformer, Malik al-Muvarrikhin, believed that Iran produced all the shawls, fur, and taffeta needed to clothe its inhabitants.[14] In 1903, the shah forbade the purchase of shawls from Kashmir for his royal wardrobe and instead supported the use of locally crafted shawls from Kerman.[15] Activists of the constitutional era expressed their patriotism by endorsing Iranian manufactured goods, though some advised a judicious policy that would not deprive Iran of necessary imports.[16] Female pioneers such as Muhtaram Iskandari organized conferences and gatherings to promote the use of Iranian-made goods among Iranian women and to dissuade women from buying foreign luxury items.[17]

Iranians expressed some of their ambivalence about change and modernity through the politics of dress. Qajar reformers remained at odds over the role of religion in Iran, an unresolved issue that precipitated a civil war in 1908. The victory of the constitutionalists a year later did not bring an end to these tensions, which replicated themselves in the politics of dress. In 1916, one observer had this to say about looks: "Beards, turbans, canes, and shaved heads in all places and in every instance do not result in piety and religiosity."[18] He then went on to make a similar observation about politics: "Ties and bow ties do not bring political understanding and diplomatic knowledge."[19] In short, appearances could be deceiving. The outward manifestation of virtue as embodied in turbans or beards did not necessarily induce pious behavior. Much to this observer's dismay, however, Iranian society was preoccupied with outward appearance.[20] To many, beards conveyed manliness and piety, bow ties a predilection for the Western, secular, and modern. For all its superficiality, outward appearance became a preoccupation for Iranians. As women and men became consumers of fashion, their changing taste in attire reflected the growing divide between secularism and religion. Veiling became part of this tug-of-war between the native and foreign, the traditional and modern.

In 1899, the Egyptian intellectual Qasim Amin published *The Liberation of Women*, in which among other matters he advocated changes in the veiling and seclusion of women. A partial translation of Amin's work appeared in Persian only a year later.[21] Like other Muslims in the Middle East, many Iranians grappled with the practice of veiling. In 1914, Maryam Muzayyin al-Saltanah made a vigorous argument touting the veil as a necessary barrier against moral depravity and degeneracy. In an essay entitled "The Philosophy of Veiling," she observed: "Everyone knows that unveiling causes the free interaction of men and women, and the ills resulting from this interaction . . . cannot be denied. As we can see, in Europe, where the veil has been removed and there is the free interaction of men and women, there is not a single family that has not encountered great problems."[22] She used religion, tradition, and even Firdawsi's poetry to make a case for the veil, lamenting that bit by bit this "old state law" (*qanun-i qadimah-i mamlikati*) was being eroded in Iran.[23] She had a point. The veil was becoming increasingly less popular among certain cadres of Iranians—a process that gained momentum in other Middle Eastern societies as well.[24]

Iranian men also engaged in this debate. In 1925, one gentleman asked: "What does hijab mean? It means hiding Muslim women in a black sack, which air and light can in no way penetrate." Aside from challenging religious injunctions in favor of the veil, this male writer volunteered nationalistic arguments against it: "Hijab kills the family, and since the family is the basis of nationalism and patriotism . . . we will be deprived of these blessings." And finally, this writer maintained that from an economic vantage point, "hijab causes poverty in the country. [For w]omen are deprived of all business." Such economic hardships, in turn increased the occurrence of prostitution.[25] These views, however, were not widespread. The question of women and veiling would instigate further debate, particularly since the decision to make unveiling a state policy was a novel concept.[26]

In 1927, a journal with an Islamic bent, *Dabistan*, argued against unveiling and enjoined women to uphold their Islamic and familial duties while pursuing education. Unveiling, regarded as an imitative Western custom, did not necessarily have to be an element of women's cultural enlightenment; rather, veiling could be reflective of women's purity and honor, even amidst the emergent modernist mores of the nation.[27]

After his coronation in 1926, Reza Shah and his coterie of reformers initiated several policies intended to transform the national culture. The question was no longer "Who is the Iranian?" but rather "Who is the *modern* Iranian?" This was not a question left to the ordinary citizen to answer. Rather than invent this persona from naught, the architects of Reza Shah's nationalist policies forged the modern Iranian through "renewal" (*tajaddud*)—that is, the remaking of every Iranian, whether man or woman. It is no surprise, then, that such a process required cosmetic changes, as well as intellectual indoctrination. In other words, the modern Iranian literally had to embody this message of renewal, a distinction that set apart the modernist debates of the Pahlavi era from those of the Qajar period. While Qajar thinkers had broached the theme of modernity, they had lacked the power to make it a state policy that concerned the private and public facets of the citizen's life.

Women with different political inclinations also voiced their opinions on veiling, though at times obliquely. Citing an interview with Queen Sorayya of the Afghan royal family, Rawshanak Naw'dust, editor of the women's journal *Payk-i Sa'adat-i Nisvan*, addressed the historical significance of the veil, arguing that it had become associated with seclusion through a gradual process. Naw'dust quoted the queen as asserting that in the early community of Islam women actively performed their social and religious obligations alongside men. Veiling, however, had posed an obstacle to women's education and advancement in the modern societies of the East.[28] Queen Sorayya described veiling as a "tribal custom slowly linked to religion." The veil was intended to bring about social decency and was not intended as a social threat or restriction.[29]

In March 1928, the Persian queen traveled to Qum to take part in the events marking the Persian New Year. Apparently, while in the mosque "she inadvertently exposed her face during the service." As a result, "she was severely admonished by the officiating mullah who proceeded to denounce the tendencies of modern Persian women to depart from the traditional customs of the Islamic faith." The crowd of people then protested against the queen.[30] Once word reached the shah about this spontaneous demonstration, he went to the mosque in Qum and "entered its portals without removing his boots." This act was considered sacrilegious and a breach of Islamic tradition, since shoes and boots were regarded as soiled objects that polluted the mosque. When he found the mullah who had reprimanded the queen, he administered "corporal punishment to him." As reported by American foreign service officer J. Rives Childs, the shah took this "occasion for striking most effectively at the prestige of the clergy . . . From that time on, throughout 1928, one reform after another, touching the vested interests and the prejudices of the mullahs, was introduced with scant regard for their susceptibilities."[31] The tensions between religious groups and the state intensified as a result of these targeted programs.[32]

In the summer of 1928, the government loosened restrictions and "made possible the admission of Moslem women to cinemas, restaurants and other public places, granted them the right to speak to men in the streets, to ride with men in carriages (with the top down), and, more important than all, authorized police protection for those Moslem women who might choose to appear unveiled in public."[33] The arrest of the popular religious scholar Sayyid Hasan Mudarris did little to assuage the disgruntlement of the 'ulama and only fueled their tacit disapproval of the shah and his policies.

In 1928, amidst this uncertainty, the government took a portentous step toward launching its renewal project by passing a law outlining the proper dress code for its male citizens. Although Islam does not dictate headgear for men, many Iranian men customarily wore hats in public. Iranian men were enjoined to wear "Pahlavi hats" (although the style of hat would later be remodeled), jackets, shirts, and pants. Moreover, the Pahlavi hats were not to contain any "distinguishing marks" or to be in "off-putting colors."[34] Religious scholars and students were exempted from this law if they could provide necessary documentation verifying their vocation. Those who did not abide by this directive faced punishment in the form of either fines or incarceration.[35]

The state, rather than the individual, decided what was modern and appropriate even in something as personal as someone's daily attire. While socially enforced dress codes expressing ethnic, social, professional, and gender status had existed previously, only under the Pahlavi state was dress nationally legislated and enforced. As in other arenas, European mores influenced modern Iranian sartorial choices. Such legislation, while defining the modern Iranian male citizen, suppressed individual choice. The individual became a medium for the implementation of social and cultural policy and could not assert himself or diverge from the norm through the use of conspicuous and suggestive signs, colors, or fashions, for such differentiation might breed subversion. Perhaps most important to the official nationalist project, other individual distinctions such as ethnicity or religion would also be effaced through uniform clothing, since at least in their outward appearance most Iranian men, regardless of geographic or linguistic ties, looked like they had something in common.[36]

In 1931, the shah decreed that employees of various ministries "put on homespun clothing." The government planned to purchase clothing for minor employees. This law amended an earlier measure passed by the Majlis in 1922. To meet the demand, "woolen mills are operated on rather a large scale at Ispahan while much woolen cloth is woven by hand looms at Yezd." To set an example, Reza Shah appeared "in a homespun uniform."[37] Although the legislation aimed to promote the local economy, it created unintended difficulties. An editorial in a Persian newspaper, *Kushesh*, found that the order "has given the profiteering craftsmen a chance to charge exorbitant prices for home-made commodities and clothes."[38] An inadequate supply of cloth and the dearth of textile factories made it difficult for government employees to fulfill this decree.

Women, too, had to be made modern, and in May 1935, the Society for Women (Kanun-i Banuvan) was founded to "renew" the

Iranian woman. One of Reza Shah's daughters, Shams Pahlavi, presided over the Society for Women in an honorary capacity, since, as exemplars of the state, the members of the royal family were to embody its message of renewal as well.[39] The modernized Iranian woman, who was charged to become both patriotic mother and skilled professional, would not project an image of progress if dressed in the traditionalist garb of the veil.

A government memorandum assessed the women's movement in Iran through the range of activities undertaken by the society during its first year of existence. These activities included the establishment of classes for illiterate women, encouragement of women in the pursuit of physical fitness and exercise, hygiene, the arts, and the hosting of public lectures.[40] The Society for Women offered other venues for the expression of patriotic womanhood, as endorsed by the nationalist program of the state. Patriotic women aspired not just to motherhood and basic literacy but also to physical exercise and charitable work.

In 1936, patriotic womanhood would be expressed through the removal of the veil. According to Badr al-Muluk Bamdad, one of the members of the Executive Committee of the Society for Women, "One of the center's main purposes was to promote abandonment of the veil. . . . The women who joined the center began to persuade their relatives one [by] one by one to drop the black shroud, and the lectures emboldened other ladies to do likewise."[41] Social pressure existed in certain circles that impelled some middle- and upper-class women to conform to the state's vision of patriotic womanhood.

Some outside observers remained concerned about the shah's plans to proceed with unveiling. William Hornibrook, appointed U.S. minister to Iran in 1933, reported on these social developments with a keen eye and, as it turned out, with justifiable worries about the systematic disempowerment of the religious classes in Iran. In several dispatches, Hornibrook expressed ambivalence about the shah's assault upon the religious classes. As he averred, "No innovation inaugurated during the reign of Reza Shah has caused the same feeling of unrest and uncertainty, or the same feeling of open resentment to the present regime as the proposal for the unveiling of Moslem women."[42] He went on to say "with certainty" that the 'ulama classes and "the great majority of Moslems are enraged" at the proposed change. Hornibrook compared the unveiling program with the replacement of the Pahlavi hat by another type of hat, noting that many Iranians of the upper and middle classes accepted these changes, whereas members of the lower classes were being intimidated into accepting them.[43]

Hughe Knatchbull-Hugessen, the British minister in Tehran, put it another way. "Articles of clothing," he averred, "have in recent years become more and more typical of political movements. In Europe the shirt is an essential item in many modern creeds. In Asia the hat has played a no less conspicuous part. . . . In Persia renaissance has equally had its hat, if not its head."[44] Writing in 1935, Knatchbull-Hugessen was referring to the replacement of the Pahlavi hat just days earlier. But the politics of dress was becoming an increasingly volatile discourse in Iran.

Mashhad, a religious city and the burial site of Imam Reza (the eighth Imam of Twelver Shi'ism), became the center of religious protests months before the decree for unveiling became law. Demonstrations at the Gawharshad Mosque in July 1935, which resulted in several deaths, illustrated the popular resistance to the unveiling issue.[45] The uprising had apparently been instigated by Shaykh Buhlul, a man with a history of disturbance and intrigue against the regime. It was believed that Buhlul "harangued his congregation into a frenzy" at the mosque.[46] British sources noted that Buhlul "ascended the 'Manbar' (pulpit) and proceeded to make an inflammatory address" in which he "roundly abused" the shah and his local supporters. Subsequently, people took to the streets and allegedly cried, "Hussain protect us from this Shah!"[47] During this interval Syrian, Egyptian, and Turkish newspapers reported a "plot to kill the Shah and overthrow the Government," reflecting popular discontentment with the regime's social policies.[48]

Some prophesied that the rioting marked the end of the Pahlavi dynasty since "the dome of the Shrine was damaged by the fire of the soldiers, who in order to terrify the insurgents, first fired into the air."[49] Regardless, opposition to "changing the hat and chaddur was sufficiently strong for people to lay down their lives rather than submit to the reforms."[50] Perhaps, the rioting hardened the shah, who planned on moving ahead with unveiling, undeterred by the public resistance to it. In October 1935, during a private gathering at Golestan Palace he made his intentions known.[51] Outside of Mashhad, the shah's social reforms met with little popularity. In Kermanshah, men and women "looked upon with great disfavour" his plans for unveiling.[52]

To complete the women's renewal project, Reza Shah decreed the mandatory unveiling of women in 1936. Although there was widespread resistance to the unveiling law, poets such as Mohammad Taqi Bahar, Malik al-Shu'ara, and Parvin I'tisami welcomed the change.[53] Yet clothing was at best a poor national adhesive. The dress code regulations for women of the Reza Shah regime would not only alienate the religious classes and many women accustomed to veiling, but they were also short-lived, as they ceased to be enforced after Reza Shah's 1941 abdication.[54] Furthermore, despite their limited success as national policy, they provided a blueprint for the Islamic Republic of Iran to enforce its unique dress codes for women and men decades later.

Historical assessments of unveiling in Iran suggest that Reza Shah may have gotten the idea to prohibit the veil from Ataturk. This argument has even been put forth by one of the archival centers of the Islamic Republic of Iran, which several years ago published a collection of documents concerning the decision to ban the veil. As stated in the introduction to that volume, Reza Shah's "trip to Turkey nurtured this inclination [to remove the veil]."[55] The reference here is to a historic trip that Reza Shah made to Turkey in June 1934—a journey that lasted several weeks.[56] However, documents from the Iranian Ministry of Foreign Affairs do not support such a theory. In an official report chronicling the specifics of this trip, there is little to suggest that Reza Shah was emboldened to push for the mandatory unveiling of women because of Ataturk's policies. According to this report, in meetings between Ataturk and Reza Shah frontier disputes were resolved, and the desire to form what became the Sa'd Abad Pact (1937) was broached. There is no mention of social policies or discussions that may have influenced Reza Shah to go ahead with the decision to ban the veil.[57] That said, it cannot be denied that Reza Shah admired Ataturk's modernizing policies. In a note thanking Ataturk for his hospitality, he remarked: "It was with complete pleasure that I witnessed the enormous progress of the nation of my friendly neighbor, which was accomplished with complete speed in a short period of time under the patriotic guidance of its august leader."[58] This admiration, however, did not necessarily mean that Ataturk encouraged Reza Shah to proceed with outlawing the veil, particularly since Iran, *not* Turkey, was the first country to impose such legislation.

On 7 January 1936, when the unveiling decree was officially promulgated, there was much public celebration in official circles. In an
upbeat speech before female instructors in Tehran, the shah affirmed:
"You women must regard this day as a big day and use the opportunities that you have for advancing the country. . . . My sisters and
daughters, now that you have entered society . . . know that your duty
is to work for your homeland."[59] Patriotic womanhood would thus
become inextricably linked to the state's policy of unveiling. Patriotic
women also had an obligation to participate in the workforce, even if
they could not easily enter certain professions. Although their domestic roles as mothers and nurturers of the next generation of Iranian
patriots persisted, it was now accompanied by other explicit patriotic
responsibilities.

Various official memoranda highlighted the public's positive
reaction to this law. A formal report written ten days after the unveiling decree stated that the women's movement and the removal of the
veil "was greeted quickly with complete eagerness by the general
population of the country . . . whether by official authorities, ministries, or private individuals, celebrations and festivities are taking
place everyday across the country."[60] Official celebrations and functions enabled the wives of government personnel to appear in public
unveiled and thus show support for this change not only as patriotic
women but also as law-abiding citizens.[61]

Nearly a week after the pronouncement of unveiling in January
1936, the British minister in Tehran, Hughe Knatchbull-Hugessen,
wrote, "[After] Meshed, the pace was deliberately slowed down. . . .
There will certainly be underground hostility on the part of the elder
generation and the strongly religious element." This prediction turned
out to be accurate.[62] Less than a month after the circulation of the
decree, another British report found that in the provinces the government exerted pressure to force the unveiling of women publicly:

At Hamadan, for instance, droshky drivers and crossing sweepers have been compelled
by the police to parade their womenfolk unveiled. At Shiraz, Sultan Rakhshani, the
Rais-i Malieh and a capable official, has been suspended because his wife attended,
wearing the chaddar, an official reception given for the Minister of Finance. At Kerman,
the Governor-General is said to be showing tact and patience in the face of general
ill-will roused by the campaign, and from Bushire passive resistance is reported to what
is regarded as a sacrilegious change.[63]

Enforcement of the law became difficult, but the state devised creative methods to put the unveiling decree into effect. The police identified particular streets "to be out of bounds to veiled women." Service providers such as "cab drivers, restaurant proprietors, bath keepers, and even chemists" were barred from serving "women who wear the veil."[64] The public hardly embraced this quintessential symbol of the women's renewal movement. Even some state officials sympathized with the resistance, although they lacked the authority to modify social policy. In Tabriz, the government specifically targeted members of the 'ulama to attend a state function with their wives, unveiled, by sending out "written invitations marked 'compulsory.'"[65] Attempts to enlist the participation of the 'ulama, albeit coercively, in the realization of the unveiling project underscored the state's recognition of the need to win religious support for its social policies.

Some members of the religious classes opted for arrest rather than succumbing to state pressure. In Khoi, for instance, "it is rumoured that a seyyid [a person claiming descent from the Prophet Muhammad] prominent . . . in resisting the orders to unveil, was arrested, shaved and sent home wearing a European hat, and that he was found dead in bed on the following morning."[66] The 'ulama especially rejected the dramatic shift in cultural practices forcibly brought on by the unveiling decree, lamenting "the rape of Islamic tradition"; the state's inability to acknowledge a place for Islam, even a limited one, in its cultural policies only polarized the opposition, led principally by the 'ulama. The erosion of Islam from public life would be further evidenced three years later when the king apparently "set up a special commission of experts to investigate the possibility of distilling alcohol from the surplus rice crops of Mazanderan and Gilan."[67]

Later in 1936, the religious mourning rituals of 'Ashura, commemorating the death of the Prophet Muhammad's grandson and the third Shi'i imam, Husayn ibn 'Ali, tested the regime's unveiling policy. Anticipating dissent, the municipal police had taken "appropriate precautions" to defuse antigovernment protests, according to one report in Isfahan. Women wearing veils were banned from entering *rowzeh khanis*, or public mourning events. In addition, preachers were expected to recite their sermons calmly, to avoid inciting the public. The same report indicated that veiled women were no longer spotted on the main avenues. It was anticipated that after the municipal authorities distributed appropriate clothing to the destitute, veiled women would no longer be frequenting the side streets and alleyways, either.[68] Despite the regime's regulatory mechanisms, many women found a way to defy its norms of modernity and patriotic womanhood. The remaking of Iranian women— or *tajaddud-i nisvan*, as the state preferred to call it—and the recasting of patriotic womanhood would not come about without significant resistance and dissent. In 1938, for instance, one provincial document indicated that "in the division of women's renewal, in the past year much significant progress has been made," pointing out further that "every day in each area the municipal authorities and security forces fiercely struggle and overcome the negative actions of the 'worshipers of the old' [*kuhnih parastan*]."[69] This report indicated that despite top-down measures to enforce the legislation, two years later the state faced serious resistance against the law from various quarters.

In Damavand, more than a year after the promulgation of the unveiling decree, an official testified that "four women with chadors had come outside in the evening." The head of the local security forces had confronted them and subsequently confiscated and burned their chadors. At a public celebration in Reza'iyah all the women except for the wives of three officials appeared with long white headgear. The telegram reporting the event stated that because of the lack of enthusiasm of the people in charge, the "renewal of women" (*tajaddud-i nisvan*) had not progressed in this area.[70] Notices from other regions of the country, such as Kashan, Khorasan, and Kerman, mentioned the use of headgear by urban and rural women.[71]

Regional informational sessions were set up to educate women on the proper modes of dress and behavior. A report from Damavand in 1937 indicated that in a girls' elementary school, local women and men were invited to attend a gathering at which "the necessary points regarding the acquisition of attire and social interactions" was conveyed, and "two pictures were taken of those who were present."[72] Careful records such of photographs were kept of those openly participating in the women's renewal movement, as the state strove to recognize individuals who supported its programs. According to an Interior Ministry report from Isfahan in 1937, progress was being made in terms of feminine fashions, particularly given that "the inhabitants of Isfahan had been drowning in the sea of superstition" prior to that time. This same source indicated that young female students and other young women in general upheld their duties to the renewal movement (*vaza'if-i tajaddud khahi*), but that "older women do not leave their homes" so that they would not appear unveiled in public. Moreover, the official making this statement noted that in the countryside, "where from the beginning there was no veil," the situation has stayed the same.[73] Given the impact of religious tradition and generational preferences, the unveiling of women necessitated a gradual and carefully orchestrated agenda for its execution. Older women were disinclined to participate willingly in the unveiling project, whereas younger women seemed more malleable.

The state planned public celebrations on the second anniversary of the unveiling decree to mark the occasion. The day's festivities included athletic presentations at the Amjadiyih Arena, which served to link the newly fashionable culture of physical fitness with the women's cause. The Society for Women invited various dignitaries to an "elegant" gathering. Representatives of the Society for Women remarked that in addition to encouraging physical fitness, its membership had reached out to destitute women by providing them access to educational and medical facilities. Finally, a play in three acts, appropriately titled *Why Won't You Get a Wife?* (*Chira Zan Nemigirid?*), was performed, no doubt to encourage familial relations and to promote marriage among Iranian youth, reflecting nationalists' desire to increase the country's population and to reduce the social ills of venereal disease.[74] Poor women faced additional hardships in trying to comply with the new regulations of dress. The cost of living steadily increased, and the "disappearance of the chaddur and the obligation to wear European dress hats" placed financial burdens on Iranian families.[75]

Attire was only one facet of the regime's "renewal" project. The citizen's body itself became a corner of nationalist topography, stirring debate and spurring the rise of supporting institutions. Bodily "renewal" of the modern Iranian would be incomplete without a concomitant transformation of the citizen's mind. Intellectual indoctrination occurred in schools through the publication of carefully crafted texts, and an institution was formed expressly for this purpose toward the end of Reza Shah's reign. On January 2, 1939, almost three years after the promulgation of the unveiling law, the Organization for the Cultivation of Thought (Sazman-i Parvarish-i Afkar) was created to herald the virtues of the women's renewal movement, among other goals. As stated in its bylaws, the Organization for the Cultivation of Thought would sponsor regular lectures on approved topics.[76] These talks included, but were not limited to, women's issues. Fairly careful records were kept regarding the number of speeches held in various parts of the country, as well as the number of attendees. Between 1939 and 1940, there were numerous well-attended gatherings.[77]

The themes addressed at these sessions concerned the importance of forming a family, child care, household management, and women's duties in society—clearly topics intended primarily for the modern patriotic woman—as well as less gender-specific events on national unity, the necessity of sports, and industriousness.[78] The archetypal modern Iranian woman, though unveiled, could escape neither the cult of domesticity nor the burdens of patriotic womanhood. Despite the institutional measures that had been taken to educate women about their rights and their role in the regime's "renewal" or modernity movement, social limitations and politics undermined women's control over their lives.

The founding of girls' schools and the expansion of women's curricula offered new possibilities of learning and professional development for certain women, especially urban and upper-class women. It did so not by obliterating the traditional markers of female identity as mother and wife but rather by fully embracing them. Women's education developed within the context of patriarchy to support the modernizing objectives of the men in politics who were crafting their vision of the nation. Nowhere does this distinction appear as pointedly as in the decision to force the unveiling of Iranian women. Barely giving lip service to Islam, the state introduced multiple cultural reforms intended to ingrain secularism. For many, the unveiling decree contradicted the message of virtue and morality implicit in discussions of ethics and the "proper" Iranian wife, who, despite the propaganda of the renewal movement, was still subjected to Islamic tradition in her private and public comportment.

The 'ulama took up the cause of women and veiling after Reza Shah was ousted from Iran with the encouragement of the Allied powers. In 1944, under the leadership of Grand Ayatollah Tabataba'i Qumi (d. 1947), religious groups pressed for giving women the right to wear the veil without penalty, and the government acceded to this demand.[79] The unveiling decree had created widespread malaise not only among the religious classes but even among some secular women. Its impact was assessed that same year by Nayyir Saʻidi who would eventually go on to serve as a delegate for the Nuvin Party in the twenty-second Majlis.[80] She had witnessed a revealing incident on Istanbul Avenue in Tehran involving some foreign soldiers. Apparently in jest, the officers had barred a woman wearing a chador from crossing the street. The veiled woman, exasperated, finally removed her chador and, although exposing an unkempt appearance, managed to cross. Just then, another woman, unveiled and dressed in a neat outfit, appeared, and the soldiers graciously let her through without incident. As Saʻidi commented: "Yes, dear ladies! The importance of the seventeenth of Dey—the festival of our freedom—lies not only in the fact that outfits changed, but also that women's characters and spirits became transformed. Women freed themselves from slavery [*bardegi*] and considered themselves worthy of serving their nation. . . . Unfortunately, some women have not understood the meaning of freedom and have confused freedom with taking off veils and donning feathered hats. . . . These are not the women of whom we are proud. . . . Those women are ones who are devoted mothers, thoughtful spouses, and productive members of society; they exercise, read books, participate in charitable activities, and raise capable children."[81] Feminists such as Nayyir Saʻidi subscribed to the ideal types that they imparted to other Iranian women. Whether women's freedom to participate fully in Iranian society ought to have been linked expressly with unveiling remains an unresolved matter. The legacy of this radical reform elicited contradictory opinions even after the state agreed to relax enforcement of unveiling.[82]

What impact did the ideology of "renewal" have on women and the politics of gender in Iran? The reforms of the Reza Shah era undoubtedly left an imprint on Iranian women and society. By 1941, when Reza Shah was forced out of office, the appearance of Iranian women in the media and in state-sponsored events looked markedly different. From hairstyle to attire, the Iranian woman looked more Western and less like her counterparts at the turn of the century. Women and men interacted regularly in public arenas. Women could take pleasure in lavishing attention on their looks within acceptable social norms. Boys and girls could occupy certain public spaces together, even

17th of Dey Picture. *Banu.*

though the mixing of sexes did not always produce salutary results. In 1944, Nayyir Sa'idi reported that many girls had stopped attending the School for Beaux Arts (Hunaristan-i Ziba), established in 1932, when it became coeducational after the unveiling decree.[83]

Many women felt alienated by such reforms and opted not to participate in the renewal movement. Writing in 1953, more than a decade after the deposition of Reza Shah, Najmeh Najafi remarked, "Some new rich who have taken on Western ways very rapidly allow their women to meet in public places and to drink tea and other things, to play cards, to shop in the Westernized stores. But in the old conservative families men will not allow their wives and daughters such liberties."[84] The battle between tradition and modernity continued.

Perhaps the most enduring legacy of the renewal movement was not its emphasis on women's secular education and health but rather its expansion of choices for modern Iranian women. Women's capacity to imagine new roles for themselves eventually enabled them to stride into untrodden public spaces and to discover identities beyond their reproductive selves.

PART THREE

Politics and Reproduction

CHAPTER 8

ᴄᴠᴐ

From Mothers to Voters

Suffrage, Literacy, and Family Dynamics

While the women's renewal movement had broadened educational access for women, it did not grapple with the weighty issue of women's political emancipation. Women's enfranchisement gained support after the fall of Reza Shah. After 1941, as the number of educated Iranian women grew, so did their campaign for political parity. Feminism, as opposed to maternalism, became a rallying point for women activists. The exigencies of the war years ushered in poverty and famine, intensifying public frustration. In 1942, thousands of Iranians, "including women and children have been demonstrating all day in front of Majlis crying, 'You may kill us but we must have bread."[1] Food shortages exacerbated public malaise about the country's taxing economic conditions. Iranians also confronted the experience of foreign occupation as a result of the Allied invasion. These tensions spilled into the realm of gender relations. Iranian officials could not handle the misconduct of occupying American troops even when the rights, lives, and dignity of Iranian women were at stake. This emasculation of Iranian men was reflected in their lack of control over Iranian women, an imbalance in power that generated unease.

In 1943, Louis Dreyfus, the American minister in Iran, expressed concern about the inappropriate behavior of some American soldiers, emphasizing that the "question of misconduct and drunkenness is becoming increasingly serious."[2] Qazvin residents complained about "the drunken conduct of American troops which involve accosting women, entering houses," and the like.[3] Although Dreyfus acknowledged that the low morale of the American troops likely contributed to their poor conduct—given that they had been assigned "a dull task under difficult conditions"—he remained concerned about "reports from all sides of drunkenness, disorderly conduct and molestation of women by American officers and men."[4] These telling episodes point to social tensions resulting from the stress of wartime occupation, anxieties that also expressed themselves in the context of gender.[5]

Men could, however, exert some control over family life through the medium of print. It is partly within this context that the writings of historian Ahmad Kasravi should be assessed. The dislocating effects of women's participation in the workforce, as well as the mixed reactions to the state's platform of "women's renewal" (*tajaddud-i nisvan*), contributed to a need to reassess the multiple aims of the Iranian women's movement, which never fully dissociated women from their maternalist responsibilities.

In 1944 Kasravi published *Khvaharan va Dukhtaran-i Ma* (Our Sisters and Daughters), his one and only monograph on women.[6] Kasravi's views on motherhood and women's education reflected the impact of maternalism but also its limitations in granting women equality in Iranian society. From the outset, Kasravi criticized those participants in the women's movement who divorced women's issues from men's concerns. In his view women and men performed different, complementary roles, and depended upon each other in partnership. While articulating differences between the two genders, he reinforced women's primacy in the domestic sphere. Women could participate as bystanders in politics, but becoming delegates and judges "is not their job."[7] Maternalism as a social ideology could effectively be marshaled against women's participation in male-dominated spheres of power such as politics and business.

As Kasravi opined, women reserved the unequivocal right (*haqq-i bi chun va chira*) to have husbands and children—a right that he claimed had been "trampled upon" (*paymal migardad*). Men who reached the age of marriage but refused to wed were in effect trampling upon the rights of women. In fact, he stated that marriage should be mandatory (*ijbari bashad*). Another social inequity he acknowledged was that when women and men engaged in untoward courtship, only women earned a bad reputation. Kasravi believed that both parties needed to be held equally responsible. He particularly criticized the law of temporary marriage and divorce, which satisfied men's desires but offered little security to women.

Kasravi staunchly opposed women's active participation in politics as ministers, parliamentarians, and the like. He maintained that Iranian women remained best suited to domesticity and child care, a responsibility he considered no less significant than politics. As Kasravi explained: "Military service and warring are not the work of girls and women. Women were not created for these tasks, nor will they be able to shine in these fields."[8] Nature had similarly endowed men with distinct societal responsibilities. If men devoted themselves to housework and child rearing, their deficits would become clear.[9] Kasravi considered the social roles of women and men to be complementary but distinct. Kasravi's reflections on stereotypical gender roles echoed the opinions of other intellectuals of his generation who had shaped educational content and health care policies affecting women. His emphasis on stereotypical gender roles stemmed from a fear of social deviance. What might actually happen to the Iranian nation and family if men became homemakers and women served in the army? To maternalists, such social upheaval seemed unimaginable, and their ideology was intended to prevent social subversion. While Kasravi's views did not produce legal precedents or translate automatically into public policy, it is telling that the fields that witnessed a marked growth in women's participation included public health and education.[10]

At least one of Kasravi's contemporaries, Fatimah Sayyah, took issue with his views on women.[11] In particular, she denied that reproduction and child rearing were obstacles to women's political participation. As she maintained, "Women's political participation will not harm their natural responsibilities and will not have any harmful effects on the next generation."[12] Sayyah affirmed that in countries where women had gained political parity there had been no evidence of depopulation. Her arguments, however, did not sway many opponents of women's enfranchisement.

Kasravi composed this work at a critical moment in Iranian history. His views would not only elicit rebuke from feminists such as Sayyah but eventually bring about his assassination by an Islamic radical in 1946. Five years earlier, a young and inexperienced monarch—only twenty-one years old—had ascended the throne, a transition that energized the press and electorate. Political parties mushroomed, with the leftist Tudeh Party garnering unrivaled populist support.[13] The impact of maternalism became reflected in the platform of political parties that appeared during this time. One group, Hizb-i Iran-i Naw (New Iran Party), included in its charter the following points: the mandatory education and behavioral training of Iranian women, provisions for public sanitation in an attempt to increase the population, mandatory participation in athletics, and battling substance abuse. Regarding family life, Hizb-i Iran-i Naw even waged war on celibacy by stipulating the need to create families, as well as to protect existing families, in order to combat prostitution and to promote population growth.[14] The charter of the Democratic Faction (Fraksiyon-i Dimukrat), a group founded after the Second World War, included articles supporting population increase, employment for the able-bodied, and the creation of institutions serving the disabled and the poor. It also declared a campaign against opium cultivation and use.[15]

The question of women's suffrage, which had been effectively quashed after the constitutional era, reemerged as a topic for political debate. In 1943, the Tudeh organized a women's branch called Tashkilat-i Zanan-i Iran, and later that year existing women's groups came together to form the Women's Party.[16] In 1944, a Tudeh member pushed for women's suffrage, but the effort foundered.[17] A year later, parliamentary debates concerning the revision of election laws invited discussion of women's voting rights. As the women's suffrage movement witnessed another burst of activity, women managed to express their political opinions in flourishing women's journals.[18] In 1944 the women's magazine *Banu*, edited by Nayyir Saidi, published a timeline of the international suffrage movement marking the dates when women achieved voting rights. The entry for Iran noted, however, that "this story should wait for another time."[19] In a subsequent issue, *Banu* reported that Dr. Fatimah Sayyah and Hajar Tarbiyat, founding members of the Women's Party, had taken a trip to Turkey to forge ties with activist women there. Another women's journal, *Alam-i Zanan*, managed by the British embassy, also published an interview with Sayyah and Tarbiyat on the subject of this trip.[20] Sayyah summarized the legal milestones that Turkish women had reached, including the right to vote in municipal and parliamentary elections, as well as equal rights in marriage and divorce. This legal equality, Sayyah believed, made social progress possible for Turkish women. By contrast, Sayyah noted that in Iran the parliament refused to draft equitable legislation for marriage and divorce. To make matters worse, Sayyah contended, the state had allowed women to wear the chador again, making no effort to restrict the activities of those opposed to the women's movement: "They tell us that women's duties are motherhood and child care, duties that have nothing to do with rights and emancipation."[21] Sayyah's public disavowal of maternalist ideology showed the ways in which motherhood was being used to deny women equal political participation and access in Iranian society. Nowhere did the distinction between maternalist and feminist ideologies diverge as conspicuously as they did on the subjects of suffrage and emancipation.

For feminists, the battle for suffrage waged on. Sayyah, the first female professor at the University of Tehran, countered the arguments of another writer, Hasan Naziyah, in which Naziyah had contended that "from a psychological perspective, women have no talent for obtaining political positions."[22] Sayyah gave as her evidence the effective political rule of sovereigns such as Queen Victoria and Catherine the Great (though, ironically, she excluded sovereigns of ancient Iran such as Purandokht and Azarmidokht). She further asserted that contemporary Iran had not yet entrusted women with political responsibilities and therefore had not tested their political acumen. Conclusions about women's political ineptitude were spurious at best.[23]

Sayyah stood out from among her contemporaries in terms of both her education and her intellectual acumen. Labeled a "genius" (*nabighah*), Sayyah began working in the Cultural Ministry in 1935, and a year later she formally assumed her post as a professor of literature at the University of Tehran. Conversant in German, English, Russian, Arabic, Turkish, and French, Sayyah had completed her higher education abroad. When she first began teaching, she had no female students.[24] Her unusual status as a university professor as well as her intellectual prowess positioned her well to dismantle the specious arguments of those opposed to women's political empowerment. Yet the debate itself reflected a deep-seated fear among certain intellectuals over the social ramifications of broadening women's participation in Iranian civic life.

The issue of women's suffrage compounded the unease of religious intellectuals, who actively debated social policy after 1941. With the abdication of Reza Shah, an interval of political openness emerged, and Islam slowly reentered Iranian public discourse through the medium of print. In addition to relaxing the unveiling decree, Iranian authorities allowed once again public mourning on 'Ashura, the anniversary of the martyrdom of Imam Husayn, as prime minister Morteza Quli Bayat "countermanded earlier orders forbidding all demonstrations."[25] Even the American-trained minister of education at the time, Dr. 'Isa Sadiq, "felt it necessary to bow before aroused feeling to extent of ordering all public school teachers to take pupils to Mosque once every day, girls in veils, for prayers."[26] After two decades of suppression, religious sentiment was reaching new heights. Bowing to public pressure, Iranian officials carved a small niche for the participation of Islamic thinkers.

While the Shi'i 'ulama of Iran maintained institutional bases in shrine cities such as Qum and Mashhad, they had lacked a women's group that gave voice to Shi'i visions of Iranian womanhood, akin to the Catholic women's organization Union Féminine Civique et Sociale.[27] In the absence of such religiously inspired women's associations that articulated a position on reproduction, suffrage, veiling, and family life, writers with a religious bent broadcast their opinions through their literary output or in public sermons. Although Reza Shah had curtailed public manifestations of Islam during his reign, many Iranians retained a popular interest in Shi'i traditions, which these writers tapped into.

This interval saw the efflorescence of the press and the emergence of journals with an Islamic bent, such as *A'in Islam*, which covered themes of religious import including Islamic jurisprudence (*fiqh*) and Qur'anic exegesis (*tafsir*). Such publications also considered the politics of dress and documented the response of the religious classes to the cultural policies of the Pahlavi regime, including marriage and divorce. Shi'i scholars often addressed women's issues from the vantage point of family life.

Although this weekly apparently enjoyed only a short life span with limited circulation—indeed, in its second year, *A'in-i Islam* faced the threat of shutdown and frequently published appeals to its readership for support—it nonetheless provides a rare glimpse of the popular views of religious conservatives and the lower-ranking 'ulama of the Pahlavi era, a time when publications with Islamic themes remained scarce and lacked state backing.[28]

Nusrat Allah Nuriyani, editor of *A'in-i Islam*, invested his money to launch the journal in an effort to promote Islamic values in Iranian society. Described by his readers as "young" and "zealous" about his religion, Nuriyani strove to enhance the appeal of Islam in Iranian society, which had undergone nearly two decades of secular reform often aimed at minimizing the role of religion in the country. As he explained, "Today, because of the coded propaganda of the enemies of Islam, its followers have fallen victim to lethargy in their faith."[29]

Writing in 1945, Nuriyani appealed to the character and example of Islam's first family to promote traditional norms of family life and womanhood. Concerns about prostitution and sexual promiscuity, reflected in discussions of venereal disease and unveiling, impelled Nuriyani and intellectuals with a conservative leaning to rely on Islam's teachings as a social corrective to the seeming erosion of morality in Iranian public life.[30] Who better than the Prophet's youngest daughter to embody this message of social change? Fatima, despite her "short life, in the narrow society of Arabia, with meager means," raised the "greatest young men of religion" and the "worthiest daughters and women of the world beneath her veil of chastity."[31] Fatima's Islamic purity contrasted with the secular, unveiled image of the modern Iranian woman in mid-twentieth-century Iran, where social ills such as venereal disease and illicit sex became openly discussed in the mainstream press.[32]

The appeal of Islam's first family was reflected in the enduring popularity of Fatima's son Husayn ibn Ali. The Islamic Advertising Office (Anjuman-i Tabligat-i Islami) was distributing a biography of the Prophet's grandson, which readers could purchase at various bookstores around Tehran.[33] The publication of Husayn's biography pointed to the draw of the *ahl-i bayt*, or the family of the Prophet, for many Iranians despite efforts by secular ideologues to minimize the country's Islamic culture in official nationalist discourse.

Nuriyani exhorted the Ministry of Culture to include religious education as part of the state curriculum beginning in kindergarten. University education similarly needed to make training as a religious scholar optional for its students. He acknowledged the existence of small private schools among the religious classes but viewed them as "disorganized." To reform religious education in Iran, Nuriyani recommended the involvement of mujtahids from Iran and the 'Atabat (the holy Shi'i shrine cities in Iraq). According to him, "the independence of our country will remain in danger until our religious scholars are organized."[34] In a subsequent issue, Nuriyani reported that the minister of culture, 'Isa Sadiq, had granted a request presented by the 'ulama of Shiraz to include religious education as part of the middle school curriculum.[35]

Recognizing the potential secular backlash against his ideas, Nuriyani cleverly couched them within a nationalist rhetoric. Islamic ideals, he argued, promoted national weal with their emphasis on family life and sexual morality. In his journal, he frequently discussed the theme of moral degeneracy in Iranian society, a common topic of concern for maternalists of both secular and religious persuasion. While Iranian intellectuals of this era did not neatly sort themselves into such categories, it is worth recognizing that many secular reformers who promoted hygiene often couched their arguments within an Islamic context.[36] By the middle of the twentieth century, the divide between religious writers and secular ones had widened. *A'in-i Islam* cautiously forged a politicized religious discourse that not only considered the role of Islam in modern societies but also addressed perceived social crises such as the impact of adultery and the weakening of age-old institutions such as marriage. The modern secular woman, unveiled, educated, and now in pursuit of suffrage, was perceived as inviting immorality and social disorder.

Some contributors to *A'in-i Islam*, such as Muhammad Ardahali, used arguments similar to those of secular reformers. He drew a connection between the prevalence of venereal disease and this moral degeneracy. Ardahali explored the subject of adultery as a threat to the human race, a condition that inhibited Iranian youth from engaging in marriage and family life. As he argued, an hour of lust could bring on a lifetime of misery by exposing adulterers to syphilis and other venereal illnesses.[37] At the time that Ardahali expounded these ideas, Arthur Millspaugh, who headed the third American financial mission to Iran, observed: "Diseases—typhoid and typhus, the dysenteries, malaria, trachoma, small-pox, and syphilis—are tragically prevalent."[38] The tragedy that Ardahali also perceived was one of the consequences of venereal disease infection: infertility. These familiar arguments were recast in an Islamic context to dissuade the public from seeking out prostitutes and to discourage sexual experimentation.

Sexual relations between young women and men remained a slippery slope. As Ardahali observed, women weren't born into prostitution. The absence of Islamic ethics and poor parenting likely contributed to its proliferation, he argued. But who were these generic prostitutes so feared by Ardahali? The prostitute, and perhaps the unveiled Iranian woman, loomed as a cunning temptress, an alluring siren who enticed impressionable young men with her "pleasing" (*khush nama*) outward appearance. When faced with such seduction, Ardahali urged young men to exercise composure and to recognize her temptations, so beautifully camouflaged in a "lovely crystal bottle" (*shishah-i buluri-yi qashang*), as deadly poison (*samm-i kushandah*).[39] The "deadly poison" referred to a venereal disease that could undermine a couple's fertility and cause marital discord. The prostitute not only endangered the population through the spread of venereal disease but also contributed to the erosion of contemporary marriages.

Islamic thinkers such as Nuriyani and Ardahali supported sexual control of Iranian women and men. For some, unveiling reflected sexual promiscuity and had worsened the moral degeneracy of Iranian youth. An embrace of Islamic values such as chastity and modesty might restore honor and lessen the temptations of vice. Because religious intellectuals had failed to thwart the unveiling of Iranian women during the reign of Reza, they seized this brief interval of political openness during his son's regime to voice dissent. Along with their criticism of unveiling, many religious scholars also denounced the women's suffrage movement, regarded as overturning the accepted and necessary gender divisions in Iranian society.

The women's suffrage movement in Iran gained momentum at a time when religious opposition also gathered strength. Like the unveiling decree, suffrage elicited charged emotions that further cleaved Iranian society. In 1946, Minister Muzaffar Firuz proposed the adoption of the UN Charter with its support of women's enfranchisement, a point opposed by members of the 'ulama.[40] One newspaper, *Nida-yi Haqq*, expressly challenged the state organ of the women's movement—Sazman-i Zanan (Women's Association)—and its push for women's political rights and equality. Its editor, Sayyid Hasan Adnani, expressed his grievances against the reforms adopted by the secular Pahlavi regime, changes that, in his view, had eroded the fabric of Iranian society. These unwelcome and imposed transformations had promoted "lustful behavior of women" in "cinemas, theaters, inns, hotels," and gambling houses and allowed women and men to mingle and dance. Adnani scathingly concluded that this debauchery resulted from the liberation and secular education of women over the previous twenty-five years.[41] What more did women want from men? Some of Iran's most educated women, he charged, committed unflattering acts but carried on their business as if they were innocent and still sought more freedom. To make matters worse, they rejected Islamic precepts and instead looked to the UN Charter for redress and political parity. However, Adnani contended, "An Islamic nation does not need the reviled charter of the United Nations, which contradicts the bases of Islam."[42] These incendiary words represented the polarizing views from within the alienated 'ulama community. Adnani's comments made the secular women's movement a target of political protest, reflecting the growing antagonism of a class of men against the newfound privileges of Iranian women in the workplace and in the public sphere. In another essay, Adnani warned that women's agitation for the vote created dangerous precedents because it emboldened schoolgirls and young female university students to interfere in politics and to organize protest demonstrations.[43]

In several issues, *Nida-yi Haqq* condemned members of Iran's parliament for endorsing a statement by the United Nations that recognized equal rights for women and men. In replying to the Women's Association, Adnani objected to the absence of chastity, veiling, and respect among contemporary women (*bi 'iffati, bi 'ismati, bi hijabi, bi tarbiyati, va bi ihtirami*).[44] In particular, he singled out Majlis representative 'Abd al-Qadir Azad, who initially supported the statement made by the UN. *Nida-yi Haqq* argued that the Islamic community had no need for United Nations statements that contradicted the teachings of Islam. It explained that "this freedom and equality are good for Christian, Jewish, Zoroastrian, Buddhist, sun-worshipping, and cow-worshipping nations, not for the Muslim nation." In Islam, Adnani contended, "the limits between women and men are explicit and determined and there is no confusion or complication about it."[45] The desire to provide a uniform Islamic position on the question of equal rights between women and men was an aggressive response on the part of Iran's religious community to the secular women's movement, as well as an attempt to suppress dissent in the name of Islamic uniformity.

The chasm between secularism and religiosity was expressed in health-related matters as well. In one issue, *Nida-yi Haqq* protested the treatment that veiled women received at state-run birthing clinics. It reported that women who sought medical help at Fawzia Hospital or the hospital of the Society for the Protection of Women were turned away if they wore a chador. These actions raised concerns as to whether the Ministry of Health had set a policy denying veiled women medical care at such facilities. Since Iran "at the present time respects the veil" and allowed for the coming and going of veiled women, it should not subject women wearing a chador to such insults at birthing clinics or deprive them of the state's welfare programs. This reporter implored the minister of health to investigate these actions and to give all women access to medical help "regardless of what outfit or predicament" she may have. "Alas," the reporter concluded, "the problem of oil" has overwhelmed everyone. Otherwise, the unfair treatment of veiled women could be given full consideration."[46]

At stake remained the disenfranchisement of the religious classes. The issue of women's suffrage, which had gained international attention since the creation of the United Nations, fueled the religious opposition. In 1949, the United Nations Commission on the Status of Women had gathered in Beirut, where "votes for women was on every tongue."[47] Iran also sent delegates to this function. That year, Syria became the first Arab country to grant women the right to vote.

Even as Iranian politics entered a volatile stage that culminated with the campaign to nationalize the oil industry, women continued making pleas in favor of suffrage. A deputation of women led by Princess Firuz approached the parliament in 1952 "to demand voting rights in the coming election.[48] Reza Hekmat presided over the Majlis and "hurried off the floor to sign" the petition presented by the women.[49] Members of the Iranian Women's Organization also approached the United Nations to protest their exclusion from voting in the upcoming national elections. They maintained that the constitution did "not bar women from voting."[50] In addition, to show their support for national politics, some women spoke in favor of lending economic aid to Iran during the nationalization crisis. Some bought government loans in a symbolic gesture intended to show women's economic solidarity with the nation. Others urged women not to spend money on luxury items.[51] A group of women led by the shah's second wife, Princess Soraya, also formed an anti-nylon-stocking league and planned a "bonfire of hosiery" in an effort "to save foreign exchange by discouraging the wearing of foreign nylons."[52] Despite adopting such creative approaches to international politics, Iranian women could not convince their government to embrace women's suffrage.

In 1956, when Egyptian women gained the right to suffrage after the victory of Gamal Abdul Nasser and the Free Officers, Iranian women agitated once again to win the right to vote. As the *New York Times* reported, "For electoral purposes Persian women are still grouped with the insane." By 1959, Iran—along with Iraq, Jordan, Lichtenstein, and Switzerland—still had the unenviable distinction of being among a small number of countries worldwide that barred women from voting.[53] Although the shah annulled national elections in 1960, he was not able to silence the demands of Iranian women. As one journalist reported, "The women of Iran started talking during the campaign, and they showed no sign of stopping. . . . Teheran in the last fortnight has been the scene of a suffragettes' march in the best tradition of Susan B. Anthony and Carrie Chapman Catt. Swinging banners, the women of Teheran assembled one recent morning at the base of the massive stairs of the new Senate Palace. There they waylaid Premier Ja'far Sharif-Imami and members of his new cabinet."[54] The suffrage movement became part of the process of political turmoil that Iran experienced in the early 1960s. The shah's regime had turned repressive, creating an environment of political authoritarianism that paid only lip service to institutions intended to safeguard the country's democratic processes. Badr al-Muluk Bamdad summed up the situation best: "[My] reply to those who say that the Iranian women are not ready or capable of voting is that neither the men nor the women seem ready to take part in a democratic action. So why are only women barred?"[55]

Despite continued setbacks, the women's suffrage movement in Iran gained momentum. In September 1960 various women's organizations had planned a session to discuss women's suffrage, but the Ministry of Education did not approve of the gathering. Undeterred, women leading various organizations vowed to collaborate and to coordinate activities by holding informational sessions.[56] Weeks later, women's groups pressured the government to allow women to vote in elections for the city council (*anjuman-i shahr*). They argued that no legal impediment barred women either from voting or from being elected. In an interview with the daily newspaper

Ittila'at, Dr. Mehrangiz Dawlatshahi, founder of the women's group Rah-i Naw (A New Way), referred to specific articles of the law to argue that women could in fact participate in municipal elections and that there was no legal ambiguity necessitating judicial intervention. Women's groups kept up the pressure to allow women the right the vote. Dowlatshahi forcefully concluded that "every Iranian" regardless of gender could vote in the elections for the Municipal Society.[57] Women's groups worked in unison during this interval to achieve political and social progress.[58] Iranian women were not alone in sensing political isolation. In 1960, a survey conducted by the United Nations found that "in seventy-one countries women have the right to vote and are eligible for election on an equal basis with men. In seven others, they have no such voting privileges. . . . In still others, they can vote only in local elections."[59]

Iranian electoral politics had entered a turbulent phase. As women pressed for suffrage, they expressed their frustration about national elections. In 1960, the shah had promised free elections, but allegations of fraud and wrongdoing launched by the leading candidate, Asadollah 'Alam, against the incumbent prime minister, Manuchehr Iqbal, convinced the shah to cancel elections. Iqbal and Sharif Imami, his successor, eventually resigned, and finally Ali Amini became prime minister. During this confusing time, the Kennedy administration took office in the United States and encouraged the shah to implement social programs and to increase political openness in Iran.[60] The shah inaugurated his reform agenda under the name "White Revolution"—a phrase that contrasted his social agenda with the "red" and sometimes bloody Communist revolutions of the Eastern bloc. Among other issues, the shah addressed land reform, women's suffrage, and the formation of a literacy corps. Though less politically contentious, the Sipah-i Danesh (Literacy Corps) attracted much support for its campaign to address the high rates of illiteracy in rural communities.[61] Census records indicate that literacy for girls seven and older in Iran had increased from just over 7 percent in 1956 to eighteen percent in 1966. In the rural areas, however, the literacy rate among girls and women was less than 5 percent in 1966.[62]

Women's suffrage became part of a broad range of social reforms initiated by the king in his increasingly repressive second phase of rule. In January 1963, the shah called a referendum in support of the White Revolution (later renamed the Revolution of the Shah and the

People). Although women were technically barred from voting on the referendum, they set up ballot boxes, voted, and broadcast their results. Women's votes were not included in the final count, but this act impelled the shah finally to grant women suffrage shortly after.[63] In September 1963, six women were elected to serve in parliament and two were appointed to serve as senators. The elected officials were Mehrangiz Dawlatshahi, Farrokhrou Parsa, Nayyereh Ebtehaj Sami'i, Hajar Tarbiyat, Shawkat Malik Jahanbani, and Nizhat Nafisi. These female representatives had benefited from the educational opportunities of the modern era and had later advanced the cause of women's empowerment. The two appointed senators were Shams al-Muluk Musahib and Mehrangiz Manouchehrian. In October 1963, Dr. Mehrangiz Dawlatshahi addressed the parliament and made the following historic remarks: "Today, a great honor has been bestowed upon us women for the first time in this parliament which we can truly call national and historic. For during the entire constitutional period half of the nation was deprived of its political and social rights. In reality in the twenty-first Majlis for the first time Iranian constitutionalism is complete, that is, the other half of the Iranian nation has gained the right to participate in shaping its future."[64] Dawlatshahi expressed gratitude to the shah for forging ahead with women's enfranchisement despite the implacable opposition of conservatives. Once in office, this first group of state officials pursued its activism. In the Senate, Dr. Mehrangiz Manouchehrian pushed for Iran's recognition of the equal rights platform issued by the United Nations, with unfavorable results.[65]

Women's cries for political inclusion, however, met with opposition from the 'ulama. As some Islamic thinkers became radicalized in their politics, they targeted feminists and challenged the secular mores of the modern Iranian women's movement. By 1963, when Iranian women finally gained the right to vote, the chasm between secularism and religion had widened. The experience of foreign occupation and the battle to nationalize the Iranian oil industry formed a backdrop to this debate. The shah's association with the West, especially the United States, made women's suffrage less palatable to conservative groups such as the 'ulama who already objected stridently to the land reform program. Tensions erupted on 'Ashura, when demonstrators shattered and set fire to various official vehicles.[66] Martial law was declared in Shiraz and Tehran. At issue remained the opposition of the 'ulama to the shah's land reform program as well as his endorsement of women's suffrage.[67] Ayatollah Ruhollah Khomeini, a Shi'i jurist in Qum and author of important religious tracts, seized this opportunity to denounce the shah's reforms. Khomeini had organized a meeting with leading religious scholars Ayatollahs Kazem Shariatmadari and Muhammad Reza Golpaygani to elicit support for the opposition.[68] With the death in 1961 of the quietist religious scholar Ayatollah Borujerdi, a vacuum had emerged in Iran's Shi'i leadership. Khomeini looked to fill this void. Unlike Borujerdi, Khomeini had no intention of pacifying the shah. Instead, Khomeini ascended the pulpit, making incendiary speeches about the monarch and his White Revolution. Police forces intervened when he delivered remarks of an increasingly political nature during the Muharram ceremonies and rioters began attacking unveiled women.[69] Although the king eventually exiled Khomeini to Turkey and, later, Iraq, the ayatollah's departure did not quell the dissent.

Nonetheless, by 1966, the official women's movement gained traction, and a new umbrella group—the Women's Organization of Iran (WOI)—came into existence under the leadership of the shah's twin sister, Princess Ashraf Pahlavi. The WOI replaced the High Council of Women's Organizations (established in 1961) and strove to provide uniformity and cohesion to the women's movement, as well as to bring it under state control.[70] Prominent women as well as representatives from various ethnic communities and women's organizations joined the WOI.[71] A nonprofit organization, the WOI functioned with the support of volunteers drawn from the ranks of teachers, government employees, and homemakers and strove to expand literacy among women. Mahnaz Afkhami served as secretary general of the WOI, and in 1976 she was appointed to the newly created cabinet post of minister for women's affairs.[72]

In 1967, the WOI cosponsored a bill known as the Family Protection Law.[73] The marriage laws of 1931 and 1937 had denied women equality in divorce and had protected the institution of *mut'a*. The limitations of Iran's legal reforms stood in sharp contrast to those of neighboring Turkey, which had granted women equality with men in divorce and child custody in 1926.[74] The Family Protection Law, approved on 12 June 1967, made it difficult for men to divorce their wives at whim, as stipulated in Islamic law. Instead, couples had to go to court and receive an order recognizing irreconcilable differences.[75]

The law raised the age of marriage for women to fifteen and to eighteen for men.[76] In addition, the Family Protection Act made polygamy difficult, since men had to demonstrate the financial ability to provide for more than one wife and to pledge equal treatment of their wives. Finally, women gained the right to petition for divorce under certain circumstances, such as spousal imprisonment for more than five years or addiction.[77] In 1975, the parliament passed an amendment to the law that raised the age of marriage to twenty for men and eighteen for women, though courts could deliberate marriage petitions from women over fifteen. The amendment also empowered the court to grant men the right to take a second wife with the consent of his first wife, or if the first wife was found to be barren, to be mentally incapacitated, or to refuse sex.[78]

Literacy and education remained a focus of women's activism. In October 1962, the Ministry of Education announced a plan to fight

Sipah-i Danesh Lady Reading. *Ittila'at.*

illiteracy, estimated at 60 percent, in rural communities. The army conscription department was set to recruit male high school graduates, who would be trained and sent to rural areas.[79] Initially, it was unclear what role women would play in the literacy corps, though mothers were urged to encourage their children to volunteer for the campaign against illiteracy.[80] In 1968, Dr. Farrokhrou Parsa was appointed minister of education. A member of parliament and daughter of activist Fakhr Afaq Parsa, Dr. Farrokhrou Parsa became the first woman to serve in the cabinet. Women's literacy also gained support with the implementation of the Women's Literacy Corps in September 1968.[81] Women trained during the first six months of the program to serve in rural communities for the following twelve months. At the end of the eighteen-month program, women qualified to become formal instructors through the Ministry of Education.[82] By 1971, the proportion of rural women who were literate, though still less than 10 percent, had doubled since 1966.[83]

Rising literacy enabled women to enter the workforce in record numbers, contributing to the country's economic development and social welfare. In addition, the Family Protection Law made it difficult for fathers and husbands to restrict their daughters or wives from entering professionals considered dishonorable or harmful to family life by requiring court injunctions.[84] By 1967, more than three thousand female employees in professional fields had earned a university education. The majority of female students graduated with degrees in literature, while others earned degrees in medicine and scientific fields. More than fifty-five thousand women worked for the government, while nearly half a million women were employed in the private sector, nationalized businesses, or factories. Others engaged in agriculture and animal husbandry. The majority of professional working women were between twenty and thirty years of age, and they served in diverse fields such as medicine, education, benevolent organizations, libraries, museums, and research institutions.[85] Women also participated in the workforce as police officers, although they faced harassment on the job.[86] Although these numbers show progress, some female employees were illiterate or could barely read and were employed in low-tier jobs.[87]

In 1968, on the anniversary of the unveiling decree, *Ittila'at* featured an article on the progress of women in Iran since the rise of the

Female Police Officer. *Ittila'at.*

Pahlavis. With state support, Iranian women founded benevolent associations to support indigent mothers and children, organized arts shows, and attended school in growing numbers. One women's activist, Nur al-Huda Manganah, recalled that women could not go to cinemas. Instead, women were told: "Go to *ta'ziyah* [passion plays] and *rowzeh khanis* [public mourning ceremonies]; other places are forbidden to you."[88] Iranian women had reached many milestones, including the right to vote.

Iran's embrace of women's suffrage and its passage of the Family Protection Law, however, had deeply divided the country. For decades, women's empowerment had come through a celebration of motherhood, and the maternalist discourse advanced women's health and education without threatening patriarchy. But women's suffrage could not be achieved without recognition of the need for gender parity. For religious scholars such as Ayatollah Khomeini, who associated women's suffrage in Iran with the global feminist movement originating in the West, this change underscored the emasculation of

Iranian men and Islam itself. In reality, Iranian women never gained true political parity. Rather, they won a political prerogative that brought them a step closer to the ideal of gender equality. Women's ability to break into politics meant that they no longer needed to advance their causes through secondary channels of power. Instead, they could initiate social reforms as insiders. Although Iran's first generation of female politicians did not disavow maternalism, they exuded an unrelenting feminist spirit.

CHAPTER 9

∾

Managing Birth

Family Planning and Health Care

In 1948, two Middle Eastern monarchs—Malik Faruq of Egypt and Muhammad Reza Shah Pahlavi—announced the termination of their respective marriages. Queen Farida of Egypt had borne Faruq three daughters but no sons, and Faruq's sister, Fawzia, had given the shah of Iran a daughter.[1] In both cases, the monarchs divorced their wives because of the absence of a male heir to the throne (and likely for other reasons, too). The shah's desire for a son seemed only natural to his entourage, as did his decision to divorce Fawzia. Yet the premium on the male heir seemed strangely incongruous when placed within the context of Middle Eastern women's movements of the postwar years. For one thing, it reinforced the notion of political patriarchy. Although women were entering new professions and attending schools in unprecedented numbers, they were not considered equal partners in a traditionally male sphere: politics. Second, it implied that although for two decades the state had strenuously espoused a policy of high fertility for Iranian couples—a rhetoric that had remained gender neutral in its endorsement of high rates of childbirth—gender preferences still mattered in Iranian families. After all, the shah himself used the absence of a firstborn male heir as a justifiable reason to end his marriage to Fawzia.

The shah's personal life became a matter of public debate because he and his family embodied the state. Having authorized a machismo rhetoric that lauded the vigor and virility of men, especially military men, the shah himself needed to embody similar strength and manliness, which was measured not just by his prowess as a pilot but also by his ability to sire male offspring. It is not coincidental that the king himself had attended a military academy in Switzerland and often participated in sporting events during his youth. The public seemed no more ready than the shah to endorse a woman at the helm. The desire for a male heir preserved men's political dominance by excluding women from the possibility of attaining the highest office in the land. Finally, the politics of reproduction affected the shah's marriage, a union that initially had seemed to fulfill the expectations of his office.

In February 1951, three years after his divorce, Muhammad Reza Shah married Soraya Esfandiyari Bakhtiary in a lavish ceremony, in which the bride wore a dress designed by Christian Dior. After becoming a member of Iran's first family, Queen Soraya reflected upon the complex world of relationships among its royal women. She remarked that the king's mother, Taj al-Muluk, guarded her privileged status as the woman from whose "loins . . . the Kings of Persia were born."[2] Soraya joined the royal family at a turbulent time. Politics focused on the movement to nationalize Iranian oil under the charismatic leadership of the premier, Dr. Muhammad Musaddiq. Queen Soraya recalled the nationalization of the oil industry as a passive observer of the events much like any ordinary Iranian. As she wrote with some sarcasm, "In the street, on the roads, in the countryside the signs for petrol stations were torn down to be replaced by inscriptions in Iranian. Everywhere there was joy, exhilaration, euphoria. Everyone imagined that the oil would flow in rivers and be delivered free from Allah to people's houses."[3] Once the story of oil had subsided, the nation could focus again on the reproductive status of its queen.

Somewhat predictably, Soraya viewed her mother-in-law as a woman who "tried to impose her way of thinking on Mohammed Reza who listened to her respectfully."[4] As Soraya sardonically concluded, "In Iran, sons listen to and respect their mothers. 'Yes mother . . . No, mother.'"[5] But with her husband, the maternal bond "went no further than that," principally because in "Persia, even if she were the Empress Mother, a woman cannot make an appearance in political life. Her destiny is to obey men and their laws."[6] Queen

Soraya's reflections on the position of women in Iranian life seemed to negate the decades of activism of upper-class women. Her words may have had more to say about the role of the queen in Iranian public life than about the impediments women faced by seeking a role in the civic community.

After enduring the turbulent oil nationalization movement led by Dr. Muhammad Musaddiq, the shah and his wife began planning for an heir. As Queen Soraya recounts, "I knew that he was waiting for me to bear him a child, a child to succeed him, a child I denied him in the first year because I was too ill."[7] Reportedly, Soraya had difficulty recovering from typhoid. In her casual encounters with members of the court, from whispers in the corridors to scrutiny surrounding the size of her waist, the queen felt the pressures of producing an heir.

In the meantime, Soraya devoted herself to charitable work. In particular, she was committed to the children she "had to snatch back from the brink of death every day in the country's hospitals."[8] The queen reported unsatisfactory conditions for the disabled, as well as for indigent women and children. For example, after five years of planning, a hospital for the poor was only partially built. In addition, she notes, "At an orphanage which I visited unannounced, I discovered children covered in filth and with abscesses all over their bodies. They did not have heating and it was winter."[9] Further, the queen discovered that many children had died at the orphanage. As she remarked, "I asked to see the records and I noticed to my horror that many of the little girls and boys registered were no longer alive. This scandalous rate of mortality was higher than in any old people's home."[10] Disappointed at the lack of support she received from the ministry of health, the queen approached women in Iran's "high society" and succeeded in organizing a benefit ball—and eventually the Soraya Foundation—to bring money, blankets, clothes, and sewing machines to the orphanage.[11] The queen's involvement in the work of benevolence not only benefited poor children but also helped her shape social welfare policy. At her behest, clothes were distributed to poor families on the occasion of the Persian New Year. She was also credited with founding two orphanages in Tehran.[12] Despite her benevolent works, Queen Soraya's marriage was doomed to failure. The outside world noted with some justification that "worries over an heir to the throne are certainly preferable to plots to topple it."[13] In 1958, international headlines reported that the couple had divorced, as Queen Soraya had not provided the shah with a son.

A male heir to the Iranian throne finally arrived after the shah's marriage to his third wife, Queen Farah Diba. The crown prince, Reza Pahlavi, was born on 31 October 1960. Although the public officially rejoiced at the news, Queen Farah recalled some of the unpleasant canards that had spread about her and the shah: "As usually happens in our country, the most improbable rumors circulated. It was claimed, for example, that I was not really pregnant but had put a cushion on my stomach. . . . It was also said that the shah was not the father because he could not have children. . . . Then there was the idea that I had the baby in the big public hospital in the south of the city so that the girl I gave birth to could be exchanged for a boy."[14] Her reflections point to the lack of public trust in the first family, as well as to the ways in which the shah's masculinity had been undermined. The arrival of a male heir did not fully repair the image of a feeble king, but it did solidify the shah's third marriage.

The queen's first experience with labor showed just how much the culture of health care and birthing had changed. She delivered in a hospital at a time when hospital use remained limited in rural areas. In fact, a survey on demographic conditions in Iranian villages completed by the Iranian Ministry of Health and by the Rockefeller Foundation in 1951 found that "of 4,700 births, only 40 were delivered in a hospital; and only 16 of the total were delivered by physicians." Midwives, "few of whom were professionally trained," ministered to the other women.[15] The prince's birth was not uneventful. Toward the end of her labor, the queen had needed anesthesia, and apparently "the anesthetist overdid it somewhat (which enraged the obstetrician who was attending me)." The obstetrician was Dr. Jahanshah Saleh, who had served as minister of health and who had helped shape policies on maternal and child care in Iran. The use of anesthesia during labor reflected changes in the culture of pain management during birth as well.

Iran revamped its health care program as a part of several consecutive development plans. During the first development plan, which lasted from 1948 to 1955, new hospitals emerged. An assessment completed midway through the second Seven-Year Plan, which began in 1955, showed a significant increase of government investment in preventive medicine and the treatment of infectious diseases.[16] With the inauguration of the third Five-Year Plan, from 1962 to 1967, the government invested in developing a national health services network, paying more attention to the training of health care personnel. To fulfill their military obligations, physicians worked for eighteen months in rural areas. In addition, health services became more specialized during this time, with a demand for a rural midwifery training program.[17]

Assistant nurses, or *behyars*, offered necessary aid to medical professionals and for this purpose received rudimentary training in health and hygiene, usually a two-year course of study after completing the ninth grade. *Behyars* often worked in hospitals or health clinics under the direction of more advanced nurses and sometimes served as midwives in rural communities.[18] By 1970 Iran had sixteen nursing schools, three of which operated in Tehran. Of these, only the High Institute of Nursing in Tehran offered a four-year course of study directed toward a bachelor's degree. The others provided a three-year training program in nursing that culminated in a nursing diploma. Except for the newly established schools, the nursing programs graduated approximately 350 nurses per year.[19]

In just over fifty years, the country rapidly multiplied the number of hospitals and clinics to meet the growing public demand for health care services. The immunization program succeeded in substantially cutting down on the incidence of diseases such as smallpox and diphtheria, which a century earlier had taken many lives and contributed to the high rate of infant mortality in Iran.[20] Despite these advances, by 1975 Iran still lacked sufficient nurses in the workforce as compared with other nations, especially in provinces outside the capital.[21]

Queen Farah Pahlavi went on to bear three other healthy children, including a male "spare," and during the same decade the state ironically took the decision to introduce family planning. The emergence of Iran's family planning policies reflected new public health concerns and efforts to manage the fertility of Iranian women. The founder of the Family Planning Association of Iran, Sattereh Farman Farmaian, observed in her memoirs that "population growth was the most important social problem we faced." According to her, Iranian parents, "made desperate by the arrival of babies they couldn't afford," often felt they had no choice but to abandon their children. Sattereh Farman Farmaian acknowledged the obstacles that lay before her and other family planners in traditional Middle Eastern societies that revered the culture of childbearing. As she noted, "In the Middle

East, feelings about the importance of having many children are extremely strong, and it was difficult to convince old-fashioned, traditional Persians like my mother that birth control was not against God's law."[22] Iranians were not the only ones steeped in tradition, however; many religiously inspired movements in the West voiced similar ambivalence toward family planning policies.[23]

Family planning was intended not to discourage mothering but to manage it. In 1966, the national census determined that Iran's population had an increase rate of approximately 2.5 to 3 percent in a decade.[24] Based in part on this data, Iranian officials introduced population control programs. In 1967, the shah, along with twenty-nine other world leaders, signed a declaration on population that was presented to the UN secretary general, U Thant.[25] That year, Iran introduced programs in support of family planning, which Ayatollah Shariatmadari also endorsed.[26]

Considering the impassioned debates surrounding fears of depopulation during the interwar years, this development may seem surprising. As Ali Asghar Zahedi, who directed research and planning at the Family Planning Division of Tehran, acknowledged, "Prior to 1967 no official steps were taken regarding family planning. On the contrary, the general attitude and the national laws were, essentially, encouraging large families." In fact, "mothers-of-the-year were selected solely on the basis of the number of children they had raised."[27] In 1966, for example, the mother of the year had given birth to eighteen children.[28]

Like other countries, Iran experienced an about-face in the use of birth control and the evolution of reproductive politics after World War II. The decline in death rates (particularly in developing countries), the increasing independence of women in asserting control over their sexuality, and a belief that a large number of pregnancies eventually threatened the well-being of mother and child contributed to a reversal of earlier ideology and an endorsement of family planning.[29] Improved sanitation, physical activity, and attention to personal hygiene had been mantras for Iranian women, and a reduction in childbearing was added as a necessary step in maintaining the health of young women. The initial campaign to keep women's bodies healthy and strong—albeit intended principally to enable women to birth multiple children—contributed to a reduction in maternal deaths by the second half of the twentieth century. What remained consistent was the state's continued desire to impose social control over women's bodies and their reproductive choices. The debate surrounding reproduction demonstrated that, despite the success of Iranian women in gaining the vote, maternalist ideology nonetheless attempted to circumscribe their freedoms in other ways, often by influencing their private reproductive decision making and, by extension, their presence in the professional workplace. Although the Population Council, which informed Iranian family planning, urged that the "role of government in promoting family planning should be facilitative and permissive, and in no degree coercive," the absence of an alternative state discourse on the subject sometimes made it difficult for some citizens to embrace other choices, particularly in places where the state exerted undue influence.[30] Just as the state had at one time viewed large families as patriotic, it shifted to a discourse of small families, pinpointing differences in class and education of its citizens.[31]

The state-sponsored family planning program aimed to "lower the rate of population growth" and to "raise the overall status of the family."[32] In 1967, the Population Council submitted a report to Iran's Ministry of Health highlighting changes in the demographic composition of the country, shifts that had occurred in part because of improvement in public health services. Both economic and social considerations had influenced changes in the perceived ideal Iranian family size. The report addressed the issue that "the declining death rate and the likelihood of a higher population growth rate will reduce the pace of increase in per capita income. Thus for both economic and general welfare considerations, in the next decade or two, family planning should be popularized and it should constitute one of our important welfare programmes in the future plans."[33] The Population Council recognized that family planning would be unsuccessful in areas where infant mortality remained high: "Programs of education and assistance in family planning should therefore concentrate on areas where mortality has fallen. In areas where 50 per cent or fewer children survive to adult ages there is little reason to promote contraception and little chance that it would be accepted."[34] According to Dr. Amir Mansur Sardari, undersecretary of state for family planning, as of September 1968 more than two hundred family planning clinics had been set up in towns and cities throughout Iran.[35] By 1971, rural areas had become targets of Iran's family planning policy as well.

To promote the program, the Population Council posted a resident advisor to Iran in 1968, and a year later the United Nations assigned a Population program officer to Tehran.[36] Although Iran had numerous private and nongovernmental agencies delivering health care services, a UN report noted, the "Ministry of Health has been the most important provider of these services."[37] Local health officials disseminated information about population control as well. In November 1967, a seminar on health and family planning was convened in the northeastern province of Khurasan. Dr. Sardari spoke about the hazards of overpopulation, pointing out that economic limitations and social considerations made it difficult to reproduce and nurture families as in the past. Sardari also assured Iranian families that given Iran's "rich natural resources" (*manab'i tabi'i-yi ghani*), the purpose of health care and family planning principally remained "the well-being of families" (*rifah-i khvanavadah*).[38] Southern Iran held a similar forum two months later. In January 1968, the governor of Khuzistan, along with other government and health care professionals, presided at a three-day seminar on family planning. Participants included representatives from the provinces of Khuzistan, Luristan, and Kahkiluyah.[39] Thirteen two-day conferences were convened between 1967 and 1968, each with an attendance of three hundred. These conferences addressed the topic "Why Iran Needs a Family Planning Program" and instructed participants on the use of contraceptives.[40] By 1971, the program had trained more than two thousand physicians, nurses, and midwives, as well as members of the Health and Literacy Corps.

Existing clinics incorporated family planning services, and the School of Public Health trained students with a focus on family planning. In 1971, Dr. Sardari gauged the success of the program: "One indicator of progress is the response we are getting from the public. The annual number of clinical visits has increased fivefold from 313,000 to one and one-half million. The number of acceptors of oral contraceptives has risen from 265,000 to one and one-third million."[41] These statistics did not take account of "commercial sales, which have multiplied 26 times since the start of the family planning program."[42] Nonetheless, assessing birth and fertility rates in Iran based on data gathered from surveys or censuses, Iranian demographer Mehdi Amani concluded that "the birth rate in Iran is high" and that Iran "ranks with those having the highest rates of birth in the world."[43]

Family planning advocates relied on multiple media to communicate the aims of the program to the Iranian public. For example, at a seminar in Khurasan audiences benefited from lectures as well as films related to health care.[44] The media used "radio, television, newspapers, bulletins, films, filmstrips, flannel-graphs, flip charts, pamphlets and posters," but as Nayereh Fotouhi, director of the Women's Corps program, observed, "face-to-face communication still brings the best results."[45] Training of government personnel was conducted in tandem with other efforts directed at educating rural communities about family planning. In particular, it was believed that "pregnant and newly delivered mothers are in general more receptive than others to accept contraceptive methods for spacing or limitation of their families."[46]

In Iran, as elsewhere, the birth control pill became a popular and accepted form of contraception, though, at times, an ineffective one. In 1960 the Food and Drug Administration in the United States approved use of the first contraceptive pill, Enovid. Once the pills became widely available, the Iranian Ministry of Health authorized importing them to Iran.[47] The availability of the pill, however, did not eliminate the controversies surrounding its use. If anything, women and men raised questions about its safety and efficacy. A cartoon printed in the daily newspaper demonstrates this point. The image shows three pregnant women marching in a row to the delivery room. The picture is accompanied by a sardonic caption that reads: "Users of the birth control pill."[48] The pill's ineffectiveness as a form of birth control for women was evident in its apparent failure to prevent pregnancy. Another cartoon entitled "Quintuplets" depicted an anxious father being greeted by a delivery nurse holding three newborns in her arms. The nurse says: "Come! Hold them so I can bring the other two to you."[49] While this illustration did not specifically target users of the birth control pill, it hinted at the challenges posed by unfettered fertility for soon-to-be parents. The Iranian public also pondered the safety of the pill, which was a relatively new mode of contraception. Researchers abroad investigated the effects of hormones on women's long-term health, and the Persian press occasionally discussed the results of such scientific findings. Although one article cautioned that little correlation existed between the pill and cancer in women, nonetheless it acknowledged the difficulty doctors faced in prescribing the pill as a completely safe form of contraception.[50]

Users of Birth Control Pills Marching to Maternity Clinic. *Ittila'at.*

Despite persistent social obstacles in their use, the birth control pill and IUD became the preferred methods of contraception for Iranian family planners. The penal code prescribed imprisonment for those assisting in abortions, including mothers.[51] Abortions were allowed "only on strict medical grounds, to save the life of the woman." However, many medical professionals in Iran believed that "clandestine abortions are frequent," especially in urban areas, though "reliable data on the abortion situation in Iran [are] scarce or nonexistent." Although hospitals provided some statistics, they did not "reflect the true situation in the community as most deliveries and an unknown number of abortions take place outside any institutions."[52] Iranian law offered no indications on sterilization, which remained "a matter between the doctor and his patient." Apparently, "[very] few sterilizations are performed and are mainly tubal ligations."[53] In 1974, a study conducted at the Farah Maternity Hospital in Tehran showed an alarming number of abortions, suggesting that the family planning program had not effectively prevented unwanted pregnancies.[54] Many of the women seeking abortions were either

پنج قلو !

بيا ! اينها را نگهدار تادوتاى ديگر راهم بياورم !

The nurse says, "Come! Hold these so I can bring the other two." *Ittila'at.*

married teenagers or unmarried school-age youth.[55] Abortion was legalized in 1977, though valid reasons for the abortion needed to be provided to the physician.[56]

Rural communities depended on midwives for reproductive advice and assistance. In 1971, the United Nations reported that the "proportion of deliveries in Iran conducted by traditional midwives is estimated at about 60 per cent. It is higher in the rural areas and as low or about 10 to 20 per cent in the city of Teheran."[57] The same report indicated that "[training] traditional midwives in elementary hygiene and in simple obstetric practice, supported by UNICEF, was discontinued some six years ago. The training scheme was regarded as unsuccessful and a decision was made to replace the traditional midwives with trained health personnel."[58] Yet the United Nations committee found that midwives remained central to the birthing process in Iran, and it recommended not only that "the training of traditional birth attendants be revived" but also that "their involvement in the family planning programme be considered."[59] Midwives managed to provide health care services—albeit imperfect ones—and to reach out to communities that remained untouched by the state and its modern medical professionals.

Involving midwives in the family planning program made it possible not only to educate them in accepted medical practices but also to control their activities through "proper training." Midwives could contribute to family planning by "reporting pregnancies and births, referring abnormalities for adequate care, promoting and encouraging contraception and becoming distributors of contraceptives such as condoms."[60] In short, the United Nations found that "it seems unlikely that the national family planning programme would reach the majority of the population without the co-operation of traditional birth attendants."[61] This conclusion recognized the trust that rural communities placed in traditional birth attendants. It also highlighted the ways in which the modern health campaign needed the involvement of local communities in areas where the state retained little control over the birthing process. Even if traditional midwives received none of the credit for the reduction of infant and maternal deaths in Iran and continued to be viewed as being in need of basic hygienic knowledge, they were nonetheless regarded as crucial participants in the government's ongoing health campaigns. The development of modern clinics, nursing colleges, and medical schools had not eliminated the role of the traditional midwife in part because of a shortage of trained nurses and midwives and the preference of many rural people for traditional health care.[62] The challenges to the implementation of family planning signaled the continued popularity of traditional birthing practices among the rural population.

As the idea of family planning became reality in Iran, the popular press addressed the importance of marriage for youth. The two subjects went hand in hand and reflected maternalist preoccupations with family and reproductive policy. In fact, the state relied upon the nuclear family to instill a culture that promoted marriage as a necessary social institution defining the interaction of women and men. Lack of financial independence among youth, however, served as a disincentive for marriage. As one writer observed, "At the moment, not having a home is the biggest problem faced by a youth in creating a family." Typically, a young worker earned a meager salary and spent much of it on rent. One possible way to alleviate such economic woes was to have government ministries construct housing for their employees. While such suggestions did not always become government policy, these discussions exposed the financial challenges faced by the Iranian youth of the 1960s, economic hardships that affected personal conduct including the decision to marry.[63]

Although international organizations such as the United Nations became involved in assessing Iran's health care and welfare policies, their work rarely focused on the regulation of obstetricians. While medical advances bolstered the public's faith in doctors, hospitals, clinics, and other emblems of medical authority—as reflected in the increased involvement of such medical authorities in the health care of ordinary Iranian citizens—little public debate existed around the failures, mistakes, and limitations of modern medicine. Iranians would eventually investigate the occasional misuse of modern medicine, providing a much-needed corrective to the otherwise laudatory accounts of medical progress.[64]

Persian newspapers rarely reported medical errors, but there were exceptions. In 1967, the daily paper reported that two physicians were arrested on the charge of unpremeditated murder of a woman named Fatima who had given birth at their office. The woman's brother reported that after his sister began experiencing labor pains, he obtained an automobile and took her to the office of the physician, Dr. Isma'ili. After assisting with labor, Dr. Isma'ili then informed the woman's brother that the child had died but that his sister was stable enough to undergo surgery at a private hospital. The woman and her brother awaited the doctor's arrival, and during this interval the patient's condition worsened. When the physician finally arrived, it was not possible to save the woman's life. The inspector's office launched an investigation of the deaths and held Dr. Isma'ili and his wife in custody.[65] Not all incidents of medical malpractice related to childbirth were reported, but it is significant that the state imposed more stringent guidelines and practices to investigate suspicious deaths occurring during labor.

Maternalism projected new images of motherhood, and both royal women and those of common stock subscribed to these emerging values. Although women expanded their participation in the field of

Queen Farah Reading to Her Children. *Zan-i Ruz.*

public health as physicians, nurses, *behyars*, and professors in the second half of the twentieth century, their commitment to family life
remained paramount. Queen Farah Pahlavi embodied the image of
modern motherhood for Iranian women. In its first issue, the popular
woman's magazine *Zan-i Ruz*, which began publication in 1965,

depicted the queen in a loving pose reading to her children, Crown Prince Reza and Princess Farahnaz. This loving image of the first family attracted much attention, and apparently the first printing of the magazine sold out.[66]

To embrace motherhood, Iran commemorated Mother's Day annually on the twenty-fifth of Azar (December 16). It coincided with the anniversary of the establishment of the Institute for the Protection of Mothers, first opened in 1939–1940. In 1960, the board of the institute made the decision to celebrate Mother's Day. Queen Farah Pahlavi embraced the plan, and in celebration of the day, she supported the construction of maternity clinics in remote sections of the country.[67]

The celebration emerged in part as a response to the pressures of modernity on traditional family life. Instituting Mothers' Day gave the state another means of implementing its maternalist vision for Iranian women. Women's organizations such as the WOI supported Mother's Day by distributing fifty thousand celebration cards and giving a scholarship to a child of an exemplary woman.[68] Mothers of the year also received a royal medal in recognition of their service and became honorary members of the WOI.[69] In 1967, an essay explored

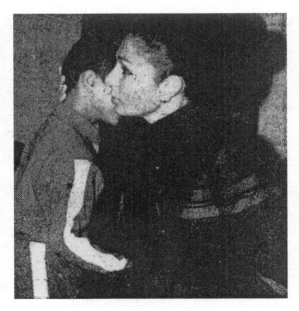

Queen Farah in a Maternal Pose. *Ittila'at.*

the reverence for mothers in Iranian society and conceded that celebration of Mother's Day was perhaps one of the best traditions that
Iranians had adopted from the West. The writer went on to argue that
although the celebration itself was a novelty, reverence for mothers
had historical precedent in Iran, going back to the pre-Islamic period
and continuing into the contemporary era.[70]

In 1967, the daily newspaper *Ittila'at* ran a feature celebrating the
"exemplary mothers" (*madaran-i barjastah*) of the year. The mothers
feted had birthed numerous children, although some attention was
also paid to the upbringing of children by exemplary mothers.[71] One
woman, for example, had fourteen children. She apparently also had
worked hard to raise her children. Another woman, a mother of six,
had attended the American College and sent a message to other
mothers encouraging them to play an active role in the "correct"
(*sahih*) upbringing of their children.[72] Also noteworthy is that ideal
mothers seemed to come from a number of different social backgrounds. In 1967, one of the mothers of the year, Bulqhays, a mother
of ten, appeared veiled.[73]

Iranian television also broadcast programs associated with Mother's Day.[74] As one writer argued, Mother's Day gained support precisely because it embraced the long-standing tradition of respect that

Celebration of Mother's Day at the Association of Young Ladies and Women. *Ittila'at.*

استقبال مردم تهران از

فروشگاه بزرگ ایران

بی‌نظیر است

قیمت قسمتی از اجناس فروشگاه بزرگ ایران

۱ ـ سینه‌بند کوتاه نایلونی گلدار خارجی
مارک ناتورانا
.

۲۴۵ ریال

۲ ـ سینه‌بند رکاب کشی رو به کوتاه پشت
دکلته در رنگهای سعید و مشکی

۳۴۵ ریال

۳ ـ شورت شکم‌بندی بادار بلند لب توری

۶۰۵ ریال

۴ ـ شلوار مردانه فلاش حبی بارنگهای
مشکی ـ سوسی سیر و سوسی روشن
اداره‌های مختلف

۶۹۵ ریال

۵ ـ شلوار مردانه مقدم دربکی وسوسی
سرمه‌ای ـ قهوه‌ای و اندازه‌های مختلف
۱۱۰ ۰۱ ۳۸

Starlight Pantyhose Ad. *Ittila'at.*

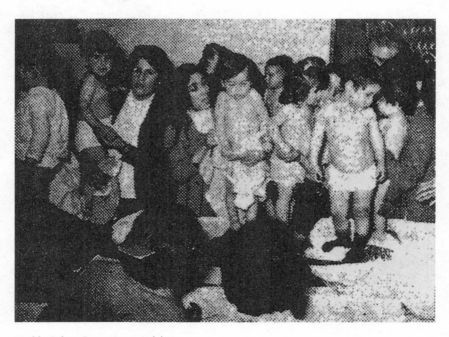

Healthy Babies Competition. *Ittila'at*

Iranian society accorded mothers: "The belief of the people of Iran in the honorable position of mothers is to a degree that even to this day many of the Iranian families believe that if a mother is not satisfied with her child, it is impossible for that child to have good fortune in his life."[75] While the importance of such adages cannot be quantified, such popular sentiments help to explain the public reception of Mother's Day, which was even endured in the Islamic Republic.

Mother's Day was used to create commercial opportunities in Iran, as elsewhere. In 1967, it coincided with the opening of a grand department store (*furushgah-i buzurg*).[76] Numerous advertisements featuring the new department store waxed rhapsodic about the love between mothers and their children even while reminding readers that the new store facilitated the purchase of appropriate gifts for mothers. Even advertisements for products that had little to do with family life, such as those for Starlight brand pantyhose, displayed touching photographs of mother and child. The mother, in other words, had become a public relations coup.

In 1967, a competition was set up in Kermanshah that rewarded the mothers of the healthiest babies.[77] The mothering of healthy children remained a focus of state interest and women's propaganda.

Although women would go on to vote and to participate in professional fields in record numbers, the emphasis on maternalism ensured that women would uphold traditional family values. Patriarchy need not be threatened by the educated, enfranchised Iranian woman, since she guarded her virtue and maintained her commitment to the family. Even if the size of the Iranian family shrank, its moral fabric would remain intact. The emphasis on "appropriate" mothering and the recognition accorded to mothers of healthy children served as reminders that women could not easily extricate themselves from the web of maternalist demands placed upon them. Nor did maternalist ideology invite dissenting opinions in its endorsement of modern medical techniques related to childbirth and child rearing.

Nonetheless, maternalist debates enabled women to transform notions of motherhood from a perfect and unattainable ideal into a realistic accounting of the complex relationship between mothers and children. Women voiced their opinions about mothering, health care, and eventually politics in the burgeoning press. Some women also perceived the limitations of the maternalist discourse, with its emphasis on family life, and encouraged Iranian women to pursue careers in fields outside of nursing and education, two professions that traditionally had attracted women workers to their ranks. The distinctions between maternalists and feminists came to the fore as the political process in Iran continued to deny women equal representation and participation.

CHAPTER 10

✧

Civil Liberties, Civic Wombs

Women in the Islamic Republic

The reforms of the Pahlavi era had often targeted the ʿulama, and mainstream Islam became dissociated from the women's movement.[1] State-supported organs of women's activism such as the Society for Women (Kanun-i Banuvan) and its subsequent incarnation, the Women's Organization of Iran (Sazman-i Zanan-i Iran), did not often challenge the philosophical and secular underpinnings of the Pahlavi regime. The official women's movement thus dissociated itself from mainstream Islamic ideology. Themes of religious import and profiles of noteworthy religious women rarely were featured in their activities or publications.

Despite the absence of Islamic rhetoric from the women movement, many Iranian families embraced popular Shiʿi traditions in their daily lives. In the 1920s, even young Muslim women studying at the American Girls' School, which was administered by Presbyterian missionaries in Tehran, adhered to their faith. In her annual report to the Board of Foreign Missions, Jane E. Doolittle, the principal of the school, reported that some boarders "wanted to fast and of course I gave the older ones Permission if they wished—but the mere idea of being allowed to, was all they wanted, and we have heard nothing more of it."[2] The popularity of Shiʿi traditions could be seen in the naming of Iranian Muslim children as well. In 1925, the American chargé in

Iran, W. Smith Murray, observed that "as regards the most common masculine given-names in use until recently in Persia, they are all either those of the Prophet, of members of his immediate family, or else attributes of Allah." He listed the following as the most popular masculine names: Mohammad, Hasan, Husayn, Mahmud, and Akbar, among others. Murray reported that women's names derived from the names of the Prophet's wives or family members, such as Fatima, Saffia, Ayesha, Masoumah, and Khadijah, among others.[3]

After the fall of Reza Shah, some journals such as *Nida-yi Haqq* lamented the absence of Islam from Iranian cultural life, citing the dearth of Islamic schools as well as the low turnout for annual Islamic rituals such as the hajj. By 1953, however, the mayor of Najaf, Haj Said, reported that Iranian "pilgrims are again coming to Najaf in large numbers."[4] The secularizing tendencies of the Pahlavi ruling elite had widened the chasm between social conservatives and westernizing modernists. In the 1960s and 1970s there was a backlash against the regime's cosmetic consumerism, as conservative intellectuals and clerics challenged publicly the dominant secular nationalist culture of Iran. Critics of the regime such as Jalal Al-i Ahmad—whose condemnatory essay, *Westoxication*, published in 1961, defined the ethos of the revolutionary movement of 1979—strove to locate indigenous cultural roots to effect social change in Iranian society. These rifts replicated themselves in the women's movement as well.

A contemporary of Al-i Ahmad, Ali Shari'ati emerged as a leading advocate of change in women's lives. Shari'ati was born in 1933, three years prior to the promulgation of the unveiling decree. Considered one of the ideologues of the 1979 Iranian Revolution, Shari'ati attended the Sorbonne in 1960 to study sociology and Islam. Upon his return to Iran in 1965, he went to his hometown for a brief period before moving to Tehran to lecture at the Husayniya Ershad, a religious establishment funded by merchants.[5] A sprawling conference hall, the Husayniya Irshad became the first modern Islamic center that housed not only a mosque but also space for classes, a dining room, and a library.[6] Shari'ati's Western education alienated him from the 'ulama, who distrusted his notions of reform. His works are imbued with Marxist and existentialist leanings, drawn from his studies at the Sorbonne, and his treatise on Fatima exposes some of these ideological biases.[7]

Fatima Is Fatima emerged from lectures that Shariʿati delivered in 1971 at the Husayniya Ershad on the anniversary of Fatima's birth.[8] On that occasion, Shariʿati addressed the identity crisis that he perceived Iranian women to be facing and exhorted them to follow the example of Fatima. Shariʿati was not the first Islamic writer to invoke Fatima's memory in the context of modern Iranian womanhood. In 1961, as the rift grew between conservative groups and advocates of women's suffrage, a magazine published from Astan-i Quds, a religious center in Mashhad, remembered Fatima, that "dame of Islam." The issue was printed in the Islamic month marking her birthday. Fatima stood out as "immaculate," holy, and chaste. She taught the women of the world the meaning of chastity. In short, "it is hoped that our women will follow in the footsteps of Fatima."[9]

Because of its polemical tone, Shariʿati's work cannot be dissociated from its historical context of prerevolutionary Iran—a period of ideological flux and questioning for many Iranians. Much of his speculation about the role and position of Fatima related to Shariʿati's larger intellectual concerns about socialism and revolution.[10] As the translator of this work, Laleh Bakhtiar, writes, Shariʿati "cries out the question which is upon all women's lips, 'Who am I?' 'Am I a mother?' 'A wife?' 'A daughter?' 'A friend?' 'A biologist?' 'A chemist?' 'A doctor, nurse, mid-wife, laborer, writer, human being . . . ?' 'Who am I?"[11] These questions showed the multifarious functions of women in society. Through them, Shariʿati aimed at developing a feminine ideal that would encompass those female identities within an Islamic context. Though he offered new ways of imagining Fatima, Shariʿati extolled the ideals of propriety and motherhood. He, too, privileged women's role as mothers and matriarchs of Iranian society in his hagiography of Fatima. Shariʿati's work illustrated the ways in which Islam can be reinterpreted in the modern period to empower or suppress Iranian women. Though Shariʿati acknowledged the multiple roles women assumed in society, he nevertheless glorified the traditional womanly values that made Fatima a beloved figure in Shi'i culture, including chastity, religiosity, and domesticity.

Yet Shariʿati believed that women themselves also played a part in reinforcing their subjugation. The propagation by women and men of "superstitious" notions of family and patriarchy—or "father power," as Shariʿati termed it—contributed to the suppression of women: "All of this occurs in the name of Islam . . . and worst of all, in the name of

'similarity to Fatima.'"[12] Fatima, an icon of Persian womanhood virtually ignored for much of the century, regained her glorified status as
the quintessential source of imitation for Shiʻi women after the establishment of the Islamic Republic.

Media reinforced and popularized the image of Fatima as a liber-
ator of modern Shi'i women. For example, in the aftermath of the
Islamic Revolution, Mother's Day in Iran was celebrated on Fatima's
birthday—an overt attempt by the nascent regime to link its agenda
on Islamic womanhood with the sacred persona of Fatima.[13] In 1980
a group of students issued a statement on Women's Day, also commemorated on the birthday of Fatima, to stamp her imprimatur on
Iran's revolutionary agenda. As the announcement proclaimed, "It
befits the revolutionary women of the Iranian society to become
more acquainted with the Imam's line concerning women and their
mission and to invite women of our age to study the position of
women in Islam and to show them how Islam and the Islamic revolution glorifies women. . . . They should teach human society about
giving and sacrifice, which resulted in the sacrifice of great martyrs at
the threshold of Islam."[14] By connecting revolutionary Islam with
Fatima and the cult of martyrdom already predominant in Shi'i literature, Iranian students lent legitimacy and historicity to their cause.

Even politicians invoked Fatima's memory. In 1983, at a seminar on
women and Islam at al-Zahra University, Mrs. Monireh Gorji, formerly a representative to the Assembly of Experts, "called on Iranian
women to be inspired by the exemplars"—Khadija, Asiyeh, Mary, and
Fatima.[15] Ayatollah Azari-Qumi, who served in the Council of Experts
of the Iranian parliament, depicted Fatima as the quintessence of
Islamic womanhood in his writings. Qumi even traces the tradition of
veiling women in chadors to Fatima: "The Prophet's daughter called
the Jews to Islam by her hejab, in particular by wearing the chador. In
observing hejab, she is a perfect example for our women."[16]

During the 1979 Islamic Revolution, other Islamic symbols of
womanhood supplanted secular ideals of feminism. The veil, once a
mark of backwardness, was resurrected as a sign of empowerment. To
Western observers who had been watching the volatile events unfurl
in Iran since 1978, the uprisings represented a "push for more mor-
alism." In the immured and religious city of Qum caustic slogans
appeared written in blood promising "death to the shah," a refrain
that would galvanize the demonstrators.[17]

The revolution had been an exhilarating moment for women activists, many of whom were educated and donned the veil as a show of opposition against the shah.[18] Women became symbols of the revolution by defying the secular vision of womanhood embraced by the Pahlavi state and its benign organs of institutional reform. Since the early Pahlavi regime had made women's appearance a key to the state's renewal project, especially with its emphasis on the removal of the veil, opposition to the regime occurred in the act of re-veiling. To many women the shah had represented an authoritarian presence, and their choice to re-veil represented an anti-shah stance.

The ambiguities over the politics of dress manifested themselves in March 1979 on the occasion of International Women's Day. A month had passed since the heady days following the defeat of the Pahlavi regime. Uncertainty and fear supplanted the initial public jubilation over the momentous political change. Many women who had supported the revolution struggled to make sense of the political chaos that accompanied the toppling of the shah's regime. Murmurings about an Islamic dress code for women raised questions about the political direction of the fledgling government. In early March Ayatollah Khomeini voiced criticism that female government employees were reporting to work without a chador.[19] His public comments became fodder for women activists, some of whom had already made the decision to rally in protest at the University of Tehran on International Women's Day when an announcement suspended the Family Protection Act of 1967.[20] Then, on March 8, military squads fired upon female demonstrators who had put on blue jeans, as well as the approved chador, to call for "freedom of dress."[21]

The unity forged in the overthrow of the Pahlavi dynasty dissipated shortly after the establishment of the Islamic Republic.[22] L. Bruce Laingen of the American Embassy in Tehran, later a hostage, reported on the deteriorating condition of Iranian women, noting that the emphasis on motherhood and marriage seemed to be an "open-ended invitation to limit" women's freedom to choose careers outside the home.[23] As public demonstrations showed, women of varying backgrounds marched in protest, fearing the curtailment of women's liberties. Hecklers hurled invectives, calling unveiled women "whores."[24] Educated and professional women worried that their hard-won struggles and rights remained threatened.

While dress codes became open to debate, Ayatollah Khomeini called on women and men to appear en masse at polling stations to select the first president of the republic. Re-veiling became the norm through intimidation and coercive policies at the workplace and in public. Women clad in the black chador and holding rifles represented a new brand of feminism and female militarism in Iran. Leftist guerilla organizations such as the Mujahidin-i Khalq and the Fidaiyan-i Khalq recruited many young female students who dressed modestly and eschewed makeup and other outward manifestations of femininity.[25] The success of leftist organizations in recruiting young educated women showed the ways in which dissenting women defied the feminine ideals of womanhood embraced by the Pahlavi state. Some young women such as Ashraf Dihqani, a member of the Fidaiyan's central committee, had even been tortured by the shah's secret police, SAVAK.[26] Such images overturned stereotypical depictions of veiled women as meek and subservient. Rather, the defiance of veiled "sister zaynabs" (*khaharan-i zaynab*) introduced a new expression of female activism in Iran that forced a more subtle explanation for veiling in the postrevolutionary climate.

For the ordinary woman, the distinction between "good hijab" and "bad hijab" was not always an easy one. Although women's magazines such as *Zan-i Ruz* quickly adapted themselves to the revolutionary environment and depicted acceptable models of Islamic dress, Iranian women did not always know what constituted improper veiling. In 1987, the Women's Association of the Islamic Republic, directed by Zahra Mostafavi, Ayatollah Khomeini's daughter, formed a Hijab Commission to curtail the appearance of "bad hijab."[27] The consequences of being singled out as a woman with "bad hijab," however, were grave, for "bad hijab" women ran the risk of being subjected to harassment and, in extreme cases, lashings.

Schools, media outlets, and security personnel worked to impose Islamic uniformity through dress. The Islamic Republic cast its authority by requiring women to comply with its newfangled dress codes, which were not always clear-cut. This ambiguity had its benefits. On one hand, women could still express their individuality through their choice of head scarf and *rupush* (long coat). On the other hand, women could be subjected to harassment for failing to comply with permissible modes of dress.[28] The Islamic dress code introduced new standards of beauty for Iranian women. One might even argue that the Islamic government shattered the "beauty myth" well before a young writer named Naomi Wolf took on that crusade with the publication of her provocative work in America. Women employees in government offices could not wear makeup or distinguishing clothing. Instead, the work culture imposed an austere dress code that discouraged bright colors in Islamic covering.[29]

Girls in Schoolbooks: Second Grade Religious Instruction Textbook (1998).

After the revolution, school curricula portrayed veiling as the rule for Iranian women and girls, even though many girls remembered the experience of going to school unveiled. The protagonist in Marjane Satrapi's highly popular book and film *Persepolis* describes a scene in which she derides the silliness and artificiality of the compulsory veiling program in schools. The young girl had previously attended the same school unveiled.[30] Even elementary school books that targeted prepubescent girls and boys depicted the girls with a head covering.[31] Iran eventually created its domestic version of Barbie and Ken dolls for children, renamed Sara and Dara and created as an alternative to the sexually revealing Western dolls.[32]

The stringency with which veiling was enforced in the Islamic Republic shifted with the vicissitudes of Iranian politics and economic life. In addition, the veil on occasion became simply a tool of public conformity rather than a successful weapon of ideological indoctrination. It is telling, for example, that beneath her veil, Fatimah Hashemi Rafsanjani, daughter of the Iranian president, preferred to wear a Western-looking Chanel-style suit rather than a traditional Persian outfit.[33] The timing here is no less significant, since by 1997 the war with Iraq had long ended, Ayatollah Khomeini had been deceased for nearly a decade, and a new forward-thinking politician named Mohammad Khatami had appeared on the horizon. Even if publicly women still looked eerily similar, dressed in various incarnations of Islamic covering, behind closed doors their choice of attire expressed not just individuality but also ideological differences.

Textbooks on Islamic culture (*farhang-i Islami*) and religious lessons (*ta'limat-i dini*) instilled other virtues through religiosity. Whereas state ideology during the Pahlavi era had exalted traditional family relations, morality, and appropriate attire as nationalist norms, the Islamic republic recast these maternalist ideals as Islamic objectives. The contents of a second-grade textbook on religious education provided not only simple explanations of Islam but also a road map to individual morality. Cleanliness through maintenance of the body, belief in God (*khuda shinashi*), and productive labor became individual ideals inculcated through religion. A short but telling vignette portrayed the Prophet Muhammad as a messenger "who loved children and who was very kind to them." The children climbed on his shoulders and walked along with him. They enjoyed their merriment with the Prophet, and he delighted in hearing their laughter. One day, when the Prophet was playing with his grandchildren, Hasan and Husayn, he expressed his tenderness toward them by caressing and kissing them. A passer-by who observed the scene was taken aback by the Prophet's expression of affection toward his grandchildren. The moral of the story was clear: the Prophet's community of faith needed to heed his example and cherish children: "O Muslims! O fathers and mothers! Hold children dear and be kind to them. For anyone who is not kind to children is not a Muslim among us."[34] The first Shi'i imam, Hazrat Ali, was similarly depicted as a family-loving man.

Respect for mothers remained an important theme in the upbringing of Iranian children. A poem entitled "A Mother's Story" again depicted an ideal Islamic family in which the mother affectionately cared for her child in "a pure world" (*jahan-i pak*) and with a "good God."[35] By connecting veiling to women's virtue, supporters of the Islamic Republic extolled the maternalist goals of promoting conventional family life, healthful reproduction, and personal hygiene, themes recast within an Islamic framework.

How did maternalist policies guide the state's latest position on women and reproduction? When the Islamic Republic was established,

Girl Praying: Second Grade Religious Instruction Textbook (1998).

it overturned the 1967 Family Protection Law on grounds of Westernism, and initially it was unclear whether contraceptives would be made legally available.[36] The regime encouraged high fertility, adopted a pro-natalist stance (partly because of the increased fatalities resulting from the Iran-Iraq War), and provided added economic incentives to larger families. In 1986 the national census indicated that the population growth rate was increasing by more than 3 percent. At first officials of the Islamic Republic of Iran lauded the country's considerable population.[37]

After the publication of the 1986 census and the conclusion of the war two years later, the government launched a campaign to control population growth. The Ministry of Health and Medical Education began discussing family planning options and even invited public debate on the population question in popular daily newspapers.[38] In 1989, a Five-Year Plan to control population growth was put forth, which was approved by the parliament.[39] The Ministry of Health and Medical Education also began distributing contraceptives, including pills and condoms, free of charge through its various networks. In 1991, a distinct department for family planning existed, and women health practitioners played an important role in educating rural communities about contraceptive use.[40] By 1999 the nation's supreme leader had passed decrees legalizing contraceptives and sterilization, including vasectomies. The country's only condom factory at the time produced approximately seventy million condoms annually to help with the government's campaign to limit family size among Iranians and to control the nation's swelling population.[41]

At the same time the Islamic Republic has striven to control infant mortality through its health care policies. Breast-feeding was stressed in an effort to promote infant health. A study conducted in 1993 recommended that medical education in Iran should place more emphasis on nutrition and especially breast-feeding. The same study further advised that there "is a need for widespread and serious public health education efforts through the mass media (especially radio and television), by religious leaders and clergymen, as well as through textbooks and face-to-face encounters," to promote breast-feeding and to educate mothers about how to maintain their milk supply.[42] In 1999 it was found that the average duration of breast-feeding in Iran, especially in urban centers, was less than the four to six months recommended by the World Health Organization. An experimental study conducted in Shiraz, Iran, argued that educating lactating mothers about the benefits of exclusive breast-feeding during the first four months after delivery not only increased the percentage of mothers who breast-fed but also enhanced the health of their infants.[43]

Nonetheless, infant mortality persisted as a pressing concern in hygiene and population politics. In 1985, the dearth of clean drinking water in some rural communities had been identified as a stumbling block in the government's efforts to improve public health, especially for small children. At that time only 50 percent of Iranian villages had access to clean water. Despite these existing challenges, Ali Reza Marandi, the Iranian health minister in 1985, claimed a significant drop in mortality figures since 1979.[44] Other studies suggest a decline in infant mortality as well. According to demographers Akbar Aghajanian and Amir Mehryar, there was a significant decline in infant mortality, which they attributed the decline to increased access to clean water and electricity in rural areas.[45]

Like its previous incarnations, the Islamic state was far from rational in executing its maternalist policies. In 1990, for example, President Hashemi Rafsanjani endorsed temporary marriage— sigheh—as a legitimate form of relationship between women and men. Yet Fatemeh Karrubi, who directed the Martyrs' Foundation Hospital Center and whose husband, Mehdi Karrubi, served as speaker of the parliament, criticized the endorsement of sigheh. As Fatemeh Karrubi explained, "To establish a permanent foundation for marriage it must be a permanent marriage, not a temporary one."[46] The prevalence of sigheh might be a deterrent against commitment to a conventional marriage, not to mention a cause in the spread of venereal disease.

To combat newly discovered illnesses, the country recast its campaign against sexually transmitted diseases and drug abuse. In Iran AIDS appeared publicly in 1987, when a child was found to be infected after a blood transfusion. In 1990, the Iranian government reported that eleven Iranians had died of AIDS and that 138 individuals carried the virus thought to trigger AIDS. Indeed, the government asserted that the carriers were hemophiliacs who prior to 1983 had received transfusions of blood contaminated with the virus. According to news reports, by 1999 there had been 203 recorded deaths from AIDS. By 2002 the number of HIV-positive patients in Iran as well as cases of full-blown AIDS had increased, and many individuals carrying the AIDS virus were identified as male drug users.[47]

The spread of AIDS challenged Iran's Islamic mores and its emphasis on traditional family roles. President Ahmadinejad's infamous denial of the existence of homosexuality in Iran on his trip to the United States in 2007 only underlined the stigma attached to homosexual behavior in Iran. Just as the Qajar state found it more convenient to attribute the spread of syphilis and gonorrhea to the sharing of opium pipes, the Islamic Republic preferred to explain the spread of AIDS by focusing on the circumscribed population of drug addicts.

Although it was becoming socially imperative to teach the public about the hazards of AIDS, social obstacles compounded the government's efforts to inform citizens and adolescents about modes of contracting the disease. In particular, physicians felt uncomfortable discussing sexuality and the use of condoms. For instance, a brochure apparently distributed to teenagers taught abstinence in the following terms: "The best way to avoid AIDS is to be faithful to moral and family obligations and to avoid loose sexual relations. Trust in God in order to resist satanic temptations."[48] Dr. Mohammad Mehdi, an infectious disease specialist who headed the Iranian Center for Disease Control, admitted that "[we] cannot talk about things that are opposed to our culture, opposed to our religious beliefs. Premarital sex is inappropriate and un-Islamic. So we can't say things to teen-agers like, 'Use a condom.'"[49] Nonetheless, Dr. Mehdi, acting on an order from Iran's supreme leader, Ayatallah Khamenei, worked to prevent the proliferation of AIDS.

A major step in the government's efforts to acknowledge publicly the spread and threat of AIDS came in 2002 when the National Committee to Fight AIDS recommended that Iranian students receive AIDS awareness information. Although the government's position, in observance of Islamic law, endorsed abstinence until marriage as the best way of avoiding AIDS, it nonetheless planned to inform students about the use of condoms and the possibility of the transmission of AIDS through intercourse.[50] In 2003 the government also decided to start distributing gratis clean syringes to drug users, officially estimated at 140,000, partly in an effort to limit the spread of AIDS.[51]

The Islamic Republic has at times approached veiling, women's health, family relations, and reproduction with little recognition that women actually have civil liberties as well as "civic wombs." Women's perspectives on politics and reproduction mattered not only because of their reproductive status but also because of their rights as citizens. An analysis of Iran's cultural and reproductive policies since 1979 becomes revealing less for the data it includes than for the dearth of women's voices setting the debate or providing oppositional views. It is this silencing—if not muting—of dissenting opinions that shows the subtle and conspicuous ways in which patriarchy ingrains itself in Iranian society.

Epilogue

It is because of men's lack of interest in promoting the enlightenment of women that today our sisters have been deprived of all humanistic progress.
—Rawshanak Naw'dust

To disregard women and bar them from active participation in political, social, economic and cultural life would in fact be tantamount to depriving the entire population of every society of half its capability. The patriarchal culture and the discrimination against women, particularly in the Islamic countries, cannot continue for ever.
—Shirin Ebadi, winner of the Nobel Peace Prize, 2003

Rawshanak Naw'dust and Shirin Ebadi inhabited different worlds. A journalist in interwar Persia, Naw'dust wrote about the hardships of peasant women toiling in the rice fields of Gilan. A lawyer in contemporary Iran, Ebadi built a career on defending disenfranchised women. Their opinions, spanning nearly a century, remind us that patriarchy in Iran remains entrenched. The power to engage, suppress, or recast Iranian women has often reflected on the political strength and viability of the Iranian state in the modern era. If the mandatory unveiling of women in 1936 embodied the secular nationalist objectives of the Reza Shah era (1926–41), the compulsory veiling of women after 1979 demonstrated the political will of the newly instated Islamic Republic.

It is perhaps ironic that within this patriarchal framework a discourse on maternalism should emerge giving women unexpected privileges and opportunities even while reinforcing their traditional identities as mothers and wives. Although Islam legislated norms of behavior regarding sexual relations, marriage, and divorce, it left room for interpretation in concepts related to reproduction, education, and mothering. Maternalism impinged on women's ability to make personal choices regarding their looks, health, and upbringing. While maternalists wrote about women's health, many approached the subject with little recognition that women actually had informed opinions on reproduction and maternal health care. As Iran faced social challenges, state policy reinforced maternalism as a prevailing ideology in national culture and local politics. Just as women dared to confront the issue of syphilis in the mid-1930s, many in the Islamic republic are now taking on the equally controversial and troubling spread of AIDS, alongside familiar debates over veiling, marriage laws, and political empowerment.

At key junctures, Iranian women have symbolized the nation's turbulent struggles. In the famous tobacco crisis of 1891–92, the women in the shah's harem, along with members of the merchant and religious classes, boycotted the use of tobacco—a popular consumer good at the time—for political purposes. During the constitutional revolution of 1906, women demonstrated alongside the men to demand the creation of a parliament. When the Pahlavi dynasty was installed in 1926, women embodied the ideology of renewal (*tajaddud*) that strove to recast the modern Iranian citizen in attire, body, and mind. Under the Islamic Republic, veiled women became the most conspicuous symbol of the regime's Islamist ideology and social policies. Finally, in the summer of 2009, Iranian women took to the streets to protest the results of the June 12 elections.

The tension between religion and secularism has played out poignantly during crucial moments in Iran's modern history, not least in the lives of Iranian women, whose status in society has been legislated by virtually every regime the country has endured over the last century. This control has spilled into the realms of women's sexuality, reproductive status, and health care.

As Iran marks the thirtieth anniversary of the Islamic Republic, women have embodied the nation's popular will and its silent dissent. They have endured violent backlash against their activism. Some, such as former minister of education Dr. Farrokhrou Parsa, lost their lives when the regime changed hands.[1] The anxiety over women's independence pits supporters of women's rights against its detractors. The need to watch over women and the need to secure men's control remain key issues, couched in the language of religion. Conservatives have drawn upon Islam to recast maternalism and to create a rationale for the social objectives of the revolution.

Even while pursuing maternalist aspirations, record numbers of Iranian women now participate in the workforce, either by choice or by necessity.[2] Major universities in Iran have women's studies departments.[3] Women have pushed ahead on the political front as well. A women's bloc of MPs in the sixth Majlis (2000–4) emerged and was headed by Elaheh Koulaee. In June 2005, women coming from different social backgrounds joined a sit-in outside the University of Tehran to encourage women to run for president.[4]

Other women, such as Shirin Ebadi, have carved a niche for themselves in the legal system. Forced out of her position as one of the country's first female judges, Ebadi resumed her work as a human rights lawyer, striving to protect political dissidents and defend the rights of women and children. She has been arrested for her activism, but even the fear of imprisonment and death has not stopped her from continuing the struggle against political oppression. In an interview with the *Sunday Times* of London in 2003, Ebadi is quoted as saying, "All I want is legal equality between men and women. What I represent is a small part of a deep-rooted reform movement in Iran that cannot be stopped. In every society there comes a time when people want to be free. That time has come in Iran."[5] Ebadi may not have coordinated the timing of her predictions with the political currents of the nation, but nearly six years later, Iran buzzed with the spirit of her message during the election campaign.

In the summer of 2009 women and men from all walks of Persian society took to the streets to challenge the outcome of the June 12 elections, giving rise to the most significant protests in the country since 1979. A harsh and violent response from the government to these demonstrations has not only polarized the public but also lent credence to the supporters of opposition candidate Mir Hossein Mousavi, who claim that the election was stolen from their man.

From the far corners of Tehran arose an unlikely rebel. Neda Agha Soltan, a university student, was killed in the violent protests that ensued after the announcement of the election results. For many, Neda became the icon of Iran's "green" movement. That a young female scholar emerged as the symbol of this inspiring movement defied stereotypes of Persian women as politically deferential. The impact of Neda's death signaled the legacy of patriotic womanhood which she perhaps unknowingly inherited. In her death, Neda joined the pantheon of famous and unknown women who have sacrificed their lives so that others might come one step closer to realizing the full meaning of political freedom.

Perhaps it is fitting that in her grief Neda's mother has united with countless other grieving mothers of Iranian youths to denounce the tragic killings of their children. Shortly after the bloody demonstrations that cost many young lives, the Mourning Mothers of Iran organized vigils in public parks to protest in silence the senseless murders of their children.[6] These women have conveyed dissent and given political expression to their losses by invoking motherhood. Though they, too, face coercion and threats, the Mourning Mothers have not backed down. In their muted defiance these mothers carry on as thunderous icons of liberty and human dignity.

NOTES

ACKNOWLEDGMENTS

1. Ta'ib, *Bimaristan'hayih Rasht az Mashrutah ta 1357* (Rasht, 1384/2005). This fascinating study documents the contributions of our family members and many others to the development of health care in Gilan. This work also highlights my grandmother's charitable activities and her leadership role in the women's clinic of Rasht.

INTRODUCTION

1. Mary E. Fissell, *Vernacular Bodies* (Oxford: Oxford University Press, 2004). This section is drawn from my review essay of Fissell's work, "Stepping Out of the Womb: Women and the Politics of Reproduction," *Journal of Women's History* 22, 3 (2010): 195–99.
2. "Az tavvalud-i bachih'ha chih midanid?" [What do you know about the birth of babies?], *Banu*, No. 1, Azar 1323/November–December 1944, 7–8. Some of the questions included the following: Do women give birth to more boys during wartime? (yes); Is it possible to determine the gender of a fetus from the heartbeat of a woman? (no); Do women who master domesticity tend to give birth to boys? (no); Do the main causes of infertility have more to do with a woman's body? (yes); Does the use of birth control bring about infertility? (no).
3. As Koven and Michel have argued, "Maternalism always operated on two levels: it extolled the private virtues of domesticity while simultaneously legitimating women's public relationships to politics and the state, to community, workplace, and marketplace." Seth Koven and Sonya Michel, "Womanly Duties: Maternalist Politics and the Origins of Welfare States in France, Germany, Great Britain, and the United States, 1880–1920," *American Historical Review* 95, 4 (1990), 1079.
4. Camron Amin, *The Making of the Modern Iranian Woman: Gender, State Policy, and Popular Culture, 1865–1946* (Gainesville: University Press of Florida, 2002). Amin discusses the many professional opportunities that opened up to Iranian women in the interwar era. For women as embodiments of the nation, see Afsaneh Najmabadi, "The Erotic *Vatan* [Homeland] as Beloved and Mother: To Love, to Possess, and to Protect," *Comparative Studies in Society and History* 39, 3 (1997): 442–67. Also, F. Kashani-Sabet, "The Frontier Phenomenon: Perceptions of the Land in Iranian Nationalism," *Critique* 38, 3 (1997): 19–38; F. Kashani-Sabet, *Frontier Fictions: Shaping the Iranian Nation, 1804–1946* (Princeton: Princeton University Press, 1999), chs. 4, 6; F. Kashani-Sabet,

"Hallmarks of Humanism: Hygiene and Love of Homeland in Qajar Iran," *American Historical Review* 105, 4 (2000): 1171–203. Related studies include Mohamad Tavakoli-Targhi, "Going Public: Patriotic and Matriotic Homeland in Iranian Nationalist Discourses," *Strategies: Journal of Theory, Culture and Politics* 13, 2 (2000): 175–200, and Camron Amin, "Selling and Saving 'Mother Iran': Gender and the Iranian Press in the 1940s," *International Journal of Middle East Studies* 33, 3 (2001): 335–61.

5. Anthropologist Ziba Mir-Hosseini defines feminism another way: "as a general concern with women's issues; an awareness that women suffer discrimination at work, in the home, and in society because of their gender; and action aimed at improving their lives and changing the situation." Ziba Mir-Hosseini, *Islam and Gender: The Religious Debate in Contemporary Iran* (Princeton: Princeton University Press, 1999), 6. For a critique of feminism (*'aqayid-i feministi*) in a Persian journal, see *Payk-i Sa'adat-i Nisvan*, Nos. 4–5 (May–July, 1928), 98.

6. Yoshikuni Igarashi, *Bodies of Memory: Narratives of War in Postwar Japanese Culture, 1945–1970* (Princeton: Princeton University Press, 2000); Gail Kligman, *The Politics of Duplicity: Controlling Reproduction in Ceausescu's Romania* (Berkeley: University of California Press, 1998).

7. As Offen has shown, France, along with Great Britain and Germany, recorded declining population rates in the nineteenth century. Karen Offen, "Depopulation, Nationalism, and Feminism in Fin-de-Siècle France," *American Historical Review* 89, 3 (1984): 648–52.

8. Matthew Connelly, *Fatal Misconception: The Struggle to Control World Population* (Cambridge: Harvard University Press, 2008).

9. Marcia Inhorn, ed., *Reproductive Disruptions: Gender, Technology, and Biopolitics in the New Millennium* (New York: Berghahn, 2007).

10. Khaled Fahmy, "Women, Medicine, and Power in Nineteenth-Century Egypt," in *Remaking Women*, ed. Lila Abu-Lughod (Princeton: Princeton University Press, 1998). However, Fahmy's article leaves out the crucial connection between maternalism and the practice of midwifery and obstetrics in the modern era. For studies of reproduction in contemporary Iran, see Homa Hoodfar, "Devices and Desires: Population Policy and Gender Roles in the Islamic Republic," *Middle East Research Report* 24, 190 (1994): 11–17; Akbar Aghajanian, "A New Direction in Population Policy and Family Planning in the Islamic Republic of Iran," *Asia-Pacific Population Journal* 10, 1 (1995): 3–20; Akbar Aghajanian and Amir H. Mehryar, "Fertility Transition in the Islamic Republic of Iran: 1976–1996," *Asia-Pacific Population Journal* 14, 1 (1999): 21–42.

11. Kashani-Sabet, "Hallmarks of Humanism"; Firoozeh Kashani-Sabet, "'The City of the Dead': The Frontier Polemics of Quarantines in the Ottoman Empire and Iran," *Comparative Studies of South Asia, Africa, and the Middle East* 18, 2 (1998): 51–58; Firoozeh Kashani-Sabet, "Giving Birth: Women, Nursing and Sexual Hygiene in Iran," paper presented at the Fourth Biennial Conference of Iranian Studies, May 2002; Firoozeh Kashani-Sabet, "The Politics of Reproduction: Maternalism and Women's Hygiene in Iran, 1896–1941," *International Journal of Middle East Studies* 38, 1 (2006): 1–29; Cyrus Schayegh, *Who Is Knowledgeable Is Strong: Science, Class, and the Formation of Modern Iranian Society, 1900–1950*

(Berkeley: University of California Press, 2009); Amir Arsalan Afkhami, "Iran in the Age of Epidemics: Nationalism and the Struggle for Public Health, 1889–1926," Ph.D. diss., Yale University, 2003; Hormoz Ebrahimnejad, "Un traité d'épidémiologie de la médecine traditionnelle persane: *Mofarraq ol-Heyze va'l-Vaba* de Mirza Mohammad-Taqi Shirazi (ca. 1800–1873)," *Studia Iranica* 27 (1998): 83–107; Hormoz Ebrahimnejad, "La médecine d'observation en Iran du XIXe siècle," *Gesnerus: Swiss Journal of the History of Medicine and Sciences* 55, 1–2 (1998): 33–57; Willem Floor, *Public Health in Qajar Iran* (Washington, DC: Mage, 2004). Islamic and Persian historiography effervesces with the brilliant contributions of intellectuals and physicians such as Muhammad ibn Zakaria Razi (d. 932) and Ibn Sina (d. 1037). Not only did the writings of these medieval intellectual giants guide physicians for centuries, but their insights continue to inspire historical analysis and interpretation. By contrast, we know rather little about the social history of hygiene and the popular practices of health and healing in the Middle East. In the case of Persian historiography, we still have limited data on Iranian physicians and their involvement in the creation of modern society. This lacuna in Persian historiography has sometimes been explained away by saying that "nineteenth-century Iranian medicine also lacked celebrities of Avicenna or Razi's calibre" (Ebrahimnejad, *Medicine, Public Health, and the Qajar State* [Leiden: Brill, 2004], 6) and thus the subject did not warrant intense scholarly scrutiny.

12. Compare with Laurel T. Ulrich, *A Midwife's Tale: The Life of Martha Ballard Based on Her Diary, 1785–1812* (New York: Knopf, 1990). These historiographical difficulties, however, should not deter social historians from delving into the field of public health. Even if accurate data are at times wanting, available documentation in the form of historical manuscripts, travelogues, and journalistic accounts can chronicle the social circumstances and cultural milieux in which ideas of maternalism and hygiene took shape and gained institutional backing. Moreover, Iranian and other international libraries contain valuable and overlooked medical manuscripts from the nineteenth century—barely referenced by historians—that shed light on the medical culture and social evolution of the field.

13. Several works in the last fifteen years have addressed the history of Iranian women: Parvin Paidar, *Women and the Political Process in Twentieth-Century Iran* (Cambridge: Cambridge University Press, 1995); Amin, *The Making of the Modern Iranian Woman*; Afsaneh Najmabadi, *Women with Mustaches, Men Without Beards: The Sexual and Gender Anxieties of Iranian Modernity* (Berkeley: University of California Press, 2005); Hamideh Sedghi, *Women and Politics in Iran: Veiling, Unveiling, and Reveiling* (Cambridge: Cambridge University Press, 2006); Nikki Keddie, *Women in the Middle East: Past and Present* (Princeton: Princeton University Press, 2007); Janet Afary, *Sexual Politics in Modern Iran* (Cambridge: Cambridge University Press, 2009). All of these works deal with various questions (including education, marriage laws, and veiling), and each has significantly expanded our general understanding of women's lives in Iran.

14. See my article "Hallmarks of Humanism," in which I laid out a case first for the study of hygiene as distinct from medicine, and second as an argument for

broadening the study of hygiene to include discussions of humanism, politics, and gender. See F. Kashani-Sabet, "Politics of Reproduction: Maternalism and Women's Hygiene in Iran, 1896–1941," *International Journal of Middle East Studies* 38, 1 (2006): 1–29, for a study of venereal disease, nursing, and reproductive politics. Also, Floor, *Public Health in Qajar Iran.* Floor's volumes on health and sexual relations provide useful and broad historical surveys. They rely extensively on European travel accounts, thus inviting analyses that include an array of indigenous sources and that provide a theoretical framework for the discussion of sexuality and health.

15. Najmabadi's engaging analysis and creative reliance on art historical data provide a fresh interpretation of women's lives in the Qajar era. A pioneer in the field of Middle Eastern women's history, Najmabadi has published a work that stands out for its inclusion of hitherto unexplored subjects such as homoerotic love. In addition, Najmabadi's thoughtful discussions of women's education, though drawing at times on a different set of primary texts, complement my views on the subject. Whereas Najmabadi often relies on literary criticism to shape her historical arguments, my interpretations tend to be more political in orientation. In addition, some of the themes I cover, particularly the subjects of reproductive politics and midwifery, are not explored in her work. Amin's well-written analysis of Qajar and Pahlavi women leaves room for a systematic discussion of hygiene and reproductive politics as well.

16. See the following important studies: Amin, *The Making of the Modern Iranian Woman*; Afsaneh Najmabadi, "Crafting an Educated Housewife in Iran," in *Remaking Gender: Feminism and Modernity in the Middle East,* ed. Lila Abu-Lughod (Princeton: Princeton University Press, 1998), 91–125; Paidar, *Women and the Political Process in Twentieth-Century Iran*; Nikki Keddie and Beth Baron, *Women in Middle Eastern History* (New Haven: Yale University Press, 1991); Lois Beck and Nikki Keddie, eds., *Women in the Muslim World* (Cambridge: Harvard University Press, 1980); Jasamin Rostam-Kolayi, "The Women's Press, Modern Education, and the State in Early Twentieth-Century Iran, 1900–1930s," Ph.D. diss., University of California, Los Angeles, 2000; Michael Zirinsky, "Harbingers of Change: Presbyterian Women in Iran, 1883–1949," American Presbyterians: Journal of Presbyterian History 70, 3 (1992): 173–86; Michael Zirinsky, "A Panacea for the Ills of the Country: American Presbyterian Education in Inter-War Iran," Iranian Studies 26, 1–2 (1993): 119–37; Dror Ze'evi, *Producing Desire: Changing Sexual Discourse in the Ottoman Middle East, 1500–1900* (Berkeley: University of California Press, 2006).

17. As Dye and Smith have contended, "Mothering is far more than a biological constant; it is an activity whose meaning has altered considerably over time. Changes in cultural values, maternal self-perceptions, and attitudes toward children—all these factors underscore the historical dimensions of motherhood." Nancy Schrom Dye and Daniel Blake Smith, "Mother Love and Infant Death, 1750–1920," *Journal of American History* 73, 2 (1986): 329.

18. *Salnamah-i Sazman-i Zanan,* 100, mentions the existence of a Hygiene Association (Anjuman-i Haygan). Precursors to these organizations existed during the Constitutional period as well.

19. Kristin Luker, "Sex, Social Hygiene, and the State: The Double-Edged Sword of Social Reform," *Theory and Society* 27, 5 (1998): 606.

20. *Tarbiyat*, 2nd year, No. 113, 23 June 1898, 452. This issue announced the publication of works by Miftah al-Mulk called *Ta'lim al-Atfal* and *Ta'dib al-Atfal*. It was hoped that teachers would regard this work as a model for the instruction of children.

21. As Fernea has maintained, "In the Middle East, the child is seen as the crucial generational link in the family unit, the key to its continuation, the living person that ties the present to the past and to the future." Yet while Fernea has contended that "child rearing and the concept of childhood in the Middle East were until recently based on widely accepted assumptions," I argue that child care and mothering in Iran were hotly contested subjects. Elizabeth Fernea, *Children in the Muslim Middle East* (Austin: University of Texas Press, 1995), 4–5.

CHAPTER 1 : HEALING IRAN

1. J. D. Tholozan, *Histoire de la peste bubonique en Perse, ou la détermination de son origine, de sa marche, du cycle de ses apparitions, et de la cause de sa prompte extinction* (Paris: Masson, 1874), 25.

2. Public Record Office, F.O. 248/330, Resht, 24 May 1877, 1–2.

3. *International Sanitary Conference* (Paris, 1851), 31st séance, M. le Docteur Monlau, Secrétaire Rapporteur; *International Sanitary Conference* (Constantinople, 1866), No. 1, séance du 13 Février 1866, 3.

4. MH 98/24/51345, "Les symptomes de la peste de Rescht d'après Hassan Khan."

5. FO 248/330, Churchill to Thomson, Anzali, 11 July 1877. Churchill was not alone in thinking that British habits and cleanliness were a breed above the rest. In a report on the plague in Baghdad, Dr. Colvill remarked on the cleanliness of the average Englishman: "In a house usually clean and well drained, such a dwelling as a middle-class Englishman inhabits . . . there would be no danger of plague spreading." See MH 98/24/51345, Surgeon-Major Colvill to Consul-General Nixon, Baghdad, September 4, 1877, 2.

6. For reference to I'tizad al-Saltanah's comment, see MH 98/24/51345, "Memorandum by Sir J. Dickson of the Meeting of the Board of Health on Sunday, January 14, 1877." For a discussion of hygiene and cleanliness in nineteenth-century Iran, see my essay "In Sickness and in Health."

7. Many of these treatises can be found at the National Library in Tehran, Iran. See the following works as representative samples: *Dastur al-Attiba fi Daf' al-Ta'un va al-vaba* (F/605); *Risalah dar Vaba va Ta'un* (2767/3); *Maraz-i Abilih* (F-1227/7); *Hafiz al-Sihhi-yi Nasiri* (RF-447); and *Hifz-i Sihhat* (132/1).

8. Firoozeh Kashani-Sabet, "Hallmarks of Humanism: Hygiene and Love of Homeland in Qajar Iran," *American Historical Review* 105, 4 (2000): 1179–80.

9. F.O. 248/326/51262, "Memo of the Board of Health, Sunday, February 18, 1877," 2.

10. *Ruznamah-i 'Ilmi*, No. 1, 22 Dhul-hijja 1293/8 January 1877, 4.

11. *Ruznamah-i 'Ilmi*, No. 10, 3 Rabi' al-Avval 1294/19 March 1877, 1. Cf. Michel Foucault, *Birth of the Clinic: An Archaeology of Medical Perception*, trans. A. M. Sheridan Smith (New York: Pantheon, 1973). In his study of tuberculosis in

nineteenth-century France, Barnes has discussed the term "hygienic gaze," which he argues "did indeed represent a strategy of controlling pathology through surveillance, knowledge, and writing" (David Barnes, *The Making of a Social Disease* [Berkeley: University of California Press, 1995], 213). It may be argued that a similar "hygienic" or sanitizing gaze was developing in nineteenth-century Iran.

12. For related discussions, see H. Ebrahimnejad, "Les épidémies et l'évolution de la médecine en Iran du XIXe siècle," *Medicina Nei Secoli* 11, 1 (1999):167–96.

13. *Ruznamah-i Vaqayi' Ittifaqiyah*, No. 45, 10 December 1851, 1.

14. F.O. 248/330, 25 April 1877.

15. F.O. 248/326/51262, "Proceedings of the Board of Health," 15 April 1877, 2–3.

16. F.O. 248/326/51262, "Memo of the Board of Health," 25 March 1877, 3.

17. *Farhang*, No. 76, 6 Muharram 1298/9 December 1880, 2–4. Also, *Farhang*, No. 75, 28 Dhul-hijja 1297/2 December 1880, 2–4. This topic is continued in other numbers as well.

18. *Farhang*, No. 84, 3 Rabi'al-Avval 1298/3 February 1881, 2–3.

19. *Ittila'*, No. 186, 26 Safar 1305/13 November 1887, 3.

20. As Abrahamian explains, "Each *mahalah* [quarter] had its own *kadkhuda*, who was usually chosen by the prominent families in the ward and was then confirmed in office by the city administration." Ervand Abrahamian, "Oriental Despotism: The Case of Qajar Iran," *International Journal of Middle East Studies* 5, 1 (1974): 23.

21. For more on the history of germs, see John Waller, *The Discovery of the Germ* (New York: Columbia University Press, 2002); Sherwin B. Nuland, *The Doctor's Plague: Germs, Childbed Fever, and the Strange Story of Ignac Semmelweis* (New York: W. W. Norton, 2003).

22. Qahraman Mirza Ayn al-Saltanah Salur, *Ruznamah-i Khatirat-i Ayn al-Saltanah* (Tehran: Asatir, 1374–79/1995–2000), 1:771, 28 June 1895.

23. Malik al-Muvarrikhin, *Qanun-i Muzaffari*, manuscript at the National Library, Tehran, #314, ch. 19. For studies of Tehran in the nineteenth century, see Nasir Najmi, *Dar al-Khilafah-i Tehran* (Tehran: Amir Kabir, 1977); Nasir Najmi, *Tehran-i 'Ahd-i Nasiri* (Tehran: Gulsha'i, 1990).

24. *Nasiri*, No. 1, 3 Shavval 1314/7 March 1897, 6.

25. Khan-i Khanan, *Risalah-i dar Siyasat*, manuscript at the National Library, Tehran, #385 RF, 110. Unfortunately, this manuscript offers little information on the background of the writer.

26. Ibid., 111–12.

27. *Tarbiyat*, 11 Ramadan 1315/3 February 1898, 239. It is important to note that the study of the human anatomy and physiology had roots in medieval Islamic medical literature. A fifteenth-century Persian manuscript, *Tashrih al-Badan* (Description of the Body), by Mansur ibn Muhammad ibn al Faqih Ilyas, provided a drawing of the circulatory and nervous systems of the human anatomy. As Turner explains, "Medieval Muslim physicians added significantly to our knowledge of anatomy and physiology. Diagrams such as this fifteenth-century example reveal considerable understanding of the body's vital processes." Howard R. Turner, *Science in Medieval Islam: An Illustrated Introduction* (Austin: University of Texas Press, 1995), 144.

28. *Adab*, No. 181, 6 Safar 1324/1 April 1906, 5.
29. *Adab*, No. 185, 11 Rabi' al-Avval 1324/6 May 1906, 7; *Adab*, No. 178, 5 Muharram 1324/1 March 1906, 6. This point is also reinforced by Foucault, who wrote, "Medicine must no longer be confined to a body of techniques for curing ills and of the knowledge that they require; it will also embrace a knowledge of *healthy man*, that is, a study of *non-sick man* and a definition of the *model man*" (*The Birth of the Clinic*, 34).
30. *Encyclopaedia of Islam*, "al-Insan al-Kamil." The idea of the "perfect man" also occurs in Islamic mysticism, in particular the philosophy of Ibn al-'Arabi (d. 1240). As Gerhard Böwering has noted, "The idea of the Perfect Human Being may best be understood in the Sufi paradigm that depicts the human race as taking its origin from God in cosmic descent and returning to God in mystic ascent" (*Encyclopaedia Iranica*, "Ensan-e Kamel"). For use of the term in Persian constitutionalist literature, see *Iblagh*, No. 2, 23 Dhul-hijja 1324/7 February 1907, 2.
31. *Qur'an*, Sura IV, Verse 43 & Sura V, Verse 6.
32. *Qur'an*, trans. by Mohammed M. Pickthall, 52. Sura II, Verse 222.
33. *Adab*, No. 32, 28 November 1904, 1.
34. *Adab*, No. 179, 19 Muharram 1324/15 March 1906, 8. Also, *Adab*, No. 185, 11 Rabi' al-Avval 1324/6 May 1906, 7.
35. N. Keddie, *An Islamic Response to Imperialism: Political and Religious Writings of Sayyid Jamal ad-Din "al-Afghani"* (Berkeley: University of California Press, 1968), 183–84. It is worth noting that one of Afghani's works was put on sale and advertised during the constitutional period. See *Khayr al-Kalam*, No. 78, 6 Shavval 1328/10 October 1910, 4.
36. *Tarbiyat*, No. 94, 11 Dhul-hijja 1315/3 May 1898, 376.
37. *Tarbiyat*, 14 Shavval 1314/18 March 1897, 55. I cannot agree with Foucault's assertion that "Renaissance 'humanism' and Classical 'rationalism' were indeed able to allot human beings a privileged position in the order of the world, but they were not able to conceive of man" (Michel Foucault, *The Order of Things: An Archaeology of the Human Sciences* [New York: Pantheon, 1971], 318). Indeed, the sculptures of Michelangelo, for instance, attest to Renaissance fascination with male forms and the male anatomy as categories of art and knowledge.
38. *Tarbiyat*, 3 Dhul-hijja 1314/6 May 1897, 84. The newspaper *Ruznamah-i 'Ilmiya-i Iran* also devoted several issues to the sciences.
39. The word *pathology* was not unknown to Qajar doctors and intellectuals. There is a manuscript with that title dating to the thirteenth century AH/nineteenth century CE at the National Library in Tehran: Pathologie—2777/F. In fact, there is also an explanation of the term in the journal *Hifz al-Sihhat*, No. 4, Jumada al-Avval 1324/1906, 2.
40. *Tarbiyat*, No. 59, 4 Ramadan 1315/27 January 1898, 233.
41. *Tarbiyat*, No. 88, 4 Dhul-hijja 1315/26 April 1898, 350. Also *Tarbiyat*, 14 Safar 1315/15 July 1897, 124; and *Tarbiyat*, 4 Ramadan 1315/27 January 1898, 234.
42. *Ma'arif*, No. 32, 10 Shavval 1317/10 February 1900, 2. Other related subjects that would form part of the school curriculum included ophthalmology, surgery, dentistry, physiology, and pharmacology. Other than the term *physiology*, which

was given a Persian transliteration of the equivalent French term, the aforementioned subjects were noted using Persian/Arabic words, which I have rendered into English equivalents.

43. *Ma'arif*, Tehran, No. 34, 1 Dhul-qa'da 1317/3 March 1900, 3.

44. Ibid. Here, I want to stress the very significant *public* recognition accorded the subject of women's education by the mouthpiece of the Society of Education, an influential group in establishing schools and promoting education in Qajar Iran. These themes would recur in many newspapers published later during the Constitutional period. This is more than an "oblique" reference, as Asfaneh Najmabadi claims in "Crafting an Educated Housewife in Iran," in *Remaking Women: Feminism and Modernity in the Middle East* (Princeton: Princeton University Press, 1998), 103.

45. For a discussion of female education and patriotic womanhood based on textbooks used in women's schools in late-Qajar Iran, see Firoozeh Kashani-Sabet, "Frontier Fictions: Land, Culture, and Shaping the Iranian Nation, 1804–1946," Ph.D. diss., Yale University, 1997, and Kashani-Sabet, *Frontier Fictions: Shaping the Iranian Nation, 1804–1946* (Princeton: Princeton University Press, 1999), ch. 6. For related discussions using educational texts from an earlier period, see Najmabadi, "Crafting an Educated Housewife in Iran."

46. *Adab*, 5 Sha'ban 1321/26 October 1903, 13–14.

47. *Hifz al-Sihhat*, No. 4, Jumada al-Avval 1324/1906, 18–23.

48. Women's mothering, in particular their breast-feeding abilities, remained an important theme of public hygiene in Iran. For another reference, see *Khayr al-Kalam*, No. 32, 4 Rabi' al-Avval 1328/16 March 1910, 3. Here, women are told to be careful when supplementing their breast milk with other milk. It is pointed out that a decent alternative to mother's milk is sterilized cow's milk. Women are also told to sterilize bottles before putting them in the infant's mouth. In addition, there was interest in treating diseases with sensitive social implications, such as syphilis. For instance, see *Nasiri*, No. 4, 1 Dhul-qa'da 1313/15 April 1896, 38–39.

49. For one such example, see *Nawruz*, 22 Jumada al-Avval 1321/16 August 1903, 2–3.

50. *Akhtar*, No. 20, 30 December 1890, 155.

51. Ibid.

52. *Nawruz*, 1 Rabi' al-Avval 1322/17 May 1904, 3–4. The newspaper *Nasiri* also stressed the importance of engaging in moderate physical activity and movement to maintain bodily health. See *Nasiri*, No. 17, 1 Jumada al-Thani 1312/30 November 1894.

53. *Mirrikh*, 28 April 1879, 2.

54. *Akhtar*, No. 20, 30 December 1890, 155.

55. *Tarbiyat*, 21 Safar 1315/22 July 1897, 125.

56. For a discussion of Voltaire's ideas on Mirza Fath 'Ali Akhundzadah, see Maryam B. Sanjabi, "Rereading the Enlightenment: Akhundzada and His Voltaire," *Iranian Studies* 28, 1–2 (1995): 39–60.

57. For discussions of the homeland, see Kashani-Sabet, *Frontier Fictions*. For an analysis of related Qajar political terminologies like *millat*, see Mohamad Tavakoli-Targhi, *Refashioning Iran: Orientalism, Occidentalism, and Historiography* (New York: Palgrave, 2001).

58. *Umid*, No. 9, 12 Dhul-qa'da 1324/28 December 1906, 3.

59. For similar expressions of patriotism and nostalgia for "old Iran," see *Umid*, No. 18, 1 Safar 1325/16 March 1907, 2.

60. *Ruh al-Quds*, No. 1, 25 Jumada al-Thani 1325/5 August 1907, 4. In several issues, this newspaper used medical and anatomical metaphors to discuss the problems of Iran.

61. For a study of the geographic boundaries of Iran, see Firoozeh Kashani-Sabet, "Fragile Frontiers: The Diminishing Domains of Qajar Iran," *International Journal of Middle East Studies* 29, 2 (1997): 205–34; Kashani-Sabet, *Frontier Fictions*.

62. Eric Hobsbawm and Terence Ranger, eds., *The Invention of Tradition* (Cambridge: Cambridge University Press, 1983).

63. For an interesting study on these themes using Foucauldian analysis, see David Armstrong, *Political Anatomy of the Body: Medical Knowledge in Britain in the Twentieth Century* (Cambridge: Cambridge University Press, 1983), xi, 1–18.

64. For one example, see *Hifz al-Sihhat*, No. 10, 1 Shavval 1324/1906, 24.

65. *Taraqqi*, No. 5, 5 Rabi' al-Avval 1325/1907, 1.

66. *Adab*, No. 178, 5 Muharram 1324/1 March 1906, 6.

67. *Nida-yi Vatan*, No. 46, 23 July 1907, 1.

68. *Tamaddun*, No. 45, 26 Shavval 1325/2 December 1907, 4.

69. *Nida-yi Vatan*, No. 46, 23 July 1907, 1.

70. *Tamaddun*, No. 54, 26 Muharram 1326/29 February 1908, 1–2.

71. *Baladiyya*, No. 19, 11 Jumada al-Thani 1325/22 July 1907, 4.

72. *Baladiyya*, No. 36, 19 Dhul-hijja 1325/24 January 1907, 4.

73. Mansoureh Ittihadiyeh, ed., *Maramnamah'ha va Nizamnamah'ha-yi Ahzab-i Siyasi-yi Iran dar Duvvumin Dawrah-i Majlis-i Shaura-yi Milli* (Tehran: Nashr-i Tarikh-i Iran, 1361/1982), 149, 163. During the constitutional period, efforts to promote institutions that supported public health and hygiene spread more rapidly to the provinces, in part because of the creation of provincial societies. See *Khayr al-Kalam*, No. 59, 22 Sha'ban 1328/28 August 1910, 3–4, on efforts to revamp the hospital in Rasht, Gilan. Also, *Khayr al-Kalam*, No. 51, 25 Rajab 1328/1 August 1910, 4, mentions the existence of a medical council (*shaura-yi tibbi*) that included some of the well-known doctors of Gilan and would convene twice a week. In addition, a hygiene assembly (*majlis-i hifz al-sihhi*) existed there. For a list of its members and some of its instructions, see *Khayr al-Kalam*, No. 51, 25 Rajab 1328/1 August 1910, 3.

74. *Khurshid*, Mashhad, 1328/1910, 2.

75. *Khayr al-Kalam*, No. 59, 28 August 1910; *Khayr al-Kalam*, No. 51, 1 August 1910, 4; *Khayr al-Kalam*, No. 51, 1 August 1910, 3; *Habl al-Matin*, Tehran, No. 27, 19 May 1908, 5–6.

76. Sayyid Zia' al-Din Tabataba'i, *Ta'limat-i Muduniyya* (Tehran, 1329/1911), 40–41.

77. Mirza Sayyid Muhammad Taqi, *Ta'limat-i Muduniyya* (Tehran, 1330/1912), 31–32; Mir 'Imad Naqibzadah Tabrizi, *Ma'lumat-i Muduniyya* (Tehran, 1331/1913), 125–27.

78. *Shikufah*, No. 15, 2 Shavval 1333/13 August 1915, 1–4. Some Persian illustrations and writings hallowed women as caring mothers, while others disparaged them as nags or temptresses.

79. For other examples of this, see Afsaneh Najmabadi, "The Erotic *Vatan* [Homeland] as Beloved and Mother: To Love, to Possess, and to Protect," *Comparative Studies in Society and History* 39, 3 (1997): 442–67.
80. *Shikufah*, No. 10, 14 Jumada al-Thani 1333/29 April 1915, 4.
81. For an analysis of erotic love and the motherland, see Najmabadi, "The Erotic *Vatan*." Also, Firoozeh Kashani-Sabet, "The Frontier Phenomenon: Perceptions of the Land in Iranian Nationalism," *Critique* 38, 3 (1997): 19–38; Kashani-Sabet, *Frontier Fictions*, chs. 4, 6; Kashani-Sabet, "Hallmarks of Humanism." Related studies include Mohamad Tavakoli-Targhi, "Going Public: Patriotic and Matriotic Homeland in Iranian Nationalist Discourses," *Strategies: Journal of Theory, Culture, and Politics* 13, 2 (2000): 175–200, and Camron Amin, "Selling and Saving 'Mother Iran': Gender and the Iranian Press in the 1940s," *International Journal of Middle East Studies* 33, 3 (2001): 335–61.
82. Kashani-Sabet, "Hallmarks of Humanism."
83. Other samples of Persian literature depict a less flattering image of mothers. Women appear alternatively as saintly or satanic in Persian literature. Scholars have discussed these multiple characterizations of women. See the following important studies: Hasan Javadi, "Women in Persian Literature: An Exploratory Study," in *Women and the Family in Iran*, ed. Asghar Fathi (Leiden: Brill, 1985); Farzaneh Milani, "The Mediatory Guile of the Nanny in Persian Romance," *Iranian Studies* 32, 2 (1999): 181–201; Afsaneh Najmabadi, "Reading and Enjoying 'Wiles of Women' Stories as a Feminist," *Iranian Studies* 32, 2 (1999): 203–22; and Paul Sprachman, *Suppressed Persian* (Costa Mesa, CA: Mazda, 2005).

CHAPTER 2 : POPULATION POLITICS

1. Justin Perkins, *A Residence of Eight Years in Persia, Among the Nestorians, with Notices of the Muhammedans* (Andover: Allen, Morrill and Wardwell, 1843), 408.
2. Ibid.
3. Lady Mary Sheil, *Glimpses of Life and Manners in Persia* (London: J. Murray, 1856), 149.
4. This practice apparently continued into the twentieth century. An American physician, Adelaide Kibbe, noted in 1930 that babies are "soothed with a 'bit' of opium from the day they are born." PHS, RG 91, Box 20, Fifteenth Annual Report of the American Christian Hospital, Meshed, Persia, 1929–1930, 9.
5. George Nathaniel Curzon, *Persia and the Persian Question* (London: Longmans, Green, 1892), 2:492.
6. James Bassett, "Child Life in Persia," *The American Magazine* 36 (1893), 174.
7. The discrepancy in Sheil's and Curzon's observations about breast-feeding may reflect class differences. It is likely that some women from affluent families who could afford to employ wet nurses seemed less inclined to breast-feed, whereas the majority of nineteenth-century Iranian women had little choice but to breast-feed their infants. As Sheil writes, "Ladies, of even moderate wealth and station, never nurse their children." *Glimpses of Life and Manners in Persia*, 149.
8. Mustafa ibn 'Aqil al-'Alavi Isfahani, trans., "Risalah-i Mukhtasar dar Bab-i Vaksan, Ya'ni Kubidan-i Abilah Az Ta'lifat-i Hakim Tholozan-i Farangi Ast," Malik Library, Tehran, 1.

9. Napier Malcolm, *Children of Persia* (Edinburgh: Oliphant, Anderson, and Ferrier, 1911), 84–85.
10. *Nasiri*, No. 4, 15 Dhul-qa'da 1311/21 May 1894, 30.
11. *Tarbiyat*, 2nd year, No. 74, 10 April 1898, 296.
12. *Nasiri*, 21 May 1894, 30.
13. *Tarbiyat*, 2nd year, No. 75, 11 April 1898, 300.
14. It is important to highlight here that many graduates of colleges in the 1920s and 1930s frequently served in the government. As Arasteh writes, these graduates "filled many key government posts." A. Reza Arasteh, "The Role of Intellectuals in Administrative Development and Social Change in Modern Iran," *International Review of Education/Internationale Zeitschrift für Erziehungswissenschaft/Revue Internationale de l'Education* 9, 3 (1963): 328.
15. Alisa Klaus, "Depopulation and Race Suicide: Maternalism and Pronatalist Ideologies in France and the United States," in *Mothers of a New World: Maternalist Politics and the Origins of Welfare States*, ed. Seth Koven and Sonya Michel (New York: Routledge, 1993), 188–212.
16. Qur'an, "The Cave," 18:46.
17. F.O. 248/326/51262, "Memo of the Meeting of the Board of Health, 11 February 1877," 2–3.
18. F.O. 248/326/51262, "Memo of the Board of Health," 18 February 1877, 2.
19. F.O. 248/326/51262, 25 March 1877, "Memo of the Board of Health," 1.
20. C. J. Wills, "Medicine in Persia," *British Medical Journal* 1, 956 (April 26, 1879): 624.
21. Yahya Dawlatabadi, *Hayat-i Yahya* (Tehran: Sazman-i Intisharat-i Javidan, 1362/1983), 1:12.
22. Abdollah Mostofi, *The Administrative and Social History of the Qajar Period: From Agha Mohammad Khan to Naser ed-Din Shah (1794–1896)*, trans. Nayer Mostofi Glenn (Costa Mesa, CA: Mazda, 1997), 1:116.
23. According to Floor, "Many of the therapies prescribed by Persian doctors were indeed just ridiculous.... What to think of treatments 'such as the placing of a live pigeon or disemboweled fowl or lamb to the feet of a dying patient.'" Willem Floor, *Public Health in Qajar Iran* (Washington, DC: Mage, 2004), 120, 123.
24. "Nizamnamah-i madrasah-i tibb va davasazi va qabiligi," 27 Shahrivar 1307/18 September 1928, in *Dawlat-i Illiyah-Iran, Vizarat-i Ma'arif va Awqaf va Sanayi' mustazrafah, Salnamah-i ihsa'iyah, 1307–1308* (n.p.: Rawshana'i, 1929), 100–4.
25. *Adab*, Nos. 9–10, 30 January 1899, 36–38.
26. Ibn Khaldun, *The Muqaddimah: An Introduction to History* (Princeton: Princeton University Press, 1967), 319.
27. Ibid., 323.
28. Jamal Khvansari, *Kulthum Nanah*, ed. Bizhan Asadipur (Tehran: Intisharat-i Murvarid, 1976). For an interesting study, see Kathyrn Babayan, "The 'Aqa'id al-Nisa': A Glimpse at Safavid Women in Local Isfahani Culture," in *Women in the Medieval Islamic World*, ed. Gavin R. G. Hambly (New York: St. Martin's, 1999), 349–81. For another informative discussion of this text, see Hasan Javadi, "Women in Persian Literature: An Exploratory Study," in Asghar Fathi, ed., *Women and the Family in Iran*, 37–59 (Leiden: Brill, 1985).

29. Khvansari, *Kulthum Nanah*, 59–67; James Atkinson, *Customs and Manners of the Women of Persia and Their Domestic Superstitions* (London: Oriental Translation Fund of Great Britain and Ireland, 1832), 47–53.

30. J. J. Morier, *A Second Journey Through Persia, Armenia, Asia Minor to Constantinople* (London: Longman, Hurst, Rees, Orme, and Brown, 1818), 105.

31. Ibid.

32. Ibid.

33. Muhammad Baqir Majlisi, *Hilyat al-Muttaqin* (Tehran, 1959), 72. Majlisi's works were known to Qajar-era Shi'i 'ulama and even today are relied upon by contemporary Shi'i scholars.

34. Marion Holmes Katz, *Body of Text: The Emergence of the Sunni Law of Ritual Purity* (Albany: State University of New York Press, 2002); Kathleen M. Brown, *Foul Bodies: Cleanliness in Early America* (New Haven: Yale University Press, 2009), 16.

35. Majlisi, *Hilyat al-Muttaqin*, 73, 79. For related discussions, see Shireen Mahdavi, "Muhammad Baqir Majlisi and Family Values," in *Safavid Iran and Her Neighbors*, ed. Michel Mazzaoui (Salt Lake City: University of Utah Press, 2003).

36. Majlisi, *Hilyat al-Muttaqin*, 87.

37. Ibid.

38. *Journal de médecine, de chirurgie et de pharmacologie* 91 (1890): 68. This journal was published by La Société royale des sciences médicales et naturelles de Bruxelles.

39. Wills, "Medicine in Persia," 624. For related discussions, see Floor, *Public Health*, 141.

40. *Revue médico-chirurgicale des maladies des femmes* 7 (1885): 187, 196.

41. Ibid., 196–97.

42. To read about Duhousset and the contributions of other French individuals in Iran, see Nader Nasiri-Moghaddam, "France viii. Travelogues of the 18th–20th Centuries," *Encyclopaedia Iranica*, online version.

43. *Bulletins de la Société d'anthropologie de Paris* (1883), 796–97.

44. Samuel Graham Wilson, *Western Mission* (Philadelphia: Presbyterian Board of Publication and Sabbath School Work, 1896), 273–74.

45. Isaac Adams, *Persia by a Persian* (n.p., 1900), 17.

46. Ibid., 209.

47. Mooshie G. Daniel, *Modern Persia* (Toronto: Henderson, 1898), 208. Daniel was a Nestorian whose family had settled in Iran in the eighteenth century. He attended some of the schools run by the American Presbyterian missionaries in Urumiyah.

48. Schneider's reference to "many cases of puerperal fever" is important, since Elgood writes that in Safavid times, "puerperal fever was almost non-existent" in Iran. Cyril Elgood, *Safavid Medical Practice* (London: Luzac, 1970), 272.

49. Jean-Etienne Schneider, "Les Médecins français en Perse," *Revue medicale de l'est* 43 (1911): 546–51.

50. *Tarbiyat*, 3rd year, No. 22, 27 June 1904, 176.

51. "Risalah dar qabilagi," manuscript at Malik Library, Tehran, #805, completed 5 Jumada al-Thani 1294/17 June 1877, 1–3.

52. Ibid., 7.

53. "Amraz al-Nisa,'" manuscript at Malik Library, Tehran, #805, completed May 1877.
54. *Tarbiyat*, 2nd year, No. 75, 11 April 1898, 300.
55. Tarbiyat, 2nd year, No. 122, 22 August, 1898, 487.
56. *Adab*, Nos. 9–10, 30 January 1899, 36–38. Browne notes that the "scientific articles" in *Adab* were likely composed by Mirza Najaf Quli Khan, not Adib al-Mamalik, the journal's editor. See E. G. Browne, *The Press and Poetry of Modern Persia* (Cambridge: Cambridge University Press, 1914), 38.
57. C. J. Wills, *Persia As It Is: Being Sketches of Modern Persian Life and Character* (London: S. Low, Marston, Searle, and Rivington, 1886), 66.
58. Eustache de Lorey and Douglas Sladen, *Queer Things About Persia* (Philadelphia: J. B. Lippincott, 1907), 160–61. De Lorey and Sladen considered this matter to be especially true of the women in the shah's harem. As they observed, "Maternity becomes a passion for every woman of the Imperial harem, and her sole object. A child is the most valuable pledge of favour of the King" (161). Curzon mentions another pilgrimage site for women in Tehran in *Persia and the Persian Question*, 1:309.
59. Zahir al-Dawlah, *Khatirat va asnad-i Zahir al-Dawlah*, ed. Iraj Afshar (Tehran, 1351/1972), 98.
60. Abraham Valentine Williams Jackson, *Persia Past and Present: A Book of Travel and Research* (New York: Macmillan, 1906), 160. Williams Jackson also refers on page 422 to the site mentioned by Curzon.
61. *Jahan-i Zanan*, No. 3, 4 April 1921, 15.
62. *Tarbiyat*, 2nd year, No. 122, 22 August 1898, 485. The total population amounted to approximately 8.848 million. Compare with Bharier listing the population of Iran as 9.860 million for 1900.
63. J. Bharier, *Economic Development in Iran, 1900–1970* (New York: Oxford University Press, 1971), 26–27.
64. *Ruh al-Quds*, No. 1, 25 Jumada al-Thani 1325/5 August 1907, 4.
65. *Tarbiyat*, No. 370, 20 July 1905, 1880.
66. *Adab*, No. 180, 26 Muharram 1324/22 March 1906, 8.

CHAPTER 3 : FROM CELIBACY TO COMPANIONSHIP

1. Muhammad Baqir Majlisi, *Hilyat al-Muttaqin* (Tehran, 1959), 67–68. Majlisi's works were known to Qajar-era Shi'i 'ulama and even today are relied upon by contemporary Shi'i scholars. For an announcement in a Qajar newspaper about the printing of one of Majlis's other works, *Zad al-Ma'ad*, see *Ittila'*, No. 15, 10 November 1903, 8.
2. *Akhtar*, 24 Safar 1294/10 March 1877, 53.
3. Cf. Nancy F. Cott, *Public Vows: A History of Marriage and the Nation* (Cambridge: Harvard University Press, 2002), 1–17, for an important theoretical discussion of marriage.
4. Mary Lynn Stewart, "'Science Is Always Chaste': Sex Education and Sexual Initiation in France, 1880s–1930s," *Journal of Contemporary History* 32, 3 (1997): 382.
5. Maulana Muhammad Ali, *A Manual of Hadith* (Lahore: The Ahmadiyya Anjuman Ishaat Islam, 2001), 219.

6. Sayyid Muhammad Shirazi, *Bulugh al-Ibtihaj fi sihhat al-izdivaj* (n.p., n.d.), 6–9. The text appears to have been translated in the late nineteenth century. Shirazi relied upon a Hindi edition to translate this work into Persian.

7. Ibid., 9–10.

8. For a comparable text, produced by Mirza Muhammad Malik al-Kuttab, see *Kitab-i Vasa'il-i Ibtihaj fi Hifz Sihhat al-Izdivaj* (Tehran 1325/1907). This text appears very similar to Shirazi's work.

9. Shirazi, *Bulugh al-Ibtihaj*, 14.

10. Ibid., 17.

11. Ibid., 19–20.

12. Ibid., 21–22.

13. Majlisi, *Hilyat al-Muttaqin*, 69.

14. Shirazi, *Bulugh al-Ibtihaj*, 55. Yet Shirazi also noted that to avert disgrace, some mothers would examine their daughters' private parts before the wedding. If they detected a broken hymen, they would give their daughters a thin hide covered with pigeon's blood that could be used instead to provide evidence of virginity.

15. Majlisi, *Hilyat al-Muttaqin*, 70.

16. Nasir al-Din Shah was the reigning monarch of Iran's Qajar dynasty from 1848 until his assassination in 1896.

17. Shireen Mahdavi, "Taj al-Saltaneh, an Emancipated Qajar Princess," *Middle Eastern Studies* 23, 2 (1987): 188–93. Shi'ism allowed men to take on temporary wives for a limited period. Some Shi'is believe that this practice was allowed in the time of the Prophet Muhammad and was only forbidden during the reign of the second caliph, 'Umar. For more on this subject, see Moojan Momen, *An Introduction to Shi 'i Islam: The History and Doctrines of Twelver Shi 'ism* (New Haven: Yale University Press, 1987), 182.

18. Taj al-Saltanah, *Crowning Anguish: Memoirs of a Persian Princess from the Harem to Modernity, 1884–1914*, trans. Anna Vanzan and Amin Neshati (Washington, DC: Mage, 1993), 150.

19. Ibid., 158.

20. Ahmed Bey, "La Femme Persane," *La Nouvelle Revue* 69 (1891), 378. Bey also provides an unflattering portrayal of Persian mothers, who, he believed, shirked their maternal responsibilities until their daughters reached the age of twelve, at which point they would "leave their torpor" to prepare the girls' dowry. Ibid., 382.

21. Hyacinthe Ringrose, *Marriage and Divorce Laws of the World* (New York: Musson-Draper, 1911), 142.

22. PHS, RG 91, Box 1, Folder 18, "Missions in Persia—East Persia Mission," 12.

23. PHS, RG 91, Box 1, Folder 18, "Hamadan Medical Report, July 1921—June 1922," 4.

24. For more on honor and shame, see Keddie's introduction in Nikki Keddie and Beth Baron, eds., *Women in Middle Eastern History: Shifting Boundaries in Sex and Gender* (New Haven: Yale University Press, 1993), 5–10.

25. Napier Malcolm, *Children of Persia* (Edinburgh: Oliphant, Anderson, and Ferrier, 1911), 79.

26. Cf. Cott, *Public Vows*, for a comparable discussion in the United States.
27. *Habl al-Matin*, Tehran, No. 60, 6 July 1907, 1.
28. *Habl-al-Matin*, Tehran, No. 103, 29 August 1907, 1.
29. John G. Wishard, *Twenty Years in Persia: A Narrative of Life under the Last Three Shahs* (New York: Revell, 1908), 244.
30. Ibid.
31. For a complementary discussion of this issue, see Janet Afary, *The Iranian Constitutional Revolution of 1906–1911: Grassroots Democracy, Social Democracy and the Origins of Feminism* (New York: Columbia University Press, 1996), 201.
32. *Habl-al-Matin*, Tehran, No. 103, 29 August 1907, 1–2.
33. *Rahnima*, No. 8, 24 September 1907, 4.
34. Janet Afary, *Sexual Politics in Modern Iran* (Cambridge: Cambridge University Press, 2009), 77.
35. *Habl al-Matin*, Tehran, 1 Shavval 1325/8 November 1907, 1.
36. Deniz Kandiyoti, "Introduction," in *Women, Islam, and the State*, ed. D. Kandiyoti (Philadelphia: Temple University Press, 1991), 13.
37. Ibid.
38. *Parvanah*, No. 31, 22 Dhul-qa'da 1329/14 November 1911, 4. Mu'minzadah then extended the analogy to praise the men who had sacrificed their children to preserve the Iranian homeland in the fight against Muhammad Ali Shah and the preservation of Iranian parliamentarianism.
39. *Amuzgar*, No. 14, 10 Ramadan 1329/4 September 1911, 4.
40. Hasan Javadi, Manijeh Marashi, and Simin Shekarloo, eds., *Ta'dib al-Nisvan va Ma'ayib al-Rijal* (Piedmont, CA: Jahan, 1992).
41. *Amuzgar*, No. 14, 10 Ramadan 1329/4 September 1911, 4.
42. *Danish*, No. 1, 10 Ramadan 1328/14 September 1910, 5. For a complementary discussion of these essays, see Camron Amin, *The Making of the Modern Iranian Woman: Gender, State Policy, and Popular Culture, 1865–1946* (Gainesville: University Press of Florida, 2002), 117.
43. *Danish*, No. 3, 9 Shavval 1328/14 October 1910, 7.
44. *Danish*, No. 6, 7 Dhul-qa'da 1328/10 November 1910, 8.
45. *Shikufah*, No. 20, third year, 21 Dhul-hijja 1333/30 October 1915; *Shikufah*, No. 9, third year, 2 Jumada al-Thani/17 April 1915; *Shikufah*, No. 1, fourth year, 1 Safar 1334/8 December 1915.
46. *Shikufah*, No. 10, 20 Jumada al-Avval 1332/16 April 1914, 1.
47. *Shikufah*, No. 9, third year, 2 Jumada al-Thani/17 April 1915, 1.
48. *Shikufah*, No. 20, third year, 21 Dhul-hijja 1333/30 October 1915, 2–3.
49. Hamideh Sedghi, *Women and Politics in Iran: Veiling, Unveiling, and Reveiling* (Cambridge: Cambridge University Press, 2007), 80.
50. *Jahan-i Zanan*, No. 2 (1921), 26–28.
51. *Jahan-i Zanan*, No. 4 (1300/1921), 82–83.
52. *Majallah-i Nisvan-i Vatankhvah-i Iran*, No. 3 (1924), 3–11.
53. *Jahan-i Zanan*, No. 5 (1921), 105–6.
54. *Majallah-i Nisvan-i Vatankhvah-i Iran*, Nos. 7–8, 22–31.
55. *Majallah-i Nisvan-i Vatankhvah-i Iran*, No. 3 (1924), 17–23.

56. "Preliminary Report on Medical Education in Persia," July 1926, 15. Prepared by Information Service of the Rockefeller Foundation. Rockefeller Archive Center, RF, RG 1.1, Box 1.
57. *Alam-i Nisvan*, ninth year, No. 3 (May 1929), 108–9.
58. *Majallah-i Nisvan-i Vatankhvah*, Nos. 5–6 (1924), 51.
59. Ibid., 50–51.
60. *Majallah-i Nisvan-i Vatankhvah*, Nos. 7–8 (1924), 5–7.
61. *Majallah-i Nisvan-i 'Vatankhvah*, Nos. 5–6 (1924), 51.
62. "Varzish va ta'ahul," *Ittila'at*, 30 Mehr 1317/22 October 1938.
63. "Zan va varzish," *Ittila'at*, 18 Aban 1318/10 November 1939.
64. Badr al-Muluk Bamdad, *Tadbir-i Manzil va Dastur-i Bachih-dari* (Tehran: Firdawsi, 1931). For the term *shawhardari*, see *Ittila'at*, 28 July 1938, 1.
65. *Ittila'at*, No. 524, 12 Tir 1307/3 July 1928, 3.
66. *Ittila'at*, No. 543, 25 July 1928, 3.
67. *Alam-i Nisvan*, fifth year, No. 2 (March 1925), 38.
68. "Preliminary Report on Medical Education in Persia," July 1926, 15. Rockefeller Archive Center, RF, RG 1.1, Box 1.
69. "Islahat-i ijtima'i," *Ittila'at*, 9 October 1928, 1. Also, *Ittila'at*, 11 October 1928, 1. For another article, see "Chira izdivaj dar Iran kam mishavad," *Ittila'at*, No. 524, 3 July 1928, 3.
70. "Persia's 1931 Marriage Law Has Practically Stopped Child Marriage," Charles Hart to Secretary of State, Tehran, 7 April 1933, 1, RG 59, U.S. Department of State Records.
71. Ibid. For more on this, see Amin, *Making of the Modern Iranian Woman*, 129–32.
72. *'Alam-i Nisvan*, twelfth year, No. 5 (1932), 193. For an alternative translation of this passage, see Jasamin Rostam-Kolayi, "Expanding Agendas for the 'New' Iranian Woman: Family Law, Work, and Unveiling," in *The Making of Modern Iran: State and Society Under Riza Shah, 1921–1941*, ed. Stephanie Cronin (London: Routledge-Curzon, 2003), 157.
73. *Ittila'at*, 3 Mordad 1310/26 July 1931, 1. Related discussions are continued in the next issue.
74. Parvin Paidar, *Women and the Political Process in Twentieth-Century Iran* (Cambridge: Cambridge University Press, 1995), 109.
75. "Report on Muharram Ceremonies of the Current Year," in *British Documents on Foreign Affairs. Part II, From the First to the Second World Wars. Series B, Turkey, Iran and the Middle East*, ed. Kenneth Bourne and D. Cameron Watt (Frederick, MD: University Publications of America, 1985), 27:140.
76. Paidar, *Women and the Political Process in Iran*, 110.
77. "Transmitting Test of New Persian Law on Offenses Against Decency and Morality," George Wadsworth to Secretary of State, Tehran, 3 February 1934, 2, RG 59, U.S. Department of State Records.
78. Ibid.
79. Shahla Haeri, *Law of Desire: Temporary Marriage in Shi'i Iran* (Syracuse: Syracuse University Press, 1989), 215 n. 15.
80. For more on homosexuality in Iran, see Afsaneh Najmabadi, *Women with Mustaches and Men Without Beards: The Sexual and Gender Anxieties of*

Iranian Modernity (Berkeley: University of California Press, 2005); Afary, *Sexual Politics in Iran.*

81. *Ittila'at,* No. 524, 3 July 1928, 3.
82. *Banu,* No. 6 (Urdibihisht 1324/April–May 1945), 3.
83. *Nisvan-i Vatankhvah-i Iran,* No. 9, 6 July 1925, 12–13. This is a long and fascinating article that touches on many other aspects of the marital relationship. In conclusion, the author found that both men and women were complicitous in bringing about the decline in marriage, but that men were guiltier than women in this matter (21).
84. M. B. Mashayekhi and Guy S. Hayes, "Some Demographic and Health Characteristics of 173 Villages in a Rural Area of Iran," 22, Rockefeller Archive Center, RF, RG 1.1, 771, Box 1. The survey was finished in 1951.
85. Ibid.
86. Amin, *Making of the Modern Iranian Woman,* 136–38, for press coverage and discussion of this marriage.
87. Bourne and Watt, eds., *British Documents on Foreign Affairs,* 28:314.
88. Ibid., 28:315.
89. Ibid., 28:392.
90. Amin, *Making of the Modern Iranian Woman,* 136–37. Also, Bourne and Watt, eds., *British Documents on Foreign Affairs,* 28:327.
91. Bourne and Watt, eds., *British Documents on Foreign Affairs,* 28:395.
92. Ibid., 28:454.
93. *Banu,* No. 6, Urdibihisht 1324/April–May 1945), 1.

CHAPTER 4 : SEXUAL MORES, SOCIAL LIVES

1. Abu al-Hasan Khan Tafrishi, *Masa'il-i 'Umdah-i Hifz-i Sihhat* (1894), 2–3. Unfortunately, Tafrishi does not mention either the title or author of the original French text, making it difficult to provide comparisons or any assessment of editorial liberties that he may have taken.
2. Ibid., 202.
3. Ibid., 203.
4. Cf. Mary E. Fissell, *Vernacular Bodies: The Politics of Reproduction in Early Modern England* (Oxford: Oxford University Press, 2004), and my review of Fissell's work, "Stepping Out of the Womb: Women and the Politics of Reproduction," *Journal of Women's History* 22, 3 (2010): 195–99.
5. Jean-Etienne Schneider, "Discussion," *Revue d'hygiène et de police sanitaire* 30 (1908): 453–54.
6. Ibid., 453–54. Although apparently a colleague of Fournier's (Schneider refers to Fournier as "mon vénéré maître," "my venerated master"), Schneider believed that syphilis alone did not cause general paralysis.
7. "Amraz al-Nisa," manuscript at Malek Library, #805, ch. 12.
8. Jakob Polak, "Ueber den Gebrauch des Quecksilbers in Persien," *Wiener Medizinische Wochenschrift* (1860). Cited in New Sydenham Society, *A Year-Book of Medicine, Surgery, and their Allied Sciences* (1862), 136. Also cited in *Cincinnati Lancet and Observer,* vol. 5 (1862), 93.
9. William Sanger, *The History of Prostitution* (New York: Harper and Brothers, 1858), 417.

10. Ibid. Also see Rudi Matthee, "Prostitutes, Courtesans, and Dancing Girls: Women Entertainers in Safavid Iran," in *Iran and Beyond: Essays in Middle Eastern History in Honor of Nikki Keddie*, ed. Rudi Matthee and Beth Baron (Costa Mesa, CA: Mazda, 2000), 121–50.

11. Sanger, *History of Prostitution*, 418. For reports of prostitution in various cities, see Willem Floor, *A Social History of Sexual Relations in Iran* (Washington, DC: Mage, 2008), 239–51.

12. Matthee, "Prostitutes, Courtesans, and Dancing Girls," 123–24.

13. Muhammad Husayn Tabataba'i and Seyyed Hossein Nasr, *Shi'ite Islam* (St. Leonard's, Australia; Allen and Unwin, 1975).

14. James Bassett, *Persia: Eastern Mission: A Narrative of the Founding and Fortunes of the Eastern Persia Mission, with a Sketch of the Versions of the Bible and Christian Literature in the Persian and Persian-Turkish Languages* (Philadelphia, 1890), 66.

15. Robert Elliott Speer, *Missionary Principles and Practice* (New York: Revell, 1902), 308.

16. Homa Hoodfar, "The Veil in Their Minds and on Our Heads: Veiling Practices and Muslim Women," in *Women, Gender, Religion: A Reader*, ed. Elizabeth Anne Castelli and Rosamond C. Rodman (New York: Palgrave, 2001), 427.

17. Speer, *Missionary Principles and Practice*, 307.

18. Qahraman Mirza Ayn al-Saltanah Salur, *Ruznamah-i Khatirat-i Ayn al-Saltanah* (Tehran: Asatir, 1374–79/1995–2000), 1:781.

19. Khan-i Khanan, "Risalah-i dar siyasat" (1314 AH/ 1896), manuscript at Kitab-khanah-i Melli, Tehran, #RF 385, 109–10. Khan-i Khanan discussed the need to institute hygiene in Iran: 52–57, 104–12, 125–26.

20. *Adab*, fourth year, No. 177, 7; *Adab*, fifth year, 29 April 1906, 5. Also *Tarbiyat*, 18 May 1905, 1862.

21. *Bulletin de la société belge d'études coloniales*, 1904, 615.

22. *Adab*, fourth year, No. 180, 22 February 1906, 4.

23. *Khayr al-Kalam*, third year, No. 91, 13 Rabi' al-Thani 1329/13 April 1911, 4.

24. *Muzaffari*, 11 July 1903, 589; *Muzaffari*, 26 July 1903, 604–5.

25. *Adab*, second year, No. 9, 19 February 1902, 68.

26. *Hadid*, No. 8, 19 Jumada al-Akhivah 1323/21 August 1905, 8.

27. *Adab*, second year, No. 9, 19 February 1902, 68.

28. John Gilmour, *Report on an Investigation into the Sanitary Conditions in Persia Undertaken on Behalf of the Health Committee of the League of Nations at the Request of the Persian Government* (Geneva: Imp. Atar, 1925), 57–58; Rosalie Slaughter Morton, *A Doctor's Holiday in Iran* (New York: Funk & Wagnalls, 1940), 217–28.

29. I borrow the term "medical popularizer" (to mean "hygienist") from Mary Lynn Stewart, "'Science Is Always Chaste': Sex Education and Sexual Initiation in France 1880s–1930s," *Journal of Contemporary History* 32, 3 (1997): 382.

30. See http://www.niaid.nih.gov/factsheets/stdsyph.htm.

31. See http://www.nlm.nih.gov/exhibition/islamic_medical/islamic_14.html.

32. Sheldon Watts, *Epidemics and History: Disease, Power and Imperialism* (New Haven: Yale University Press, 1997), 150.

33. Jill Harsin, "Syphilis, Wives, Physicians: Medical Ethics and the Family in Late Nineteenth-Century France," *French Historical Studies* 16, 1 (spring 1989) 74.

34. *Muzaffari*, No. 38, 26 July 1903, 604–5.

35. *Tamaddun*, No. 70, 25 April 1908, 4; *Tamaddun*, No. 74, 30 April 1908, 3.

36. *Shikufah*, second year, No. 20, 1 Dhul-hijja 1332/21 October 1914, 3. Also, *Hifz-i Sihhah*, Nos. 7 and 8, Sha'ban and Ramadan 1324/September–October 1906, 59.

37. For more on syphilis, see M. Maurice Cohen, *Défense Sanitaire de la Perse* (Paris: 1912), 77. As late as 1914, the lack of attention to hygiene and the absence of clean supplies of water remained a problem. Islam and the example of the Prophet Muhammad was once again called upon to impel Iranians and Muslims more globally to live their lives in a hygienic way and to promote cleanliness. The writer singled out women who washed dirty clothes in communal sources of water. *Jarchi-yi Millat*, fourth year, No. 27, 6 Rabi' al-Thani 1332/3 March 1914.

38. Yusuf Mughis al-Saltanah, *Namah'hayah Yusuf Mughis al-Saltanah*, ed. Ma'soumah Mafi (Tehran: Nashr-i Tarikh-i Iran, 1362/1983), 176.

39. *Nida-yi Vatan*, No. 31, 21 May 1907, 7.

40. *Jarchi-yi Millat*, 5 Shavval 1335/25 July 1917, 3.

41. *Nahid*, No. 15, 1923, 5.

42. Iran, Prime Ministry Archives, File Number 293, 2/16/44, "I'lan: Idarah-i Institut Pasteur-i Dawlat-i Iran."

43. C. Christidi, "La Syphilis en Perse à travers les siècles," *La Presse Medicale*, 15 March 1922, 425.

44. PHS, RG 91, Box 1, Folder 18, "Report of Medical Work Outside of Meshed, Year Ending June 30, 1922," 2.

45. PHS, RG 91, Box 1, Folder 20, "Report of the Medical Work in Meshed, July 1, 1924–June 30, 1925," 2.

46. *Jahan-i Zanan*, first year, No. 3, 4 April 1921, 10–11. Also, Allan Brandt, *No Magic Bullet: A Social History of Venereal Disease in the United States Since 1880* (New York: Oxford University Press, 1987), 147.

47. *Jahan-i Zanan*, first year, No. 3, 4 April 1921, 12–13.

48. *Dabistan*, No. 2, December 1922, 26–27.

49. Ibid., 27.

50. *Nahid*, No. 11, 8 June 1924, 6.

51. '*Alam-i Nisvan*, fifth year, No. 2, March 1925, 36–39.

52. Rockefeller Archive Center, RF/RG1.1, Series 771, Box 1, "Preliminary Report on Medical Education in Persia," July 1926, 38.

53. Ibid.

54. *Avvalin Rapurt-i Shish-mahah-i Sihhiyah-i kull* (1926), 11–15.

55. *Salnamah-i Pars*, 1307/1928, "Vizarat-i Dakhilah," 14.

56. Onera Amelia Merritt, *Persia: Romance and Reality* (London: Nicholson, 1935), 289. Iran had signed the International Convention for the Suppression of the Traffic in Women and Children in 1921. See *Encyclopedia of the United Nations and International Agreements*, ed. Edmund Jan Osmanczyk and Anthony Mango, vol. 4 (New York: Taylor & Francis, 2003), 2344. U.S. diplomats in Iran also wrote about this issue. See RG 59, Charles Hart to Secretary of State, "League of Nation's [*sic*] Commission's Report on White Slave Traffic in Oriental Countries Touches Persian Amour Propre," Tehran,

June 14, 1922. RG 59, Charles Hart to Secretary of State, No. 1047, Tehran, February 9, 1932.

57. *Payk-i Sa'adat-i Nisvan*, Nos. 4–5, May–June 1928, 98–100; *Payk-i Sa'adat-i Nisvan*, No. 2, December 1927–January 1928, 61.

58. Merritt, *Persia*, 289.

59. *Majallah-i Baladiyyah*, 15 Day 1306/6 January 1928, 16.

60. *'Alam-i Nisvan*, fifth year, No. 2, March 1925, 38.

61. *Payk-i Sa'adat-i Nisvan*, Nos. 4–5, May–June 1928, 128.

62. *'Alam-i Nisvan*, fifth year, No. 2, March 1925, 39.

63. *Salnamah-i Pars*, 1308/1929, "Mu'assassat-i Sihhiyah dar 1307," 78.

64. *'Alam-i Nisvan*, fifth year, No. 2, March 1925, 39.

65. *'Alam-i Nisvan*, twelfth year, 1932, 195.

66. *Ittila'at*, 21 November 1932, 1. Discussions on venereal disease were continued in other issues. See *Ittila'at*, 6 November 1932, 9 November 1932, 10 November 1932, and 20 November 1932.

67. Jasamin Rostam-Kolayi, "The Women's Press, Modern Education, and the State in Early Twentieth-Century Iran, 1900–1930s," Ph.D. diss., University of California, Los Angeles, 2000, 190.

68. *Ittila'at*, 22 Khordad 1306/13 June 1927, 2. For another advertisement promising a cure for gonnorhea, see *Ittila'at*, 21 June 1928, 4.

69. *Ittila'at*, 22 Khordad 1306/13 June 1927, 2.

70. *Ittila'at*, No. 611, 21 October 1928, 4.

71. *Sihhat-Nimayi Iran*, No. 1, March–April 1933, 23. For more on syphilis, see *Sihhat Nimayi Iran*, Nuskhah-i Fawq al-'Adah, 1934, 38–44; also, 70–72 is of interest.

72. *Sihhat-Nimayi Iran*, No. 2, April–May 1933, 3.

73. Harsin notes that the practice of using silver nitrate on newborns to prevent blindness was introduced in 1884. Jill Harsin, "Syphilis, Wives, Physicians: Medical Ethics and the Family in Late Nineteenth-Century France," *French Historical Studies* 15, 4 (1989): 78.

74. *Salnamah-i Pars*, 1307/1928, 47–48.

75. "Sifilis-i madarzadi," *Ittila'at*, 1 May 1937, 2.

76. PHS, RG 91, Box 2, "Meshed Medical Report, 1935–1936," 4.

77. PHS, RG 91, Box 2, "Meshed Medical Report, 1935–1936," 4.

78. Iran, Prime Ministry Archives, File 290000, 5/532/3, Mordad Mah 1315/1936.

79. Iran, National Archives, Ministry of Internal Affairs, "Guzarish-i 'Umumi: Vaz'iyat-i bihdari," 24 Farvardin 1317/13 April 1938, 4.

80. *Ittila'at*, 9 Azar 1315/30 November 1936, "Mubarizah ba Amraz."

81. *Ittila'at*, 18 Dey 1318/9 January 1939, "Suzak va vagiri-yih an." Other public lectures on hygiene included one given by Amir A'lam, published in *Salsalah Intisharat-i Mu'assassah-i va'az va khattabah*, Lesson No. 7, 1315/1936. Also see *Ittila'at*, 11 Dey 1318/2 January 1940, and ttila'at, 12 Dey 1318/3 January 1940.

82. *Sihhat Nimayih-i Iran*, No. 4, Tir 1312/June–July 1933, 102.

83. *Sihhat Nimayih-i Iran*, No. 6, Shahrivar 1312/August–September 1933, 132–33.

84. For example, see Badr al-Muluk Bamdad, *Tadbir-i Manzil* (Tehran: Iqbal, 1310/1931). Also see Firoozeh Kashani-Sabet, "The Politics of Reproduction:

Maternalism and Women's Hygiene in Iran, 1896–1941," *International Journal of Middle East Studies* 38, 1 (2006): 1–29.

85. *Sihhat-Nimayi Iran*, No. 2, April–May 1933, 3. For more discussions of syphilis and gonorrhea, see *Salnamah-i Pars*, 1307 [1928], 1308 [1929], 1309 [1930].

86. *Sihhatnima-yi Iran*, first year, No. 2, April–May, 1933, 2–6.

87. League of Nations Secretariat, Committee of Enquiry into Traffic in Women and Children in the East, Summary of Report to Council, 1934, 30–31.

88. Ibid., 14.

89. Ibid.

90. Ibid.

91. Ibid.

92. *Ittila'at*, 14 Mehr 1317/6 October 1938; *Ittila'at*, No. 3627, 19 Mehr 1317/11 October 1938.

93. *Ittila'at*, 22 Aban 1317/November 1938. Also, Dr. Nijat's views on this bill are in *Ittila'at*, No. 3677, 10 Azar 1317/1 December 1938. Dr. Nijat primarily supported this legislation as a way of curbing the spread of syphilis.

94. "Barrisihayih pizishki dar barayah-i banuvan-i 'aqim," *Banu*, 1945, 13.

95. *Ittila'at*, No. 2022, 9 Tir 1314/April 1935.

96. *Ittila'at*, No. 2576, 30 Mordad 1317/1938, 7.

97. Amin talks about Iran's beauty culture of the 1930s in comparison with Western models of feminine beauty; see Camron Amin, *The Making of the Modern Iranian Woman: Gender, State Policy, and Popular Culture, 1865–1946* (Gainesville: University Press of Florida, 2002), 208–12, and Amin, "Importing 'Beauty Culture' into Iran in the 1920s and 1930s: Mass Marketing Individualism in an Age of Anti-Imperialist Sacrifice," *Comparative Studies of South Asia, Africa and the Middle East* 24, 1 (2004): 81–100. For historical background, see Fatemeh Soudavar Farmanfarmaian, "*Haft Qalam Arayesh*: Cosmetics in the Iranian World," *Iranian Studies* 33, 3–4 (2000): 285–326, and Niloufar Jozani, *La Beauté Menacée: Anthropologie des maladies de la peau en Iran* (Tehran: Institut Français de Recherche en Iran, 1994). Also, F. Kashani-Sabet, "Giving Birth: Women, Nursing, and Sexual Hygiene in Iran." Paper presented at the Biennial Conference of Iranian Studies, May 2002. Published as "The Politics of Reproduction."

98. "Arayesh va zibayi: Ziba kardan-i bini bih vasilah-i jarrahi," *Ittila'at*, 21 Mehr 1317/ September–October 1938. Cf. Elaine Sciolino's article discussing Iranian women's enthusiasm for nose jobs: "Iran's Well-Covered Women Remodel a Part That Shows," *New York Times*, 22 September 2000.

99. For advertisements regarding these products, see *Ittila'at*, No. 629, 13 November 1928, 4; *Ittila'at*, No. 603, 11 October 1928, 1; *Ittila'at*, December 7, 1932; *Ittila'at*, No. 1824, 6 February 1933; *Ittila'at*, No. 1829, 12 February 1933; *Salnamah-i Pars*, 1310/1931, center ad section.

100. Houchang Chehabi, "Staging the Emperor's New Clothes: Dress Codes and Nation-Building Under Reza Shah," *Iranian Studies* 26, 3–4 (1993): 209–33.

101. *Ittila'at*, No. 630, 14 November 1928, 4.

102. *Pars Yearbook*, 1927, 1928, 1929.

103. Michel Foucault, *A History of Sexuality*, trans. Robert Hurley (New York: Pantheon, 1978), 1:11.

104. *Salnamah-i Aryan,* 1322/1943, 14; Vizarat-i Farhang, *Kitab-i Bihdasht, sal-i avval-i dabirestanha,* 1319/1940, 92–94, 97.

CHAPTER 5 : GIVING BIRTH

1. This section is adapted from my review article of Fissell's work, "Stepping Out of the Womb: Women and the Politics of Reproduction." *Journal of Women's History* 22, 3 (2010): 195–99.
2. Cyril Elgood, *A Medical History of Persia and the Eastern Caliphate from the Earliest Times Until the Year A.D. 1932* (Cambridge: Cambridge University Press, 1951).
3. Leila Ahmed, "Arab Culture and Writing Women's Bodies," in *Women and Islam: Critical Concepts in Sociology,* ed. Haideh Moghissi (London: Routledge, 2005), 205–8. Also, Basim Musallam, *Sex and Society in Medieval Islam* (Cambridge: Cambridge University Press, 1983). Other important works on women in Islam include the following: Leila Ahmed, *Women and Gender in Islam: Historical Roots of a Modern Debate* (New Haven: Yale University Press, 1993); Lois Beck and Nikki Keddie, eds., *Women in the Muslim World* (Cambridge: Harvard University Press, 1980); and Barbara Freyer Stowasser, *Women in the Qur'an, Traditions, and Interpretation* (Oxford: Oxford University Press, 1994).
4. Sherry Sayed Gadelrab, "Discourses on Sex Differences in Medieval Scholarly Islamic Thought," *Journal of the History of Medicine and Allied Sciences,* April 2010, 1–42. Also, Dror Ze'evi, *Producing Desire: Changing Sexual Discourse in the Ottoman Middle East, 1500–1900* (Berkeley: University of California Press, 2006), 16–47.
5. Cyril Elgood, *Safavid Medical Practice* (London: Luzac, 1970), 208–10, 217.
6. "Amraz al-Nisa," Jumada al-Avval 1294/May 1877, manuscript at Astan Quds Razavi, Mashhad, Iran, #805, ch. 12.
7. Firoozeh Kashani-Sabet, "The Politics of Reproduction: Maternalism and Women's Hygiene in Iran, 1896–1941," *International Journal of Middle East Studies* 38, 1 (2006): 1–29.
8. "Ihsa'iyah-i attiba'-i shahr-i Tehran dar amordad mah-i sal-i 1313," *Majallah-i Baladiyyah,* December 1934.
9. For an article encapsulating this idea, see "Sihhat-i 'umumi," *Ittila'at,* No. 582, 17 September 1928, 2.
10. For more on this idea, see Firoozeh Kashani-Sabet, "Patriotic Womanhood: The Culture of Feminism in Modern Iran, 1900–1941," *British Journal of Middle Eastern Studies* 32, 1 (2005): 29–46.
11. The statement about *Tamaddun* comes from E. G. Browne, *The Press and Poetry of Modern Persia* (Cambridge: Cambridge University Press, 1914), 63.
12. *Tamaddun,* No. 75, 2 Rabi' al-Thani 1326/3 May 1908, 4; *Tamaddun,* No. 76, 4 Rabi'al-Thani, 1326/5 May 1908, 3–4.
13. As McGregor has argued in her study of midwifery in America, "Physicians came into cultural authority as representing science and the social structure of the larger political and economic system when they began to supervise child-birth. . . . Physicians with forceps in hand, even though they would not use them for decades, became a symbol of power." See Deborah Kuhn McGregor, *From*

Midwives to Medicine: The Birth of American Gynecology (New Brunswick: Rutgers University Press, 1998), 122.

14. *Sur-i Israfil*, No. 24, 24 Muharram 1326/27 February 1908, 5.
15. The two main journals published for women in the early twentieth century were *Danish* and *Shikufah*, and parts of these journals have recently been reprinted in Iran. See *Shikufah bih Inzimam-i Danish* (Tehran: Kitabkhanah-i Milli-yi Jumhuri-yi Islami-yi Iran, Fall 1377/1998). *Danish* began publication in 1910 under the editorship of Banu Kahhal and *Shikufah* in 1912 under the editorship of Maryam Muzayyin al-Saltanah, both in Tehran.
16. *Shikufah*, No. 6, 8 Rabi' al-Thani 1333/23 February 1915, 4.
17. *Danish*, No. 14, 17 Muharram 1329/18 January 1911, 2.
18. *Hifz-i Sihhah*, No. 4, Jumada al-Avval 1324/June–July 1906, 18–23.
19. Qur'an, Sura 2:233.
20. No. 4, Jumada al-Avval 1324/June–July 1906, 20–22.
21. Ibid., 22.
22. According to Giladi, "Approval of maternal breastfeeding seems to have been unanimous among Muslim doctors," among them Ibn Sina. Avner Giladi, *Infants, Parents and Wet Nurses: Medieval Islamic Views on Breastfeeding and Their Social Implications* (Leiden: Brill, 1999), 48.
23. Ibid., chapter 2.
24. *Jahan-i Zanan*, No. 2, 15 Hawt 1299/1921, 38.
25. *Jahan-i Zanan*, No. 1, 15 Dalv 1921, 12.
26. *Shikufah*, 2nd Year, No. 12, 1 Rajab 1332/26 May 1914, 4.
27. *Shikufah*, 2nd Year, No. 10, 20 Jumada al-Avval 1332/16 April 1914, 3. For a continuation of these themes in another journal, see *Farhang*, Nos. 4–5, Summer 1928, 149–60.
28. *Shikufah*, 2nd year, No. 10, 20 Jumada al-Avval 1332/16 April 1914, 2.
29. *Jahan-i Zanan*, No. 2, 15 Hawt 1299/1921, 39. This advice is not much different from the information given to parents of newborns today. This discussion continues in the fourth issue of this journal, 11–12, where recommended amounts of milk consumption (both breast milk and artificial milk) are given for newborns.
30. *Jahan-i Zanan*, Mashhad, No. 1, 1921, 10–11.
31. Ibid., 18.
32. *Majallah-i Nisvan-i Vatankhvah-i Iran*, No. 1, 1924, 15.
33. Ibid., 16.
34. Ibid., 16–17.
35. Ibid., 24.
36. *Nisvan-i Vatankhvah-i Iran*, No. 9, 6 July 1925, 2–3.
37. Camron Amin, *The Making of the Modern Iranian Woman: Gender, State Policy, and Popular Culture, 1865–1946* (Gainesville: University Press of Florida, 2002), 165–68.
38. *Shikufah*, fourth year, No. 7, 6 Jumada al-Avval 1334/11 March 1916, 2–3.
39. *CENTO Conference on Nursing Education, Held in Tehran, Iran, April 14–25 1964* (Ankara: Office of the U.S. Economic Coordinator for CENTO Affairs, 1964), 62.

40. PHS, Record Group (hereafter RG) 91, Box 4, Folder 11, Received 23 November 1916, "Medical Report," Urumiyah 1916, 2.

41. Ibid.

42. Ibid.

43. PHS, RG 91, Box 4, Folder 14, "Report of American Hospital, Tabriz, 1919–1920," 2.

44. PHS, "Report of Women's Work in Tabriz, Persia, August 1918 to August 1919."

45. PHS, "Report of the American Mission Hospital at Tabriz, to the Annual Meeting held at Tabriz, Persia, August 1922."

46. PHS, RG 91, Box 4, Folder 14, "Report of American Hospital, Tabriz, 1919–1920," 2.

47. PHS, "Tabriz Women's Work, 1923," 1.

48. PHS, RG 91, Box 1, Folder 18, "Report of Medical Work, Hamadan, 1910/1911," 4.

49. PHS, RG 91, Box 1, "Report of Medical Work in Meshed, July 1st, 1920—June 30th, 1921," 5.

50. PHS, RG 91, Box 1, Folder 20, "Resht Medical Report 1924–5," 6.

51. Ibid.

52. *The Iranian Red Lion & Sun (Red Cross) Bulletin*, no. 1, March 1947, 22–23.

53. John Gilmour, *Report on an Investigation into the Sanitary Conditions in Persia Undertaken on Behalf of the Health Committee of the League of Nations at the Request of the Persian Government* (Geneva: Imp. Atar, 1925), 52.

54. *Bakhtar*, No. 6, April/May 1935, 421–24. This writer advocated decent treatment of orphans using the Prophet Muhammad as an example to show that other orphans, too, could achieve extraordinary feats during their lifetime if given the opportunity.

55. Prince Nusrat al-Dawlah Firuz gave impetus to the creation of the Pasteur Institute in Iran. While in Paris to attend the peace conference, he visited the Pasteur Institute in Paris and advised Iranian officials to start a similar institution there. Dr. Joseph Mesnard was appointed its director. Rockefeller Archive Center, RF, RG1.1, Series 77, Box 1, "Preliminary Report on Medical Education in Persia," 31. For more on the history of the Pasteur Institute, see Amir A. Afkhami, "Institut Pasteur," *Encyclopaedia Iranica*, online version. Also, Mohammad-Hossein Azizi and Touraj Nayernouri, "The Establishment and the First Four Decades of the Activities of the Pasteur Institute of Iran," *Archive of Iranian Medicine* 11, 4 (2008): 477–81.

56. PHS, RG 91, Box 20, Annual Report of the Medical Work at Meshed, Persia, American Hospital, Year Ending June 30th, 1929, 1.

57. *Ittila'at*, 12 Mehr 1305/5 October 1926, 2. The services of Mme. Chichlo, a midwife certified by a school in Petrograd, were publicized.

58. *Ittila'at*, December 7, 1932, 4. Five years later, another private maternity clinic was in need of nurses and placed an announcement for this purpose. *Ittila'at*, 18 October 1938.

59. *Payk-i Sa'adat-i Nisvan*, No. 2, January 1928, 44.

60. Ibid.

61. Dr. Amir 'Alam had headed the Sanitary Council from 1914 until it was subsumed under the newly established Ministry of Health in 1921. He contributed regularly to the society's journal.

62. *Majallah-i shir va khurshid-i surkh-i Iran*, first year, nos. 2–3 (Tehran: Sa'adat Press, Isfand 1305/February–March 1926): 4–21.

63. *Payk-i Sa'adat-i Nisvan*, No. 1, October–November 1927, 6.

64. *Ittila'at*, No. 385, 24 Aban 1306/1927, 2.

65. *Sihhat-Nimayah-i Iran*, No. 6, Shahrivar 1312/August–September 1933, 140.

66. *'Alam-i Nisvan*, tenth year, No. 6, November 1930, 281.

67. Ibid., 282–83.

68. Vizarat-i Farhang, *Salnamah va Amar, 1315–1316 va 1316–1317*, 608–9. Also, *Salnamah-i Pars*, 1309/1930, 154–55.

69. *Ittila'at*, 20 Azar 1314/12 December 1935, 1. Also, *Ittila'at*, 22 Azar 1314/14 December 1935.

70. *Ittila'at*, 19 Mehr 1315/11 October 1936, 1.

71. Vizarat-i Farhang, *Salnamah va Amar, 1315–1316 va 1316–1317*, 747–72.

72. Ibid., 490–91.

73. R. M. Burrell, ed., *Iran Political Diaries, 1881–1965* (Farnham Common, UK: Archive Editions, Ltd., 1997), 7:441.

74. Ibid.

75. Ibid., 7:442–43.

76. U.S. Confidential Department of State Records, RG 59, Iran, 1925–1941, Charles Hart to Secretary of State, 11 March 1931, and enclosure: "Death Toll of the City of Teheran During the Month of Dey, 1309."

77. PHS, RG 91, Box 20, "Fifteenth Annual Report of the American Christian Hospital, Meshed, Persia, 1929–1930," 9.

78. Ibid., 9.

79. PHS, RG 91, Box 20, Folder 2, "Eighteenth Annual Report of the American Christian Hospital, Meshed," 1 July 1932–June 30, 1933, 4; *Ittila'at*, 27 February 1933, "Dar Jashn-i Madrasah-i Qabilagi," 2.

80. PHS, RG 91, Box 20, "Fifteenth Annual Report of the American Christian Hospital, Meshed, Persia, 1929–1930," 35. Kibbe's comments echoed the observations of Lady Sheil and others who had first broached these subjects in the nineteenth century.

81. Iran, Prime Ministry Files, "Sazman-i Parvaresh-i Afkar Records," The Situation of Kerman, 5, 13.

82. PHS, RG 91, Box 20, Folder 2, "Eighteenth Annual Report of the American Christian Hospital, Meshed," 1 July 1932–June 30, 1933, 4.

83. Ibid.

84. *Salnamah va amar: 1315/1316, 1316/1317*, 747–48.

85. *Encyclopaedia Iranica*, "Faculties of the University of Tehran, Faculty of Medicine."

86. PHS, RG 91, Box 19, Folder 30, "Medical Report Kermanshah, 1937," 3.

87. Ibid., 4.

88. Iran, National Archives, File 291, *Vizarat-i Dakhilah, Sihhiyah-i kul-i mamlikati*, "Nizamnamah-i Asasi-yi Abilih kubi-yi majjani," September 1932.

89. *Khatabah-hayah kanun-e banuvan* (Tehran, 1314/1935), 13.

90. Iran, National Archives, Prime Ministry Files, File 290, 23 Mordad 1315/1936.

91. *Alam-i Zanan*, No. 5, Aban 1323, October–November 1944, 3.

92. *Alam-i Zanan*, No. 2, Murdad 1323/June–July 1944.

93. Kenneth Bourne and D. Cameron Watt, eds., *British Documents on Foreign Affairs. Part II, From the First to the Second World Wars. Series B, Turkey, Iran and the Middle East* (Frederick, MD: University Publications of America, 1985), 28:66 (dated 20 February 1936).

94. Ibid. After the fall of Reza Shah in 1941, women gradually gained the privilege of choosing whether to veil or not to veil. In theory, clinics could once again revert to ministering to pregnant women regardless of their public appearance or expressions of religiosity.

95. *Ittila'at*, 22 Mehr 1317/14 October 1938, 10.

96. *Ittila'at*, 20 Aban 1317/11 November 1938, 10; *Ittila'at*, 21 Aban 1317/12 November 1938.

97. *Ittila'at*, 6 Bahman 1318/27 January 1940, "Sanjish-i mama-yi, diruz va imruz."

98. Firoozeh Kashani-Sabet, "The Haves and the Have Nots: A Historical Study of Disability in Modern Iran," *Iranian Studies* 43, 2 (2010): 167–95.

99. *Sihhatnima-yi Iran*, first year, No. 3, May–June 1933, 59–63.

100. *Sihhatnima-yi Iran*, first year, No. 1, March–April 1933, 12–13.

101. Carrie Yang Costello, "Teratology: 'Monsters' and the Professionalization of Obstetrics," *Journal of Historical Sociology* 19, 1 (2006), 1–2, 10.

102. *Sihhatnima-yi Iran*, first year, No. 3, May–June 1933, 59–63.

103. Ibid., 59. A subsequent discussion of physical deformity, entitled the "oddities of nature" (*aja'ib-i tabi'at*), was rendered into French as "les monstres."

104. Byron J. Good, "The Transformation of Health Care in Modern Iranian History," in *Modern Iran: The Dialectics of Continuity and Change*, ed. Michael Bonine and Nikki Keddie (Albany: State University of New York Press, 1981), 72.

105. Rosalie Morton, *A Doctor's Holiday in Iran* (New York: Funk and Wagnalls, 1940), 243–45.

106. *Alam-i Zanan*, No. 6, Azar 1323/November–December 1944.

107. Ibid.

CHAPTER 6 : SCHOOLING MOTHERS

1. *Habl al-Matin*, Tehran, No. 103, 19 Rajab 1325/29 August 1907, 1.

2. *Nijat*, No. 22, 19 Ramadan 1327/5 October 1909, 4.

3. For studies of women in the constitutional period, see Mangol Bayat-Philipp, "Women and Revolution in Iran, 1905–11," in *Women in the Muslim World*, ed. Lois Beck and Nikki Keddie (Cambridge: Harvard University Press, 1978); Janet Afary, "On the Origins of Feminism in Early 20th-Century Iran," *Journal of Women's History*, 1 (1989): 65–87; Eliz Sanasarian, *The Women's Rights Movement in Iran* (New York: Praeger, 1982); Afsaneh Najmabadi, "Women or Wives of the Nation?" *Iranian Studies*, 26 (1993): Huma Natiq, "Nigahi bih barkhi nivishtiha va mubarizat-i zanan dar dawran-i mashrutiyat," *Kitab-i Jum'a* 30 (1979):45–54; 'Abdul Husayn Nahid, *Zanan-i Iran dar junbish-i mashrutiyat* (Saarbrucken: Nuvid, 1989); for an excellent article on women under the Qajars, see Mansoureh Ettehadieh, "Zan dar jami'ah-i qajar," *Kilk*, 55–56 (Fall 1373/1994): 27–50.

4. Monica Ringer, *Education, Religion, and the Discourse of Cultural Reform in Qajar Iran* (Costa Mesa, CA: Mazda, 2001); A. Reza Arasteh, *Education and Social Awakening in Iran, 1850–1968* (Leiden: Brill, 1969).

5. Khan-i Khanan, "Risalah-'i dar siyasat," 1897, Manuscript at the National Library, #RF 385, 75–76. I am in the process of editing this manuscript for publication.

6. Afsaneh Najmabadi, "Crafting an Educated Housewife in Iran," in *Remaking Women: Feminism and Modernity in the Middle East*, ed. Lila Abu-Lughod (Princeton: Princeton University Press, 1998); Firoozeh Kashani-Sabet, *Frontier Fictions: Shaping the Iranian Nation, 1804–1946* (Princeton: Princeton University Press, 1999), ch. 6.

7. *Ittila'*, No. 20, 19 January 1904, 8.

8. PHS, RG 91, Box 1, "Tehran Station, 1910–1911." The newspaper *Danish* also reported the opening of a school for orphan girls. *Danish*, No. 4, 22 Shavval 1328/27 October 1910, 2.

9. *Danish*, No. 4, 22 Shavval 1328/26 October 1910, 2. (I refer to the copies of *Danish* published by the National Library of Iran.) *Ruh al-Quds* also reports the opening of a school for orphans in Bujnurd. *Ruh al-Quds*, No. 10, 6 Ramadan 1325/14 October 1907, 4.

10. *Khayr al-Kalam*, second year, No. 21, 6 Dhul-hijja 1327/19 December 1909, 4.

11. Arasteh, *Education and Social Awakening in Iran*, 53.

12. PHS, RG 91, Box 1, "Report, 1911–1912," 1.

13. Ibid.

14. Jasamin Rostam-Kolayi, "Origins of Iran's Modern Girls' Schools: From Private/National to Public/State," *Journal of Middle East Women's Studies* 4, 3 (2008): 58–88.

15. For some statistics on women's schools in 1912–13, see *Shikufah*, second year, No. 20, 1 Safar 1332/1913, 3–4. See also Najmabadi, "Crafting an Educated Housewife in Iran," 107–11.

16. *Ruh al-Quds*, No. 25, 4 May 1908, 2. The article notes that European teachers at the Dar al-Funun were getting paid, while the Iranian instructors were not.

17. *Junub*, No. 22, 25 May 1911, 6.

18. Huma Rizvani, *Lavayih-i Aqa Shaykh Fazl Allah Nuri* (Tehran: Nashr-i Tarikh-i Iran, 1983), 28. Other religious scholars, however, such as Mirza Hadi Dawlatabadi, father of Sadiqih Dawlatabadi, endorsed the founding of girls' schools, and female members of their family became activists in the cause of women's education. Najmabadi, "Crafting an Educated Housewife," 123 n. 103.

19. Badr al-Muluk Bamdad, *From Darkness into Light: Women's Emancipation in Iran*, ed. and trans. F. R. C. Bagley (New York: Exposition, 1977), 44–45.

20. *Habl al-Matin*, No. 105, 14 September 1907, 4. For related discussions, see Janet Afary, *The Iranian Constitutional Revolution of 1906–1911: Grassroots Democracy, Social Democracy and the Origins of Feminism* (New York: Columbia University Press, 1996), 191; Najmabadi, "Crafting an Educated Housewife," 107.

21. Nazim al-Islam Kirmani, *Tarikh-i Bidari-yi Iranian* (Tehran: Bunyad-i Farhang-i Iran, 1357/1978), 1:244. Also, Kashani-Sabet, *Frontier Fictions*, ch. 6.

22. *Khayr al-Kalam*, second year, No. 31, 27 Safar 1328/9 March 1910, 1.

23. *Khayr al-Kalam,* second year, No. 24, 24 Dhul-hijja 1327/6 January 1910, 1–2.
24. For accounts of the constitutional revolution that have significantly informed Western accounts of the subject, see Ahmad Kasravi, *Tarikh-i Inqilab-i Mashruti- yat* (Tehran: Intisharat-i Amir Kabir, 1984), and Mehdi Malikzadeh, *Tarikh-i Inqilab-i Mashrutiyat-i Iran* (Tehran: 'Ilmi, 1984). Other accounts have been written by Abrahamian, Afary, Bayat, Ettehadieh, Keddie, Najmabadi, and Sedghi.
25. "The Persian Problem," *The Times,* March 25, 1912,
26. "Suffragists Hold Congress," *Chicago Daily Tribune,* 16 June 1913, 2.
27. Kashani-Sabet, "Frontier Fictions," ch. 6. The content of many schoolbooks used in women's schools in the 1920s is a focus of this chapter. Unfortunately, it is often overlooked in studies of women's education and nationalism in Iran despite the value of the schoolbooks themselves. I must also take this opportunity to correct an error that appears in the text: Muhtarim Iskandari's name is misidenti- fied as Muhtaram Ikhtisari on 183. I have no reasonable explanation for this over- sight other than to attribute it to human error.
28. For discussions of the nation as a motherland, see Afsaneh Najmabadi, "The Erotic *Vatan* [Homeland] as Beloved and Mother: To Love, to Possess, and to Protect," *Comparative Studies in Society and History* 39, 3 (1997): 442–67. For related discussions, see Firoozeh Kashani-Sabet, "The Frontier Phenomenon: Perceptions of the Land in Iranian Nationalism," *Critique* 38, 3 (1997): 19–38. For one reference to mothers and patriotism, see *Shikufah,* third year, No. 19, 4 Dhul-hijja 1333/1915, 2–3. Also, *Shikufah,* fourth year, No. 5, 3 Jumada al-Avval 1334/1916. There are numerous other references to patriotism in *Shikufah* as well, though it is significant to point out that *Danish* placed less emphasis on this issue.
29. *Hadid,* No. 13, 25 Rajab 1323/25 September 1905, 4.
30. *Tarbiyat,* No. 75, 11 April 1898, 300, for reports of a measles epidemic killing children.
31. *Hadid,* no. 13, 25 Rajab 1323/25 September 1905, 6. On the same page, this ar- ticle notes further that knowing that lack of sanitation causes disease is impor- tant, since such ignorance breeds epidemics: "In India there is always plague, [whereas] the English, who maintain sanitary habits, do not become victims [of this disease]." Therefore, women had to be equipped with such knowledge to help limit the spread of disease in their family and in their nation.
32. *Hadid,* No. 13, 25 Rajab 1323/25 September 1905, 4.
33. This point has been eloquently argued and supported in a study by Camron Amin, *The Making of the Modern Iranian Woman: Gender, State Policy, and Popular Culture, 1865–1946* (Gainesville: University of Florida Press, 2002).
34. *Danish,* No. 1, 10 Ramadan 1328/14 September 1910, 2. Several editions of *Danish* and *Shikufah,* another women's journal that began publication in 1912, have been edited in Iran. See *Shikufah bih Inzimam-i Danish: Nakhustin Nashriyah'hayah Zanan-i Iran* (Tehran: Kitabkhanah-i Milli-yi Jumhuri-yi Islami-yi Iran, 1377/1999). In some instances, my references to these jour- nals refer to original copies.
35. *Danish,* No. 6, 7 Dhul-qa'da 1328/9 November 1910, 3.

36. *Amuzgar*, No. 14, 10 Ramadan 1329/4 September 1911, 4.
37. *Amuzgar*, No. 14, 10 Ramadan 1329/4 September 1911, 4.
38. *Junub*, No. 16, 11 April 1911, 4.
39. *Shikufah*, fourth year, No. 1, 1 Safar 1334/8 December 1915, 3–4.
40. These ideas would be institutionalized through the textbooks published and used in the late Qajar period. See Kashani-Sabet, *Frontier Fictions*, ch. 6, for more on this issue and for detailed discussions of the textbooks.
41. *Shikufah*, No. 8, 13 Jumada al-Avval 1333/29 March 1915, 2.
42. This point has not been lost on the Islamic Republic of Iran, either, which has allowed republication of many issues of these journals.
43. For more on the history of hygiene in nineteenth- and early twentieth-century Iran, see Firoozeh Kashani-Sabet, "Hallmarks of Humanism: Hygiene and Love of Homeland in Qajar Iran," *American Historical Review* 105, 4 (2000): 1171–1203.
44. *Shikufah*, second year, No. 22, 5 Rabi' al-Avval 1332/1 February 1914, 3–4.
45. Mirza Sayyid Muhammad Qummi, *Ta'limat-i Muduniyah* (Tehran: Shams, 1330/1912), 34. According to its title page, this textbook was approved and written according to the "program and instructions" of the Education Ministry.
46. Samuel Jordan, "The New Spirit in Persia," *Women's Work* 31 (1916): 273–75.
47. PHS, RG 91, Box 4, Folder 1, Mary Lewis Shedd, "Report of Urumia Station, 1916–7," 3.
48. Zohreh T. Sullivan, "Eluding the Feminist, Overthrowing the Modern? Transformations in Twentieth-Century Iran," in *Remaking Women*, ed. Lila Abu-Lughod (Princeton: Princeton University Press, 1998), 229. Sullivan provides a fascinating and informative discussion of Dawlatabadi's career.
49. Bamdad, *From Darkness into Light*, 56.
50. *Sitarah-i Iran*, No. 27, 23 September 1923, 4. In 1924, the newspaper *Vatan* reported the existence of what appears to be a small private school for girls in Tehran, *Vatan*, 6 November 1924, 4. Mirza Yusuf Khan Mua'dib a al-Mulk Richard had founded the Ecole Franco-Persane during the constitutional period. Richard's mother was an Iranian and his father was a Frenchman employed at the Dar al-Funun. Bamdad, *From Darkness into Light*, 52.
51. "Suffrage Congress Demands Vote for Women of All Lands," *New York Times*, February 13, 1919.
52. In 1949, the United Nations Commission on the Status of Women completed its fourth yearly session and focused on the status of women in politics worldwide. "Women as Voters," *New York Times*, May 28, 1950.
53. "Women Assemble from 40 Nations," *New York Times*, 26 May 1926, 10. Sullivan, "Eluding the Feminist," 230, notes that Sadiqah Dawlatabadi was Iran's delegate. Dawlatabdi's participation is confirmed in a governmental memo, which erroneously cites the date of the conference as 1306 Shamsi/1927. Sazman-i Asnad-i Milli-yi Iran, Interior Ministry, Report on Women's Movement (*nihzat-i banuvan*), 290/5-194-4, 5 April 1936.
54. *Muzakirat-i Majlis*, fourth Majlis, 16 Safar 1340/18 October 1921, 172–80.
55. *Nahid*, no. 3, 26 April 1921, 1. This is a general essay on the moral corruption of Iranian society, entitled "Fisad-i muhit," in which women's illiteracy is considered a contributing factor to this general condition.

56. *Majallah-i Nisvan-i Vatankhvah,* Nos. 5–6, 1924, 19.
57. Ibid., 18–20.
58. One notable dissenter from the Qajar period was Mirza Malkum Khan, who frequently talked about nineteenth-century Iran's backwardness vis-à-vis the civilized world.
59. *Bahar,* second year, No. 7, Rajab 1340/1922, 430.
60. Ibid., 431.
61. *Jahan-i Zanan,* No. 2, 4 March 1921, 32–35.
62. *Jahan-i Zanan,* No. 1, February 1921, 7.
63. Ibid., 8.
64. *Jahan-i Zanan,* No. 5, 1921, 108.
65. *Jahan-i Zanan,* No. 3, 4, April 1921, 68.
66. Ibid., 69.
67. Kashani-Sabet, *Frontier Fictions,* ch. 6.
68. *Jahan-i Zanan,* first year, No. 1, 4 February 1921, 5–6. For a complementary essay on similar subjects, see *Majallah-i Nisvan-i Vatankhvah,* No. 2, 1923, 11–13.
69. *Jahan-i Zanan,* No. 5, September 1921, 9–13.
70. Parvin Paidar, *Women and the Political Process in Twentieth-Century Iran* (Cambridge: Cambridge University Press, 1995), 94.
71. Sazman-i Asnad-i Milli-yi Iran, Interior Ministry, Report on Women's Movement (*nihzat-i banuvan*), 290/5-194-4, 5 April 1936. This report provides a history of the women's movement since 1921. Iskandari is credited with being the first woman to advocate women's renewal.
72. *Majallah-i Nisvan-i Vatankhvah,* No. 1, 1923, 4–7. For similar arguments, see *Jahan-i Zanan,* No. 2, 1921, 1–4.
73. *Majallah-i Nisvan-i Vatankhvah,* No. 2, 1923, 7.
74. *Shikufah,* No. 21, 6 Muharram 1334/14 November 1915, 1–2; *Shikufah,* No. 1, 6 Muharram 1333/24 November 1914, 2–3.
75. Ahmad Sa'adat, *Rahnima-yih Sa'adat* (Tehran, 1923), 97.
76. *Vizarat Ma'arif,* 172.
77. *Majallah-i Nisvan-i Vatankhvah,* No. 1, 1923, 21–22.
78. *Majallah-i Nisvan-i Vatankhvah,* Nos. 5–6, 1924, 2–4. For an interview with Nur al-Huda Manganah, in which she discusses the founding of the league and women's activism during this era, see *Ittila'at,* "Siy va do Sal Nabard-i Tarikhi-yi Zanan-i Iran," 17 Day 1346/7 January 1968, 14.
79. *Majallah-i Nisvan-i Vatankhvah,* Nos. 7–8, 1924, 41–43.
80. Sazman-i Asnad-i Milli-yi Iran, Interior Ministry, Report on Women's Movement (*nihzat-i banuvan*), 290/5-194-4, 5 April 1936.
81. Kashani-Sabet, *Frontier Fictions,* ch. 6.
82. *Majallah-i Nisvan-i Vatankhvah,* for example, discusses these ideas, No. 1, 1302/1923, 21–22.
83. *Namah-i Farangistan,* No. 3, 1 July 1924, 110–12.
84. *Farhang,* second year, No. 4, June–July 1925, 153–55.
85. Ibid., 156–59.
86. For background information, see Paidar, *Women and the Political Process,* 90–101.
87. Ibid., 97.

88. *Payk-i Sa'adat-i Nisvan*, No. 1, 15 Mehr 1306/1927, 6.
89. *Payk-i Sa'adat-i Nisvan*, Nos. 4–5, 1928, 98–100.
90. *Payk-i Sa'adat-i Nisvan*, No. 2, January 1928, 42.
91. "Ihsa'iyah-i madaris-i Iran," *Ittila'at*, Murdad 1305/1926.
92. Rockefeller Archive Center, RF, RG1.1, Series 77, Box 1, "Preliminary Report on Medical Education in Persia," 16.
93. Ibid., 16.
94. Ibid., 17.
95. Ibid., 17–18.
96. Ibid., 17.
97. PHS, Fifteenth Annual Report of the American Christian Hospital, 35.
98. "Preliminary Report on Medical Education in Persia," 17.
99. Agha Mirza Sayyid Ali Khan, *Hunar Amuz-i Dushizigan* (Tehran: Nihzat-i Sharq, 1343/1944), 2, 10–11.
100. Dawlat-i 'Illiyah-i Iran, Vizarat-i Ma'arif, *Salnamah-i Ahsa'iyah, 1307–1308* (1929), 168.
101. Ibid., 143.
102. Muhammad Hijazi, *Mihan-i Ma* (Tehran: Intisharat-i Vizarat-i Farhang, 1338/1959), 285.
103. *Payk-i Sa'adat-i Nisvan*, No. 6, Shahrivar 1307/August 1928, 166.
104. *Pahlavi*, No. 19, 19 Jumada al-Ukhra 1342/1923, 3–4.
105. PHS, RG 91, Box 20, "Report of Iran Bethel School, 1925–1926," Tehran, 2.
106. Michael Zirinsky, "Harbingers of Change: Presbyterian Women in Iran, 1883–1949," *American Presbyterians: Journal of Presbyterian History* 70, 3 (1992): 173–86; Zirinsky, "A Panacea for the Ills of the Country: American Presbyterian Education in Inter-War Iran," *Iranian Studies* 26, 1–2 (1993): 119–37.
107. *Vizarat-i Ma'arif va Awqaf va Sana'i-yi Mustazrafah: Ihsa'iyah-i Ma'arif va Madaris(1307–1308)* (Tehran: Matba'a-yi Rawshana'i, n.d.), 27.
108. Firoozeh Kashani-Sabet, "Cultures of Iranianness: The Evolving Polemic of Iranian Nationalism," in *Iran and the Surrounding World*, ed. Nikki Keddie and Rudi Matthee, 162–81 (Seattle: University of Washington Press, 2002). For a recent article by my former student, see Mikiya Koyagi, "Moulding Future Soldiers and Mothers of the Iranian Nation: Gender and Physical Education Under Reza Shah, 1921–41," *International Journal of the History of Sport* 26, 11 (2009): 1668–96.
109. Sa'id Nafisi, *Sukhanranihayah sazman-i parvarish-i afkar* (Tehran: Chapkhanah-i Firdawsi, 1318/1939), 154–55.
110. *Khattabahhayah Kanun-i Banuvan*, Tehran, 1935, 1; also Kashani-Sabet, "Cultures of Iranianness," 170–74.
111. Mirza Sayyid Ali Khan, *Hunar amuz-i dushizigan: sal-i duvvum, madaris-i nisvan* (Tehran: Nihzat-i Sharq, 1303/1924); Ahmad Sa'adat, *Rahnima-yi sa'adat: Makhsus-i muhassilat-i madaris-i nisvan* (Tehran, 1342/1923).
112. *Dukhtaran-i Iran*, No. 3, May–June 1932, 15.
113. Ibid., 16.
114. *Akhlaq* literature has been discussed in my work *Frontier Fictions*, ch. 6, and in Najmabadi, "Crafting an Educated Housewife in Iran." From my reading of

the *akhlaq* texts from the late Qajar period, I have rendered the term *akhlaq* into English as "manners" because of their heavy behavioral stress and their emphasis on feminine virtues. While Najmabadi has referred to them as ethics books, my sources were concerned less with ethics in the Aristotelian sense and more with the proper modes of social behavior for young Iranian women.

115. Bamdad, *Akhlaq*, 8.
116. Ibid., 32.
117. Ibid., 43.
118. Ibid., 41.
119. *Dukhtaran-i Iran*, No. 3, May–June 1932, 23.
120. "Bafandigi, bihtarin sargarmi-yih banuvan," *Ittila'at*, 14 Bahman 1317/February 1939, 10.
121. Sazman-i Asnad-i Milli-yi Iran, Interior Ministry, Report on Women's Movement (*nihzat-i banuvan*), 290/5-194-4, 5 April 1936.
122. *Dukhtaran-i Iran*, No. 3, May–June 1932, 6.
123. Ibid., 10–11.
124. Ibid., 12.
125. Badr al-Muluk Bamdad, *Tadbir-i Manzil* (Tehran: Iqbal, 1310/1931).
126. Ibid., 1.
127. Ibid., 3–4.
128. Ibid., 177–90.
129. See Kashani-Sabet, *Frontier Fictions*, ch. 6, for more on the role of education in Iranian nationalism and in domesticating the homeland.
130. *Ta'lim va Tarbiyat*, sixth year, No. 12, Isfand 1315/February–March 1937, 864.
131. *Salnamah-i Zanan-i Iran*, 100. Contrast views on "cult of domesticity" with Najabadi, "Crafting an Educated Housewife."
132. Hammed Shahidian, *Women in Iran: Emerging Voices in the Women's Movement* (Westport, CT: Greenwood, 2002), 36.
133. *Ta'lim va Tarbiyat*, seventh year, No. 8, 1937.
134. Bamdad, *From Darkness into Light*, 98.
135. Sazman-i Asnad-i Milli-yi Iran, Interior Ministry, Report on Women's Movement (*nihzat-i banuvan*), 290/5-194-5, 5 April 1936. No figures were cited for girls attending specialty schools.
136. "Nihzat-i Banuvan-i Iran az sal-i 1301 shuru' shud," *Ittila'at*, 7 January 1968, 7. *Ittila'at* based this analysis on an article it had published decades earlier in Day 1316/January 1937 that compared statistics on female school enrollment.
137. *British Documents on Foreign Affairs. Part II, From the First to the Second World Wars. Series B, Turkey, Iran and the Middle East*, ed. Kenneth Bourne and D. Cameron Watt (Frederick, MD: University Publications of America, 1985), 27:268.
138. David Menashri, *Education and the Making of Modern Iran* (Ithaca: Cornell University Press, 1992); Seyed Farian Sabahi, "The Literacy Corps in Pahlavi Iran (1963–1979): Political, Social and Literary Implications," *Cahiers d'études sur la Méditerranée orientale et le monde turco-iranien* 31 (2001).
139. Hijazi, *Mihan-i Ma*, 226.

140. *British Documents on Foreign Affairs*, 28:373.

141. *Zaban-i Zanan*, No. 1, December 1942, cover.

142. *Zaban-i Zanan*, No. 3, June 1945, 17–21.

143. For related discussions of this issue, see Najmabadi, "Crafting an Educated Housewife in Iran."

144. *Alam-i Zanan*, No. 1, Tir 1323/June–July 1944, No. 1. For Musahab's biography, see the same issue, 13.

145. Ibid., 13.

CHAPTER 7 : DEFROCKING THE NATION

1. My discussion of the politics of dress in this chapter has been informed by Victoria de Grazia, "Introduction," in *The Sex of Things: Gender and Consumption in Historical Perspective*, ed. Victoria de Grazia with Ellen Furlough (Berkeley: University of California Press, 1996), 5. Also see the review essay by Mary Louise Roberts, "Gender, Consumption, and Commodity Culture," *American Historical Review* 103, 3 (June 1998): 821.

2. Edward Scott Waring, *A Tour to Sheeraz, by the Route of Kazroon and Feerozabad* (1807), 61.

3. Ibid., 57.

4. Ibid., 62.

5. Cf. Edward Said, *Orientalism* (New York: Pantheon, 1978).

6. Homa Hoodfar, "The Veil in Their Minds and on Our Heads: Veiling Practices and Muslim Women," in *Women, Gender, Religion: Troubling Categories and Transforming Knowledge*, ed. Elizabeth Anne Castelli and Rosamond C. Rodman (New York: Palgrave, 2001), 427. As Hoodfar has argued, "Both Muslim oriental and Christian occidental women were thought to be in need of male protection and intellectually and biologically destined for the domestic domain."

7. Justin Perkins, *A Residence of Eight Years in Persia, Among the Nestorians, with Notices of the Muhammedans* (Andover: Allen, Morrill and Wardwell, 1843), 152.

8. Frederick Shoberl, *Persia: Containing a Description of the Country, with an Account of its Government, Laws, and Religion* (Philadelphia: J. Grigg, 1828), 124.

9. Abdollah Mostofi, *The Administrative and Social History of the Qajar Period: From Agha Mohammad Khan to Nasir ed-Din Shah*, 1:318.

10. Ibid.

11. See Dust Ali Khan, Muayyir al-Mamalik, *Yad'dashthayi az zindagiyih khususiyah Nasir al-Din Shah* (Tehran: Nashr-i Tarikh-i Iran, 1983), 29.

12. Eustache de Lorey and Douglas Sladen, *Queer Things About Persia* (Philadelphia: J. B. Lippincott, 1907), 107; Nasir al-Din Shah, *The Diary of H.M. the Shah of Persia During His Tour Through Europe*, trans. James William Redhouse (London: Jonathan Murray, 1874), 38.

13. Perkins, *A Residence*, 149.

14. Firoozeh Kashani-Sabet, *Frontier Fictions: Shaping the Iranian Nation, 1804–1946* (Princeton: Princeton University Press, 1999), 89; Malik al-Muvarrikhin, "Qanun-i Muzaffari," manuscript at the Kitabkhanah-i Milli, #314, 14–16.

15. *Iran-i Sultani*, No. 7, 16 June 1903, 1.

16. *Subh-i Sadiq*, No. 37, 20 May 1907, 1; *Nida-yi Vatan*, No. 40, 2 July 1907, 3.

17. *Majallah-i Nisvan-i Vatankhvah*, Nos. 5–6, 1924, 3, 40–44.
18. *Jarchi-yi Millat*, No. 16, 6 Dhul-qa'da 1335/24 August 1917, 1.
19. Ibid.
20. Afsaneh Najmabadi, *Women with Mustaches and Men Without Beards*. Also, Faegheh Shirazi, "Men's Facial Hair in Islam: A Matter of Interpretation," in *Hair: Styling Culture and Fashion*, ed. Geraldine Biddle-Perry and Sarah Cheang (New York: Berg, 2008).
21. Najmabadi, *Women with Mustaches*, 193. For studies of Qasim Amin and the Egyptian women's movement, see Leila Ahmed, *Women and Gender in Islam* (New Haven: Yale University Press, 1992), and Beth Baron, *The Women's Awakening in Egypt: Culture, Society, and the Press* (New Haven: Yale University Press, 1994).
22. *Shikufah*, second year, No. 23, 20 Rabi' al-Avval 1332/16 February 1914, 4.
23. *Shikufah*, second year, No. 24, 5 Rabi' al-Thani 1332/2 March 1914, 3.
24. Huda Shaarawi, *Harem Years*, ed. Margot Badron (London: Virago, 1986).
25. *Farangistan*, Nos. 9–10, January–February 1925, 439–43.
26. For a study of the veil and Iranian sartorial fashion in the Pahlavi period, see Houchang Chehabi, "Staging the Emperor's New Clothes: Dress Codes and Nation-Building Under Reza Shah," *Iranian Studies* 26, 3–4 (1993): 209–29. For other important studies, see Eliz Sanasarian, *The Women's Rights Movement in Iran: Mutiny, Appeasement and Repression from 1900 to Khomeini* (New York: Praeger, 1982), and Parvin Paidar, *Women and the Political Process in Twentieth-Century Iran* (Cambridge: Cambridge University Press, 1995).
27. *Dabistan*, No. 9, 26 Safar 1346/24 August 1927, 385–89.
28. *Payk-i Sa'adat-i Nisvan*, Nos. 4–5, Urdibihisht and Tir 1307/Spring-Summer 1928, 121–26. For more reaction on the queen of Afghanistan, see Rosalie Morton, *A Doctor's Holiday in Iran* (New York: Funk and Wagnalls, 1940), 294–97.
29. *Payk-i Sa'adat-i Nisvan*, Nos. 4–5, Urdibihisht and Tir 1307/Spring-Summer 1928, 121–26.
30. J. Rives Childs, "The March of Modernism in Persia," Enclosure No. 1 to Despatch of 18 October 1934 from Legation at Tehran, 8, RG 59.
31. Ibid., 9.
32. Mohammad H. Faghfoory, "The Ulama-State Relations in Iran: 1921–1941," *International Journal of Middle East Studies* 19, 4 (1987): 413–32.
33. J. Rives Childs "The March of Modernism in Persia," Enclosure No. 1 to Despatch of 18 October 1934 from Legation at Tehran, 9, RG 59. For arrest of Mudarris, see ibid., 10.
34. Iran, National Archives, Ma'arif "B," File 51006, Document 324, "Nizamnamah-i Muttahid al-Shikl Nimudan-i Albasah," 3 Bahman 1307/23 January 1928.
35. Iran, National Archives, Ma'arif "B," File 51006, Document 324, "Qanun-i muttahid al-shikl nimudan-i albasah-i atba'-i Iran dar dakhilih-i mamlikat," 10 Day 1307/1928.
36. Chehabi, "Staging the Emperor's New Clothes," 225. In this article Chehabi has translated the dress code law into English.
37. RG 59, U.S. Confidential Department of State, No. 384, Charles C. Hart to Secretary of State, 19 February 1931, 1–2.

38. U.S. Confidential Department of State, RG 59, No. 451, Charles C. Hart to Secretary of State, 18 March 1931, 2.

39. Iran, National Archives, Ma'aref "A," File 51006, Document 568, "Nezamnameh-e Kanun-e Banovan."

40. National Archives, Tehran, Foreign Ministry Files, 2910001495, 20 Day 1315/10 January 1937.

41. Badr al-Muluk Bamdad, *From Darkness into Light: Women's Emancipation in Iran*, ed. and trans. F. R. C. Bagley (New York: Exposition, 1977), 94.

42. RG 59, No. 503, Hornibrook to Department of State, 9 July 1935, 1.

43. This passage is cited in full in Mohammad Gholi Majd, *Great Britain and Reza Shah: The Plunder of Iran* (Gainesville: University Press of Florida, 2001), 212–13. For additional discussion of the Gawharshad incident based upon these and other U.S. diplomatic documents, see Camron Amin, *The Making of the Modern Iranian Woman*, 85–90.

44. Knatchbull-Hugessen to Sir Samuel Hoare, Tehran, 14 June 1935, in Kenneth Bourne and D. Cameron Watt, eds., *British Documents on Foreign Affairs. Part II, From the First to the Second World Wars. Series B, Turkey, Iran and the Middle East* (Frederick, MD: University Publications of America, 1985), 27:380.

45. Sina Vahid, *Qiyam-i Gawharshad* (Tehran: Vizarat-i Farhang va Irshad-i Islami, 1366/1987).

46. RG 59, U.S, Department of State, "Memorandum," Enclosure No. 1 from the Legation at Tehran, 21 July 1935, 1.

47. Consul-General Daly to Mr. Knatchbull-Hugessen, 15 July 1935, in Bourne and Watt, eds., *British Documents on Foreign Affairs*, 27:398.

48. Ibid., 27:396.

49. RG 59, U.S. Department of State, "Memorandum," Enclosure No. 1 from the Legation at Tehran, 21 July 1935, 1.

50. Ibid., 2.

51. RG 59, Hornibrook to Department of State, No. 613, "Shah Prepares to Ban Chador from Iran," 30 October 1935. Also, Amin, *Making of the Modern Iranian Woman*, 90.

52. Bourne and Watt, eds., *British Documents on Foreign Affairs*, 27:404.

53. Parvin I'tisami, *Divan-i Qasa'id va Masnaviyat va Tamsilat va Muqatta'at* (Tehran, 1977); and Muhammad Taqi Bahar, Malik al-Shu'ara, *Divan-i ash'ar-i shadravan Muhammad Taqi Bahar Malik al-Shu'ara* (Tehran: Firdawsi, 1956).

54. Vahid, *Qiyam-e Gawharshad*.

55. *Vaqa'ih-i Kashf-i Hijab* (Tehran: Mu'assassah-i Mutali'at-i Farhangi, 1371/1992), 21.

56. For an interesting article on the trip, see Afshin Marashi, "Performing the Nation: The Shah's Official State Visit to Turkey, June to July 1934," in Stephanie Cronin, *The Making of Modern Iran: State and Society Under Riza Shah, 1921–1941* (London: Routledge-Curzon, 2003), 99–119.

57. Ministry of Foreign Affairs, Tehran, "Guzarishi dar barayih-i musafarat-i A'la Hazrat Reza Shah Kabir bih Turkiyah," 1313/1934—Carton 20. A translation of the official program of the king's visit did not contain any information on this issue, either. See "Tarjumah-i Program," 1313/1934—Carton 20.

58. Ministry of Foreign Affairs, Tehran, Note to Ataturk, 1313/1934—Carton 20.

59. National Archives, Tehran, Prime Ministry Files, 2910001495, 20 Day 1314/11 January 1936, 2.

60. Ibid.

61. National Archives, Tehran, Prime Ministry Files, 2910001495, 27 Day 1314/1936 discusses one such occasion at which the wives of various government officials were present.

62. Dated 11 January 1936, in Bourne and Watt, eds., *British Documents on Foreign Affairs* 28:45. Knatchbull-Hugessen further speculated that "one of the causes of the fall of the late Prime Minister, M. Feroughi, is thought to have been his opposition to the rapidity with which the Shah proposed to press on the unveiling."

63. Dated 7 February 1936, in Bourne and Watt, eds., *British Documents on Foreign Affairs*, 28:56.

64. Dated 22 February 1936, in Bourne and Watt, eds., *British Documents on Foreign Affairs*, 28:64.

65. Dated 3 February 1936, in Bourne and Watt, eds., *British Documents on Foreign Affairs*, 28:60–61.

66. Bourne and Watt, eds., *British Documents on Foreign Affairs*, 28:61.

67. Ibid., 28:426.

68. Iran, National Archives, Prime Ministry Files, File 103013/9692, 18 Farvardin 1315/7 April 1937.

69. National Archives, Tehran, Prime Ministry Files, 103013/9950, 24 Farvardin 1317/1938, 3.

70. National Archives, Tehran, Ministry of Post and Telegraph, Bahman 1316/1938.

71. *Khushunat va Farhang: Asnad-i Mahramanah-i Kashf-i Hijab* (Tehran: Intisharat-i Sazman-i Asnad-i Milli-yi Iran, 1371/1992), 102, 227, 231.

72. National Archives, Tehran, Prime Ministry Files, 103013/9886, "Guzarish-i Damavand," 16 Khurdad 1316/1937.

73. National Archives, Tehran, Isfahan Records, 2910001495, 4 Bahman 1315/1937.

74. Iran, National Archives, Ministry of Foreign Affairs, 19 Day 1316/9 January 1938, Weekly Report, 1. For more on the subject of marriage, hygiene, venereal disease, and population concerns, see Kashani-Sabet, "The Politics of Reproduction."

75. Bourne and Watt, eds., *British Documents on Foreign Affairs*, 28:128.

76. National Archives, Tehran, Ministry of Culture, 2910002573, 12 Day 1317/2 January 1939.

77. National Archives, Tehran, Prime Ministry Files, 108011/3268, "Amar-i Jalisat-i Sukhanranihayih Parvarish-i Afkar."

78. National Archives, Tehran, Prime Ministry Files, 108011/3268, "Fihrist-i Mawzu'hayih Sukhanraniha."

79. Said Amir Arjomand, ed., *From Nationalism to Revolutionary Islam* (Albany: State University of New York Press, 1984), 204–10. Also, Janet Afary, *Sexual Politics in Modern Iran* (Cambridge: Cambridge University Press, 2009), 187–88.

80. *Iran Almanac and Book of Facts* (1970), 773.

81. *Banu*, No. 2, Dey 1323/December 1944–January 1945, 1.

82. In the same issue of *Banu*, No. 2, December 1944/January 1945, 11–12, 28–29, another writer, Abul Qasim Azad Maragha'i, wrote about his support for the

unveiling movement and recounted the resistance the idea of unveiling had originally encountered in the 1920s.

83. *Banu*, No. 1, Azar 1323/November–December 1944, 29–31. The article is also revealing in its discussion of the condition of the School of Beaux Arts. Sa'idi noted that students often had to provide their own supplies. While schools had proliferated in Iran, the conditions of schools sometimes raised questions about their management and efficacy, as in this instance.

84. Najmeh Najafi, *Persia Is My Heart* (New York: Harper, 1953), 83.

CHAPTER 8 : FROM MOTHERS TO VOTERS

1. *Foreign Relations of the United States* (FRUS), 1942, IV:207–8. This series is available online at http://digicoll.library.wisc.edu/FRUS.
2. FRUS, 1943, IV:497–98. Also, Bill, *The Eagle and the Lion*, 47.
3. FRUS, 1943, IV:498.
4. Ibid., IV:500–1.
5. I delve into these concerns in more detail in my forthcoming book, *American Crosses, Persian Crescents: A History of U.S.-Iranian Relations.*
6. Ahmad Kasravi, *Khvaharan va Dukhtaran-i Ma*, ed. M. A. Jazayery (Bethesda, MD: Iranbooks, 1992), 5–9.
7. Ibid., 33.
8. Ibid., 34–36. Also see Camron Amin, *The Making of the Modern Iranian Woman: Gender, State Policy, and Popular Culture, 1865–1946* (Gainesville: University Press of Florida, 2002), 232, for more on the issue of soldiering and women.
9. Kasravi, *Khvaharan va Dukhtaran-i Ma*, 39.
10. Sedghi notes that "although nursing was almost exclusively a female-dominated field, women were mostly concentrated in secondary positions" Hamideh Sedghi, *Women and Politics in Iran: Veiling, Unveiling, and Reveiling* (New York: Cambridge University Press, 2007), 121 n. 39).
11. Janet Afary, *Sexual Politics in Modern Iran* (Cambridge: Cambridge University Press, 2009), 182, provides a complementary analysis of this exchange.
12. Iraj Parsinejad, *A History of Literary Criticism in Iran, 1866–1951: Literary Criticism in the Work of Enlightened Thinkers* (Bethesda, MD: Ibex, 2003), 185. Also, Fatimah Sayyah, *Naqd va Siyahat: Majmu'ah-i maqalat va taqrirat-i Doktor Fatimah Sayyah*, ed. Muhammad Gulbun (Tehran: Tus, 1354/1975), 145.
13. Fakhreddin Azimi, *The Quest for Democracy in Iran: A Century of Struggle Against Authoritarian Rule* (Cambridge: Harvard University Press, 2008).
14. Iran, National Archives, Prime Ministry Files, 109063/2304, "Bayaniyah: Hizb-i Iran-i Naw."
15. Iran, National Archives, Prime Ministry Files, 109001, "Maram-i Fraksiyun-i Dimukrat."
16. L. P. Elwell-Sutton, "Political Parties in Iran 1941–1948," *Middle East Journal* 3, 1 (January 1949), 45–632.
17. Camron Amin, "Globalizing Iranian Feminism, 1910–1950," *Journal of Middle East Women's Studies* 4, 1 (2008), 8–10.

18. Hossein Shahidi, "Women and Journalism in Iran," in *Women, Religion and Culture in Iran*, ed. Sarah Ansari and Vanessa Martin (Richmond, Surrey: Curzon, 2002), 70–87.

19. *Banu*, No. 1, Azar 1323/November–December 1944, 13.

20. For an important discussion of this interview, see Amin, "Globalizing Iranian Feminism," 22–23. Also, *Alam-i Zanan*, No. 7, Dey 1323/December 1944–January 1945, 13–14.

21. *Banu*, No. 2, Dey 1323/December 1944–January 1945, 10.

22. Sayyah, *Naqd va Siyahat*, 144–45.

23. Ibid.

24. For these biographical notes, I rely on an article published on Sayyah's life in the daily *Ittila'at*, 30 December 1967, 7. In this article, Sayyah is referred to as "*banuyih nabighah.*"

25. Microfilm 4457, U.S. Department of State Records, 1945–1949, Richard Ford to the Department of State, 6 January 1945.

26. Department of State Records, 1945–1949, Allen to Dept. of State, 12 January 1948, 1.

27. Susan Pedersen, "Catholicism, Feminism, and the Politics of the Family during the Late Third Republic," in *Mothers of a New World: Maternalist Politics and the Origins of Welfare States*, ed. Seth Koven and Sonya Michel (New York: Routledge, 1993), 247–48.

28. *A'in-i Islam*, "Yik khabar-i ta'asuf angiz," 14 Dey 1324/4 January 1946. It is interesting to note, however, that the journal makes no mention of the unveiling decree, or the subject of unveiling in general, in the days before and after the anniversary of the promulgation of the unveiling decree of 1936. For 'ulama support of this publication, see *A'in-i Islam*, 12 Bahman 1324/1 February 1946, 11, which cites 'ulama financial contributions to the journal.

29. *A'in-i Islam*, "Talashi-yi 'Aqidah," 17 Farvardin 1324/6 April 1945, 1.

30. For more on this subject, see Firoozeh Kashani-Sabet, "The Politics of Reproduction: Maternalism and Women's Hygiene in Iran, 1896–1941," *International Journal of Middle East Studies* 38, 1 (2006): 1–29.

31. *A'in-i Islam*, "Yik Banuyi Islami-yi Buzurg va nimunah-i kamil-i madar," 7 Urdibihisht 1324/27 April 1945, 2.

32. *Ittila'at*, 18 Dey 1318/9 January 1940.

33. *A'in-i Islam*, "Tarikh-i Husayn ibn Ali Alayhasalam," 7 Day 1324/28 December 1945.

34. *A'in-i Islam*, "Tashkilat-i yik millat," 31 Farvardin 1324/20 April 1945, 2.

35. *A'in-i Islam*, "Aqa-yi Abulfazl Haziqi namayandah-i Muhtaram-i Majlis-i Shaurayah Milli," 31 Farvardin 1324/20 April 1945, 6.

36. See for example, Emir Faradj Khan, "Hygiène et Islamisme," dissertation (Lyon, 1904).

37. *A'in-i Islam*, 17 Farvardin 1324/6 April 1945, 11.

38. Arthur Millspaugh, *Americans in Persia* (Washington, DC: Brookings Institution, 1946), 73.

39. *A'in-i Islam*, 17 Farvardin 1324/6 April 1945, 11.

40. Afary, *Sexual Politics in Modern Iran*, 193.

41. *Nida-yi Haqq*, No. 18, second year, 2 Bahman 1330/23 January 1952, 1–2. Sayyid Hasan Adnani owned and oversaw its publication. In No. 11 (1 Azar 1329/22 November 1950, 1–2), he talked about the ills of unveiling and its impact on undermining the honor of Iranian women.

42. *Nida-yi Haqq*, No. 19, 9 Bahman 1330/30 January 1952.

43. *Nida-yi Haqq*, No. 7, 15 Aban 1330/7 November 1951, 1.

44. *Nida-yi Haqq*, No. 18, second year, 2 Bahman 1330/23 January 1952, 1–2.

45. *Nida-yi Haqq*, 9 Bahman 1330/30 January 1952, 1–2.

46. *Nida-yi Haqq*, No. 10, 2nd Year, 6 Azar 1330/28 November 1951, 1–2.

47. Dorothy Kenyon, "Woman Suffrage in East: Syrian Law Regarding Arabian Voting Hailed as Entering Wedge," *New York Times*, 21 September 1949,

48. "Iran Women Press for Suffrage," *New York Times*, 9 January 1952.

49. "Princess Leads Iranian Women in Vote Demand: Ignore Rules, March Into Parliament," *Chicago Daily Tribune*, 9 January 1952, A7. Also, "Iran Princess Leads Women Asking Vote," *Los Angeles Times*, 9 January 1952.

50. "Iran's Women Seek Vote: Organization Protests to U.N., Saying Ban Violates Charter," *New York Times*, 17 January 1952, 2. The Iranian newspaper *Ittila'at* also reported on these developments. See Afary, *Sexual Politics in Modern Iran*, 195.

51. *Ittila'at*, 18 Day 1330/9 January 1952.

52. "Princess Leads Iranian Women in Vote Demand," *Chicago Daily Tribune*, 9 January 1952.

53. "Women Voteless in Ten Countries," *New York Times*, 16 August 1959.

54. "Women of Iran Seek the Ballot," *New York Times*, 25 September 1960.

55. Ibid.

56. "Vizarat-i farhang ba miting-i zanan mukhalifat kard," *Ittila'at*, 31 Shahrivar 1339/22 September 1960.

57. "Zanan bayad dar intikhabat-i anjuman-i shahr shirkat konand," *Ittila'at*, 18 Mihr 1339/10 October 1960, 16.

58. "Shura-yi 'ali-yi jamiyat-hayeh zanan tashkil-i jalisah dad," *Ittila'at*, 8 Azar 1341/29 November 1962.

59. "Male Bias Found in Governments," *New York Times*, March 27, 1960.

60. Mohsen M. Milani, *The Making of Iran's Islamic Revolution*, 2nd ed. (Boulder: Westview, 1994), 43–45.

61. Seyed Farian Sabahi, "The Literacy Corps in Pahlavi Iran (1963–1979): Political, Social and Literary Implications," *Cahiers d'études sur la Méditerranée orientale et le monde turco-iranien* 31 (2001).

62. Hammed Shahidian, *Women in Iran: Emerging Voices in the Women's Movement* (Westport, CT: Greenwood, 2002), 38. Also, Gholam-Reza Vatandoust, "The Status of Iranian Women During the Pahlavi Regime," in *Women and the Family in Iran*, ed. Asghar Fathi (Leiden: Brill, 1985), 126.

63. Haleh Esfandiari, "The Role of Women Members of Parliament, 1963–88," in *Women in Iran: From 1800 to the Islamic Republic*, ed. Lois Beck and Guity Nashat (Urbana: University of Illinois Press, 2004), 139–40.

64. *Muzakirat-i Majlis-i Shura-yi Milli*, second session, 23 Mehr 1342/15 October 1963, 3–4.

65. *Muzakirat-i Majlis-i Sina*, 2 Bahman 1342/ 22 January 1964, 5–7.

66. "Iran Quells Riot by Moslem Sect Fighting Reforms," *New York Times*, 6 June 1963.

67. "Mullahs in Revolt," *Times* (London), 7 June 1963.

68. Baqer Moin, *Khomeini: Life of the Ayatollah* (New York: St. Martin's, 1999), 75–76.

69. George C. Denney to U.S. Department of State, "The Iranian Riots and Their Aftermath," RNA-30, 26 June 1963, National Security Archive (online), George Washington University, item IR00483.

70. Parvin Paidar, *Women and the Political Process in Twentieth-Century Iran* (Cambridge: Cambridge University Press, 1995), 142, 148.

71. "Asasnamah-i Jadid-i Sazman-i Zanan-i Iran Tasvib Shud," *Ittila'at*, 18 Day 1346/8 January 1968, 4.

72. Mahnaz Afkhami, "The Women's Organization of Iran: Evolutionary Politics and Revolutionary Change," in *Women in Iran: From 1800 to the Islamic Republic*, ed. Lois Beck and Guity Nashat (Urbana: University of Illinois Press, 2004), 115.

73. Paidar, *Women and the Political Process*, 153. Also Nikki R. Keddie, *Women in the Middle East: Past and Present* (Princeton: Princeton University Press, 2006), 153.

74. Deniz Kandiyoti, "Introduction," in *Women, Islam and the State* (Philadelphia: Temple University Press, 1991), 22–23.

75. *Ittila'at*, 14 Day 1346/4 January 1968, 14.

76. Ziba Mir-Hosseini, *Marriage on Trial: Islamic Family Law in Iran and Morocco* (London: I. B. Tauris, 2000), 24.

77. Vatandoust, "The Status of Iranian Women During the Pahlavi Regime," 116–18.

78. Paidar, *Women and the Political Process*, 154–55.

79. Ben M. Harris, "Literacy Corps: Iran's Gamble to Conquer Illiteracy," *International Review of Education/Internationale Zeitschrift für Erziehungswissenschaft/ Revue Internationale de l'Education* 9, 4 (1963–1964): 430–37.

80. *Ittila'at*, 8 Azar 1341/29 November 1962, 7.

81. Farian Sabahi, "Gender and the Army of Knowledge in Pahlavi Iran," in *Women, Religion, and Culture in Iran*, ed. Sarah Ansari and Vanessa Martin (Richmond, Surrey: Curzon, 2002), 109–12.

82. *Ittila'at*, 19 Azar 1346/10 December 1967.

83. Vatandoust, "The Status of Iranian Women During the Pahlavi Regime," 126.

84. Sedghi, *Women and Politics in Iran*, 146. According to Sedghi, Article 1117 of the Civil Code had granted this privilege to fathers and husbands.

85. *Ittila'at*, "Zanan-i huquq bigir," 9 Day 1346/30 December 1967. This is a very important analysis based on census records in Iran. For example, the article maintained that women working for the Ministry of Foreign Affairs earned the highest salaries, while women employed in the railroad service earned the least.

86. *Ittila'at*, 12 Day 1346/3 January 1968, 7.

87. "Zanan-i huquq bigir," *Ittila'at*, 9 Day 1346/30 December 1967.

88. "Siy va do Sal Nabard-i Tarikhi-yi Zanan-i Iran," *Ittila'at*, 17 Day 1346/7 January 1968, 14.

CHAPTER 9 : MANAGING BIRTH

1. "Two Moslem Rulers Divorce Wives Who Bore No Sons," *New York Times*, 20 November 1948.
2. Soraya Esfandiary Bakhtiary in collaboration with Louis Valentin, *Palace of Solitude*, trans. Hubert Gibbs (London: Quartet, 1992), 71.
3. Ibid., 85. For more on the Musaddiq crisis, see ch. 8.
4. Bakhtiyari, *Palace of Solitude*, 71.
5. Ibid.
6. Ibid.
7. Ibid., 115.
8. Ibid.
9. Ibid., 116.
10. Ibid.
11. Ibid., 116–17.
12. Muhammad Hijazi, *Mihan-i Ma* (Tehran: Intisharat-i Vizarat-i Farhang, 1338/1959), 314–17.
13. *Time*, December 8, 1958.
14. Farah Pahlavi, *An Enduring Love: My Life with the Shah, A Memoir* (New York: Miramax Books, 2004), 108. For news of rejoicing, 109–10. For public anticipation of the birth of the queen's first child, see *Ittila'at*, 10 Mehr 1339/2 October 1960.
15. Rockefeller Archive Center, RF, RG1.1, 771, Box 1, "An Appraisal of Iranian Rural Life," 27.
16. Sazman-i Barnamah, *Sanjish-i pishraft va 'amalkard-i barnamah-i 'umrani-yi haft sal-i duvvum-i Iran* (Tehran, 1959), 111–12.
17. Ernest L. Stebbins, "Stebbins Evaluation: Preliminary Report of the Consultant to the U.S. Economic Coordinator for CENTO," *CENTO Conference Series on the Teaching of Public Health and Public Health Practice* (Ankara: Office of United States Economic Coordinator for CENTO Affairs, 1970), 130–31.
18. G. Saroukhanian, "The Present Situation of Teaching Public Health and Public Health Practice in Iran," in *CENTO Conference Series on the Teaching of Public Health and Public Health Practice*. Ankara: Office of United States Economic Coordinator for CENTO Affairs, 1970, 85–86.
19. Ibid., 85–88.
20. Salnamah-i Amar-i Kishvar, Sal-i 1349/1970, 134; Salnamah-i Amar-i Kishvar, Sal-i 2535 Shahanshahi, 124. Also, H. Mirchamsy, H. Taslimi, and M. Aghdachi, "Résultats des vaccinations collectives," *Acta Medica Iranica* 2, 3 (1960): 33.
21. Farideh Kiyumehr, "Shakhishayah Bihdasht va Darman," in *Shakhishayah ijtima'i-yi Iran 1357* (Tehran, 1978), 162. I thank Prof. Ahmad Ashraf for pointing out this source to me and for encouraging me to include relevant statistics based on the government's annual reports. Professor Ahmad also provided me with copies of several statistical annual reports on Iran.
22. Sattareh Farman Farmaian, *Daughter of Persia* (New York: Crown, 1993), 238.
23. Daniel Callahan, "Contraception and Abortion: American Catholic Responses," *Annals of the American Academy of Political and Social Science* 387, 1 (1970): 109–17.

24. Ferydoon Firoozi, "Iranian Censuses 1956 and 1966: A Comparative Analysis," *Middle East Journal* 24, 2 (1970): 221.

25. Charles Prigmore, *Social Work in Iran Since the White Revolution* (Tuscaloosa: University of Alabama Press, 1976), 62.

26. Farman Farmaian, *Daughter of Persia*, 258–59.

27. *CENTO Workshop Series on Clinical and Applied Research in Family Planning*, 1971, 65.

28. *Iran Almanac and Book of Facts* (Tehran: Echo of Iran, 1966), 585.

29. Jan Stepan and Edmund H. Kellogg, "The World's Law on Contraceptives," *American Journal of Comparative Law* 22 (1974): 615.

30. Population Council, "Iran: Report on Population Growth and Family Planning," *Studies in Family Planning* 1, 20 (1967): 4.

31. For example, a report by the United Nations stated that there "is a high rate of illiteracy especially among women and lack of schools and teachers in rural areas where fertility is high." United Nations, "Population and Family Planning in Iran," prepared for the Government of Iran by a United Nations Interagency Mission, 1971, 23.

32. *CENTO Workshop Series on Clinical and Applied Research in Family Planning*, 43.

33. As cited in Population Council, "Iran: Report on Population Growth and Family Planning," 3.

34. Ibid., 4.

35. A. M. Sardari and R. Keyhan, "The Prospect of Family Planning in Iran," *Demography* 5, 2 (1968): 782. For another helpful article, see Mehdi Amani and Nancy Hatch Dupree, "Family Planning," *Encyclopaedia Iranica*, online version.

36. *CENTO Workshop Series on Clinical and Applied Research in Family Planning*, 1971, 74.

37. United Nations, "Population and Family Planning in Iran," 9. One of the non-governmental agencies providing health services remained the Red Lion and Sun Society. Another was the Institute for the Protection of Mothers and Children.

38. *Ittila'at*, 4 Azar 1346/25 November 1967.

39. *Ittila'at*, 16 Day 1346/January 6, 1968. Dr. Sardari also participated in this seminar.

40. Sardari and Keyhan, "The Prospect of Family Planning in Iran," 781.

41. *CENTO Workshop Series on Clinical and Applied Research in Family Planning*, 44.

42. Ibid.

43. Ibid., 49–50.

44. *Ittila'at*, 4 Azar 1346/25 November 1967.

45. *CENTO Workshop Series on Clinical and Applied Research in Family Planning*, 78.

46. United Nations, "Population and Family Planning in Iran," 10.

47. Sardari and Keyhan, "The Prospect of Family Planning in Iran," 780. For discussion of the pill in the United States, see Cathy Booth Thomas, "The Pill that Unleashed Sex," *Time*, 31 March 2003; "Pregnancy Control," *Time*, 11 April 1960. The researcher cited in "Pregnancy Control" was John Rock. According to Booth, Margaret Sanger became a crusader for birth control after watching her mother die at the age of fifty after having endured eighteen pregnancies.

48. *Ittilaʿat*, 26 Dey 1346/16 January 1968.
49. *Ittilaʿat*, 6 Azar 1346/28 November 1967.
50. Ibid.
51. Jacqueline Rudolph Touba, "Effects of the Islamic Revolution on Women and the Family in Iran: Some Preliminary Observations," in *Women and the Family in Iran*, ed. Asghar Fathi (Leiden: Brill, 1985), 140–41.
52. United Nations, "Population and Family Planning in Iran," 15.
53. Ibid., 16. In fact, the United Nations recommended that sterilization "be made available more widely to women and men."
54. G. H. Jalali, H. Peyman, and A. Majd, "Study of Abortion at Farah Maternity Hospital, Teheran," *Iranian Journal of Public Health* 2, 4 (1974): 1–7. Parvin Paidar also refers to this study in her work *Women and the Political Process in Twentieth-Century Iran* (Cambridge: Cambridge University Press, 1995), 155.
55. Jalali, Peyman, and Majd, "Study of Abortion," 3.
56. Paidar, *Women and the Political Process*, 155.
57. United Nations, "Population and Family Planning in Iran," 18. Also, ibid., 66.
58. Ibid., 19.
59. Ibid., 19, 77–79.
60. Ibid., 19.
61. Ibid.
62. Ibid., 18. See also Soodabeh Ghavami, "The Role of the Medical Profession in Family Planning," in *CENTO Conference on Family Planning, Health and Demographic Statistics Held in Tehran, Iran, August 12–16, 1973* (Ankara: CENTO, 1973), 95–96.
63. "Chih konim ta javanan izdivaj konand?" *Ittilaʿat*, 16 Azar 1346.
64. Sima Amidi, Steven Solter, Bagher Rashidian, Ali-Reza Zokaian, and Feraidon Razmjoian, "Antibiotic Use and Abuse Among Physicians in Private Practice in Shiraz," *Medical Care* 13, 4 (1975): 341–45. Also, *Ittilaʿat*, "Tibabat," 25 Azar 1346/16 December 1967.
65. *Ittilaʿat*, 16 Azar 1346/7 December 1967.
66. *Zan-i Ruz*, No. 1, 1965, cover.
67. "Madaran va ruz-i madar," *Ittilaʿat*, 23 Azar 1346/14 December 1967.
68. "Jashn-i Ruz-i Madar," *Ittilaʿat*, 13 December 1967.
69. "Az madar, barjastah tarin ʿuzv-i ijtimaʿ dar jashn-i anjuman-i dushizigan va banuvan tajlil shud," *Ittilaʿat*, 28 Azar 1346. Also, "Muhhim tarin vazifah-i to inast kih madar-i shayestah-i bashi," *Ittilaʿat*, 26 Azar 1346.
70. "Salam bih Madar," *Ittilaʿat*, 23 Azar 1346/14 December 1967.
71. Ibid.
72. "Madaran-i Barjastah-i Sal,"*Ittilaʿat*, 21 Azar 1346/12 December 1967.
73. *Ittilaʿat*, 23 Azar 1346/14 December 1967.
74. "Tiliviziyon-i Iran," *Ittilaʿat*, 25 Azar 1346/16 December 1967.
75. "Salam bih Madar," *Ittilaʿat*, 23 Azar 1346/14 December 1967.
76. *Ittilaʿat*, 5 Azar 1346/26 November 1346; *Ittilaʿat*, 18 Azar 1346/9 December 1967.
77. "Kudakan-i Kermanshah dar mosabiqah-i salamat," *Ittilaʿat*, 18 Azar 1346/9 December 1967, 9.

CHAPTER 10 : CIVIL LIBERTIES, CIVIC WOMBS

1. Firoozeh Kashani-Sabet, "Cultures of Iranianness."
2. PHS, Jane Elizabeth Doolittle File, RG 360, Box 39, Folder 12, "Personal Report of Jane E. Doolittle, July 1st 1927 to July 1st, 1928," 3.
3. U.S. Department of State, RG 59, W. Smith Murray to the Secretary of State, 4 February 1925. My copy of the microfilm was rather unclear, but I believe the date to be 4 February 1925.
4. Confidential U.S. State Department central files, Iran, 1950–1954, Philip W. Ireland, Baghdad, to Department of State, 30 March 1953.
5. Ervand Abrahamian, "Ali Shari'ati: Ideologue of the Iranian Revolution," in *Islam, Politics, and Social Movements*, ed. Edmund Burke III and Ira M. Lapidus (Berkeley: University of California Press, 1988), 291.
6. *Ittila'at*, 14 Day 1346/4 January 1968, 7.
7. Marcia Hermansen, "Fatimeh as a Role Model in the Works of Ali Shari'ati," in *Women and Revolution in Iran*, ed. Guity Nashat (Boulder: Westview, 1983), 87–88.
8. Ali Shari'ati, *Fatima Is Fatima*, trans. Laleh Bakhtiar (Tehran: Shari'ati Foundation, 1980), 5. See also Hermansen, "Fatimeh as a Role Model," 88–89.
9. "Banuyi Islam," *Namah-i Astan-i Quds*, No. 9, Azar 1340/November–December 1961, 2–5.
10. Nahid Yeganeh, "Women's Struggles in the Islamic Republic of Iran," in *In the Shadow of Islam: The Women's Movement in Iran*, ed. Azar Tabari and Nahid Yeganeh (London: Zed, 1982), 48–49. Also Abrahamian, "Ali Shari'ati," 292–95.
11. Shari'ati, *Fatima Is Fatima*, 5.
12. Ibid., 109.
13. Afsaneh Najmabadi, "Power, Morality, and the New Muslim Womanhood.," in *The Politics of Social Transformation in Afghanistan, Iran and Pakistan*, ed. Myron Weiner and Ali Banuazizi (Syracuse: Syracuse University Press, 1994), 366–89.
14. "Iranian Muslim Students' Announcement on Role of Women," Summary of World Broadcasts, BBC, 8 May 1980,
15. "Women's Rights in Iran," Summary of World Broadcasts, BBC, 9 April 1983,
16. Cited in Ziba Mir-Hosseini, *Islam and Gender: The Religious Debate in Contemporary Iran* (Princeton: Princeton University Press, 1999), 56.
17. *Wall Street Journal*, "Religious Revival," 15 August 1978.
18. Nayereh Tohidi, "Gender and Islamic Fundamentalism: Feminist Politics in Iran," in *Third World Women and the Politics of Feminism*, ed. Chandra Talpade Mohanty, Ann Russo, and Lourdes Torres (Bloomington: Indiana University Press, 1991), 251–69. Also, Farah Azari, *Women of Iran: The Conflict with Fundamentalist Islam* (Ithaca, NY: Ithaca Press, 1983), and Anne H. Betteridge, "To Veil or Not to Veil: A Matter of Protest or Policy," in *Women and Revolution in Iran* (Boulder, CO: Westview, 1983), 109–28.
19. "Iran: Women's Movement," 14 March 1979, Central Intelligence Agency National Foreign Assessment Center, 1, National Security Archive (online), George Washington University.

20. Jonathan C. Randal, "Iran's Revolution Stirs Fears of Islam-Based Law; Threat of Islamic Justice Arouses Fears in Iran," *Washington Post*, 5 March 1979.

21. Philip Dopoulos, "Today's Focus: Off with the Veil," Associated Press, 14 March 1979.

22. Mahnaz Afkhami and Erika Friedl, *In the Eye of the Storm: Women in Post-Revolutionary Iran* (Syracuse: Syracuse University Press, 1994).

23. L. Bruce Laingen to the United States Department of State, "Women's Rights in Revolutionary Iran," Confidential, Cable Tehran, 06563, 24 June 1979, National Security Archive (online), George Washington University.

24. Jonathan C. Randal, "Militant Women Demonstrators Attack Khomeini Aide Who Heads Iran Radio," *Washington Post*, 13 March 1979.

25. Janet Afary, *Sexual Politics in Modern Iran*, 245; Ervand Abrahamian, *The Iranian Mojahedin* (New Haven: Yale University Press, 1989), 185, 233–35.

26. Hamideh Sedghi, *Women and Politics in Iran*, 182–86; Afary, *Sexual Politics in Modern Iran*, 248. Also, Haideh Moghissi, *Populism and Feminism in Iran* (New York: St. Martin's, 1996); and Minoo Moallem, *Between Warrior Brother and Veiled Sister: Islamic Fundamentalism and the Politics of Patriarchy in Iran* (Berkeley: University of California Press, 2005), 78–79. For Dihqani's memoirs, see *Hamasah-i Muqavimat* (Tehran: Nashr-i Mardum, 1970).

27. Ziba Mir-Hosseini, "Women and Politics in Post-Khomeini Iran: Divorce, Veiling, and Emerging Feminist Voices," in *Women and Politics in the Third World*, ed. Haleh Afshar (London: Routledge, 1996), 156.

28. Even today these difficulties continue. In June 2010 the Iranian police gave out 62,000 warnings to women who were inappropriately veiled in the religious city of Qum. See "Iranian Police Issue 'Badly Veiled' Warnings to 62,000 Women," *Daily Telegraph*, 21 June 2010.

29. Naomi Wolf, *The Beauty Myth: How Images of Beauty Are Used Against Women* (New York: Morrow, 1991). Between 1995 and 1996, I spent approximately seven months in Iran conducting research and spending considerable time in government offices and archives. Women typically wore *rupush* that were navy, black, or gray, along with dark veils. I complied with those standards as well. For more on dress codes in the Islamic Republic, see Hammed Shahidian, *Women in Iran: Emerging Voices in the Women's Movement* (Westport, CT: Greenwood, 2002), 197–98.

30. Marjane Satrapi, *Persepolis: The Story of a Childhood* (New York: Pantheon, 2003). This was also my personal experience, attending school briefly in Iran after the revolution.

31. *Ta'limat-i Dini, duvvum-i dabistan* (Tehran: Vizarat-i Amuzish va Parvarish, 1998), 10.

32. Elaine Sciolino, "The Chanel Under the Chador," *New York Times*, 4 May 1997. Also, Afshin Valinejad, "Sara Is Substituted for Barbie," *Philadelphia Inquirer*, 25 October 1996; Helena Smith, "Iranian Police Raid Shops to End the Scourge of Barbie," *Guardian*, 25 May 2002.

33. Sciolino, "The Chanel Under the Chador."

34. *Ta'limat-i Dini, duvvum-i dabistan* (1998), 29–31.

35. Ibid., 40.

36. Homa Hoodfar and Samad Assadpour, "The Politics of Population Policy in the Islamic Republic of Iran," *Studies in Family Planning* 31, 1 (March 2000): 10–34.

37. Farzaneh Roudi, "Iran's Revolutionary Approach to Family Planning," *Population Today* 27, 7 (1999); Mohammad Jalal Abbasi, Amir Mehryar, Gavin Jones, and Peter McDonald, "Revolution, War and Modernization: Population Policy and Fertility Change in Iran," *Journal of Population Research* 19, 1 (2002): 25–46.

38. Hoodfar and Assadpour, "The Politics of Population Policy."

39. Abbasi et al., "Revolution, War and Modernization."

40. Akbar Aghajanian and Amir H. Mehryar, "Fertility Transition in the Islamic Republic of Iran: 1976–1996," *Asia-Pacific Population Journal* 14, 1 (1999): 21–42. Also, Charles Kurzman, "A Feminist Generation in Iran?" *Iranian Studies* 41, 3 (June 2008): 297–321.

41. Brian Murphy, "Iran's Birth Control Drive Blessed," Associated Press, 11 October 1999.

42. A. Marandi, H. M. Afzali, and A. F. Hossaini, "The Reasons for Early Weaning Among Mothers in Teheran," *Bulletin of the World Health Organization* 71, 5 (1993): 561–69.

43. M. D. Froozani, K. Permehzadeh, A. R. Dorosty Motlagh, and B. Golestan, "Effect of Breastfeeding Education on the Feeding Pattern and Health of Infants in Their First 4 Months in the Islamic Republic of Iran," *Bulletin of the World Health Organization* 77, 5 (1999): 381–85.

44. "Iran: Water Supply and Infant Mortality," BBC Monitoring Service: The Middle East, 30 July 1985.

45. Aghajanian and Mehryar, "Fertility Transition in the Islamic Republic of Iran."

46. Elaine Sciolino, "From the Back Seat in Iran, Murmurs of Unrest," *New York Times*, 23 April 1992. It is curious and not entirely surprising that more than a hundred years after the arrival of the first American visitors to Iran, Sciolino has continued perpetuating the notion of *sigheh* as prostitution or "call-girl business." According to Sciolino, "The world's oldest profession is practiced largely in the form of 'sigheh,' the Islamic practice by which a couple can get married for a few years or months, or, if the rules are stretched, a few hours."

47. "Iran in Brief: Iranian Health Official on Blood Donations," BBC Summary of World Broadcasts, 28 July 1990; "Iran Records More than 200 AIDS-related Deaths," Agence France-Presse, 1 December 1999.

48. "Doctors Urge 'Moral' Behaviour," *APS Diplomat Recorder*, 6 April 2002.

49. Ibid.

50. "In Brief: National Committee to Fight AIDS," *International Family Planning Perspectives* 28, 2 (2002): 56–57.

51. *Alcoholism and Drug Abuse Weekly*, 18 August 2003, 8.

EPILOGUE

1. Dr. Farrokhrou Parsa, an educator, politician, physician, and supporter of women's causes, was executed—"wrapped in a dark sack and machine-gunned" to death—in 1979. At her trial, conducted by hooded judges, she was denied a

defense attorney and an appeal. Her crimes were stated as promotion of prostitution and fighting against God. In other words, she was found guilty of supporting the unveiling of Iranian women. See Mahnaz Afkhami, "Iran: A Future in the Past: The 'Prerevolutionary' Women's Movement," *in Sisterhood Is Global: The International Women's Movement Anthology*, ed. Robin Morgan (New York: Feminist Press, 1996), 330.

2. Hammed Shahidian, *Women in Iran: Gender Politics in the Islamic Republic* (Santa Barbara, CA: Greenwood, 2002), 241.
3. Roksana Bahramitash, "Iranian Women During the Reform Era (1994–2004): A Focus on Employment," *Journal of Middle East Women's Studies* 3, 2 (2007): 86–109.
4. Ibid.
5. *The Sunday Times*, London, 19 November 2003.
6. Elahe Amani with Lys Anzia, "'Mourning Mothers Iran' Stand with Activist Mothers Worldwide," Women News Network, 8 October 2009, http://womennewsnetwork. net/2009/10/08/mourning-mothers-iran-stand-with-activist-mothers-worldwide.

BIBLIOGRAPHY

ARCHIVES

Great Britain

Public Record Office, Kew. Foreign Office. FO: 248/326, 248/330, 924
Public Record Office, Kew. Ministry of Health. MH: 98/24/51345

Iran

Malik Library, Tehran
National Library of Tehran
National Archives:
Prime Ministry Files: 290, 293, 103013/9692, 103013/9886, 108011/3268, 109001, 109063, 290000, 2910001495
Ministry of Internal Affairs Files: 290; 291, 310
Ma'arif "B," File 51006/324, 51006/402
Ma'arif "A," File 51006/441, 51006/568
Ministry of Foreign Affairs Files: Carton 20, 2910001495
Ministry of Health and Charitable Matters Files: 293
Ministry of Education and Foundations Files: 297
Ministry of Post and Telegraph
Isfahan Records, 2910001495
Ministry of Culture (Vizarat-i Farhang), 2910002573

United States

National Archives:
Confidential U.S. State Department Central Files, Iran, 1925–1941, RG 59: 491, 503 Department of State Records, 1945–1949: Microfilm 4457
Confidential U.S. State Department Central Files, Iran, 1950–1954
Foreign Relations of the United States (FRUS), accessed online at: http://digital.library.wisc.edu/1711.dl/FRUS
Presbyterian Historical Society (PHS), Record Group (hereafter RG) 91: 1/18, 1/20, 1/21, 4/11, 4/14, 20/2; RG 360: 39/12
Rockefeller Archive Center, Rockefeller Foundation, RG 1.1, 771: Box 1

MANUSCRIPTS

Al-Muvarrikhin, Malik. *Qanun-i Muzaffari*. MS 314. Kitabkhanah-i Milli.

"Dastur al-Attiba fi Daf' al-Ta'un va al-vaba." MS F/605. Kitabkhanah-i Milli.

"Hafiz al-Sihhi-yi Nasiri." MS RF-447. Kitabkhanah-i Milli.

"Hifz-i Sihhat." MS 132/1. Kitabkhanah-i Milli.

Ibn 'Aqil al-'Alavi Isfahani, Mustafa, trans. "Risalah-i Mukhtasar dar Bab-i Vaksan, Ya'ni Kubidan-i Abilah Az Ta'lifat-i Hakim Tholozan-i Farangi Ast." Malik Library, Tehran.

Khan-i Khanan. *Risalah-'i dar Siyasat*. MS 385 RF. Kitabkhanah-i Milli.

"Risalah dar qabilagi." MS 805. Malik Library.

"Risalah dar Vaba va Ta'un" MS 2767/3. Kitabkhanah-i Milli.

"Amraz al-Nisa'," Malik Library #805.

PERIODICALS AND NEWSPAPERS

A'in-i Islam

Adab

Adamiyat

Akhtar

'Alam-i Nisvan

'Alam-i Zanan

Alcoholism and Drug Abuse Weekly

al-Hadid

Amuzgar

Anjuman (Tabriz)

Bahar

Bakhtar

Baladiyya

Banu

Chicago Daily Tribune

Dabistan

Danish

Dukhtaran-i Iran

Farhang

Habl al-Matin

Hifz al-Sihhat

Iblagh

Ittila'

Ittila'at

Jahan-i Zanan

Jarchi-yi Millat

Junub

Khayr al-Kalam

Khurshid

Los Angeles Times

Ma'arif

Majallah-i Mahanah-i Shir va Khurshid Surkh-i Iran
Majallah-i Mahiyanah, Shir va khurshid
Majallah-i Nisvan-i Vatankhvah-i Iran
Majallah-i Qiyam-i Zan
Majlis
Mihrigan
Mirrikh
Muzaffari
Namah-i Astan-i Quds
Namah-i Farangistan
Nasiri
Nawruz
New York Times
Nida-yi Haqq
Nida-yi Vatan
Pahlavi
Parvanah
Payk-i Sa'adat-i Nisvan
Qanun
Rahnima
Ruh al-Quds
Ruznamah-i 'Ilmi
Ruznamah-i Iran-i Sultani
Ruznamah-i Milli
Shikufah
Sihhat-Nimayi Iran
Subh-i Sadiq
Ta'lim va Tarbiyat
Tamaddun
Taraqqi
Tarbiyat
The Iranian Red Lion and Sun Bulletin
Time
Umid
Vaqayi' 'Ittifaqiyah
Vatan
Wall Street Journal
Washington Post
Zaban-i Zanan
Zan-i Ruz

IRANIAN OFFICIAL SOURCES

Vizarat-i Ma'arif va Awqaf va Sanayi' mustazrafah:
    Salnamah-i ihsa'iyah, 1307–1308, 1309–1310, 1312–1313, 1313–1314 (n.p.:
    Rawshana'i, 1929)

Vizarat-i Farhang:
  Kitab-i Bihdasht, sal-i avval-i dabirestanha
  Salnamah va amar: 1315–1316, 1316/1317
  Salnamah va Amar, 1315–1316 va 1316–1317 (Tehran, 1939)
Vizarat-i Sihhat:
  Avvalin rapurt-i shish mahah-i sihhiyah-i kull (1926)
Vizarat-i Dakhilah:
  Sihhiyah-i kull-i mamlikati (1932)
Muzakirat-i Majlis-i Shura-yi Milli, 2nd Session, 23 Mihr 1342/15 October 1963
Sazman-i Barnamah, *Sanjish-i pishraft va 'amalkard-i barnamah-i 'umrani-yi haft sal-i
    duvvum-i Iran* (Tehran, 1959)
Sazman-i Barnamah va Budjih, Markaz-i Amar-i Iran, *Bayan-i Amari: Tahavvulat-i Iqti-
    sadi va Ijtima'i-yi Iran dar dawran-i por Iftikhar-i dudman-i Pahlavi, 2535* [1976]
Salnamah-i Pars, 1307 [1928], 1308 [1929], 1309 [1930], 1310 [1931], 1311 [1932]
Salnamah-i Ma'arif-i Isfahan, sal-i tahsili-yi 1313/1934 (n.p., n.d.)
Salnamah-i Aryan
Salnamah-i Zanan-i Iran
Salnamah-i Kishvar-i Iran 1326/1947
Salnamah-i Amar-i Kishvar, 1349/1970 and 2535 shahanshahi
Salnamah-i Sazman-i Zanan

INTERNATIONAL OFFICIAL SOURCES

Central Intelligence Agency National Foreign Assessment Center (accessed via Digi-
    tal National Security Archive).
International Sanitary Conference: Paris, 1851; Constantinople, 1866.
League of Nations Secretariat, Committee of Enquiry into Traffic in Women and Chil-
    dren in the East. "Summary of Report to Council." 1934.
Overseas Consultants Inc. *Report on Seven-Year Development Plan for the Plan Organi-
    zation of the Imperial Government of Iran.* New York, 1949.
United Nations. "Population and Family Planning in Iran." Prepared for the Govern-
    ment of Iran by a United Nations Interagency Mission. 1971.

WEBSITES

BBC Summary of World Broadcasts
BBC Monitoring Service: The Middle East (http://www.monitor.bbc.co.uk)
Digital National Security Archives
Encyclopaedia Iranica (www.iranica.com)
Iranian.com (http://www.iranian.com)
National Institute of Allergy and Infectious Diseases (http://www.niaid.nih.gov)
United States National Library of Medicine—National Institutes of Health (http://
    www.nlm.nih.gov)
Women News Network (http://womennewsnetwork.net)

OTHER PUBLISHED PRIMARY AND SECONDARY SOURCES

Abbasi, Mohammad Jalal, Amir Mehryar, Gavin Jones, and Peter McDonald. "Revolution, War and Modernization: Population Policy and Fertility Change in Iran." *Journal of Population Research* 19, 1 (2002).

Abrahamian, Ervand. "Ali Shari'ati: Ideologue of the Iranian Revolution." In *Islam, Politics, and Social Movements*, ed. Edmund Burke III and Ira M. Lapidus. Berkeley: University of California Press, 1988.

————. *Iran Between Two Revolutions*. Princeton, NJ: Princeton University Press, 1982.

————. *The Iranian Mojahedin*. New Haven, CT: Yale University Press, 1989.

————. "Oriental Despotism: The Case of Qajar Iran." *International Journal of Middle East Studies* 5, 1 (1974): 3–31.

Adamiyat, Fereydun. *Fikr-i Azadi va Muqaddamah-i Nihzat-i Mashrutiyat-i Iran*. Tehran, 1981.

Adams, Isaac. *Persia by a Persian*. n.p., 1900.

Afary, Janet. *The Iranian Constitutional Revolution of 1906–1911: Grassroots Democracy, Social Democracy and the Origins of Feminism*. New York: Columbia University Press, 1996.

————. "On the Origins of Feminism in Early 20th-Century Iran." *Journal of Women's History* 1 (1989): 65–87.

————. *Sexual Politics in Modern Iran*. Cambridge: Cambridge University Press, 2009.

Afkhami, Amir Arsalan. "Iran in the Age of Epidemics: Nationalism and the Struggle for Public Health, 1889–1926." Ph.D. dissertation, Yale University, 2003.

Afkhami, Mahnaz. "Iran: A Future in the Past: The 'Prerevolutionary' Women's Movement." In *Sisterhood Is Global: The International Women's Movement Anthology*, ed. Robin Morgan, 330–38. New York: Feminist Press, 1996.

————. "The Women's Organization of Iran: Evolutionary Politics and Revolutionary Change." In *Women in Iran: From 1800 to the Islamic Republic*, ed. Lois Beck and Guity Nashat. Urbana: University of Illinois Press, 2004.

Afkhami, Mahnaz, and Erika Friedl. *In the Eye of the Storm: Women in Post-Revolutionary Iran*. Syracuse, NY: Syracuse University Press, 1994.

Afshar, Haleh, ed. *Women and Politics in the Third World*. London: Routledge, 1996.

Aghajanian, Akbar. "A New Direction in Population Policy and Family Planning in the Islamic Republic of Iran." *Asia-Pacific Population Journal* 10, 1 (1995).

Aghajanian, Akbar, and Amir H. Mehryar. "Fertility Transition in the Islamic Republic of Iran: 1976–1996." *Asia-Pacific Population Journal* 14, 1 (1999): 21–42.

Ahmed, Leila. "Arab Culture and Writing Women's Bodies." In *Women and Islam: Critical Concepts in Sociology*, ed. Haideh Moghissi. London: Routledge, 2005.

————. *Women and Gender in Islam: Historical Roots of a Modern Debate*. New Haven, CT: Yale University Press, 1992.

Akhundzadah, Mirza Fath 'Ali. *Alifba-yi Jadid va Maktubat*, ed. Hamid Muhammadzadah. Tabriz: Nashr-i Ihya,' 1357/1978.

A'lam, Amir. Lecture published in *Salsalah Intisharat-i Mu'assassah-i va'az va khattabah*. Lesson No. 7. Tehran: 1315/1936.

al-Dawlah, Zahir. *Khatirat va asnad-i Zahir al-Dawlah/* Ed. Iraj Afshar. Tehran: Kitab-ha-yi jibi, 1351/1972.

Algar, Hamid. *Mirza Malkum Khan: A Study in the History of Iranian Modernism.* Berkeley: University of California Press, 1973.

Al-Husayni al-Najafi, Muhammad Ja'far. *Kitab-i Tabayi'i Zanan.* Tehran: Maṭba'ah-i Barādarān-i Bāqirzādah, 1926.

Ali, Maulana Muhammad. *A Manual of Hadith.* London: Curzon, 1983.

al-Kulayni, Muhammad ibn Yaqub. *al-Usul min al-Kafi.* Tehran: Intisharat-i 'Ilmiyah-i Islamiyah, n.d.

al-Mulk, Majd. *Risalah-i Majdiyyah.* Tehran: Chapkhanah-i Bank-i Melli, 1321/1942.

al-Saltanah, Yusuf Mughis. *Namah'hayah Yusuf Mughis al-Saltanah,* ed. Ma'soumah Mafi. Tehran: Nashr-i Tarikh-i Iran, 1362/1983.

Amani, Mehdi, and Nancy Hatch Dupree, "Family Planning," *Encyclopaedia Iranica,* online version.

Amidi, Sima, Steven Solter, Bagher Rashidian, Ali-Reza Zokaian, and Feraidon Razmjoian. "Antibiotic Use and Abuse Among Physicians in Private Practice in Shiraz." *Medical Care* 13, 4 (1975): 341–45.

Amin, Camron Michael. "Globalizing Iranian Feminism, 1910–1950." *Journal of Middle East Women's Studies* 4, 1 (2008): 6–30.

———. "Importing 'Beauty Culture' into Iran in the 1920s and 1930s: Mass Marketing Individualism in an Age of Anti-Imperialist Sacrifice." *Comparative Studies of South Asia, Africa and the Middle East* 24, 1 (2004): 81–100.

———. *The Making of the Modern Iranian Woman: Gender, State Policy, and Popular Culture, 1865–1946.* Gainesville: University Press of Florida, 2002.

———. "Propaganda and Remembrance: Gender, Education, and the 'Women's Awakening' of 1936." *Iranian Studies* 32, 3 (1999): 351–86.

———. "Selling and Saving 'Mother Iran': Gender and the Iranian Press in the 1940s." *International Journal of Middle East Studies* 33, 3 (2001): 335–61.

Anderson, Benedict. *Imagined Communities: Reflections on the Origin and Spread of Nationalism.* London: Verso, 1991.

Ansari, Sarah, and Vanessa Martin, eds. *Women, Religion, and Culture in Iran.* Richmond, Surrey: Curzon, 2002.

Arasteh, A. Reza. *Education and Social Awakening in Iran, 1850–1968.* Leiden: E. G. Brill, 1969.

———. "The Role of Intellectuals in Administrative Development and Social Change in Modern Iran." *International Review of Education/Internationale Zeitschrift für Erziehungswissenschaft/Revue Internationale de l'Education* 9, 3 (1963): 326–34.

Ariès, Philippe. *Centuries of Childhood: A Social History of Family Life.* Trans. Robert Baldick. London: Jonathan Cape, 1962.

———. *L'enfant et la vie familiale sous l'Ancien Régime.* Paris: Librarie Plon, 1960.

Arjomand, Said Amir, ed. *From Nationalism to Revolutionary Islam.* Albany: State University of New York Press, 1984.

Armstrong, David. *Political Anatomy of the Body: Medical Knowledge in Britain in the Twentieth Century.* Cambridge: Cambridge University Press, 1983.

Atkinson, James. *Customs and Manners of the Women of Persia and Their Domestic Superstitions.* Translated from the original Persian manuscript *Kulthum Nanah.* London: Oriental Translation Fund of Great Britain and Ireland, 1832.

Azari, Farah. *Women of Iran: The Conflict with Fundamentalist Islam.* Ithaca, NY: Ithaca Press, 1983.

Azhakh, Susan Beth. "A Look at the Past and Present: General and Special Education in Iran." Master's thesis, Mankato State University, Minnesota, 1980.

Azimi, Fakhreddin. *The Quest for Democracy in Iran: A Century of Struggle Against Authoritarian Rule*. Cambridge, MA: Harvard University Press, 2008.

Azizi, Mohammad-Hossein, and Touraj Nayernouri. "The Establishment and the First Four Decades of the Activities of the Pasteur Institute of Iran." *Archive of Iranian Medicine* 11, 4 (2008): 477–81.

Babayan, Kathyrn. "The 'Aqa'id al-Nisa'': A Glimpse at Safavid Women in Local Isfahani Culture." In *Women in the Medieval Islamic World*, ed. Gavin R. G. Hambly. New York: St. Martin's, 1999.

Baghchihban, Jabbar. *Zindiginamah-i Jabbar Baghchihban bunyan guzar-i amuzish-i na shinavayan dar Iran, bih qalam-i khudash*. Tehran: Markaz-i Nashr-i Sepehr, 1977.

Bahar, Muhammad Taqi. *Divan-i ash'ar-i shadravan Muhammad Taqi Bahar Malik al-Shu'ara*. Tehran: Firdawsi, 1956.

Bahramitash, Roksana. "Iranian Women During the Reform Era (1994–2004): A Focus on Employment." *Journal of Middle East Women's Studies* 3, 2 (2007): 86–109.

Bakhash, Shaul. "Iran's Unlikely President." *New York Review of Books*, 5 November 1998.

Bakhtiary, Soraya Esfandiary, in collaboration with Louis Valentin. *Palace of Solitude*. Trans. Hubert Gibbs. London: Quartet, 1992.

Bamdad, Badr al-Muluk. *Akhlaq*. Tehran: Firdawsi, 1931.

———. *From Darkness into Light: Women's Emancipation in Iran*. Ed. and trans. F. R. C. Bagley. New York: Exposition, 1977.

———. *Tadbir-i Manzil va Dastur-i Bachih-dari*. Tehran: Iqbal, 1310/1931.

Barnes, David S. *The Making of a Social Disease: Tuberculosis in Nineteenth-Century France*. Berkeley: University of California Press, 1995.

Barnum, P. T. *The Life of P. T. Barnum: Written by Himself*. Chicago: University of Illinois Press, 2000 [1865].

Baron, Beth. *The Women's Awakening in Egypt: Culture, Society, and the Press*. New Haven, CT: Yale University Press, 1994.

———. *Egypt as a Woman: Nationalism, Gender, and Politics*. Berkeley: University of California Press, 2005.

Bassett, James. "Child Life in Persia." *American Magazine* 36 (1893).

———. *Persia: Eastern Mission: A Narrative of the Founding and Fortunes of the Eastern Persia Mission, with a Sketch of the Versions of the Bible and Christian Literature in the Persian and Persian-Turkish Languages*. Philadelphia, 1890.

Bayat, Mangol. *Iran's First Revolution: Shi'ism and the Constitutional Revolution of 1905–1909*. New York: Oxford University Press, 1991.

Bayat-Philipp, Mangol. "Women and Revolution in Iran, 1905–11." In *Women in the Muslim World*, ed. Lois Beck and Nikki Keddie. Cambridge, MA: Harvard University Press, 1978.

Beck, Lois, and Nikki Keddie, eds. *Women in the Muslim World*. Cambridge, MA: Harvard University Press, 1978.

Benjamin, S. G. W. "The Tazieh, or Passion Play of Persia." *Harper's New Monthly Magazine* 72 (1886): 464.

Betteridge, Anne H. "To Veil or Not to Veil: A Matter of Protest or Policy." In *Women and Revolution in Iran*, ed. Guity Nashat, 109–28. Boulder, CO: Westview, 1983.

Bey, Ahmed. "La Femme Persane." *La Nouvelle Revue* 69 (1891): 378.

Bharier, J. *Economic Development in Iran, 1900–1970*. New York: Oxford University Press, 1971.

Bill, James. *The Eagle and the Lion: The Tragedy of American-Iranian Relations*. New Haven, CT: Yale University Press, 1988.

Bird, Isabella Lucy. *Journeys in Persia and Kurdistan*. London: Jonathan Murray, 1891.

Bogdan, Robert. *Freak Show: Presenting Human Oddities for Amusement and Profit*. Chicago: University of Chicago Press, 1990.

Bonner, Michael, Mine Ener, and Amy Singer. *Poverty and Charity in Middle Eastern Contexts*. Albany: State University of New York Press, 2003.

Bourne, Kenneth, and D. Cameron Watt, eds. *British Documents on Foreign Affairs. Part II, From the First to the Second World Wars. Series B, Turkey, Iran and the Middle East*. 35 vols. Frederick, MD: University Publications of America, 1985.

Brandt, Allan. *No Magic Bullet: A Social History of Venereal Disease in the United States Since 1880*. New York: Oxford University Press, 1987.

Brown, Kathleen M. *Foul Bodies: Cleanliness in Early America*. New Haven, CT: Yale University Press, 2009.

Browne, E. G. *The Press and Poetry of Modern Persia*. Cambridge: Cambridge University Press, 1914.

Burrell, R. M., ed. *Iran Political Diaries, 1881–1965*, vol. 7. Farnham Common, UK: Archive Editions, Ltd., 1997.

Callahan, Daniel. "Contraception and Abortion: American Catholic Responses." *Annals of the American Academy of Political and Social Science* 387, 1 (1970): 109–17.

CENTO Conference on Nursing Education, Held in Tehran, Iran, April 14–25 1964. Ankara: Office of United States Economic Coordinator for CENTO Affairs, 1964.

CENTO Conference Series on the Teaching of Public Health and Public Health Practice. Ankara: Office of United States Economic Coordinator for CENTO Affairs, 1970.

CENTO Workshop Series on Clinical and Applied Research in Family Planning. Ankara: Office of United States Economic Coordinator for CENTO Affairs, 1971.

Chehabi, Houchang. "The Juggernaut of Globalization: Sport and Modernization in Iran." *International Journal of the History of Sport* 19, 2–3 (2002): 275–94.

———. "The Politics of Football in Iran." *Soccer and Society* 7, 2–3 (2006): 233–61.

———. "Sport and Politics in Iran: The Legend of Gholamreza Takhti." *International Journal of the History of Sport* 12, 3 (1995): 48–60.

———. "Staging the Emperor's New Clothes: Dress Codes and Nation-Building Under Reza Shah." *Iranian Studies* 26, 3–4 (1993): 209–29.

Chelkowski, Peter. *Ta'ziyeh: Ritual and Drama in Iran*. New York: New York University Press, 1979.

Chodzko, Aleksander. *Théâtre persan*. Paris: E. Leroux, 1878.

Christidi, C. "La Syphilis en Perse à travers les siècles." *La Presse Medicale*, 15 March 1922, 425.

Clinton, Jerome. "The Uses of Guile in the Shahnamah." *Iranian Studies* 32, 2 (1999): 223–30.

Cochran, James P. "Treatment of the Sick and Insane in Persia." *American Journal of Insanity* 56 (1899): 105.

Cohen, M. Maurice. *Défense sanitaire de la Perse.* Paris, 1912.

Coleman, William. *Biology in the Nineteenth Century.* Cambridge: Cambridge University Press, 1971.

Comte, Auguste. *Positive Philosophy.* Trans. Harriet Martineau. New York: Calvin Blanchard, 1855.

Connelly, Matthew. *Fatal Misconception: The Struggle to Control World Population.* Cambridge, MA: Harvard University Press, 2008.

Costello, Carrie Yang. "Teratology: 'Monsters' and the Professionalization of Obstetrics." *Journal of Historical Sociology* 19, 1 (2006): 1–33.

Cott, Nancy F. *Public Vows: A History of Marriage and the Nation.* Cambridge, MA: Harvard University Press, 2000.

Cronin, Stephanie, ed. *The Making of Modern Iran: State and Society under Riza Shah, 1921–1941.* London: Routledge Curzon, 2003.

Curzon, George Nathaniel. *Persia and the Persian Question.* 2 vols. London: Longmans, Green, 1892.

Dabashi, Hamid. *Iran: A People Interrupted.* New York: W. W. Norton, 2007.

———. *Shi'ism: A Religion of Protest.* Cambridge, MA: Harvard University Press, 2011.

Daniel, Mooshie G. *Modern Persia.* Toronto: Henderson, 1898.

Dawlatabadi, Yahya. *Hayat-i Yahya.* Tehran: Sazman-i Intisharat-i Javidan, 1362/1983.

de Grazia, Victoria. "Introduction." In *The Sex of Things: Gender and Consumption in Historical Perspective,* ed. Victoria de Grazia with Ellen Furlough. Berkeley: University of California Press, 1996.

de Lorey, Eustache, and Douglas Sladen. *Queer Things About Persia.* Philadelphia: J. B. Lippincott, 1907.

Diba, Layla S. "Images of Power and the Power of Images: Intention and Response in Early Qajar Painting (1785–1834)." In *Royal Persian Paintings: The Qajar Epoch, 1785–1925,* ed. Layla S. Diba and Maryam Ekhtiar. New York: Brooklyn Museum of Art, 1998.

Dihqani, Ashraf. *Hamasah-i Muqavimat.* Tehran: Nashr-i Mardum, 1970.

"Doctors Urge Moral Behaviour." *APS Diplomat Recorder* 56, April 6, 2002.

Dols, Michael W. "Insanity and Its Treatment in Islamic Society." *Medical History* 31, 1 (1987): 1–14.

———. "The Leper in Medieval Islamic Society." *Speculum* 58 (1983): 891–916.

———. *Majnun: The Madman in Medieval Islamic Society.* Oxford: Oxford University Press, 1992.

Dye, Nancy Schrom, and Daniel Blake Smith. "Mother Love and Infant Death, 1750–1920." *Journal of American History* 73, 2 (1986): 329–53.

Ebrahimnejad, Hormoz. "Les épidémies et l'évolution de la médecine en Iran du XIXe siècle." *Medicina Nei Secoli* 11, 1 (1999): 167–96.

———. "La médecine d'observation en Iran du XIXe siècle." *Gesnerus: Swiss Journal of the History of Medicine and Sciences* 55, 1–2 (1998).

———. *Medicine, Public Health and the Qajar State.* Leiden: Brill, 2004.

―――. "Un traité d'épidémiologie de la médecine traditionnelle persane: *Mofarraq ol-Heyze va'l-Vaba* de Mirza Mohammad-Taqi Shirazi (ca. 1800–1873)." *Studia Iranica* 27 (1998): 83–107.

Elgood, Cyril. *A Medical History of Persia and the Eastern Caliphate from the Earliest Times Until the Year A.D. 1932.* Cambridge: Cambridge University Press, 1951.

―――. *Safavid Medical Practice.* London: Luzac, 1970.

Elwell-Sutton, L. P. "Political Parties in Iran 1941–1948." *Middle East Journal* 3, 1 (1949): 45–62.

Emami, Sayyid Hasan. *Huquq-i Madani.* Tehran: Intisharat-i Danishgah-i Tehran, 1339/1960.

Encyclopaedia of Islam, ed. H. A. R. Gibb et al. New ed. Leiden: E. J. Brill, 1960.

Encylopaedia Iranica, ed. Ehsan Yarshater. London: Routledge and Kegan Paul, 1982–.

Endress, Gerhard. *An Introduction to Islam.* Trans. Carole Hillenbrand. New York: Columbia University Press, 1988.

Ener, Mine. *Managing Egypt's Poor and the Politics of Benevolence, 1800–1952.* Princeton, NJ: Princeton University Press, 2003.

Esfandiari, Haleh. *Reconstructed Lives: Women and Iran's Islamic Revolution.* Washington: Woodrow Wilson Center Press, 1997.

―――. "The Role of Women Members of Parliament, 1963–88." In *Women in Iran: From 1800 to the Islamic Republic,* ed. Lois Beck and Guity Nashat, 136–62. Urbana: University of Illinois Press, 2004.

Ettehadieh, Mansoureh. "Zan dar jami'ah-i qajar." *Kilk,* 55–56 (Fall 1373/1994): 27–50.

Faghfoory, Mohammad H. "The Ulama-State Relations in Iran: 1921–1941." *International Journal of Middle East Studies* 19, 4 (1987): 413–32.

Fahmy, Khaled. "Women, Medicine, and Power in Nineteenth-Century Egypt." In *Remaking Women,* ed. Lila Abu-Lughod. Princeton, NJ: Princeton University Press, 1998.

Farman Farmaian, Sattareh. *Daughter of Persia.* New York: Crown, 1992.

Farmanfarmaian, Fatemeh Soudavar. "*Haft Qalam Arayish*: Cosmetics in the Iranian World." *Iranian Studies* 33, 3–4 (2000): 285–26.

Fathi, Asghar, ed. *Women and the Family in Iran.* Leiden: Brill, 1985.

Fernea, Elizabeth. *Children in the Muslim World.* Austin: University of Texas Press, 1995.

Firoozi, Ferydoon. "Iranian Censuses 1956 and 1966: A Comparative Analysis." *Middle East Journal* 24, 2 (1970): 220–28.

Fissell, Mary E. *Vernacular Bodies: The Politics of Reproduction in Early Modern England.* Oxford: Oxford University Press, 2004.

Floor, Willem. *The History of Theater in Iran.* Washington, DC: Mage, 2005.

―――. *Public Health in Qajar Iran.* Washington, DC: Mage, 2004.

―――. *A Social History of Sexual Relations in Iran.* Washington, DC: Mage, 2008.

Foucault, Michel. *Birth of the Clinic: An Archaeology of Medical Perception.* Trans. A. M. Sheridan Smith. New York: Pantheon, 1973.

―――. *A History of Sexuality.* 3 vols. Trans. Robert Hurley. New York: Pantheon, 1978.

————. *The Order of Things: An Archaeology of the Human Sciences*. New York: Pantheon, 1971.

Fraser, James. *A Winter's Journey from Constantinople to Tehran*. Bentley, 1838.

Froozani, M. D., K. Permehzadeh, A. R. Dorotsy Motlagh, and B. Golestan. "Effect of Breastfeeding Education on the Feeding Pattern and Health of Infants in Their First 4 Months in the Islamic Republic of Iran." *Bulletin of the World Health Organization* 77, 5 (1999): 381–90.

Gadelrab, Sherry Sayed. "Discourses on Sex Differences in Medieval Scholarly Islamic Thought." *Journal of the History of Medicine and Allied Sciences*, April 2010, 1–42.

Ghavami, Soodabeh. "The Role of the Medical Profession in Family Planning." In *CENTO Conference on Family Planning, Health and Demographic Statistics Held in Tehran, Iran, August 12–16, 1973*. Ankara: CENTO, 1973.

Gheissari, Ali, and Seyyed Vali Reza Nasr. *Democracy in Iran: History and the Quest for Liberty*. New York: Oxford University Press, 2006.

Gheytanchi, Elham. "Civil Society in Iran: Politics of Motherhood and the Public Sphere." *International Sociology* 16, 4 (2001): 557–76.

Giladi, Avner. *Children of Islam: Concepts of Childhood in Medieval Muslim Society*. New York: St. Martin's, 1992.

————. *Infants, Parents and Wet Nurses: Medieval Islamic Views on Breastfeeding and their Social Implications*. Leiden: Brill, 1999.

Gilmour, John. *League of Nations Health Organisation. Report on an Investigation into the Sanitary Conditions in Persia Undertaken on Behalf of the Health Committee of the League of Nations at the Request of the Persian Government*. Geneva: Imp. Atar, 1925.

Göçek, Fatma Müge, and Shiva Balaghi. *Reconstructing Gender in the Middle East: Tradition, Identity, and Power*. New York: Columbia University Press, 1994.

Good, Byron J. "The Transformation of Health Care in Modern Iranian History." In *Modern Iran: The Dialectics of Continuity and Change*, ed. Michael Bonine and Nikki Keddie. Albany: State University of New York Press, 1981.

Haeri, Shahla. *Law of Desire: Temporary Marriage in Shi'i Iran*. Syracuse, NY: Syracuse University Press, 1989.

Halm, Heinz. *Shi'ism*. Edinburgh: Edinburgh University Press, 1991.

Hanioglu, M. S. *The Young Turks in Opposition*. New York: Oxford University Press, 1995.

Harris, Ben M. "Literacy Corps: Iran's Gamble to Conquer Illiteracy." *International Review of Education/Internationale Zeitschrift für Erziehungswissenschaft/Revue Internationale de l'Education* 9, 4 (1963–64): 430–37.

Harsin, Jill. "Syphilis, Wives, Physicians: Medical Ethics and the Family in Late Nineteenth-Century France." *French Historical Studies* 16, 1 (spring 1989): 72–95.

Hermansen, Marcia. "Fatimeh as a Role Model in the Works of Ali Shari'ati." In *Women and Revolution in Iran*, ed. Guity Nashat. Boulder: Westview, 1983.

Hijazi, Muhammad. *Mihan-i Ma*. Tehran: Intisharat-i Vizarat-i Farhang, 1338/1959.

Hobsbawm, Eric, and Terence Ranger, eds. *The Invention of Tradition*. Cambridge: Cambridge University Press, 1983.

Hoodfar, Homa. "Devices and Desires: Population Policy and Gender Roles in the Islamic Republic." *Middle East Research Report* 24, 190 (1994): 11–17.

———. "The Veil in Their Minds and on Our Heads: Veiling Practices and Muslim Women." In *Women, Gender, Religion: A Reader,* ed. Elizabeth Anne Castelli and Rosamond C. Rodman. New York: Palgrave, 2001.

Hoodfar, Homa, and Samad Assadpour. "The Politics of Population Policy in the Islamic Republic of Iran." *Studies in Family Planning* 31, 1 (2000): 19–34.

Humphreys, R. Stephen. *Between Memory and Desire: The Middle East in a Troubled Age.* Berkeley: University of California Press, 1999.

Ibn Khaldun. *The Muqaddimah: An Introduction to History.* Trans. Franz Rosenthal. Princeton, NJ: Princeton University Press, 1967.

Igarashi, Yoshikuni. *Bodies of Memory: Narratives of War in Postwar Japanese Culture, 1945–1970.* Princeton, NJ: Princeton University Press, 2000.

"In Brief: National Committee to Fight AIDS." *International Family Planning Perspectives* 28, 2 (2002): 56–57.

Inhorn, Marcia, ed. *Reproductive Disruptions: Gender, Technology, and Biopolitics in the New Millenium.* New York: Berghahn, 2007.

Iran Almanac and Book of Facts. 9th ed. Tehran: Echo of Iran, 1970.

I'tisami, Parvin. *Divan-i Qasa'id va Masnaviyat va Tamsilat va Muqatta'at.* Tehran, 1977.

Ittihadiyeh, Mansoureh, ed. *Maramnamah'ha va Nizamnamah'ha-yi Ahzab-i Siyasi-yi Iran dar Duvvumin Dawrah-i Majlis-i Shaura-yi Milli.* Tehran: Nashr-i Tarikh-i Iran, 1361/1982.

Jafery, Syed Mohammed Askari. *Nahjul Balagha: Sermons, Letters and Sayings of Hazrath Ali.* Karachi: Khorasan Islamic Centre, 1971.

Jalali, G. H., H. Peyman, and A. Majd. "Study of Abortion at Farah Maternity Hospital, Teheran." *Iranian Journal of Public Health* 2, 4 (1974): 1–7.

Javadi, Hasan. "Women in Persian Literature: An Exploratory Study." In *Women and the Family in Iran,* ed. Asghar Fathi. Leiden: Brill, 1985.

Javadi, Hasan, Manijeh Marashi, and Simin Shekarloo, eds. *Ta'dib al-Nisvan va Ma'ayib al-Rijal* (Piedmont, CA: Jahan, 1992).

Jochens, Jenny. "The Politics of Reproduction: Medieval Norwegian Kingship." *American Historical Review* 92, 2 (1987): 327–49.

Jordan, Samuel. "The New Spirit in Persia." *Women's Work* 31 (1916): 273–75.

Jozani, Niloufar. *La Beauté Menacée: Anthropologie des maladies de la peau en Iran.* Tehran: Institut Français de Recherche en Iran, 1994.

Kandiyoti, Deniz. "Introduction." In *Women, Islam, and the State,* ed. D. Kandiyoti. Philadelphia: Temple University Press, 1991.

Kashani-Sabet, Firoozeh. "'The City of the Dead': The Frontier Polemics of Quarantines in the Ottoman Empire and Iran." *Comparative Studies of South Asia, Africa, and the Middle East* 18, 2 (1998): 51–58.

———. "Cultures of Iranianness: The Evolving Polemic of Iranian Nationalism." In *Iran and the Surrounding World,* ed. Nikki Keddie and Rudi Matthee, 162–81. Seattle: University of Washington Press, 2002.

———. "Fragile Frontiers: The Diminishing Domains of Qajar Iran." *International Journal of Middle East Studies* 29, 2 (1997): 205–34.

————. *Frontier Fictions: Shaping the Iranian Nation, 1804–1946.* Princeton, NJ: Princeton University Press, 1999.

————. "The Frontier Phenomenon: Perceptions of the Land in Iranian Nationalism." *Critique* 38, 3 (1997): 19–38.

————. "Giving Birth: Women, Nursing, and Sexual Hygiene in Iran." Paper presented at the Fourth Biennial Conference of Iranian Studies, May 2002.

————. "Hallmarks of Humanism: Hygiene and Love of Homeland in Qajar Iran." *American Historical Review* 105, 4 (2000): 1171–203.

————. "The Haves and the Have Nots: A Historical Study of Disability in Modern Iran." *Iranian Studies* 43, 2 (2010): 167–95.

————. "Patriotic Womanhood: The Culture of Feminism in Modern Iran, 1900–1941." *British Journal of Middle Eastern Studies* 32, 1 (2005): 29–46.

————. "The Politics of Reproduction: Maternalism and Women's Hygiene in Iran, 1896–1941." *International Journal of Middle East Studies* 38, 1 (2006): 1–29.

————. "Stepping Out of the Womb: Women and the Politics of Reproduction." *Journal of Women's History* 22, 3 (2010): 195–99.

Kashifi, Mullah Husayn Vaiz. *Rawdat al-Shuhada.* Tehran: Kitab Furushi-yi Islamiyah, n.d.

Kasravi, Ahmad. *Khvaharan va Dukhtaran-i Ma*, ed. M. A. Jazayery. Bethesda: Iranbooks, 1992.

————. *Tarikh-i Mashrutah-i Iran.* Tehran: Intisharat-i Amir Kabir, 1984.

Katz, Marion Holmes. *Body of Text: The Emergence of the Sunni Law of Ritual Purity.* Albany: State University of New York Press, 2002.

Keddie, Nikki. *An Islamic Response to Imperialism: Political and Religious Writings of Sayyid Jamal ad-Din "al-Afghani."* Berkeley: University of California Press, 1968.

————. *Roots of Revolution: An Interpretive History of Modern Iran.* New Haven, CT: Yale University Press, 1981.

————. *Sayyid Jamal ad-Din "al-Afghani": A Political Biography.* Berkeley: University of California Press, 1972.

————. *Women in the Middle East: Past and Present.* Princeton, NJ: Princeton University Press, 2006.

Keddie, Nikki, and Beth Baron, eds. *Women in Middle Eastern History: Shifting Boundaries in Sex and Gender.* New Haven, CT: Yale University Press, 1991.

Kerber, Linda. *Women of the Republic: Intellect and Ideology in Revolutionary America.* Chapel Hill: University of North Carolina Press, 1980.

Khan, Agha Mirza Sayyid Ali. *Hunar Amuz-i Dushizigan.* Tehran: Nihzat-i Sharq, 1343.

Khan, Dust Ali. *Yad'dashthayi az zindagiyih khususiyah Nasir al-Din Shah.* Tehran: Nashr-i Tarikh-i Iran, 1983.

Khan, Emir Faradj. "Hygiène et Islamisme," dissertation. Lyon, 1904.

Khan, Malkum. *Kulliyat-i Malkum Khan*, ed. Hashim Rabi'zadah. Tehran: Majlis, 1325/1907.

————. *Majmu'ah-i Asar-i Mirza Malkum Khan*, ed. Muhammad Muhit Tabataba'i. Tehran: Intisharat-i 'Ilmi, 1980.

Khan, Mirza Yusuf, and Mustashar al-Dawlah. *Yak Kalimah*, ed. Sadiq Sajjadi. Tehran: Nashr-i Tarikh-i Iran, 1364/1985.

Khatami, M. *Islam, Liberty and Development.* Trans. Hossein Kamaly. Binghamton: Institute of Global Cultural Studies, State University of New York at Binghamton, 1998.

Khattabah'hayah Kanun-i Banuvan. Tehran: Intisharat-i Kanun-i Banuvan, 1935.

Khomeini, Ruhollah. *A Clarification of Questions: An Unabridged Translation of Resaleh Towzih al-Masael.* Boulder: Westview, 1984.

Khushunat va Farhang: Asnad-i Mahramanah-i Kashf-i Hijab. Tehran: Intisharat-i Sazman-i Asnad-i Milli-yi Iran, 1371/1992.

Khvansari, Jamal. *Kulthum Nanah.* Ed. Bizhan Asadipur. Tehran: Intisharat-i Murvarid, 1976.

Kirmani, Mirza Aqa Khan. *A'inah-i Sikandari.* Tehran, 1906.

———. *Sih Maktub.* Ed. Bahram Choubine. Tehran: Intisharat-i Mard-i Imruz, 1370/1991.

Kirmani, Nazim al-Islam. *Tarikh-i Bidari-yi Iranian.* Tehran: Bunyad-i Farhang-i Iran, 1357/1978.

Kitab-i farsi-yi duvvum-i dabastan va ta'limat-i dini. Tehran: Vizarat-i Farhang, 1964.

Kiyumehr, Farideh. "Shakhishayah Bihdasht va Darman." In *Shakhishayah ijtima'i-yi Iran 1357.* Tehran, 1978.

Klaus, Alisa. "Depopulation and Race Suicide: Maternalism and Pronatalist Ideologies in France and the United States." In *Mothers of a New World: Maternalist Politics and the Origins of Welfare States,* ed. Seth Koven and Sonya Michel. New York: Routledge, 1993.

Kligman, Gail. *The Politics of Duplicity: Controlling Reproduction in Ceausescu's Romania.* Berkeley: University of California Press, 1998.

Koven, Seth, and Sonya Michel. "Womanly Duties: Maternalist Politics and the Origins of Welfare States in France, Germany, Great Britain, and the United States, 1880–1920." *American Historical Review* 95, 4 (1990): 1076–1108.

Koyagi, Mikiya. "Moulding Future Soldiers and Mothers of the Iranian Nation: Gender and Physical Education Under Reza Shah, 1921–41." *International Journal of the History of Sport* 26, 11 (2009): 1668–96.

Kraemer, Joel L. *Humanism in the Renaissance of Islam: The Cultural Revival During the Buyid Age.* Leiden: E. J. Brill, 1986.

Kurzman, Charles. "A Feminist Generation in Iran?" *Iranian Studies* 41, 3 (June 2008), 297–321.

Lambton, Ann. "Secret Societies and the Persian Revolution of 1905–1906." In *Qajar Persia,* ed. Ann Lambton. Austin: University of Texas Press, 1987.

———. *State and Government in Medieval Islam.* Oxford: Oxford University Press, 1980.

Lammens, Henri. *Fatima et les filles du Mahomet.* Rome: Sumptibus Pontificii Instituti Biblici, 1912.

League of Nations. *Statistical Year-book of the League of Nations, 1931/32.* Geneva: League of Nations, Economic and Financial Section, 1932.

Linton, Simi. *Claiming Disability: Knowledge and Identity.* New York: New York University Press, 1998.

Luker, Kristin. "Sex, Social Hygiene, and the State: The Double-Edged Sword of Social Reform." *Theory and Society* 27, 5 (1998): 601–34.

Mahdavi, Shireen. "Muhammad Baqir Majlisi and Family Values." In *Safavid Iran and Her Neighbors*, ed. Michel Mazzaoui. Salt Lake City: University of Utah Press, 2003.

———. "Shahs, Doctors, Diplomats and Missionaries in 19th-Century Iran." *British Journal of Middle East Studies* 32, 2 (2005): 169–91.

———. "Taj al-Saltaneh, an Emancipated Qajar Princess." *Middle Eastern Studies* 23, 2 (1987): 188–93.

Mahdi, Muhsin. *Al-Farabi's Philosophy of Plato and Aristotle*. Ithaca, NY: Cornell University Press, 1962.

Majd, Mohammad Gholi. *Great Britain and Reza Shah: The Plunder of Iran*. Gainesville: University Press of Florida, 2001.

Majlisi, Muhammad Baqir. *Hilyat al-Muttaqin*. Tehran, 1959.

Makdisi, George. *The Rise of Humanism in Classical Islam and the Christian West : With Special Reference to Scholasticism*. Edinburgh: Edinburgh University Press, 1990.

Malcolm, Napier. *Children of Persia*. Edinburgh: Oliphant, Anderson, and Ferrier, 1911.

Merritt, Onera Amelia. *Persia: Romance and Reality*. London: Nicholson, 1935.

Mirza Muhammad Malik al-Kuttab. *Kitab-i Vasa'il-i Ibtihaj fi Hifz Sihhat al-Izdivaj*. Tehran, 1325/1907.

Malikzadah, Mehdi. *Tarikh-i Inqilab-i Mashrutiyat-i Iran*. Tehran: 'Ilmi, 1984.

Marandi, A., H. M. Afzali, and A. F. Hossaini. "The Reasons for Early Weaning Among Mothers in Teheran." *Bulletin of the World Health Organization* 71, 5 (1993): 561–70.

Marashi, Afshin. "Performing the Nation: The Shah's Official State Visit to Turkey, June to July 1934." In *The Making of Modern Iran: State and Society Under Riza Shah, 1921–1941*, ed. Stephanie Cronin. London: Routledge-Curzon, 2003.

Martin, Vanessa. *Islam and Modernism: The Iranian Revolution of 1906*. London: I. B. Tauris, 1989.

———. *The Qajar Pact: Bargaining, Protest and the State in Nineteenth-Century Persia*. London: I. B. Taurus, 2005.

Massignon, Louis. *La Mubahala de Médine et l'hyperdulie de Fatima*. Paris: Librairie Orientale et Américaine, 1955.

Matthee, Rudi. "Prostitutes, Courtesans, and Dancing Girls: Women Entertainers in Safavid Iran." In *Iran and Beyond: Essays in Middle Eastern History in Honor of Nikki Keddie*, ed. Rudi Matthee and Beth Baron. Costa Mesa, CA: Mazda, 2000.

Mayr, Ernst. *The Growth of Biological Thought: Diversity, Evolution, and Inheritance*. Cambridge, MA: Belknap, 1982.

McGregor, Deborah Kuhn. *From Midwives to Medicine: The Birth of American Gynecology*. New Brunswick, NJ: Rutgers University Press, 1998.

The Meaning of the Glorious Qur'an. Trans. Muhammad M. Pickthall. Elmhurst, NY: Tahrike Tarsile Qur'an, 1999.

Menashri, David. *Education and the Making of Modern Iran*. Ithaca, NY: Cornell University Press, 1992.

Milani, Farzaneh. "The Mediatory Guile of the Nanny in Persian Romance." *Iranian Studies* 32, 2 (1999): 181–201.

———. *Veils and Words: The Emerging Voices of Iranian Women Writers.* Syracuse, NY: Syracuse University Press, 1992.

Milani, Mohsen M. *The Making of Iran's Islamic Revolution,* 2nd ed. Boulder: Westview, 1994.

Millspaugh, Arthur. *Americans in Persia.* Washington: Brookings Institution, 1946.

Minuchehr, Pardis. "Homeland from Afar: Iranian Diaspora and the Quest for Modernity." Ph.D. dissertation, Columbia University, 1998.

Mirchamsy, H., H. Taslimi, and M. Aghdachi. "Résultats des vaccinations collectives." *Acta Medica Iranica* 2, 3 (1960): 33–41.

Mir-Hosseini, Ziba. *Islam and Gender: The Religious Debate in Contemporary Iran.* Princeton, NJ: Princeton University Press, 1999.

———. *Marriage on Trial: Islamic Family Law in Iran and Morocco.* London: I. B. Tauris, 2000.

———. "Women and Politics in Post-Khomeini Iran: Divorce, Veiling, and Emerging Feminist Voices." In *Women and Politics in the Third World,* ed. Haleh Afshar. London: Routledge, 1996.

Moallem, Minoo. *Between Warrior Brother and Veiled Sister: Islamic Fundamentalism and the Politics of Patriarchy in Iran.* Berkeley: University of California Press, 2005.

Moghadam, Valentine M. *Women, Gender and Social Change in the Middle East.* Boulder, CO: Lynne Rienner Publishers, 2003.

Moghissi, Haideh. *Populism and Feminism in Iran.* New York: St. Martin's, 1996.

Moin, Baqer. *Khomeini: Life of the Ayatollah.* New York: St. Martin's, 1999.

Momen, Moojan. *An Introduction to Shi'i Islam: The History and Doctrines of Twelver Shi'ism.* New Haven, CT: Yale University Press, 1987.

Morier, J. J. *A Second Journey Through Persia, Armenia, Asia Minor to Constantinople.* London: Longman, Hurst, Rees, Orme, and Brown, 1818.

———. *The Adventures of Hajji Baba of Ispahan.* Chicago: Stone and Kimball, 1895.

Morton, Rosalie. *A Doctor's Holiday in Iran.* New York: Funk and Wagnalls, 1940.

Mostofi, Abdollah. *The Administrative and Social History of the Qajar Period: From Agha Mohammad Khan to Nasir ed-Din Shah (1794–1896).* 3 vols. Trans. Nayereh Mostofi Glenn. Costa Mesa, CA: Mazda, 1997.

Mottahedeh, Negar. *Representing the Unpresentable: Historical Imges of National Reform from the Qajars to the Islamic Republic of Iran.* Syracuse, NY: Syracuse University Press, 2008.

Musallam, Basim. *Sex and Society in Medieval Islam.* Cambridge: Cambridge University Press, 1983.

Nafisi, Sa'id. *Sokhanranihayeh sazman-e parvaresh-e afkar.* Tehran: Chapkhaneh-i Ferdausi, 1318/1939.

Nahid, 'Abdul Husayn. *Zanan-i Iran dar junbish-i mashrutiyat.* Saarbrucken: Nuvid, 1989.

Najafi, Najmeh, as told to Helen Hinckley. *Persia Is My Heart.* New York: Harper, 1953.

Najmabadi, Afsaneh. "Crafting an Educated Housewife in Iran." In *Remaking Women: Feminism and Modernity in the Middle East*, ed. Lila Abu-Lughod. Princeton, NJ: Princeton University Press, 1998, 91–125.

———. "The Erotic *Vatan* [Homeland] as Beloved and Mother: To Love, to Possess, and to Protect." *Comparative Studies in Society and History* 39, 3 (1997): 442–67.

———. "Power, Morality, and the New Muslim Womanhood." In *The Politics of Social Transformation in Afghanistan, Iran and Pakistan*, ed. Myron Weiner and Ali Banuazizi. Syracuse, NY: Syracuse University Press, 1994.

———. "Reading and Enjoying 'Wiles of Women' Stories as a Feminist." *Iranian Studies* 32, 2 (1999): 203–22.

———. *Women with Mustaches and Men Without Beards: The Sexual and Gender Anxieties of Iranian Modernity*. Berkeley: University of California Press, 2005.

———. "Zanha-yi millat: Women or Wives of the Nation?" *Iranian Studies* 26, 1–2 (1993): 51–71.

Najmi, Nasir. *Dar al-Khilafah-i Tehran*. Tehran: Amir Kabir, 1977.

———. *Tehran-i 'Ahd-i Nasiri*. Tehran: Gulsha'i, 1990.

Nasir al-Din Shah. *The Diary of H. M. the Shah of Persia During His Tour Through Europe*. Trans. James William Redhouse. London: Jonathan Murray, 1874.

Natiq, Huma. "Nigahi bih barkhi nivishtiha va mubarizat-i zanan dar dawran-i mashrutiyat." *Kitab-i Jum'a* 30 (1979): 45–54.

Nuland, Sherwin B. *The Doctor's Plague: Germs, Childbed Fever, and the Strange Story of Ignac Semmelweis*. New York: W. W. Norton, 2003.

Oberling, Charles. "Certain Aspects of Public Health in Persia." *Proceedings of the New York State Association of Public Health Laboratories*, 1942.

Offen, Karen. "Depopulation, Nationalism, and Feminism in Fin-de-Siècle France." *American Historical Review* 89, 3 (1984): 648–76.

Pahlavi, Farah. *An Enduring Love: My Life with the Shah, a Memoir*. New York: Miramax Books, 2004.

Paidar, Parvin. *Women and the Political Process in Twentieth-Century Iran*. Cambridge: Cambridge University Press, 1995.

Parascandola, John. "The Introduction of Antibiotics into Therapeutics." In *Sickness and Health in America: Readings in the History of Medicine and Public Health*, ed. Judith Walzer Leavitt and Ronald L. Numbers, 3rd ed. Madison: University of Wisconsin Press, 1997.

Parsinejad, Iraj. *A History of Literary Criticism in Iran, 1866–1951: Literary Criticism in the Work of Enlightened Thinkers*. Bethesda: Ibex, 2003.

Pedersen, Susan. "Catholicism, Feminism, and the Politics of the Family During the Late Third Republic." In *Mothers of a New World: Maternalist Politics and the Origins of Welfare States*, ed. Seth Koven and Sonya Michel. New York: Routledge, 1993.

Pelly, Lewis. *The Miracle Play of Hasan and Husain*, ed. Arthur N. Wollaston. London: W. H. Allen, 1879.

Perkins, Justin. *A Residence of Eight Years in Persia, Among the Nestorians, with Notices of the Muhammedans*. Andover: Allen, Morrill and Wardwell, 1843.

Pernick, Martin S. "Defining the Defective: Eugenics, Aesthetics, and Mass Culture in Early-Twentieth-Century America." In *The Body and Physical Difference:*

Discourses of Disability, ed. David T. Mitchell and Sharon L. Snyder. Ann Arbor: University of Michigan Press, 1997.

Pinault, David. "Zaynab Bint Ali and the Place of the Women of the Households of the First Imams in Shi'ite Devotional Literature." In *Women in the Medieval Islamic World*, ed. Gavin Hambly. New York: St. Martin's, 1998.

Plato. *The Republic*. Trans. Benjamin Jowett. New York: Vintage, 1991.

Poovey, Mary. *Uneven Developments: The Ideological Work of Gender in Mid-Victorian England*. Chicago: University of Chicago Press, 1988.

Population Council, "Iran: Report on Population Growth and Family Planning." *Studies in Family Planning* 1, 20 (1967): 3–6.

Potts, Malcolm, and Roger Valentine Short. *Ever Since Adam and Eve: The Evolution of Human Sexuality*. Cambridge: Cambridge University Press, 1999.

Prigmore, Charles. *Social Work in Iran since the White Revolution*. Tuscaloosa: University of Alabama Press, 1976.

Qummi, Mirza Sayyid Muhammad. *Ta'limat-i Muduniyah*. Tehran: Shams, 1330/1912.

Report of the Autopsy of the Siamese Twins: Together with Other Interesting Information Concerning Their Life. Philadelphia: J. B. Lippincott, 1874.

Ringer, Monica. *Education, Religion, and the Discourse of Cultural Reform in Qajar Iran*. Costa Mesa, CA: Mazda, 2001.

Ringrose, Hyacinthe. *Marriage and Divorce Laws of the World*. New York: Musson-Draper, 1911.

Rizvani, Huma. *Lavayih-i Aqa Shaykh Fazl Allah Nuri*. Tehran: Nashr-i Tarikh-i Iran, 1983.

Roberts, Mary Louise. "Gender, Consumption, and Commodity Culture." *American Historical Review* 103, 3 (June 1998): 817–44.

Robinson, B. W. "The Court Painters of Fath Ali Shah." *Eretz Israel* 7 (1964): 94–105.

———. *Studies in Persian Art*. London: Pindar, 1993.

Rosenthal, Erwin I. J. *Political Thought in Medieval Islam*. Cambridge: Cambridge University Press, 1958.

Rostam-Kolayi, Jasamin. "Expanding Agendas for the 'New' Iranian Woman: Family Law, Work, and Unveiling." In *The Making of Modern Iran: State and Society Under Riza Shah, 1921–1941*, ed. Stephanie Cronin. London: Routledge-Curzon, 2003.

———. "Origins of Iran's Modern Girls' Schools: From Private/National to Public/State." *Journal of Middle East Women's Studies* 4, 3 (2008): 58–88.

———. "The Women's Press, Modern Education, and the State in Early Twentieth-Century Iran, 1900–1930s." Ph.D. dissertation, University of California, Los Angeles, 2000.

Roudi, Farzaneh. "Iran's Revolutionary Approach to Family Planning." *Population Today* 27, 7 (1999).

Sa'adat, Ahmad. *Rahnima-yih Sa'adat*. Tehran, 1923.

Sabahi, Seyed Farian. "Gender and the Army of Knowledge in Pahlavi Iran." In *Women, Religion, and Culture in Iran*, ed. Sarah Ansari and Vanessa Martin, 99–126. Richmond, Surrey: Curzon, 2002.

————. "The Literacy Corps in Pahlavi Iran (1963–1979): Political, Social and Literary Implications." *Cahiers d'études sur la Méditerranée orientale et le monde turco-iranien* 31 (2001).

Said, Edward. *Orientalism*. New York: Pantheon, 1978.

Salur, Qahraman Mirza Ayn al-Saltanah. *Ruznamah-i Khatirat-i Ayn al-Saltanah*, vol. 1. Tehran: Asatir, 1374–79/1995–2000.

Sanasarian, Eliz. *The Women's Rights Movement in Iran: Mutiny, Appeasement and Repression from 1900 to Khomeini*. New York: Praeger, 1982.

Sanger, William. *The History of Prostitution*. London: Sampson Low, Son, & Co., 1858.

Sanjabi, Maryam B. "Rereading the Enlightenment: Akhundzada and His Voltaire." *Iranian Studies* 28, 1–2 (1995): 39–60.

Sardari, A. M., and R. Keyhan. "The Prospect of Family Planning in Iran." *Demography* 5, 2 (1968).

Saroukhanian, G. "The Present Situation of Teaching Public Health and Public Health Practice in Iran." In *CENTO Conference Series on the Teaching of Public Health and Public Health Practice*. Ankara: Office of U.S. Economic Coordinator for CENTO Affairs, 1971.

Satrapi, Marjane. *Persepolis*. New York: Pantheon, 2003.

Sayyah, Fatimah. *Naqd va Siyahat: Majmu'ah-i maqalat va taqrirat-i Doktor Fatimah Sayyah*. Ed. Muhammad Gulbun. Tehran: Tus, 1354/1975.

Schayegh, Cyrus. *Who Is Knowledgeable, Is Strong: Science, Class, and the Formation of Modern Iranian Society, 1900–1950*. Berkeley: University of California Press, 2009.

Schneider, Jean-Etienne. "Discussion." *Revue d'hygiène et de police sanitaire* 30 (1908): 453.

————. "Les Médecins français en Perse." *Revue medicale de l'est* 43 (1911): 546–47.

Sedghi, Hamideh. *Women and Politics in Iran: Veiling, Unveiling, and Reveiling*. New York: Cambridge University Press, 2007.

Sered, Susan. "Rachel, Mary, Fatima." *Cultural Anthropology* 6, 2 (1991): 131–46.

Shaarawi, Huda. *Harem Years*. Ed. Margot Badran. London: Virago, 1986.

Shahidi, Hossein. "Women and Journalism in Iran." In *Women, Religion and Culture in Iran*, ed. Sarah Ansari and Vanessa Martin. Richmond, Surrey: Curzon, 2002.

Shahidian, Hammed. *Women in Iran: Emerging Voices in the Women's Movement*. Westport, CT: Greenwood, 2002.

————. *Women in Iran: Gender Politics in the Islamic Republic*. Westport, CT: Greenwood, 2002.

Shari'ati, Ali. *Fatima is Fatima*. Trans. Laleh Bakhtiar. Tehran: Shari'ati Foundation, n.d.

Sheikh al-Islami, Pari. *Zanan-i Ruznamah-nigar va Andishmand-i Iran*. 1972.

Sheil, Lady Mary. *Glimpses of Life and Manners in Persia*. London: J. Murray, 1856.

Shikufah bih Inzimam-i Danish: Nakhustin Nashriyah'hayah Zanan-i Iran. Tehran: Kitabkhanah-i Milli-yi Jumhuri-yi Islami-yi Iran, 1377/1999.

Shirazi, Faegheh. "Men's Facial Hair in Islam: A Matter of Interpretation." In *Hair: Styling Culture and Fashion*, ed. Geraldine Biddle-Perry and Sarah Cheang. New York: Berg, 2008.

Shirazi, Sayyid Muhammad. *Bulugh al-Ibtihaj fi sihhat al-izdivaj*. N.p., n.d.

Shoberl, Frederick. *Persia: Containing a Description of the Country, with an Account of Its Government, Laws, and Religion.* 1828.

Sladen, Douglas Brooke Wheelton. *Queer Things About Persia.* Philadelphia: J. B. Lippincott, 1907.

Soufi, Denise L. "The Image of Fatima in Classical Muslim Thought." Ph.D. dissertation, Princeton University, 1997.

Southgate, Minoo S. "Men, Women, and Boys: Love and Sex in the Works of Sa'di." *Iranian Studies* 17, 4 (1984): 413–52.

Speer, Robert Elliott. *Missionary Principles and Practice.* New York: Revell, 1902.

Spencer, Rowena. *Conjoined Twins: Developmental Malformations and Clinical Implications.* Baltimore: Johns Hopkins University Press, 2003.

Sprachman, Paul. *Suppressed Persian.* Costa Mesa, CA: Mazda, 2005.

Stebbins, Ernest L. "Stebbins Evaluation: Preliminary Report of the Consultant to the U.S. Economic Coordinator for CENTO." *CENTO Conference Series on the Teaching of Public Health and Public Health Practice,* 130–31. Ankara: CENTO, 1970.

Stepan, Jan, and Edmund H. Kellogg. "The World's Law on Contraceptives." *American Journal of Comparative Law* 22, 4 (1974): 615–51.

Stewart, Jane A. "Origin of Mother's Day." In *Mother's Day: Its History, Origin, Celebration, Spirit, and Significane as Related in Prose and Verse.* Comp. Susan Tracy Rice. Ed. Robert Haven Schauffler. Detroit: Omnigraphics, 1990.

Stewart, Mary Lynn. "'Science Is Always Chaste': Sex Education and Sexual Initiation in France 1880s–1930s." *Journal of Contemporary History* 32, 3 (1997): 381–94.

Stowasser, Barbara. *Women in the Qur'an, Traditions, and Interpretation.* Oxford: Oxford University Press, 1996.

Sullivan, Zohreh T. "Eluding the Feminist, Overthrowing the Modern? Transformations in Twentieth-Century Iran." In *Remaking Women,* ed. Lila Abu-Lughod. Princeton, NJ: Princeton University Press, 1998.

Sykes, Ella C. *Persia and Its People.* London: Methuen, 1910.

Tabataba'i, Muhammad Husayn, and Seyyed Hossein Nasr. *Shi'ite Islam.* St. Leonard's, Australia: Allen and Unwin, 1975.

Ta'limat-i dini chaharum-i dabistan. "Hazrat-i Fatima, Banu-yi nimunah-i Islam." Tehran: Vizarat-i amuzish va parvarish, 1377/1979.

Ta'limat-i dini, duvvum-i dabistan. Tehran: Vizarat-i Amuzish va Parvarish, 1979.

Ta'ib, Sayyid Husayn. *Bimaristan'hayih Rasht az Mashrutah ta 1357.* Rasht, 1384/2005.

Tabataba'i, Sayyid Zia' al-Din. *Ta'limat-i Muduniyya.* Tehran, 1329/1911.

Tabrizi, Mir 'Imad Naqibzadah. *Ma'lumat-i Muduniyya.* Tehran, 1331/1913.

Tafrishi, Abu al-Hasan Khan. *Masa'il-i 'Umdah-i Hifz-i Sihhat.* 1894.

Taj al-Saltanah. *Crowning Anguish: Memoirs of a Persian Princess from the Harem to Modernity, 1884–1914.* Trans. Anna Vanzan and Amin Neshati. Washington: Mage, 1993.

Taqi, Mirza Sayyid Muhammad. *Ta'limat-i Muduniyya.* Tehran, 1330/1912.

Tavakoli-Targhi, Mohamad. "Going Public: Patriotic and Matriotic Homeland in Iranian Nationalist Discourses." *Strategies: Journal of Theory, Culture and Politics* 13, 2 (2000): 175–200.

———. *Refashioning Iran: Orientalism, Occidentalism, and Historiography.* New York: Palgrave, 2001.

Tholozan, J. D. *Histoire de la peste bubonique en Perse, ou la determination de son origine, de sa marche, du cycle de ses apparitions, et de la cause de sa prompte extinction.* Paris: Masson, 1874.

Tohidi, Nayereh. "Gender and Islamic Fundamentalism: Feminist Politics in Iran." In *Third World Women and the Politics of Feminism,* ed. Chandra Talpade Mohanty, Ann Russo, and Lourdes Torres, 251–69. Bloomington: Indiana University Press, 1991.

Touba, Jacqueline Rudolph. "Effects of the Islamic Revolution on Women and the Family in Iran: Some Preliminary Observations." In *Women and the Family in Iran,* ed. Asghar Fathi. Leiden: Brill, 1985.

Turner, Howard R. *Science in Medieval Islam: An Illustrated Introduction.* Austin: University of Texas Press, 1995.

Ulrich, Laurel T. *A Midwife's Tale: The Life of Martha Ballard Based on Her Diary, 1785–1812.* New York: Knopf, 1990.

Vahid, Sina. *Qiyam-i Gawharshad.* Tehran: Vizarat-i Farhang va Irshad-i Islami, 1366/1987.

Vaqa'ih-i Kashf-i Hijab. Tehran: Mu'assassah-i Mutali'at-i Farhangi, 1371/1992.

Vatandoust, Gholam-Reza. "The Status of Iranian Women During the Pahlavi Regime." In *Women and the Family in Iran,* ed. Asghar Fathi. Leiden: Brill, 1985.

Vizarat-i Ma'arif va Awqaf va Sana'i-yi Mustazrafah: Ihsa'iyah-i Ma'arif va Madaris (1307–1308). Tehran: Matba'a-yi Rawshana'i, n.d.

Waller, John. *The Discovery of the Germ.* New York: Columbia University Press, 2002.

Waring, Edward Scott. *A Tour to Sheeraz, by the Route of Kazroon and Feerozabad.* London: Printed for T. Cadell and W. Davies by W. Bulmer, 1807.

Watson, Chalmers. *Encyclopaedia Medica.* Edinburgh: Green, 1902.

Watts, Sheldon. *Epidemics and History: Disease, Power and Imperialism.* New Haven, CT: Yale University Press, 1997.

Williams Jackson, Abraham Valentine. *Persia Past and Present: A Book of Travel and Research.* New York: Macmillan, 1906.

Wills, C. J. "Medicine in Persia." *British Medical Journal* 1, 956 (April 26, 1879): 623–24.

———. *Persia As It Is: Being Sketches of Modern Persian Life and Character.* London: S. Low, Marston, Searle, and Rivington, 1886.

Wilson, Samuel Graham. *Persian Life and Customs.* New York: F. H. Revell, 1895.

———. *Western Mission.* Philadelphia: Presbyterian Board of Publication and Sabbath School Work, 1896.

Winichakul, Thongchai. *Siam Mapped: A History of the Geo-body of a Nation.* Honolulu: University of Hawaii Press, 1994.

Wishard, John G. *Twenty Years in Persia: A Narrative of Life Under the Last Three Shahs.* New York: Revell, 1908.

Wolf, Naomi. *The Beauty Myth: How Images of Beauty Are Used Against Women.* New York: Morrow, 1991.

Yeganeh, Nahid [pseud. Parvin Paidar]. "Women's Struggles in the Islamic Republic of Iran." In *In the Shadow of Islam: The Women's Movement in Iran,* ed. Azar Tabari and Nahid Yeganeh. London: Zed, 1982.

Yonan, Isaac Malek. *Persian Women: A Sketch of Woman's Life from the Cradle to the Grave, and Missionary Work Among Them, with Illustrations.* Nashville: Cumberland Presbyterian Publishing House, 1898.

Ze'evi, Dror. *Producing Desire: Changing Sexual Discourse in the Ottoman Middle East, 1500–1900*. Berkeley: University of California Press, 2006.

Zirinsky, Michael. "Harbingers of Change: Presbyterian Women in Iran, 1883–1949." *American Presbyterians: Journal of Presbyterian History* 70, 3 (1992): 173–86.

———. "A Panacea for the Ills of the Country: American Presbyterian Education in Inter-War Iran." *Iranian Studies* 26, 1–2 (1993): 119–37.

INDEX